POWERFUL CONNECTIONS

POWERFUL CONNECTIONS

The Poetics of Patronage in the Age of Louis XIII

Peter W. Shoemaker

Newark: University of Delaware Press

© 2007 by Rosemont Publishing & Printing Corp.

All rights reserved. Authorization to photocopy items for internal or personal use, or the internal or personal use of specific clients, is granted by the copyright owner, provided that a base fee of $10.00, plus eight cents per page, per copy is paid directly to the Copyright Clearance Center, 222 Rosewood Drive, Danvers, Massachusetts 01923. [978-0-87413-993-8/07 $10.00 + 8¢ pp, pc.]

Other than as indicated in the foregoing, this book may not be reproduced, in whole or in part, in any form (except as permitted by Sections 107 and 108 of the U.S. Copyright Law, and except for brief quotes appearing in reviews in the public press).

Associated University Presses
2010 Eastpark Boulevard
Cranbury, NJ 08512

The paper used in this publication meets the requirements of the American National Standard for Permanence of Paper for Printed Library Materials Z39.48-1984.

Library of Congress Cataloging-in-Publication Data

Shoemaker, Peter William, 1968–
  Powerful connections : the poetics of patronage in the age of Louis XIII / Peter W. Shoemaker.
     p. cm.
  Includes bibliographical references and index.
  ISBN-13: 978-0-87413-993-8 (alk. paper)
  ISBN-10: 0-87413-993-7 (alk. paper)
  1. French literature—17th century—History and criticism.   2. Authors and patrons—France—History—17th century.   3. Literary patrons—France.   4. France—Intellectual life—17th century.   I. Title.
PQ245.S56 2007
840.9′0032—dc22
                                                         2007005844

PRINTED IN THE UNITED STATES OF AMERICA

For my parents

Contents

A Note to the Reader	9
Acknowledgments	11
Introduction	15
1. Theorizing Patronage	26
2. Reinventing Eloquence: Balzac's *Lettres*	57
3. His Master's Voice: Poetry in an Age of Collective Authorship	94
4. The Anxiety of Influence: *Irréguliers,* Libertines, and Their Patrons	117
5. The Public and Private Lives of the Theater	152
6. Beyond Patronage	192
Conclusion	228
Notes	232
Bibliography	257
Index	280

A Note to the Reader

I HAVE REPRODUCED THE ORIGINAL FRENCH ONLY WHEN IT IS OF SCHOLarly or literary interest. Spellings follow the editions cited, except for the reciprocal substitutions of the early modern *u* and *v* and *i* and *j*. Unless otherwise noted, all translations are my own.

Sections of chapters 4 and 5 appeared in modified form in *Seventeenth-Century French Studies* and *Nottingham French Studies* and appear here by permission of the publishers of these journals.

Acknowledgments

THIS BOOK HAS HAD MANY PATRONS, THE FIRST OF WHOM WAS LIONEL Gossman, who introduced me to Guez de Balzac when I was looking for a dissertation topic and directed my research during my years at Princeton. The project would not have come to fruition without the emotional and financial support of my parents and wife, Jill Lagerstrom, who funded a much-needed sabbatical in 2004–5. A grant from the Dean of Graduate Studies at The Catholic University of America allowed me to travel to France in the summer of 2002 and start working on the book in earnest.

In addition to the anonymous readers at the University of Delaware Press, whose detailed comments helped turn a manuscript into a book, both Joan Grimbert and Robert Schneider read the manuscript in its entirety and provided invaluable feedback. Along the way, many other friends and colleagues gave advice and encouragement. I would especially like to thank Lawrence Poos (the dean of the School of Arts and Sciences at CUA), Jean-Michel Heimonet (who encouraged me to start writing), Chad Wright and Jim Gaines (who read sections of the manuscript), Nora Heimann (who gave me invaluable advice on academic publishing), Brian Ogilvie and Jennifer Heuer (who let me stay with them in Paris in the spring of 2005), as well as Daniel Solovay, David Wrisley, Julia Abramson, and Greg Brown. I owe a special debt of gratitude to the late Karl D. Uitti, for his friendship and constant encouragement.

Maxime Préaud, of the Cabinet des Estampes at the Bibliothèque Nationale, provided indispensable information while I was preparing the manuscript for publication. Over the years I have relied upon the erudition of many other anonymous librarians, particularly at the Princeton University Libraries, the Bibliothèque Nationale de France, the Folger Library, and the European and Jefferson Reading Rooms at the Library of Congress.

POWERFUL CONNECTIONS

Introduction

> Ils ont appris qu'un Ancien disoit à ceux qu'il vouloit connoistre, dy moy qui tu hantes & je te diray quel tu es: Ils croyent tirer un merveilleux avantage de la connoissance de ces honnestes gents; ils pensent qu'on dira d'eux, "il faut qu'ils soient polis & qu'ils ayent l'esprit rare puis qu'on les voit si souvent avecque ces Messieurs; & quand mesme ils ne seroient pas tels naturellement, ils le seroient devenus avecque eux."
>
> [They have learned that an Ancient told those whom he wished to know: "Tell me with whom you associate and I will tell you who you are." They think that they gain a great advantage from their well-bred acquaintances. They believe people will say of them: "since they are often seen in such company, they must be genteel and quick-witted, and even if they were not born so, it must have rubbed off on them."]
> —Pierre Guérin de La Pinelière, *Le Parnasse ou le critique des poètes*

> On loue les grands pour marquer qu'on les voit de près, rarement par estime ou par gratitude.
>
> [We praise the great to show that we are intimate with them, rarely out of esteem or gratitude.]
> —Jean de La Bruyère, *Les Caractères*

P̲ATRONAGE OF THE ARTS, AS DISTINGUISHED FROM PARTICIPATION IN THE art market, is a relatively marginal phenomenon in modern society. Today, apart from the notable exception of architecture, most artistic works are purchased rather than commissioned, and artists and writers support themselves by marketing the fruits of their labor, rather than by an independent, personal subsidy given to support artistic creation. The advance that a writer receives from a publisher is just that—a payment in advance, a speculation on future profits that takes the form of an incentive to close the deal. Even in the case of architectural commissions, where the person or persons commissioning a building often participate in its conception and design, the process is largely dominated by impersonal, market forces: a competition involving many architects followed by a fee-for-service transaction.

As we were reminded during the American "Culture Wars" of the late 1980s and early 1990s, however, patronage of the arts, although marginal within the larger economy, is still highly charged. Indeed, the most remarkable thing about the debates surrounding the National Endowment of the Arts (NEA)—ignited by the cancellation of Robert Mapplethorpe's 1989 exhibition at the Corcoran Gallery in Washington DC—was the disproportion between the actual amount of money involved (a tiny fraction of the federal budget) and the intensity of the emotions that were voiced. The debate pitted advocates of government accountability (including a number of public officials) against partisans of artistic freedom (including much of the art community and its supporters). For the art community, in the words of one commentator, the NEA's mission was to "insulate artists from the forces of the marketplace, fill the income-earnings gap of arts organizations, and publicly legitimize the tastes and judgments of the arts community."[1] Patronage, in other words, offered public recognition and a welcome bulwark against the corrupting, commercial commodification of art—as long as the government respected artistic freedom and left decisions of value to the members of the artistic community, that is. The public critics of the NEA, by contrast, invoked the populist principles of public decency and cultural consensus. Why, they asked, should a taxpayer-funded organization support artistic projects that were out of step with mainstream American values?

Leaving aside the merits of the various positions and recognizing that many of the values invoked during the debate (such as artistic freedom and populism) are foreign to the subject of this study, the episode brings to the fore two paradoxical aspects of patronage. On the one hand, patronage is often bound up with the more *elitist* aspirations of high art, its attempts to remove itself from the contingent sphere of everyday exchange and elevate itself to a higher calling. On the other hand, patronage, and especially state-sponsored patronage, inevitably raises the question of the *public*, even political, function of art. It is tightly bound up, in other words, with the exchanges between politics, economics, and art that define cultural *value*, and this is undoubtedly why the question continues to be charged even in an era when patronage has been largely overshadowed by other economic forces, most notably consumer capitalism.

In the context of seventeenth-century France, in a society where the court and other aristocratic circles possessed a kind of cultural hegemony, it is hardly meaningful to draw a sharp contrast between elitist and public values. Jürgen Habermas has famously argued that the "public sphere" of the *ancien régime* was not clearly distinct from a "private sphere" as it is today, but was rather a space within which the dominant elite (king, lords, and other members of the nobility) represented its power.[2] As Hélène Merlin has shown, however, the question of representation and its relationship to power is more complex than Habermas suggests, at least in the early modern period.[3] The model of a dominant elite representing itself before a passive audience grossly oversimplifies the nature of cultural production, just as the notion of an absolute monarchy lording its power over passive subjects oversimplifies the nature of political power. Representations were produced, and power was exerted, through networks of interpersonal relationships that bridged the public and the nonpublic.[4] Writers, historians, artists, architects, and other cultural creators specialized in the business of publicizing—and illustrating—their protectors' influence. In return, patrons provided publicity for artistic works and gave artists and writers access to social elites where the latter could promote their works.[5]

Thus charged with political and social energies, patronage was vastly more pervasive than it is today. Indeed, prior to the emergence of effective intellectual property rights that would allow writers to profit from the sales of their works, it was the predominant literary and social institution in early modern France. It was a productive system that regulated the circulation and exchange of political, literary, and social representations, shaped strategies of self-fashioning, and defined the critical articulations and boundaries between private and public life. If we are to heed Stephen Greenblatt's call for a "poetics of culture"—a poetics that apprehends the work of art as a "product of a negotiation between a creator or class of creators, equipped with a complex, communally shared repertoire of conventions, and the institutions and practices of society"—then there are few better places to start than patronage.[6]

In a widely cited synthesis, the sociologists S. N. Eisenstadt and Louis Roniger have outlined the basic characteristics of patronage relationships. They are "particularistic and diffuse," involving "simultaneous exchange of different types of resources." Although "informal," rather than "legal," these relationships are characterized by "a strong element of unconditionality and of long-range credit" and "a strong element of interpersonal obligation, loyalty, and spiritual attachment." They differ from kinship relations in that they are "theoretically voluntary" and from friendships in that there is an "inequality between patron and client" that tends to "undermine the horizontal group organization and solidarity of clients and patrons alike."[7]

Because patronage is diffuse, particularistic, and informal, its study has provided an alternative to functionalist and developmentalist approaches in the social sciences, with their characteristic focus on the process of modernization.[8] Rather than placing the emphasis on the evolution of large-scale social and political structures, such work has tended to highlight the importance of social networks that are both local and contingent. In particular, the study of patronage has been attractive to those historians who resist a modernization account of early modern society. Modernization historians (following Max Weber) tend to consider patronage as a feudal anachronism, a historical oddity in the implacable march toward capitalism and a rational, bureaucratic state. In contrast, recent work has used patronage to highlight the diffuse and personal nature of power in early modern society. Sharon Kettering, for example, has developed an account of the history of the French state in which absolutism appears not as a rational replacement for patronage, but rather as a series of strategic interventions by the crown with the intention of co-opting existing patronage networks.[9]

With its emphasis on the particular and the personal, the study of patronage can similarly serve as an antidote to monolithic, abstract models of the relationship between culture and power, such as those found in much recent cultural theory. While acknowledging the power of institutions and shared representations, a patronage-based focus recognizes the old dictum that "power is personal"—a notion that is eloquently illustrated in the two quotes that serve as epigraphs to this introduction. Although the principle still rings true today, the idea that an individual's social capital and political capital were functions of whom he or she knew was much more powerful in early modern society, where familial and corporate ties (such as participation in guilds, religious organizations, and public dignities) were at the heart of social life. Describing the case of Renaissance Italy, Ronald Weissman has written that "one did not seek to reduce all relations to the morally neutral cash nexus . . . Rather one sought to deal whenever possible with patrons, clients, family, and friends, or failing this, to convert all neutral relations, all necessary contacts with strangers, into ties of obligation, gratitude, and reciprocity."[10]

This highly personalized and hierarchical system inevitably exerted an influence on literary practice, shaping the exchanges that defined the economic, social, and political value of literature and favoring certain genres and modes of expression.[11] The promise of social advancement created a gradient of desire that generated representations and put them into circulation. In their attempts to win over patrons, writers were drawn into an elitist mode of cultural production and consumption that promoted a hierarchy of literary value based on aristocratic canons of taste. At the same time, because such relationships were fragile, strategies of authorial self-promotion and self-fashioning acquired a particular affective intensity and sense of urgency. A comprehensive picture of the relationship between literature and power in early modern France requires that we supplement the analysis of the rhetoric of royal sovereignty (for example, the king's two bodies) with an awareness of the contingent rhetorical strategies that governed the particular relationships between writers and patrons.[12]

My subject is the interplay, in the first half of the seventeenth century, between literary patronage on the one hand, and rhetoric on the other. I understand rhetoric broadly, as both a specific set of discursive practices, including the divisions of discourse, figures, and so on, and eloquence, a contested ideological framework that invests discourse with social and political values. The rhetorical focus adopted here owes much to Marc Fumaroli's seminal work on seventeenth-century French rhetoric and its antecedents. For Fumaroli, rhetoric is not a footnote to the history of seventeenth-century literature, but rather quite the opposite. Prior to our modern compartmentalization of disciplines (politics, ethics, religion, philosophy, educational theory, and so on), rhetoric—the art of human communication—provided a framework of integration and dialogue, a social form that tied together facets of human experience that we now consider distinct. To quote Fumaroli, "Rhetoric crosses the boundaries between the social, the political, and the religious. Without sacrificing its special connections with philosophy, law, morality, and theology, it takes up and embraces the entire human experience."[13] In example after example, he compellingly demonstrates the extent to which rhetoric, much like patronage, was a privileged site of negotiation and exchange between various spheres of human activity.

According to one myth dating back to antiquity, eloquence was in fact the basis of *all* exchange—the origin of society itself. In Cicero's *De inventione,* eloquent language is presented as a civilizing force that takes men from the state of nature (described in almost Hobbesian, if not Darwinian, terms) and organizes them into a rational order. Much as Orpheus, in Greek myth, tamed the wild animals with his song, the orator uses skilled and elegant language to domesticate the beast inside man, transforming him into a social animal. Cicero thus provides a historical fiction that supports his ideal of an eloquent philosophy, a wisdom that would not be merely speculative, but rather a practical tool for living an active, productive life (*vita activa*).[14] This myth of origins is retold throughout antiquity and the early modern period. For Daniel de Priézac (1652), the mellifluous tones of the orator's voice have a civilizing effect, creating social harmony and rational order. "It was the discourse of Reason that engendered the concord of civil life [by] ordering [men's] passions and adjusting them to the harmonic tones. Barely had he [the first orator] invoked the powers and charms of Eloquence, when this queen of hearts, after having drawn [men] away from the mountains where they were wandering dispersed, brought them together under the laws of civil society and, without any other chains than his voice, settled them in cities."[15] This passage evokes the early modern figure of the *Hercule gaulois*—a "Gallic" Hercules with chains attached to his tongue, symbolizing the native power of French eloquence.

In the monarchical culture of sixteenth- and seventeenth-century France, the ideal of the orator necessarily became entangled with royal patronage. The humanist who most eloquently develops this connection is Guillaume Budé, in his *De l'institution du Prince,* published in 1547.[16] In typically humanist fashion, Budé imagines Francis I as nothing less than the very source of eloquence itself, "inspir[ing] in men prompt and ingenious invention, well-ordered and appropriate disposition, copious and suitable elocution, as well as any man could desire."[17] At the same time, he seems to recognize that the royal orator will necessarily differ in important respects from his ancient predecessors. Most notably, his role is more discreet and personal: the treatise devotes an extended discussion to court oratory and lays particular emphasis on the man of letters' potential role as counselor.[18] This shift from oratory to counsel anticipates one of my principal themes, namely, that the flourishing of patronage culture in monarchical culture is bound up with a move away from the traditional *public* scope of rhetoric. It is telling, in this regard, that Cicero makes his appearance in Budé's treatise not as a public orator, but rather as a private petitioner, pleading with Caesar on behalf of his exiled friends.[19]

An illumination in the manuscript of *De l'institution* depicts the author personally presenting a copy of his book to Francis I (figure 1). Budé, we saw, described eloquence as a gift from the king; here, the gift comes back full circle, in the form of learned counsel. As Roger Chartier has shown, the iconography of this scene can be traced back to the Middle Ages, when donors were frequently depicted assuming postures of submission as they offered religious edifices, which appear as miniature models, to God. This representation of divine sovereignty was later carried over to royal iconography, with the king replacing God, the writer replacing the donor, and the book replacing the church.[20] The image thus establishes a link between the personal authority of the king and the man of letters' personal service to the crown.[21]

The notion of a personal or particularistic rhetoric dates back to

Fig. 1. Guillaume Budé presenting his book to Francis I. From Guillaume Budé, *L'Institution du prince*. Arsenal MS-5103, folio 1v. Bibliothèque Nationale de France.

antiquity. Most notably, the pseudo-Ciceronian *Rhetorica ad Herennium* allowed for multiple registers (high, middle, low) that corresponded to the varying situations in which an orator might find himself. Whereas the high style was appropriate for public oratory, the lower familiar style was considered to be better suited to private exchange between individuals. During the Renaissance, Erasmus advocated a mode of expression that eschewed the floweriness of rhetorical performance in favor of an "interior style" more suited to the spiritual growth of the individual.[22] Montaigne, in the "Au lecteur" (To the Reader) of his *Essais,* falls within this broad Erasmian tradition. Speaking as a particular person ("I have set myself no goal but a domestic and private one"), he addresses an audience of particulars ("I have dedicated it to the private convenience of my relatives and friends").[23] With their obsessive focus on the writer as embodied subject, the *Essais* represent a radically *self*-oriented rhetorical mode that contrasts sharply with the primarily *other*-oriented tendencies of seventeenth-century rhetoric. By contrast, sixteenth-century Italian models such as Baldesar Castiglione's *Book of the Courtier* more directly anticipate later developments in France. Castiglione describes conversation as an art of the particular: because no two men are totally alike, rhetoric becomes a matter of improvisation and constant adjustment to the uniqueness of one's interlocutor.[24] This principle, the basis of any sociable rhetoric, was picked up by seventeenth-century theorists of conversation such as the Chevalier de Méré (see chapter 6).

The idea of a particularistic rhetoric was given a new impetus and urgency by the rapid ascension of the early modern state, with its increasingly sharp public/private divide. Because of their associations with the civil disorder of the Wars of Religion (1559–98), public deliberation and its corollary—public rhetoric—fell out of favor and much of both private and political life was increasingly circumscribed within the *cabinet.*[25] With the Edict of Nantes, individuals were granted some degree of freedom of conscience, as long as they more or less kept it to themselves. At the same time, reason of state dictated that political deliberation be shrouded in secrecy. Thus, the rise of absolutism encouraged the expansion of two parallel realms of personalized discourse: private conversation and secret political counsel.

The prevalence of patronage could only reinforce such trends. A particularistic system, patronage required not the tools of public oratory, but rather a particularistic rhetoric, narrowly targeted to an "audience of one." This rhetoric was necessarily *ad hominem* in that the success or failure of a given performance was not a function of swaying the opinions of a broad public, but rather of seducing a single individual. Because it shaped the relationship between writer, text, and audience, patronage affected the deepest structures of literary discourse. As Robert Evans has written with respect to Ben Jonson, an English contemporary of the authors whom we will examine in the pages that follow, "[T]he text, for a patronage poet . . . was . . . closely tied to the literal act of speech, and thus to the author's personality and especially to interpersonal relationships."[26] A patronage text is always written for *someone*, a specific person or persons.

This study will examine the exchanges between patronage and literary practice within the generation of writers that came of age in the 1620s and 1630s, during Richelieu's rise to—and assertion of—power. One aspect of the analysis is essentially literary, concentrating on how rhetorical choices, fashioned identities, and literary discourses were shaped by the highly interpersonal dynamic of patronage. In addition to texts written for (and on behalf of) patrons, I will depend heavily on the rich contemporary literature dealing with the nature of human relationships, including treatises on conversation and etiquette. A second dimension is more properly historical and political. This period saw dramatic changes in the relationships between aristocratic elites and the crown (to the detriment of the former), as well as a rapid expansion and reorganization of literary culture (in the form of academies, salons, and the increased recognition of writers). To better understand these changes, I will explore how writers and patrons created and maintained personal connections, and how they leveraged these connections to fabricate and assert their authority.

In this study, I will treat patronage not as a fixed social mechanism, but rather as an indeterminate space—sitting on the thresholds between private and public, the self and the other, text and performance. Each chapter attempts to apprehend this liminality from a different angle. The first chapter situates literary patronage within the broader context of hierarchical relationships in early modern France. Such relationships were deeply ambivalent, characterized by a strange mixture of idealism and practicality, constraint and flexibility. Instead of merely assuming that patronage is constraining, I argue that we might also consider the dynamic possibilities that it offered.

The following four chapters constitute the heart of the analysis. The second chapter focuses on the case of Jean-Louis Guez de Balzac (1597–1654) and his complex relationship to rhetorical tradition and political power. His *Lettres* (1624) enact a displacement of eloquence from public contexts into the semiprivate space of the letter, which dramatizes the personal relationship between writer and patron. The second part of the chapter examines the contentious quarrel over the nature of eloquence that followed the publication of the *Lettres*. This polemic reveals the contradictions and ambiguities that eventually undermined his ambitious project.

The third chapter examines the status of occasional poems written on behalf, and at the bequest, of patrons. After an overview of the various forms of collaborative authorship in the seventeenth century, from secretarial practice to court ballet, I turn to the literary implications of these practices. Writing on behalf of a patron profoundly problematizes the relationship between historical occasion, subjectivity, and poetry. François Malherbe's "Alcandre cycle" (written for Henry IV during his infatuation with Charlotte de Montmorency) illustrates one possible response to the demands of writing for an "other." These poems adopt a technique of distancing in which the affective experience of the other is filtered by linguistic artifice and fictionalized. The occasion is ultimately not so much the pretext of poetry as it is the product of a ventriloquistic performance.

The fourth chapter continues with this question, turning to authors who have been labeled as *irréguliers* (nonconformists) and/or libertines and exploring their responses to the demands of writing for/about others. Rather than idealizing these poets as rebels, I argue that we would do better to acknowledge the extent to which their poetry is implicated in practices of patronage. Each of these poets makes a virtue of necessity, exploring the poet's protean ability to assimilate and integrate other voices. As the cases of François Tristan L'Hermite and Théophile de Viau will show, however, this assimilation is not unproblematic. The chapter concludes with an episode from Charles Sorel's comic novel *Francion* in which the eponymous hero takes advantage of his position as a ghostwriter of love poems to claim the sexual favors of a lady for himself. In positing a writer's right to the fruits of his own labor, Sorel anticipates the notion of intellectual proprietorship that would emerge in the eighteenth century.

A fifth chapter seeks to uncover the traces of the personal character of power in the most public of literary forms, the theater. I examine various forms of private intelligibility in seventeenth-century dramatic practice: private performances and readings; the single-point-perspective *scène à l'italienne* (Italian stage decor), which requires a unique ideal vantage point from within the playhouse; and dramatic prefaces (Pierre Corneille, Jean Mairet, Pierre Du Ryer). A significant portion of the chapter is devoted to a close reading of Pierre Du Ryer's *Les Vendanges de Suresnes*. Du Ryer's comedy illustrates an important claim of this chapter, namely, that patronage offered writers an alternative to spectacle (which was the territory of actors) and commercial publication (where publishers reigned supreme). Finally, the chapter examines the other side of dramatic patronage: its institutionalization and bureaucratization under Richelieu.

The last chapter is devoted to the intersections between patronage rhetoric and related social practices such as academies and conversation in the works of writers including Eustache de Refuge; Nicolas Faret; Pierre d'Ortigue de Vaumorière; Antoine Gombaud, Chevalier de Méré; and Paul Pellisson. Although these practices are often (and rightfully) considered to be distinct, I argue that they emerged out of the same general economy of personal power found in patronage. Over the course of the seventeenth century, however, each of these forms took on an increasingly specific dynamic, with the French Academy reflecting the growing bureaucratization of patronage and conversation emerging as a kind of autonomous, egalitarian social space. These trends, which correspond to efforts by various historical actors to leverage personal connections to create new bases of power and influence, anticipate aspects of literary and cultural modernity.

1
Theorizing Patronage

> Rien n'est libre en ce monde, et chaque homme dépend,
> Comte, princes, sultans, de quelque autre plus grand.
>
> [Nothing in this world is free, and every man,
> Whether he be a count, prince or sultan, depends on someone greater than he.]
>
> —Mathurin Régnier, *Satire* III

THIS CHAPTER SEEKS TO PROVIDE A SELECTIVE OVERVIEW OF RESEARCH on patronage in seventeenth-century France. The first part of the chapter will examine patronage in a broad sense, defined as a general form of social figuration, before focusing more narrowly on literary patronage and questions of terminology. We will discover that patronage is an ambiguous and paradoxical historical object—sometimes appearing as structured and hierarchical, other times revealing itself to be flexible and dynamic. Two case studies—Jean-Louis Guez de Balzac's *Mécénas* and François Le Métel de Boisrobert's *Épîtres*—will illustrate the dialectic of frustration and mobility characteristic of seventeenth-century discourses on patronage. The same factors that make patronage difficult to apprehend as a historical object, I will argue, make it central to our understanding of cultural change in early modern France.

THE SOCIETY OF ORDERS: MOUSNIER AND HIS CRITICS

The most influential account of nobiliary patronage in early modern France is contained in the work of Roland Mousnier. Patronage, or something very much like it, is central to Mousnier's famous "society of orders." "From the top to the bottom of society," he writes, "men were bound together by bonds of fealty, a man-to-man relationship between *maître* (master) and *fidèle* (dependent) which became more important under Henri IV and Louis XIII than feudalism itself."[1] Because this hierarchy was not based on land or on economic production, it cannot properly be assimilated to either feudalism or a modern class system. The basis of the society of orders, rather, is "the social esteem, honor, and dignity attached by society to different social functions, without there being any direct link between this and the production of material goods."[2] As this brief passage suggests, Mousnier stresses symbolic and affective factors over material ones. *Ancien régime* society is "a world of feelings and ideas completely alien . . . to Frenchmen of the 19th and 20th centuries."[3]

The relationship between master and dependent reproduces on a local and personal level the structure and character of the society as a whole. "It is . . . not a mere service relationship, a mere exchange of services and rewards, but a total devotion, a gift of oneself, on the one side, and a pledge of affection on the other. The bond that binds *maître* and *fidèle* is an *emotional* one."[4] Indeed this bond is so powerful that there can be a loss of individual identity, the two becoming "almost one man in two bodies."[5] Mousnier eloquently, and somewhat nostalgically, traces the gradual deterioration of this bond: first, in the seventeenth century, as the autocratic Louis XIV appropriated and reshaped existing patronage networks; and then, in the eighteenth, when "the philosophy of the Enlightenment turned men's hearts away from such relationships" and "the spirit of capitalism, accustoming everyone to translate everything in figures, gradually dried them up."[6]

Mousnier's model has obvious attractions for the literary historian/critic. First, it offers an affective landscape—a world of emotions that promises to provide rich fodder for literary texts. Indeed, as Mousnier describes it, fidelity has much in common with friendship, a central *topos* of early modern literary culture. (I will touch on the problematic relationship between friendship and patronage in chapters 2 and 4.) Second, Mousnier places the question of representation at center stage. "Esteem, honor, and dignity" only exist, after all, to the extent that they are represented—whether through words or other media such as painting, sculpture, architecture, clothing, religious ritual, civic ritual, court festivity, and so on. (For Mousnier, the social is primarily, though not exclusively, cultural.) Because Mousnier plays down conflict between orders, his influence has been especially strong on politically conservative scholars, such as Marc Fumaroli, who are drawn to his idealized vision of an organic society where everyone and everything had its place.[7]

Not surprisingly, other scholars have been less receptive to Mousnier's vision of *ancien régime* society. He has been especially criticized for neglecting material factors—both in early modern society in general, and more particularly within the patronage relationship. William Beik, Sharon Kettering, and David Parker, among others, have sought to challenge Mousnier's approach by stressing the central role of self-interest and/or class interest within early modern French society.[8] Kettering, in particular, has questioned aspects of Mousnier's methodology, most notably his use of historical sources that supposedly document the affection and loyalty between patrons and clients. Such representations, she contends, do not necessarily reflect the reality of patronage, but rather constitute the superficial veneer behind which historical players hid their real motivations and feelings. On the basis of her own study of patronage relationships, she arrives at a vision of seventeenth-century society diametrically opposed to Mousnier's. "[I]ntense emotional loyalty was not the determining characteristic of most relationships, albeit of some . . . Many relationships were characterized by self-interest and by short-term, serial loyalties in which a dependent changed protectors for reasons of self-interest; multiple loyalties were not uncommon."[9] Kettering, in sum, sees patronage as a practical business—a loose complex of alliances and interests in which concepts such as "loyalty" and "affection" are merely words.

My purpose, here, is not to settle the scholarly debate around Mousnier's work, but rather to use it to explore the attitudes and presuppositions that underlie our thinking about patronage. Broadly speaking, we find two ways of talking about patronage among recent historians and seventeenth-century writers alike. Following Mousnier, we can understand it as a relatively static social and moral model. Or, like Kettering, we can attempt to look at it in less idealized terms, as a constantly shifting network of personal interests and influence. If we embrace the latter approach, it becomes difficult to talk about a "patronage *system*" except in an extremely broad and nonspecific sense. The only thing systematic about patronage is its prevalence in the seventeenth century.

These alternatives, I would suggest, present us with a false choice. Kettering's critique certainly provides a useful reminder of the fact that historical actors cannot always be taken at their word. As she suggests, we should take the rhetoric of affection between patron and client with a grain of salt. Does this mean, however, that the elaborate declarations of loyalty found in early modern texts can simply be disregarded? If claims of fidelity and love were so transparently meaningless, why were they so prevalent? One obvious explanation is that such representations did matter. Specifically, the professions of fidelity served to reaffirm the moral and affective basis of a system that lacked a formal code of conduct. However short-term and serial they may have been, patronage relationships were not discrete transactions; instead, they depended on a fragile system of credit in which services were eventually rewarded with protection and vice versa. Moreover, since both protection and services were intangibles, it was impossible to establish a rigid formula for equitable exchange. We might therefore suppose that the notion of fidelity, of an affective bond between patron and client, served to foster a necessary but tenuous climate of trust within a system that lacked formal guarantees.

Early modern patronage, from the fifteenth to eighteenth centuries, is perhaps best understood as a transitional, hybrid form of social organization, intermediate between feudalism, a relatively static hierarchical order based on land, and the modern capitalist state, with its dynamic focus on efficiency and competition. Patronage retains the hierarchical and personal character of feudalism, but introduces a greater degree of dynamism, competition, and rationality. Because patronage, in contrast to feudalism, is not based on land, it is both more flexible and more precarious. Both the client and the patron are to some extent free agents who can choose to renegotiate or abandon the relationship.[10] There is thus a kind of market-like competition. On the one hand, clients may vie with each other for the favor of a patron. On the other hand, a client may play off potential patrons against each other. This hybrid character has led Orest Ranum to characterize early modern patronage as "bastard feudalism."[11]

Patrons, Writers, and Rewards

The central role of patronage in seventeenth-century literary culture was largely neglected by the literary historians of the late nineteenth and early twentieth century. Although prominent scholars such as Taine, Brunetière, and Lanson were aware of it, they were generally more interested in other literary institutions, most notably the salons, academies, and the court. One cannot help but suspect that the diffuse, hybrid nature of patronage played a role in this omission. Literary historians, we might presume, were uncomfortable with a phenomenon that lacked clear geographical, social, and moral boundaries.

Antoine Adam, writing in the 1930s, deserves credit for being one of the first literary historians to insist forcefully on the networks of loyalties in which writers were entangled. "At that time more than today, every writer was a publicist. He was engaged in a party. He wrote for a man who paid him."[12] Later generations of scholars, such as Henri-Jean Martin, have placed this insight within a broader socioeconomic context. Without an economic and legal framework that allowed writers to make a profit on their work, Martin argued, obtaining the personal favor of an influential patron was one of the few ways that they could make a living.[13] Patronage, in other words, was not so much a system or an institution as the *de facto* state of affairs that prevailed in the absence of modern institutions. Although seventeenth-century patronage has a number of distinctive characteristics, much of what follows is applicable to the Middle Ages and sixteenth century, both of which enjoyed flourishing patronage cultures, as well.[14]

Seventeenth-century patrons hailed from a broad and varied social spectrum. Needless to say, the royal family recruited literary talent both for official propaganda and to provide the scripts for ballets, tournaments, and other court festivities. Continuing a tradition that went back the Middle Ages, Louis XIII personally supported a number of poets, including François Malherbe and Jean Ogier de Gombauld.[15] In general, however, Henry IV and Louis XIII were not regarded as particularly generous in comparison to their Valois predecessors, who had maintained magnificent courts.[16] Indeed, according to Tallemant des Réaux, Louis XIII cut poetic pensions dramatically after the death of Cardinal Richelieu.[17] By contrast, Marie de' Medici (the queen mother), owing perhaps to her Florentine origins, was an active patron of both writers (Malherbe and Boisrobert) and artists (Rubens, most famously), as was her rival Marguerite de Valois (Maynard and Maillet).[18] Gaston d'Orléans, Louis's brother, took after his mother, surrounding himself with *gens de lettres,* including François Tristan L'Hermite, Vincent Voiture, Claude Favre de Vaugelas, Louis de Neufgermain, the baron de Blot, and André Mareschal, making him one of the most important patrons of the period.[19]

Prior to 1662, when Colbert (with the help of Chapelain) began to centralize support for writers by granting them royal pensions on a large scale, aristocratic patronage was undoubtedly more significant than royal patronage.[20] Like royal *largesse,* aristocratic patronage had a long and distinguished history in France. In the seventeenth century, Henri de Montmorency was especially generous, providing support to Jean Mairet, François Maynard, and Théophile de Viau, the last of whom he protected when the poet was being pursued for obscenity and impiety (see chapter 4). Like Gaston, Montmorency surrounded himself with literary talent, and his execution in 1632 was a devastating blow to a number of writers, including Mairet, who depended on his friendship and protection.[21] Other prominent aristocratic patrons of literature and their clients include the duc de Vendôme (Pierre Du Ryer), the duc d'Épernon (Jean-Louis Guez de Balzac), the duc de Retz (Marc-Antoine Girard de Saint-Amant), the comte de Soissons (Pierre Corneille, Jean de Rotrou, Pierre Du Ryer, Georges de Scudéry, and the theater, generally), and the duc de Longueville, who famously gave a pension to Jean Chapelain for celebrating his illustrious ancestor Dunois in the epic *Pucelle.*

Writers performed a wide variety of services for their aristocratic patrons. Some of these services were properly literary. According to Tallemant, Montmorency "always had men of learning around him whom he employed to write verses for him, to discuss a thousand matters with him, and to tell him what to think about things that were being published at the time."[22] Men of letters thus served as literary advisors, composing occasional verse and guiding their protectors in matters of taste. Other services included, but were not limited to, tutoring children, acting as a secretary, and orchestrating publicity campaigns on behalf of a patron. Significantly, many of the aristocratic patrons mentioned above participated in the opposition to the crown at one point or another, whether during the Regency (1610–14), under Richelieu, or later during the *Fronde* (France's mid-century civil war, 1648–53). Writers were therefore in a delicate position. On the one hand, their talents were sought out by factious aristocrats eager to influence public opinion. On the other hand, the risks were high if a patron were disgraced, exiled, or even executed (as in the case of Montmorency). Not all aristocratic patrons were prominent grandees (*grands*), however. François Averton, comte de Belin, for example, would probably be mostly forgotten today if it were not for his protection of dramatic authors and acting companies (see chapter 5).

The third major category of patrons included ministers and other royal officers who, more often than not, owed their influence to their office rather than their birth (although many offices were effectively hereditary). Although ministers such as Michel de l'Hôpital had supported the arts during the sixteenth century, their influence grew with the expansion of the royal administration. Since the latter was largely devoted to collecting taxes and distributing justice, these patrons had ample opportunities to provide protection and material support, both direct and indirect, to writers. Many, moreover, had social pretensions. Like aristocratic patrons, therefore, they often depended on writers and artists for their publicity value. The very act of supporting the arts was a sign of a magnanimous temperament and good taste, two noble qualities that social-climbing royal officers were eager to demonstrate.[23]

Cardinal Richelieu is undoubtedly the most famous and influential of the ministerial patrons. Among the many writers whom he supported, two deserve special mention: François le Métel de Boisrobert, who acted as his literary secretary in his dealings with other writers (see below), and Jean Desmarets de Saint-Sorlin, who was his personal playwright.[24] Richelieu's patronage was particularly important in the field of dramatic literature (see chapter 5) and in the reform of the French language. He famously transformed the French Academy from an informal gathering into an officially recognized arbiter of linguistic usage and literary taste (see chapter 6).

Other ministerial patrons who deserve special mention include Cardinal Mazarin, Pierre Séguier, and Nicolas Fouquet. Mazarin, due to personal taste (he preferred Italian opera over French theater) and political and financial constraint (the Thirty Years' War and the *Fronde* took their toll on the minister's authority and the French treasury), did not continue the level of patronage under Richelieu. Indeed one literary historian has gone so far as to speak of a crisis in literary patronage after the death of Richelieu.[25] In exile in 1652 during the *Fronde,* Paul Scarron bitterly compared the treatment of writers under the two regimes:

> Les pauvres courtisans de Muses
> Sont aujourd'huy traittez de buzes,
> Qu'autrefois defunct Richelieu
> Qu'ils ont traitté de demy-Dieu,
> Traittoit de la façon qu'Auguste,
> Prince aussi genereux que juste,

> A traitté les hommes sçavans
> Dont les vers sont encor vivans
> Et vivront malgré l'ignorance.[26]

> [The poor courtiers of the Muses
> Are now treated like fools.
> Once the late Richelieu,
> Whom they treated like a demigod,
> Treated them in the manner that Augustus,
> A generous and fair prince,
> Treated men of learning.
> Their verses are still alive
> And will survive in the face of ignorance.]

Scarron made an exception for Séguier, however, whom he viewed as continuing the legacy of Richelieu.[27] First keeper of the seals, then chancellor, Séguier was in an ideal position to offer protection to writers. As the highest officer of royal justice, his influence could be decisive in determining the outcome of lawsuits. When Boisrobert's nephews were being pursued for murder, for example, he addressed a witty epistle to Séguier, later published in his *Épîtres*, begging him to intercede on their behalf.[28] The chancellor, moreover, controlled a substantial budget from which he carved out pensions for writers. (Tallemant refers to pensions *sur le Sceau* [on the seal] that Séguier distributed in order to attract praise from writers.)[29] It certainly did not escape anyone's attention, finally, that the chancellor was in charge of royal censorship.[30] This meant not only that he could create obstacles to publication, but also that he could negotiate a favorable *privilège* on behalf of a writer or his publisher. Not surprisingly, then, many writers sought to catch Séguier's attention by dedicating their works to him. Notable among those who benefited directly from his generosity were Germain Habert, abbé de Cérisy, Daniel de Priézac, and Jacques Esprit. Many others profited indirectly, especially after the chancellor became Richelieu's successor as protector of the French Academy (see chapter 6).

The last of the great ministerial patrons was the superintendant of finances Nicolas Fouquet, immortalized in the works of Jean de La Fontaine and Madeleine de Scudéry. Before his dramatic arrest in 1661, Fouquet, advised by his secretary Paul Pellisson, lent his support to writers such as Paul Scarron, Philippe Quinault, Pierre Corneille (whose *Œdipe* he commissioned), and Molière, in addition to La Fontaine and Scudéry. After the arrest, Louis XIV appropriated many of Fouquet's artistic clients (most famously Charles Le Brun, André Le Nôtre, and Louis Le Vau), signaling that patronage would henceforth be an increasingly royal affair.[31]

Writers, finally, sought the protection of lesser ministers, royal councillors, and financiers. Financiers, or *partisans*, were generally unpopular figures, but they had social pretensions and access to vast sums of money. Pierre Corneille earned a reputation for flattery that persists to this day for his dedication of *Cinna* (1640) to Montauron, a rich *partisan*, whom he compared to Augustus Caesar. Corneille, it should be noted, was hardly the only writer to play to Montauron's legendary vanity; François Tristan L'Hermite and André Mareschal both dedicated works to him as well.[32] To the roster of lesser patrons, we can add innumerable *maîtres de requêtes, présidents de parlement*, churchmen, local magistrates, and other dignitaries whose names are often unfamiliar to modern readers, but who exerted notable influence in their own time.

How exactly did patronage benefit writers? Perhaps the most familiar form of patronage reward is the *gratification* or one-time gift. In exchange for a dedication, perhaps, or a luxuriously bound copy of a book, a patron would give a writer a sum of money.[33] Montauron, for instance, reportedly gave Corneille 200 *pistoles* for the dedication of *Cinna*. In 1624, Malherbe had similarly received 1,500 *livres* (equivalent to 150 *pistoles*) for a sonnet.[34] *Gratifications*, however, were neither the most sought after nor the most common fruits of patronage for the simple reason that they were isolated affairs and therefore did not provide financial stability. A more satisfactory solution was an annual pension or salary of some sort. A writer might receive a pension, for example, for serving a grandee as a secretary (as Pierre Du Ryer did for the duc de Vendôme) or as a *maître d'hôtel* (as Vincent Voiture did for Madame, the sister-in-law of the king). A pension, however, provided extremely limited security. Payment was intermittent at best, unless the writer had the support of an influential sponsor in the royal adminstration (see the case of Boisrobert, below). A pension, in other words, was not a measurable, exchangeable commodity in the modern sense; to be worth something, it needed to be backed up by personal influence.

Alternatively, a writer might seek to use a patron's clout to gain a lucrative *charge,* or office, in the royal administration. If the office were hereditary, this was of course an added bonus.[35] Ecclesiastical *bénéfices*, or livings tied to the church, were another source of income that could be obtained through patronage.[36] These livings carried varying degrees of responsibility. Antoine Godeau and Jean Bertaut both became bishops (of Grasse and Séez, respectively), with all of the privileges and obligations that such positions carried. As Abbot of Châtillon, Boisrobert was drawn into the sordid politics of religious orders. Isaac de Benserade, by contrast, was able to receive pensions attached to one bishopric and two abbeys while remaining a layman.[37] Like *charges*, ecclesiastical *bénéfices* allowed writers to convert the favor of a patron into financial security.

Not all of the fruits of patronage came in monetary form. A patron's generosity might also extend to room and/or board.[38] According to Tallemant, the abbé (later coadjuteur and cardinal) de Retz gave Gilles Ménage a room and welcomed him at his table, although the latter supposedly repaid this generosity with ingratitude during the *Fronde*.[39] Pierre Corneille, similarly, had a room at the Hôtel de Guise from 1662 onward.[40] In addition to being a financial boon, the privilege of sitting at the table of a great patron was a flattering sign of familiarity. In exchange for this hospitality, the writer was expected to enliven the dinner-table conversation. In his "Contemplateur," Saint-Amant describes dining at the table of the duc de Retz:

> J'entretiens mon Duc à la table.
> En-tant comme il me l'est permis,
> De quelque propos delectable.[41]
>
> [I entertain my duke at table,
> If he permits me,
> With some delectable subject.]

The social connections of the patron, finally, offered the writer the opportunity to venture into polite society, where he could present his work and expand his network of social connections. Tallemant attributed much of Ménage's social success to the influence of his protector Retz. "It is well-established that he owes almost his entire reputation and his most valued acquaintances (that is to say, the great lords and great ladies) to the coadjutor, who welcomed him into his home."[42] In particular, the protection of a noble might help a writer gain entry to a salon, such as the *chambre bleue* of Mme de Rambouillet, where polite manners were learned and literary reputations were made. In the emerging culture of the salon, wit and refined manners were generally more valued than noble birth, opening up possibilities for social advancement.[43] This symbolic and social gain often came at a price, however, as the writer could easily squander his modest savings by purchasing the expensive clothing and retinue necessary for public appearances.

What's in a Name?: Terminological Issues

In his influential *Naissance de l'écrivain,* Alain Viala has argued that it is necessary to distinguish between two distinct sociological practices of literary patronage. Following Italian usage, he proposes two terms, *clientélisme* and *mécénat,* each of which corresponds to different uses of the English word "patronage." *Clientélisme,* for Viala, is not a specifically literary practice; it encompasses, rather, all exchanges of service for favor within a hierarchical society. The writer who serves as a secretary or tutor in the household of a grandee, he contends, participates in an essentially extraliterary logic of service. By contrast, *mécénat* refers exclusively to subsidies given by a patron to an artist in support of his or her art.[44] Whereas *clientélisme* focuses on service, *mécénat* is primarily defined in aesthetic terms, modeled on the supposedly disinterested generosity of Augustus's famous companion, Maecenas (see below). Viala argues that *mécénat* tended to obscure material exchange by foregrounding a dynamic of symbolic exchange in which the writer legitimated the power of the *mécène* and the latter reciprocated by bestowing public recognition on the writer. The economic practice that arguably best captures this dynamic was the *gratification,* in that there was ostensibly no fee for service and no long-term relationship between patron and client; the money given, in principle, was a pure gift, a token of the patron's appreciation.[45]

Viala's typology reproduces the terms of the debate between Mousnier and Kettering. On the one side, we have the symbolic, the affective, and the ideal; on the other, we have self-interested material exchange. The boundary between *mécénat* and *clientélisme,* however, is tenuous at best. Even if the writer attempts to obfuscate the utilitarian character of the exchange in the practice of *mécénat,* he or she nonetheless performs a sort of service, albeit a symbolic one. This is especially true when the literary work is an exercise in panegyric—that is, the aggrandizement of the patron—or when it advances a political agenda, either overtly or covertly. The patron, to be sure, experiences aesthetic pleasure in such instances; this pleasure, however, derives from the appreciation of a job well done, a successful act of publicity and promotion. There is no particularly good reason either to limit the notion of aesthetic exchange to literary production. Aesthetic/symbolic exchange was, in fact, prevalent at all levels of court society, from the interactions between individuals to the architectural space in which these interactions took place. If, as Domna Stanton has suggested, the seventeenth-century aristocrat was in fact a "work of art," where do we draw the line between service and aesthetics?[46] Viala's tendency to relegate political and polemical treatises to *clientélisme* is similarly unfounded. It may be granted that such treatises usually rendered political services; at the same time, however, they were often read and analyzed in terms of their literary qualities. It is therefore difficult to apply Viala's criteria to works such as Jean-Louis Guez de Balzac's *Prince* or Gabriel Naudé's *Considérations politiques sur les coups d'état*, polemical texts whose efficacy depended on aesthetic and rhetorical strategies of seduction.

The problem is that Viala is comparing two basically incommensurable concepts. *Clientélisme*, as he describes it, is essentially a material and institutional practice involving the exchange of tangible services and goods. *Mécénat*, on the other hand, is an ideal—an ideology, even. It relates not to how things "really are," but rather to how social actors describe and imagine them. To use Louis Althusser's famous formulation, it is "a representation of the imaginary relationship of individuals to their real conditions of existence."[47] Without necessarily implying that the two cannot exist side by side, Viala's distinctions falsely suggest that social practices are *either* material *or* symbolic and that social agents somehow choose between the two. Thus we find claims such as the following (regarding a pamphlet written by Dubosc-Montandré): "We are *really* [*bien*] in the logic of clientelist service, *despite the protestations of disinterest that seek to accredit the impartiality of the writer*."[48] According to this kind of reasoning, however, nothing is ever "really" ideological, since ideology is never "real." But this defeats the purpose of having such a taxonomy in the first place. In fact, of course, most if not all social practices partake of both dimensions—ideal/ideological and material.

Ironically, Viala's own research illustrates the difficulty of creating rigorous distinctions in this area. In the second appendix to *Naissance de l'écrivain*, he provides an extensive list of authors with a chart indicating their relative participation in various literary institutions and practices. While numerous authors partake in *clientélisme* but not in *mécénat*, only one—Charles Sorel—supposedly participates in the latter but not in the former.⁴⁹ (Here, Viala's hairsplitting is rather puzzling. Why does Sorel's appointment as *historiographe du roi* not place him squarely within the realm of *clientélisme?*) This observation would tend to support, of course, Viala's claim that *clientélisme* was more prevalent than *mécénat*. It also suggests, however, that the two practices are in many ways two sides of the same coin. Art historian Dale Kent has warned against the temptation to establish a rigid distinction between *mecenatismo* and *clientelismo* (the terms used in Italian). "This misses the point of the patron's role in a world where patrons and artists were associated in *a network of personal bonds,* and art and literature were a major means of social and self-definition."⁵⁰ Seventeenth-century usage, we will see, underscores this point.

In the seventeenth century, none of these terms—*patronage, mécénat,* or *clientélisme*—existed. We do, however, find related forms. *Patron,* for instance, appears in all three major late seventeenth-century dictionaries, where it serves as a broad synonym for *protecteur*—a much more widely used term, along with its counterpart *créature:*

> Richelet (1680): *Patron. Protecteur, défenseur.* Someone who is interested in our fortune, who attempts to advance it [*qui tâche à la pouser*]. (When one has neither a great fortune nor an illustrious birth, one can accomplish nothing in society without a patron. For many people, a patron is a substitute for merit. To get a patron for oneself.)⁵¹

> Furetière (1690): *Patron,* is also used at court, when speaking of a lord under whose protection one puts oneself to advance one's fortune. Every man who wants to follow the court must have a patron. He will do nothing there without a patron who calls attention to his services.⁵²

> *Dictionnaire de l'Académie* (1694): *Patron. Protecteur* . . . [The term] is also used when speaking of a prince, a minister, a great lord to whom one is attached, and under whose protection one puts oneself in order to advance one's fortune, in order to have some backing [*appui*].⁵³

All three definitions convey a sense of the self-interested, interpersonal power structure of seventeenth-century society. The French Academy notes that a patron is useful for advancing one's fortunes, whereas Richelet cynically comments that patronage often serves as a substitute for wealth, noble birth, and talent. A later edition of Furetière (1727) develops this theme with a quote from Saint-Évremond: "One always appears at court in the shadow of a patron [*à l'abri d'un patron*], so [one might say] that one man is always hidden behind another."[54] In Saint-Évremond's court, every person has a patron hidden behind him, "pulling the strings," so to speak.

Etymologically derived from the Latin *patronus,* which is in turn descended from *pater, patron* evokes the powerful image of the *pater familias* of Roman law. One way to understand patronage, therefore, is as an extension of familial, and more specifically *patriarchal,* relationships.[55] It was not uncommon, for example, for aristocratic families to place their male children as pages in the households of prominent nobles.[56] In exchange for their obedience, the young men would gain a second father—a patron/protector who would stand behind them during their adult lives. Commenting in his *Nouveau traité de civilité* on the deference due to fathers and mothers, Antoine Courtin adds, "[A]nd under the name of mothers and fathers are included all those who have a comparable authority or jurisdiction over us."[57]

Both Furetière and Richelet also contain entries for *Mécénas* (or Maecenas) and/or *Mécène* (the latter term is reserved for poetry, presumably because it is more suitable for rhyming):

> Richelet (1680): *Mécénas, mécène,* n.m. In prose, we say *Mécénas* and in verse *Mécénas* and *Mécène*. The name of a man who was in favor in the time of Augustus and who supported men of letters. (The late Maecenas was courteous.)
> **Mécénas, mécène*. Protector of men of letters. (Either stop making poets, Muses, or make Maecenases for them.)[58]

> Furetière (1690): *Mecenas.* Masc. noun. The proper name of a Roman knight, a favorite of Augustus, who was fond of men of letters, and who was generous toward them, especially the poets. Since then, the name has been used to honor all rich men who have favored authors and who have purchased the dedications to their books. There are no more Maecenases. Therefore, there are no more Horaces or Virgils.[59]

Here we find the equivalent of the modern "patron of the arts"—an idealized figure modeled on the historical figure of Maecenas (70–8 BC), confidant to the emperor Augustus and supporter of the arts (see below). No sharp distinction is made between *mécène* and *patron,* however. As a matter of fact, we find the same language of personal protection ("protector" [*protecteur*], "supported" [*appuyoit*]) in both instances. Furetière does refer to the *mécène*'s love of art and artists, supporting Viala's distinction between *mécénat* and *clientél-*

isme. In the later edition of Furetière's *Dictionnaire* (1727), however, the two terms are conflated in an anonymous quote:

> Où chercher un Patron dans le siecle où nous sommes?
> Il est de grands esprits, il est de savans hommes;
> Mais il n'est plus de Mecenas.[60]

> [Where are we to find a patron in this century of ours?
> There are great minds, and wise men,
> But there are no more Maecenases.]

Contemporaries, in other words, do not seem to have considered these two terms as mutually exclusive, or even sharply distinct. Although they had different connotations—*mécène* was significantly more idealized, *patron* more socially descriptive—they were potentially reversible. As the cases of Balzac and Boisrobert will illustrate, patronage was often viewed with a paradoxical mixture of idealism and cynicism.

Guez de Balzac and the Many Faces of Maecenas

> On doit tout espérer d'un Monarque si juste
> Mais sans un Mécénas, à quoi sert un Auguste?[61]

> [We can hope for everything from a Monarch so just,
> But without a Maecenas, what good is an Augustus?]

The nostalgia for a Golden Age of patronage under Augustus and Maecenas is a recurring leitmotif of seventeenth-century literature.[62] Indeed it would not to be an exaggeration to say that Maecenas was a seventeenth-century cultural icon—the expression of the aspirations and ideals of an entire generation of writers. Jean-Louis Guez de Balzac's *Mécénas,* written around 1639 for the *salonnière* Mme de Rambouillet, seeks to make this mythical figure relevant to the contemporary political and cultural scene.

Mécénas begins with a summary of the events that led to Augustus's rise to power and, consequently, to the passage from republic to principate, and eventually empire. Balzac provides a double explanation for the change in Rome's fortunes. On the one hand, the fall of the republic was precipitated by Augustus's political cunning and military successes.[63] On the other, it reflected a calculated decision on the part of the Romans themselves. They accepted Augustus as tyrant, he explains, because they were weary of political instability and civil war. In place of the republican ethic of self-government and moral rigor, untenable in the face of recent events, the Romans accepted an ethic of prosperity and leisure:

> À la fin ils aimèrent mieux un maître certain et une paisible servitude, que des changements tous les jours, et une perpétuelle frayeur de guerre civile. Le repos qu'ils crurent être un bien essentiel, leur tint lieu de liberté, qui ne leur sembla plus qu'un plaisir de fantaisie . . . Chacun fut bien aise d'être de loisir, après tant de fâcheuses affaires; et la douceur de l'oisiveté se coula si agréablement dans leur âme qu'ils n'eussent pas voulu de leur première condition, quand Auguste la leur eût voulu rendre de bonne foi . . . "Puisqu'il nous mène, disaient-ils, dormons en assurance dans notre vaisseau; faisons la débauche si nous voulons." (Balzac, 138)

> [In the end, they preferred a sure master and peaceful servitude to daily change and the perpetual fear of civil war. In place of freedom, which now seemed like a illusory pleasure to them, they embraced peace, which they took to be the highest of goods . . . Everyone was glad to have a little leisure after so much misfortune, and sweet idleness insinuated itself so easily into their souls that frankly they would not have returned to their past lives if Augustus had offered them the choice . . . "Since he is our leader," they said, "let us sleep peacefully in our vessel. Let us enjoy ourselves if we want to."]

Balzac's tone, in judging this historical juncture, is tinged with irony and realism. Although he clearly laments the decline of Roman virtue, he recognizes the inevitability and superiority of the new order. By imposing himself on the Romans, Augustus turned the republic's weaknesses into the principate's strengths, using the rivalry and decadent tastes that had weakened the former as the basis for a new culture of leisurely self-interest. In a paradoxical inversion, political liberty became a superfluous pleasure while leisurely pleasure became a positive social force. The Roman notables whose names had once been feared by the kings of the earth were now courtiers willing to beg a former peer for favors. Rome, in sum, became a "court society" in the sense in which Norbert Elias has used the term. The pursuit of status, recognition, and reward provided a substitute for lost republican freedoms, ensuring political order.[64]

Balzac quotes his friend Jean Chapelain's rejoinder to those who sought to resist the new order:

> Qui est le présomptueux, qui se puisse plaindre que le ciel soit au-dessus de lui; qui puisse trouver étrange que la plus lumineuse des créatures soit la plus haute, et que le plus digne soit le plus grand? (Balzac, 139)

> [Who would be so presumptuous as to complain that the sky was above him? Who can find it strange that the most luminous of creatures is the highest, and that the most worthy is the greatest?]

That Chapelain, according to Balzac, raised his voice slightly underscores the gravity of these remarks, which could serve as easily as an apology for the French state of the seventeenth century as for the Roman Empire. Like Rome, after all, France had recently passed through a period of civil strife (the Wars of Religion) followed by a gradual consolidation of power under Louis XIII and Richelieu. Like the Romans, a majority of the French aristocracy seemed willing to surrender its freedoms and accept that peace and prosperity depended on the authority of a strong ruler (though not without a fight, as the *Fronde* would soon prove). Highly attuned to historical parallels between absolutist France and Augustan Rome, seventeenth-century readers could hardly have missed Chapelain's stern admonition to those contemporaries who still resisted the authority of the king and his ministers. Who could possibly yearn for a return to the years of the Wars of Religion and the League?

This historical framework sets the stage for Maecenas, whom Balzac contrasts with his military counterpart, Agrippa. The latter was a "good captain" in war, but lacked the social graces necessary in a culture of leisure and peace.[65] With his bellicose temperament and republican virtues, he was doomed to become an anachronism in the "new world order" of the *Pax Romana*. Maecenas, by contrast, was a paragon of urbanity. He possessed the advantages of birth and his manners were "polished" by exposure to fine letters and experience in the ways of the aristocratic elite. With this combination of the social grace of the courtier and the literary formation of a humanist, Maecenas was the paragon of the seventeenth-century *honnête homme* (gentleman), and indeed this is the term that Balzac uses for him (*le parfait honnête homme*).[66] Thanks to a solid moral core, moreover, he could resist the temptations of the court:

> Quoique la cour sache debaucher les saints, et d'ordinaire infecte d'abord ce qu'elle reçoit de pur, elle ne gâta point Mécénas.

[Although the court could corrupt a saint, and usually infects anything pure that it touches, it did not destroy Maecenas.]

This virtue was less Stoic than Epicurean. Elegant through and through, he reconciled outside with inside, the aesthetic realm of pleasure/appearance with the underlying truth of virtue. To paraphrase Balzac, he sought to appear exactly as he was ("Il voulut paraître ce qu'il était" [Balzac, 140]).[67]

By virtue of his *honnêteté*, Maecenas occupied a strategic position in the new political order, presiding over a series of exchanges between culture and power. Entrusted with Augustus's wealth, he redistributed it among poets and artists:

De ces biens Mécénas acheta à Auguste tous les esprits et toutes les langues; et par conséquent les luy rendit en de meilleures, de plus nobles, & de plus durables espèces. (Balzac, 142)

[With this money, Maecenas purchased for Augustus all of the minds and tongues, and thereby returned the emperor's wealth to him in a better, more noble, and more durable currency.]

In the new order, culture assumed the regulatory role that politics had played in the republic. Using a rich and suggestive monetary metaphor, Balzac describes how Maecenas converted the fruits of conquest into cultural currency (*de meilleures, de plus nobles, & de plus durables espèces*) and laid the foundation for a new hegemony by winning over the intellectual and cultural elites. With his encouragement, writers sacrificed the language of political dissent (*l'ancien langage de la République*) for material comfort and for a political and economic climate that was favorable to artistic creation (Balzac, 147).

Not all liberty was lost, however. In return for surrendering the political liberty of the republic, writers enjoyed free and easy conversation with Maecenas in his gardens. The liberty afforded by refined leisure was thus the compensation for the loss of political liberties. What is at stake, here, is nothing less than a redefinition of *liberté* itself. In his *De la conversation des Romains*, written during the same period as *Mécénas*, Balzac associates private discourse with liberty and public oratory with ideological manipulation:

[D]ans leur conversation, ils [les Romains] rendaient la liberté qu'ils avaient ôtée dans leurs harangues. (Balzac, 83)

[In their conversation, they (the Romans) gave back the freedom that they had taken away in their harangues.]

The public sphere appears not as a space of civic liberty, but rather as a degraded political battleground where orators struggle for control over men's minds. Genuine liberty is reserved for the private sphere, where men can remove their masks and reveal their true selves.

In his capacity as counselor, Maecenas enjoyed an intimate relationship with his own patron, Augustus. On occasion, he exerted a therapeutic, calming influence on the emperor:

[Il] exerçait son pouvoir sur l'âme même de l'empereur, et appaisait les mouvements qui s'y élevaient contre la raison. (Balzac, 144)

[He exercised his powers upon the very soul of the emperor and appeased the movements against reason that stirred there.]

Other times, he adopted a blunt, direct approach, chastising his master with a sharp familiarity (*familiarité piquante*). On yet other occasions, Maecenas used his eloquence to present his master with an inspiring image of the ideal ruler. Once, after a plot against the state was uncovered, he persuaded Augustus to exercise clemency by exaggerating the glory that such an action would bring him (Balzac, 146). Equal parts confidant, confessor, image consultant, and psychotherapist, Maecenas was a veritable partner in power, a kind of imperial "alter-ego." To quote Balzac:

[Auguste et Mécénas] ont partagé ensemble les diverses fonctions d'un même devoir. (Balzac, 145)

[Together, they (Augustus and Maecenas) shared the several functions of the same office.]

Maecenas's role in the Augustan state is one of mediation and persuasion: on the one hand, pushing the prince toward moderation; on the other, convincing the Roman citizens to accept the rule of a benign tyrant.[68] Because he uses language to shape political action, he is the inheritor of the great tradition of Roman eloquence:

Avec cette éloquence efficace, qui n'est autre chose que le droit usage de la prudence, qui se communique aux hommes par la parole, il fit à

Auguste une infinité de serviteurs, et, après lui avoir persuadé la modération, il persuada aux autres l'obéissance. (Balzac, 147)

[With this efficacious eloquence, which is nothing other than the true practice of prudence communicated to men through words, he attached an infinite number of loyal followers to Augustus. After persuading the latter to take the path of moderation, he persuaded the former to embrace obedience.]

Unlike a public orator, however, Maecenas always assumed this mediatory function in oblique and indirect ways, covering his involvement in state affairs with a *façade* of leisure and aristocratic disinterest. Although the public gaze did not penetrate into the shady gardens of his Roman villa, Balzac nonetheless speculates that Maecenas deserved much of the praise that was showered on Agrippa (Balzac, 143). Nor did Maecenas adopt the emphatic and ostentatious style of the orator; rather, he used a rhetoric of polite conversation to reconcile the Romans to their new government. With Maecenas, eloquence no longer appears in its public form, but instead hides its force behind ostensibly innocent forms of private social exchange.[69] An orator without a forum, he reconciles the humanist ideal of eloquence so admired in the seventeenth century with the political and social context of absolutist France.[70]

Endowed with multiple and varied functions—counselor to the prince, protector of the arts, conversationalist, minister, and man of letters among others—Maecenas is a figure of *linkage* and *connection*. By cultivating personal relationships on all sides through his formidable powers of persuasion, he assures the articulation between public and private, politics and culture, republican past and imperial future. That Balzac himself identified with Maecenas becomes clear at the end of the essay, when he undertakes a defense of Maecenas's eloquence against the criticisms of Seneca. In his letters to Lucilius, Seneca (derided by Balzac as "Nero's tutor") faulted Maecenas for abandoning the traditions of republican eloquence for the suave and refined conversation of the imperial court, thus becoming "the first corrupter of Roman eloquence."[71] Balzac seeks to rebut Seneca by discrediting his deceptive use of citation. By taking passages out of context, he suggests, Seneca distorted the meaning of the original text. This is the same accusation that Balzac and his partisans leveled against his critics in the quarrel that erupted after the publication of his letters in 1624 (see chapter 2). The autobiographical dimension of Balzac's defense of Maecenas becomes explicit a few sentences later, when he compares Seneca to "Phyllarque" (Balzac, 148). "Phyllarque" was the *nom de guerre* that Dom Goulu, Balzac's most fierce adversary, adopted during the quarrel over Balzac's *Lettres*. In fact, nearly all of Seneca's judgments of Maecenas, as Balzac characterizes them, recall Goulu's criticisms of Balzac. Like Goulu, for example, Seneca attacks stylistic liberty and mockery (*raillerie*). In response, Balzac defends the use of pleasure (*volupté*) as a legitimate component of eloquence, invoking the assertion by an unnamed philosopher (Pierre Gassendi, probably) that "il y a un art d'user innocement de la volupté" (there is an innocent art of pleasurable living) (Balzac, 149). Such passages suggest that Balzac is using the figure of Maecenas to explore his own adventure with patronage and rhetoric.

At times, Balzac's vision of a modern-day Maecenas is tinged with cynicism. In one passage, he comments dryly that the Roman minister's successors in positions of favor have not followed his example. Specifically, they have been less principled and more susceptible to the temptations that accompany power:

> Leur morale fut plus large et plus indulgente à leurs passions. Il n'eurent pas de ces délicatesses de conscience. (Balzac, 142)

> [Their morals were looser and more indulgent with regard to their passions. They did not suffer from such twinges of conscience.]

Roger Zuber, in his edition of the *Œuvres diverses,* suggests that this passage is inspired by Tacitus and that it sets up the attack on Seneca later in the essay.[72] The passage can be read in a much more concrete and direct fashion, however. When he reflects that subsequent ministers have not held themselves to the same standards as Maecenas, Balzac brings to mind those ministers (and patrons) with whom he himself has come into contact, most notably Richelieu and Séguier.[73] This allusion reframes Balzac's portrait of Maecenas, introducing a temporal rupture between the present and the past.

This contrast between the corrupt present and the idealized Golden Age of Maecenas is developed in a later work entitled "Response à trois questions." This essay recapitulates many of the themes of *Mécénas*, but focuses above all on what Balzac calls Maecenas's *facilité des mœurs*, his free and informal manner with the poets whom he protected:

Il faloit bien qu'il fust honneste-homme, & bonhomme tout ensemble, de vivre comme il faisoit avec les moindres de ses Amis, & de ne trouver pas mauvaise la liberté qu'ils prenoient quand ils traittoient aveque luy.[74]

[He had to be a polite and a good-natured fellow to get along as he did with the least of his friends and not be offended by the informality of tone that they adopted when dealing with him.]

Maecenas has the ability to transcend pomp and circumstance in such a way as to make underlings—such as writers and artists—feel like his equals. This cultivated informality contrasts sharply with the fastidiousness of modern favorites:

Mais croyez-vous que les Favoris d'aujourd'huy comme vous diriez le Comte Duc [Olivarès] en Espagne, voulust estre traitté si familierement que Mecenas, par les Poëtes de la Cour? . . . Le grand Armand mesme [Richelieu] qui caresse les Poëtes & les favorise, ne trouveroit pas bon, ou je me trompe fort, si Monsieur de l'Estoille commençoit un Sonnet, ou une Epigramme par, Cher Richelieu, ou Amy Richelieu.[75]

[But do you think that today's favorites, such as the Count-Duke (of Olivares) in Spain, would want to be treated as casually as Maecenas by the poets of the court? . . . Unless I am gravely mistaken, even the great Armand (Richelieu), who cultivates and protects poets, would not take well to being addressed as "Dear Richelieu" or "My good friend Richelieu" in one of Monsieur de L'Estoille's sonnets or epigrams.]

Continuing in this satirical verve, he recounts that one favorite, from the court of Philip of Spain, threatened to destroy an entire province because of a letter that ended with *bien–humble & tres-affectionné* (very humbly and affectionately yours) rather than *tres-humble & tres-obeisant* (very humbly and obediently yours). Although Balzac sets the episode in Spain, it recalls a famous anecdote according to which Richelieu reportedly changed *héros* to *demi-dieu* (demigod) in a dedication addressed to him.[76]

Here, Maecenas assumes the role of the ideal patron—the standard against which all other patrons are judged and against which they inevitably come up short. Although several of the passages that we have cited suggest analogies between Augustan Rome and seventeenth-century France, Balzac ultimately views antiquity as a unique moment that can never be repeated. In *De la conversation des Romains,* he writes that:

> [I]l est certain que les grandes largesses de Dieu ont été faites au commencement, et qu'encore que son bras ne soit pas plus court qu'il était, ses mains sont moins ouvertes qu'elles n'étaient . . . Ce n'est pas à nous à faire les Camilles ni les Catons.⁷⁷

> [It is certain that God's great munificence was bestowed (upon the world) in the beginning. Although his arm has not become any shorter, his hands are no longer as open as they once were . . . It is not given to us to produce Camilluses or Catos.]

A Maecenas, presumably, would be as incongruent in the modern world as a Cato or a Camillus. His combination of elegance, virtue, and an easy manner with princes and poets belongs to a bygone age. While modern-day patrons may still protect poets, the special relationship between writer and protector is gone. When viewed with the appropriate historical distance, the Golden Age of Maecenas thus calls up feelings of nostalgia and resentment.

In conclusion, Balzac's reflections on Maecenas depend on a play of contrasting perspectives. Maecenas is representative of a certain idealized type of *relationship* between culture and power, predicated on the intimate exchanges between sovereign, patron, and client. This ideal, as we have seen, is part of a larger vision of a society of peace, prosperity, and leisure. To a limited extent, this vision was realized later in the century, at Versailles, where Louis XIV strolled through his gardens with Lully and Racine. Balzac, however, seems to have believed that the seventeenth century would not—indeed could not—live up to this ideal.

The Amusing Abbot: Boisrobert and his *Épîtres*

The career and work of François Le Métel de Boisrobert (1592–1662), a correspondent and close associate of Balzac, provide an exemplary illustration of the practical workings of the patronage system that complements Balzac's reflections on the ideal patron.⁷⁸ Introduced to the court by the poet-cardinal Jacques Davy Du Perron, Boisrobert rapidly became a fixture in the household of the queen mother, Marie de' Medici. Boisrobert's duties for the queen mother included literary activities such as composing occasional verse (such as *vers de ballet* and *vers galants*) and translation, as well as nonliterary services such as traveling to England with Henrietta-

Maria, Louis XIII's sister and Charles I's French bride.[79] In Marie's entourage, he made the acquaintance of Armand-Jean du Plessis, later Cardinal Richelieu, who eventually replaced the queen as his primary patron. Boisrobert advised Richelieu on literary matters and played a critical role in mobilizing writers in support of the latter's policies. It was he, for instance, who reportedly informed Richelieu about the informal gatherings of writers at the home of Valentin Conrart that would later become the French Academy (see chapter 6). He also orchestrated the publication of two lavish volumes of laudatory poetry in which the most prominent poets of the period (including Malherbe, Racan, Scudéry, Gombauld, Chapelain, Colletet, and Desmarets) sang the praises of Richelieu and Louis XIII: *Le Sacrifice des muses* (1635) and *Le Parnasse royal* (1635). In return, Boisrobert used his position to obtain assistance for a number of writers including Balzac, Chapelain, Gombauld, and Mairet, earning for himself the title of *ardent solliciteur des muses affligées* (or *incommodées*) (ardent sollicitor for the distraught/indisposed muses).[80] A lesser Maecenas, he served as an intermediary, regulating the circulation of representations and material advantages between representatives of political authority and cultural producers.[81]

Boisrobert's enthusiastic assistance in garnering cultural support for the crown and its prime minister was richly rewarded. He accumulated numerous *bénéfices,* including (most famously) the priorship of the abbey of Châtillon. Looking back in his *Épîtres* (1647/ 1659), a collection of verse epistles, he wrote about those who were jealous of his good fortune:

> Et ces sots-là ne peuvent concevoir
> Par quelle adresse attrapant une crosse
> J'ay peu mener les Muses en carosse. (Boisrobert, 2:26)
>
> [And those idiots cannot understand
> How by snatching up a crozier
> I was able to take the Muses for a carriage ride.]

The metaphor of the carriage is apt. Perhaps more than any other writer of his generation, Boisrobert successfully used his literary career for social and financial advancement. The honeymoon with favor ended, however, on Richelieu's death in 1642. The loss, as Boisrobert describes it, was total:

J'ay perdu tout en le perdant. (Boisrobert, 1:84)

[I lost everything when I lost him.]

The vast network of patronage that Richelieu had built up during his tenure as prime minister was fractured as other players moved into positions of power. Boisrobert describes his fall in an epistle addressed to the minister Hugues de Lionne:

> J'ay passé pour le favory
> Du plus grand Homme de la Terre;
> Mais on m'a cassé comme un verre
> Dés que j'ay perdu son appuy. (Boisrobert, 2:271)

> [I was considered the favorite
> Of the greatest man on earth
> But I was shattered like a glass
> As soon as I lost his favor.]

The image of the glass/self shattered by an impersonal *on* (one) poignantly captures the fragility of a career built on personal connections and individual loyalties, and the feelings of estrangement that a loss of favor could produce. The *Épîtres* contain many other similar allusions to the vicissitudes of fortune. For a writer whose career was tied to the patronage system, such passages are more than mere conceits. They capture the experience of a life filled with cycles of euphoria, disappointment, and uncertainty.

Concretely, Richelieu's death meant that Boisrobert no longer had the same level of access to the court or to the *cabinet* of its new principal player, Mazarin, who had taken over much of Richelieu's role in government and controlled a large patronage network. Despite his success in converting patronage into lucrative *bénéfices,* Boisrobert could not entirely escape the logic of patronage. If he wanted his royal pension paid, he needed to seek (and maintain) the protection of those who were in a position of influence with respect to the treasury.[82] This meant seeking out intermediaries (much as he himself had been sought out when he was close to Richelieu). He thus courted at least two superintendents of finances (Bailleul and Fouquet) through their *serviteurs* and attempted a reconciliation with a third, Abel Servien, who had been a rival during the Richelieu years and was blocking payment of his pension (Boisrobert, 2:271). He sought the favor of other patrons as well, including the duc d'Enghien/future *Grand Condé* (through his *capitaine des gardes*, M. de la Rocque), Séguier (for a *brevet de conseiller d'état*), and the Prince of Conti (from whom he hoped to obtain another *bénéfice*).

Several passages in the *Épîtres* revolve around Boisrobert's failed efforts to obtain an interview with Mazarin.

> Hense [un garde suisse], qui m'avoit veu si bien auprez d'Armand [Richelieu],
> Me sousrit à l'abord, reconnoist mon visage,
> Favorise mon zele & me donne passage;
> Malgré ses compagnons me voila dans la Court.
> Mais voulant passer outre, on m'arreste tout court.
> Cherchant mes vieux amis, je ne voy dans la place
> Que des fronds serieux, pour moy froids comme glace;
> Pas un seul ne me dit: "Tu sois le bien venu";
> Je parois estranger, je leur suis inconnu,
> Et voy que la faveur a changé leurs visages
> En trois ou quatre mois, ainsi que leurs courages.
> Bautru, vivois-je ainsi, quand sans empeschement
> Tu me voyois passer au cabinet d'Armand? (Boisrobert, 1:49–50)

> [Hense (a Swiss guard), who knew me in my glory days with Armand (Richelieu)
> Greets me with a smile and, recognizing my face,
> Does me a favor and lets me through.
> In spite of his colleagues, I make it to the court.
> But when I try to go further, I am blocked right away
> And, looking for my old friends, I only find
> Serious foreheads glaring icily at me.
> Not a single one says: "Welcome."
> I am a stranger, unknown to them,
> And I see that in two or three months
> Favor has changed their faces as well as their hearts.
> Bautru, did I act like this when
> I had ready access to Armand's cabinet?]

In this vivid passage, Boisrobert gives poetic voice to an affectively charged social topology, contrasting the euphoria of mobility and circulation (*me donne passage, passer outre*) with the obstacles (*Malgré ses compagnons, on m'arreste tout court*) that bring frustration. Time is the enemy here, changing friendly faces into hostile glares and a familiar landscape into an inhospitable one. In a complementary epistle, addressed to Mazarin, Boisrobert imagines himself endowed with magical powers that allow him to regain his freedom of movement and mastery over time:

> Je suis reduit, tant la douleur me trouble,
> A souhaitter que je peusse estre double,
> Ou que mon corps fust un corps glorieux
> Pour penetrer & passer en tous lieux:
> Tu ne pourrais, quoy que tu peusses faire,
> En esquivant, à mes yeux te soustraire. (Boisrobert, 1:127)

> [I am reduced by my suffering
> To fantasizing that I could split myself in two,
> Or that my body could be a glorious body
> So that I could penetrate and enter anywhere.
> Whatever you did, you could not
> Slip away and hide from me.]

Although somewhat tempered with whimsy, this is nonetheless a remarkable fantasy of power. It is only by becoming a kind of "super courtier" that Boisrobert can master his social situation. Split in two, he positions himself at the different exits to the palace, awaiting Mazarin. He regains his own mobility (*penetrer, passer en tous lieux*) and immobilizes the patron, who can no longer slip away and ignore his entreaties. Mobility is arguably the key to understanding Boisrobert's relationship with his patrons. On the most obvious level, patronage offered social mobility (poetically figured by the carriage ride with the muses). The successful writer's mobility, however, was horizontal as well as vertical. As Christian Jouhaud has shown, part of his power derived from his ability to "enter anywhere," to occupy a variety of positions in the social field. This gave him a broad perspective and margin of maneuver.[83] At the height of his career, Boisrobert had a foot not only in the corridors of political power, but also in the publishing industry, the theater, and the nascent French Academy.

The *Épîtres* themselves can be understood as a strategy for regaining access to influential patrons. In a liminal poem published in the 1647 edition, Jean Ogier de Gombauld describes these short poem-letters as mirrors of the court.

> La Cour brille icy toute nue;
> Ce Beau Livre en est le miroir,
> Et ceux qui ne l'ont jamais veue
> La verront mesme sans la voir. (Boisrobert, 1:21)

> [Here the court shines in naked splendor.
> This fine book is its mirror
> And those who have never seen it
> Can see it here without seeing it.]

This description provides a starting point for reading the collection as a whole. The *Épîtres* stand in an overdetermined and paradoxical relationship to court patronage. On one level, they reproduce the social forms of the court (supplication, compliment, thankful acknowledgement, and so on) on a literary register. As the titles suggest, each poem is a social action:

A Monseigneur Le Prince de Conty: Il luy *redemande* un Prieuré

[To milord the Prince of Conti: He *asks* him anew for a priory]

A Monseigneur le Chancelier: Il se *rejouit* avec luy des Sceaux qui luy sont revenus pour la seconde fois

[To milord the chancellor: He *rejoices* with him that the seals have been bestowed upon him anew]

A Madame de Mancini: Il la *remercie* de l'avoir fait r'appeller de son exil

[To Madame de Mancini: He *thanks* her for helping him get recalled from his exile]

On a surface level, then, the *Épîtres* would appear to be a kind of verse record of Boisrobert's life at court. With a keen eye for humorous detail, he describes the crowds waiting to gain an audience with a minister, the poet standing in the rain to get a brief audience with Mazarin, and so on. On another level, the style and tone are carefully modeled on the linguistic ideals of the court. In a dedicatory epistle to Mazarin, Boisrobert describes the *Épîtres* as a *mirror of courtly style*, mentioning in particular their *graces particulières* (unique graces), and *libres et naïves expressions* (free and naïve expressions) (Boisrobert, 1:18). This is not so much the style of court as it really was, but rather as a certain elite imagined it—the rejection of contrived literary style and learned (classical) culture coupled with the valorization of innate grace and refined wit.

Much as the French stage of the period reflected a double image of high society—as object of satire (in some of Molière's most probing works) and as ideal (in the comedies of Corneille, for instance)—two different perspectives on the court emerge from the *Épîtres*.[84] At one level, Boisrobert describes himself struggling to make his way through a crowd of courtiers or ambushing his patron in a rainy street while at a second level, he and his addressee laugh together as these situations are transformed into objects of aesthetic appreciation. The sordid aspects of the court are simultaneously represented and held at a distance through irony. Like Balzac, in other words, Boisrobert alternates between idealization and frustrated cynicism in his attitude toward court patronage.

Whither Autonomy?

In his influential work on the literary field in seventeenth-century France, Alain Viala has characterized patronage as an obstacle to the "birth of the writer." His central thesis is that the seventeenth century witnessed the birth of an autonomous literary field in France—those social forces, institutions, and values that define literary culture as a distinct social phenomenon and the writer as an independent social category. At the same time, however, Viala must account for the preponderant role of patronage in cultural affairs during the period. Although the growth of academies, for example, would seem to point toward increasing writerly autonomy, the appropriation of these academies by the monarchy would seem to point in the opposite direction. Viala's solution is to contrast aspirations to autonomy with a political and social reality that could not yet fully accommodate them.[85]

Against Viala, Christian Jouhaud has suggested that patronage, far from being in conflict with autonomy, was in fact embraced by writers seeking to legitimize literature as an autonomous practice. When we speak of autonomy, we need to be clear: *autonomy from what*, precisely? Seventeenth-century France, Jouhaud points out, was a society of corporations—guilds, universities, religious orders, and other groups—each of which had its own competences, privileges, and regulations. The recognition of literature as a legitimate enterprise thus depended on achieving a degree of autonomy with regard to those corporations that claimed expertise in literary/rhetorical matters—most notably judicial institutions such as the *parlements*. State patronage, emanating from the authority of the king, offered precisely such an opportunity. By founding the French Academy (over the objections of the *parlement*), the crown created a new kind of authority, qualified to make pronouncements on matters of literary taste and linguistic usage (see chapter 6). The new *littérateurs,* Jouhaud argues, were not cast in the old professional mold. No well-defined, normative training was required, as in the *parlements.* Instead their status derived paradoxically from the non-professional character of their activity.[86] Patronage thus contributed to the creation of a properly literary sphere apart from the corporate structures of *ancien régime* France. In return, the royal state gained a valuable ally in its ongoing battle to rein in the prerogatives of the independent-minded corporations.

Mario Biagioli has similarly stressed the central role of patronage in the development of the New Science. Within the medieval university, mathematics was viewed primarily as a technical discipline and natural science fell within the purview of philosophy, which was still primarily Aristotelian and Ptolemaic. As a result, mathematically trained empiricists such as Galileo had great difficulty receiving the recognition and funding necessary to advance their work. Princely patronage, by contrast, provided fertile ground for the New Science. Eager to enhance their own prestige and outdo their rivals, princes encouraged their court mathematicians to seek out new discoveries in the heavens. In the process, they advanced not only scientific discovery, but also the social standing of the New Science and its practitioners, by giving them a place of honor in their courts. The newfound social status of court mathematicians such as Galileo was critical. Without social recognition, the latter had no chance against the scholastic establishment, no matter how compelling their discoveries might be on their own. Epistemological legitimacy, simply put, depended on social legitimacy. Patronage, finally, provided a mechanism of dissemination. As part of a coordinated publicity program on behalf of princely patrons, new books and instruments, such as Galileo's telescopes, were sent as gifts to foreign courts, where they were made available to other researchers. In sum, patronage "propelled clients, fostered and structured their communication and debates, rewarded novelties, legitimized knowledge claims that would have been unacceptable elsewhere, and gave clients the resources to legitimate unconventional socioprofessional identities."[87]

Throughout this chapter, I have stressed the ambivalent nature of patronage—structured and informal, hierarchical and diffuse, idealistic and self-interested. One of the greatest obstacles to understanding patronage and its influence is to overplay its rigidity. Following

Viala, Priscilla Parkhurst Ferguson has made the debatable claim that "[t]he logic of patronage in force during the *ancien régime* blocked a strong sense of literary self or community by subordinating literary activities to essentially aristocratic definitions of literature and culture."[88] It is true, of course, that patronage limited what a writer could say and that more than a few chafed under its constraints. (Indeed some of their stories will be told in the pages that follow.) All the same, one of my central claims, confirmed by the case examples of both Balzac and Boisrobert as well as the work of Jouhaud and Biagioli, is that the social energies created by the patronage system could be also productive and exhilarating, a decisive factor in the fashioning of literary "selves" and even "communities." Precisely because it was flexible and relatively diffuse, because it did not depend on rigid institutional hierarchies, and because it mobilized both self-interest and idealism, patronage could be a force for cultural and intellectual dynamism. It was ultimately not so much a system or an institution as a *proto*-system or *proto*-institution, a pliable but serviceable framework that could be bent into a wide variety of configurations and put to a variety of uses.

2
Reinventing Eloquence: Balzac's *Lettres*

[À] chaque tournant de siècle, sa statue de loin reparaît.

[At every turn of the century, his statue reappears from afar.]
—Sainte-Beuve, *Port-Royal*[1]

L'*UNICO ELOQUENTE*

SINCE THE SEVENTEENTH CENTURY, JEAN-LOUIS GUEZ DE BALZAC (1597–1654) has played an ambivalent role in literary history as the personification of French eloquence in all of its glory and superficiality. Nowhere is this ambivalence more evident than in Sainte-Beuve's monumental *Port-Royal* (1840–49). On the one hand, Sainte-Beuve acknowledges Balzac's importance as reformer of French prose:

> Balzac a joué un grand rôle et a gardé un rang éminent dans notre prose: il en a été le Malherbe . . . Il a régularisé la langue et, autant que cela se peut, certaines formes du beau qui ont prévalu.[2]
>
> [Balzac played a great role and continues to occupy an eminent place in our prose. He was the Malherbe of prose . . . He regularized the language and, to the extent that it is possible, certain lasting aesthetic forms.]

If the French language has become a paragon of clarity, purity, and elegance, it is in no small part, he concedes, due to the efforts of the man known to his contemporaries as the *unico eloquente*. This, by and large, is the role that literary history, from the seventeenth century onward, has assigned to Balzac. By applying the principles of the best Ciceronian Latin to French vernacular prose, he naturalized eloquence, laying the groundwork for the flourishing of French as the dominant language of the European literary elite from the seventeenth to the nineteenth centuries.

Sainte-Beuve weighs this linguistic achievement against the superficiality of Balzac's intellect and character. Echoing a critique that goes back to the seventeenth century, he characterizes Balzac as a rhetor (*rhéteur*) and a phrasemonger (*phraseur*). In contrast to Pascal, Balzac's primary concern is with the outer form of language (*une manière toute extérieure, toute rhétoricienne*) rather than with the inner man. This, as much as the reform of French prose, is his legacy to the nineteenth century:

> [Le] mal de Balzac . . . demeure plus répandu qu' on ne croit. Jamais . . . la phrase et la couleur, le mensonge de la parole littéraire, n'ont autant prédominé sur le fond et sur le vrai que dans ces dernières années.[3]

> [Balzac's malady . . . remains more widespread than one might think. Never before . . . have pretension, rhetorical color, and the falsity of literary language held sway over substance and truth as they have in recent years.]

Sainte-Beuve portrays Balzac as the archetype of the man-of-letters-as-stylist, the very antithesis of the spiritual vocation that he attributes to the *Messieurs* of Port-Royal. Balzac, it should remembered, was an apologist for orthodoxy and reason of state, qualities that could hardly have won him points with an admirer of the Jansenists. In Sainte-Beuve's hands, the history of culture thus becomes a conflict between two competing models of literature: one spiritual, the other rhetorical and official.

The contribution of twentieth-century criticism, starting with Gaston Guillaumie (1927), has been to recognize something significant and substantive at stake in Balzac's ostensibly superficial rhetoric. Guillaumie understood that Balzac was born into a moment of crisis in the history of French eloquence. Throughout the latter half of the sixteenth century, the prestige of ancient oratory among Renaissance humanists had combined with a background of political and religious conflict to create a climate favorable to public speech. As they watched magistrates, nobles, princes, and sovereigns debate matters of state, French humanists such as Guillaume Du Vair understandably believed that they were witnessing the rebirth of the civic eloquence of the Ancients. Born of political conflict, this civic eloquence could not survive the return to order after the Edict of Nantes, however. To attain a durable peace, it was necessary to put the lid back on the kettle of public debate and recognize the indivisible sovereignty of the crown.⁴ If French eloquence were to survive, its form would not be oral, nor its content explicitly political; rather, eloquence would have to become literary. As Guillaumie suggestively put it, "All that is left [is] the tiny space of literature and, more specifically, the letter."⁵ Henceforth, the space of eloquence would be constrained to the confines of the written page, the *cabinet,* and the library.

This chapter will explore Balzac's reorientation of rhetoric in practice in his *Lettres du sieur de Balzac* (1624). The first half of the chapter will focus on how he exploited the generic form of the letter to lay the foundations for a "rhetoric of patronage." Close readings of individual letters will show how Balzac sought to carve out a liminal, intermediate position between the poles of public and private, rhetoric and literature. The second half of the chapter will examine how this carefully constructed position unraveled under the weight of its own contradictions during the quarrel that followed the publication of the *Lettres.*

Epistolary Eloquence

Balzac was born into a family of bourgeois origins, but with noble titles and pretensions.⁶ His father, Guillaume Guez, had significant land holdings including an important estate near Angoulême (where Balzac was born) and performed the function of *secrétaire principal* for the duc d'Épernon, a prominent aristocrat in the entourage of the queen mother, and one of the leaders of the *parti espagnol* (the party sympathetic to Spanish influence in France). In the Jesuit *collèges* of Angoulême and Poitiers, Balzac received an education befitting his social *milieu.* Latin rhetoric was the focus of Jesuit education, and the models of learning were the great stylistic masters of Latin prose, especially Cicero and Seneca. Through exercises in emulation and imitation, Balzac learned Latin composition and the various techniques of persuasion practiced by the great classical and contemporary orators. In 1612, he met Théophile de Viau in Angoulême, inaugurating a friendship that soured in later years when Théophile was pursued for his libertine writings (see chapter 4). The two friends traveled to Holland, and eventually to the University of Leyden, where they registered as students. At Leyden, Balzac broadened his education, discovering the works of northern humanists such as Erasmus, Scaliger, and Lipsius. He was also seduced by a spirit of independence there, which found expression in the continuing Dutch struggle against the Spanish throne. Balzac's writing, we shall see, is marked by a profound tension between ideological conformity and an almost libertine spirit of individualism.

The year 1615 is a watershed date in Balzac's career because it marks his first published foray into the panegyric genre. On the occasion of the opening of the Estates General, he published a 16-page volume celebrating the king (who was entering into his majority) and the queen mother entitled *Panégyriques au Roy sur l'Ouverture de ses Estats, et à la Reine, sur l'Heureux succès de sa Régence*. There are few signs of Balzac's whereabouts or activities between 1615 and 1618. In 1618, he reemerges in the circle around the queen mother Marie de' Medici and the duc d'Épernon, a circle that included Monsieur de Luçon, the future Cardinal Richelieu. The earliest of Balzac's published letters date from this period and reveal another side to the young Balzac's character—that of the ambitious political polemicist (see chapter 3). Balzac's proximity to power failed, however, to translate into a concrete political role in the *côteries* of either Epernon or Marie de' Medici. Richelieu soon became Marie's favorite, and Balzac had to content himself with a prolonged stay in Rome from 1620 to 1622 on behalf of Cardinal La Valette, one of Épernon's sons. After two years in Rome followed by another two-year interlude in Angoulême, Balzac made his dramatic entrance on the literary scene with the publication of the *Lettres du sieur de Balzac* (1624).

The ambitious project behind the *Lettres* is articulated in a preface signed by Jacques de La Motte-Aigron. Anticipating the accusation that the letter is a minor, principally domestic genre, the preface begins by establishing a hierarchy of epistolary practices based on two criteria: the dignity of the material (*la grandeur des choses qui s'y traitent*) and style (*le soing avecque lequel il semble qu'elles ayent esté escrites*).[7] At the bottom of this scale are the letters of Germans, who delight in describing mundane subjects—household matters or schoolboy foolery. The scene of discourse is thus initially formulated in negative terms, by contrast with a *domestic* space such as a house (*maison*) or a schoolroom (*collège*). The *Lettres* must strategically *respatialize* epistolary discourse, rescuing it from its reputation as a trivial and banal genre and demonstrating that it can be both serious and dignified.

Letters, the preface insists, can be suitable vehicles for types of discourse that are usually reserved for public oratory:

> Veritablement c'est se tromper que de croire que les grands subjets doivent estre bannis de toutes les lettres; que l'eloquence mesme n'y doive paroistre que laschement, et que la majesté des deux soit reservée pour les chaires & pour les harangues, tout de mesme certes que si la vaillance ne se monstroit que dans les batailles, & qu'aux combats de seul à seul elle fut inutile pour avoir moins de tesmoins. (Balzac, 1:237–238)

> [It is truly a mistake to believe that great subjects should be banished from all letters, that eloquence itself should appear there only timidly, and that the majesty of both is reserved for the pulpit and legal harangues, as if valor could only be demonstrated on the field of battle and were useless in one-on-one combat because there are fewer witnesses to it.]

The legitimation of epistolary form relies on an extended military analogy in which public oratory is compared to the field of open battle and the letter to one-on-one combat (*combats de seul à seul*). Appealing to the contemporary fascination with duels, the preface observes that courage and valor are as praiseworthy in individual combat as in battle. Should not private eloquence, by analogy, be esteemed just as highly as public oratory, even if it is less visible? The written equivalent of a private conversation, the letter can accommodate a wide variety of subjects:

> les discours Panegyriques, les Apologies, les consolations, les jugements sur les actions morales, bonnes ou mauvaises, les opinions et sentimens des choses du temps, celles qui plaisent, & celles que l'on doit hayr, les indifferentes encore. (Balzac, 1:239)

> [panegyrics, apologies, consolations, judgments of moral actions—whether good or bad—, opinions and sentiments regarding current events, matters of good, bad, or even indifferent taste.]

All three major branches of rhetoric are represented here: political-deliberative, legal-forensic, and epideictic.

To bolster his case, the preface writer examines the historical example of Cicero's private interviews with Caesar during the collapse of the republic. Is it not reasonable to suppose, he asks, that Cicero prepared his arguments in this context *more* carefully than for a public debate? In Caesar, after all, he was dealing not only with a powerful general who held the fate of Rome in hands, but also with a learned man who was himself an orator. By contrast, the Roman populace, characterized as a "hundred-headed beast" (*beste à cent testes*), had been relatively easy to manipulate (Balzac, 1:240–41). By means of this distinction between the eloquent general and the ignorant, bestial masses, the preface establishes the aristocratic principle that the dignity of eloquence derives not from the spaces where it is traditionally deployed (forum, agora, or other public place) or from the size of the audience, as in a republican context, but rather from the audience's sophistication and stature. One enlightened noble reader represents the true *res publica* better than any crowd.

The implications of this line of argument are clear: we should judge Balzac's *Lettres* on the basis of their individual *recipients*. Most of the letters, the preface reminds us, are addressed to great men such as Cardinal La Valette, the duc d'Épernon, Cardinal Richelieu, and Louis XIII himself:

> Et puis nous nous etonnerons encore de la perfection de ces lettres dont les unes ont esté escrittes au Roy, & destinées à estre leües, ainsi qu'elles ont esté avec admiration, en plein Conseil, & la plus part des autres envoyées aux plus grands hommes de ce siecle. (Balzac, 1:141)

> [And we are surprised by the perfection of these letters, some of which were written to the king and meant to be read, as they were with admiration, in the Council itself, while most of the others were sent to the greatest men of our time.]

When we recall the etymological origin of the word *perfection* in the verb *parfaire*—"to finish" or "to complete"—we can measure the extent to which Balzac's letters are rooted in an interpersonal logic of patronage. Through the act of reading, the noble addressee completes the letter that he receives, enhancing its dignity. A quick examination of the various editions of the *Lettres* shows that letters to prominent patrons almost always occupy privileged positions. If we take the edition of 1624, for example, the first five letters are addressed to Épernon and his sons (the La Valette brothers), the following three to Richelieu, and the last to Cardinal La Valette. In the third edition, the comte de Schomberg, another important political/military figure of the period, receives the honor of ending the collection. The "sixth" edition (the 1627 *Œuvres*), finally, undertakes a complete reordering, with Richelieu, who was gradually gaining the upper hand at the French court, occupying the place of honor at the beginning of the collection. Despite this concession to the changing political climate and a gradual drift toward political conformity, the basic principle remains the same. The letters are organized so as to give visibility to Balzac's relationships with the "greatest men" of his time.

The letter, of course, is the ideal form for articulating a rhetoric of patronage. In its material aspect, first of all, each letter serves as a gift from the writer to the patron in partial repayment of the latter's generosity. It thus serves to highlight the exchange dynamic that characterizes their relationship. The letter, moreover, is an eminently rhetorical—that is to say, audience-oriented—form. Far from being merely implied, the reader-addressee is explicitly invoked throughout, from the initial address to the closing formula. Before its ultimate publication in a printed edition, each letter has a history, which is nothing less than the history of a rhetorical act involving two individuals. The letter's physical trajectory from sender to addressee parallels the process of persuasion, in which the words and thoughts of the speaker become those of the listener.[8] Because of the privileged position of the audience, finally, the letter is ideally suited to fashioning a public identity through contacts with others. It is worthy of note, in this regard, that Balzac incorporates into his collection two letters that he did not himself write. The first, from Richelieu, appears in the first edition of the *Lettres*. The second, from Schomberg, was added in the second edition. The inclusion of these letters of praise from prominent patrons establishes a principle of reciprocity, in which praise functions in both directions. The writer and patron are locked in a symbiotic relationship in which each interpellates and legitimates the other.

The goal of the preface, we have seen, is to project public forms of discourse into the private space of the letter. By exploiting the formal constraints of epistolary form (one person writing to another) and the ordering possibilities of the printed edition, the collected letters attempt to realize this goal. In place of the public circumstances of traditional oratory, Balzac offers a kind of "imagined community," a network of particular and personal relationships between himself, his friends, and (especially) his patrons.[9]

The preface writer presents this shift in the scope of rhetoric as a product of historical change:

[N]ous ne sommes plus en ce temps-là, où l'on accusait publiquement le gouvernement de l'Estat, & que les Orateurs faisoient rendre conte de leur charge aux Lieutenans Generaux des armées. (Balzac, 1:238)

[We no longer live in an era when the conduct of matters of state is subject to public criticism and orators force army lieutenant generals to account for their commands.]

There is a recognition that the age of the great orator-politician has passed, along with the accompanying political model of the Roman and Athenian democracies. As we saw in the previous chapter, Balzac is a political realist who recognizes that a strong, central authority is essential to civil peace and prosperity.

A changed political context requires a different kind of relationship between the producer of discourse and his audience, which in turn requires its own, modern, style. The preface contrasts the style of traditional oratory with that of epistolary eloquence. The author of a sustained harangue appeals to the audience with elaborate conceits and dramatic movements from register to register:

> afin qu'apres les avoir esbranlez & comme jettez hors de leur assiette, on les face tomber par apres du costé que l'on desire. (Balzac, 1:239)

> [so that after having shaken their resolve and unsettled them, one can direct their wills in the direction that one desires.]

As we saw in the previous chapter, Balzac views oratory not so much in terms of persuasion as coercion. The wills of the listeners/readers are shaken (*ébranlez*) and then reshaped according the whim of the orator. The modern, aristocratic rhetoric of the letter, by contrast, demands a less ostentatious, more conversational style—one that uses clear, elegant language to appeal to the reason of the reader:

> [L]es raisons y vont toutes seules & sans assistance, & tout ce qu'on leur permet d'ornement, c'est la liberté des pensées, le choix du langage, & de n'aller pas en desordre. (Balzac, 1:239)

> [Reason is self-sufficient and needs no assistance; all that is allowed in terms of ornamentation is audacious thoughts, well-chosen words, and a semblance of order.]

The preface compares these two rhetorics to the Atlantic and Pacific Oceans. Both are deep and thus suitable for a wide range of vessels. The latter, however, is less stormy and thus more amenable to travel (Balzac, 1:240). This metaphor illustrates the vision that Balzac and his followers had of his modern style. Although not without grandeur, it substituted a sense of harmony and limpid calm for the tempestuousness of public oratory. To quote the preface, it combined *douceur* (sweetness or softness) with *majesté, ordre,* and *nombre,* thus avoiding the excessive floweriness and sobriety of the Jesuit and parliamentary styles, respectively.[10]

Like Pierre Corneille's drama, Balzac's letters are haunted by the twin problems of historical change and the ways in which such change modifies the boundaries between private and public. The preceding pages have attempted to connect his modernization of rhetoric to changing political circumstances in seventeenth-century France. The following examples from the letters will illustrate the extent to which this project depends on a complex entanglement of private and public, literature and rhetoric. Each of the readings will focus on a different aspect of the letters: panegyric, the fictions of place, and the economy of the gift.

Overture: Balzac to Épernon (June 7, 1621)

The 1624 collection opens with a letter to the duc d'Épernon that is rich with the language of personal loyalty:

> Quand je ne serois pas nay, comme je suis, vostre tres-humble serviteur, il faudroit que je fusse mauvais François, pour ne me resjoüir pas des contentemens de vostre maison, puis que ce sont des felicitez publiques. (Balzac, 1:7)

> [If I were not born, as I am, your very humble servant, I would be a bad Frenchman if I were not to rejoice over the good fortunes of your household, for they are truly a matter of public jubilation.]

Nay (born), *tres-humble serviteur* (very humble servant), and *vostre maison* (your household) all evoke the personal, often hereditary, bonds characteristic of nobiliary patronage. Like many of his contemporaries, Balzac was born into a relationship of dependence within a noble household. His father had been Épernon's secretary, and Balzac continued in this capacity. This language of personal and hereditary allegiance contrasts with the discourse of patriotism ("bad Frenchman," "public rejoicing") that is developed in the second half of the sentence. Balzac may have been born into Épernon's *clientèle,* but he is also a French subject. The letter thus operates on two contrasting registers. On one level, it is a token of Balzac's loyalty, a gesture that serves to affirm and strengthen the personal bond between the I-servant and the you-master. On a second level, as a published letter/act of publicity, it addresses a wider audience of readers. On this higher plane, Balzac no longer speaks as Épernon's client, but rather as a patriot. This shift from personal loyalty to public acclamation is reinforced by the first-person plural of the second sentence:

> *Nous* avons sceu l'heureux succés du voyage que vous avez fait en Bearn, & les grands commencemens que vous avez donnez à tout ce que le Roy voudra entreprendre. (Balzac, 1:8)

> [*We* have learned of the brilliant success of your campaign to Béarn and the auspicious beginning that you have provided for all of the king's projects.]

Here, Balzac becomes a witness to history. Evoking Épernon's successful military expedition against the Huguenot rebels of the Béarn in the spring of 1621, he testifies to his patron's service to the crown. (In reality, Épernon was often in conflict with the young Louis XIII.)[11]

There follows a crescendo of praise that reaches its climax with Balzac's assertion of Épernon's divine election:

> Maintenant, Monseigneur, il est temps que vous recognoissiez les avantages que Dieu vous a donnez par dessus le reste des hommes. (Balzac, 1:8)

> [Now, Sir, it is time that you recognize the advantages that God has given you over the rest of mankind.]

In this impersonal formulation, the *je* (I) and the *nous* (we) have disappeared entirely. After its initial absorption into the collective, the particular is completely effaced; all that remains is the patron's contemplation of his own transcendence in the mirror of the text. The hyperbole, however, is held in check by the poised and dignified style, exemplified by the even cadence of the two three-syllabled words at the beginning of the sentence (*Maintenant, Monseigneur*). The *Maintenant* (now) has the effect momentarily arresting (or at least slowing down) time, collapsing it into an immediate present, while the *Monseigneur* (sir) adds a note of formality.

With its sense of controlled grandeur and stately rhythms, as well as its opening position within the collection, this first letter recalls a baroque orchestral overture. This is Balzac at his most ceremonious, and indeed it is in these early pages that we find some of the most oratorical flourishes in the *Lettres:*

> Dans les malheurs du temps & l'usurpation de la puissance legitime vous avez conservé tout seul la liberté de la France. Qui est-ce qui peut dire cela de soy? Où sont ceux qui se sont tenus fermes entre la rebellion & la servitude? En quel temps a-t'on veu une vieillesse si necessaire au monde, & tant de bonne et de mauvaise fortune également glorieuse? (Balzac, 1:9)

> [During the misfortunes of our times and the usurpation of legitimate authority, you have safeguarded the liberty of France all by yourself. Who else can say this of himself? Where are those who have remained firm and shunned both rebellion and servitude? In what era has the life of an old man been so important to the world? When has so much good and bad fortune been so glorious?]

From the repetition of the interrogatives (*Qui . . . Où . . . Quand?*) to the increased size of each subdivision of the period (from nine syllables, to twenty, and then to thirty in the French), this passage recalls the copious, harmonious periods of Ciceronian oratory. It is not hard to imagine the tone of voice of the orator declaiming this passage, pausing for effect after each question and rising to a final climax with *glorieuse*.

At the end of the letter, Balzac shifts register once more, turning his attention to his own writing:

> En effect, Monseigneur, je pense avoir de l'obligation à ceux qui me donnent le moyen de mettre ensemble les deux plus rares choses du monde, c'est à sçavoir la verité & l'eloquence. (Balzac, 1:9–10)

> [Indeed, Sir, I feel an obligation to those persons who give me the means to combine the two rarest things in the world—that is, truth and eloquence.]

In a later edition (1627), he adds:

> Et comme leur reputation a besoin de moy pour estre immortelle, aussi pour travailler sur de beaux sujets, je pense avoir besoin de leurs actions & de leur vie. (Balzac, 1:10)

[And as their reputations need me if they are to become immortal, so I think that I need their actions and their lives as worthy subjects for my work.]

Eloquence and heroism exist in a symbiotic relationship: Balzac's patrons need his eloquence if they are to extend their glory beyond their present lives into the future; he, inversely, depends on them to provide him with contemporary historical subjects worthy of his art. If Balzac's style evokes a musical overture, his use of contemporary history on a heroic register recalls Rubens's roughly contemporary cycle of biographical paintings for Marie de' Medici, representing various episodes from the queen's life (see chapter 3). By placing epic heroism squarely in the present, both Balzac and Rubens anticipate the official style later adopted at Versailles in Le Brun's paintings of Louis XIV's victories for the Hall of Mirrors.[12] If the pseudopreface is a kind of manifesto, this short "harangue," with its high style and its subordination of the personal to the ceremonial, is a proof of concept, a demonstration that the letter can attain the dignified sublimity of public oratory. The gesture of publication is critical, here. By disseminating the letters in print, Balzac not only immortalizes his patrons, he also immortalizes a form of writing that is usually considered to be disposable. In this respect, the *Lettres* recall another contemporaneous visual form: the engravings of ephemeral architecture used in royal entry ceremonies and court festivities. Like these records of official pageantry, they attempt to find dignity and grandeur in the temporary and fleeting.

Pastoral and Patronage: Balzac to La Motte-Aigron (September 4, 1622)

Unlike the previous example, Balzac's famous letter to La Motte-Aigron does not seem at first glance to have much to do with patronage. The subject, after all, is a bucolic *tableau* of life in the country at the writer's estate near Angoulême and it is offered to a friend, not a patron. I will argue, however, that Balzac uses the pastoral to create an idealized, imaginary place for the verbal encounter between the writer-self and the patron-other.

The description of the landscape that begins the letter is rich with literary echoes from both classical and modern texts. Its geological features, in particular, recall the beginning of Honoré d'Urfé's pastoral novel *L'Astrée* and the tradition of the pastoral *locus amoenus* in general.[13] The plain is enclosed by high mountains that isolate it from the rest of the world, protecting it from the ravages of history. Even in times of trouble, such as France's recent political and religious strife, the battling armies agree to spare the idyllic countryside. Like d'Urfé's Forez, moreover, Balzac's countryside retains vestiges of the Golden Age associated with the mythological figure of Astrea in Ovid's *Metamorphoses*:[14]

> [I]l reste encores quelques grains de cét or dont les premiers siecles ont esté faits. (Balzac, 1:133)

> [There remain a few grains of the gold of olden times.]

The people remain in a state of prelapsarian innocence, protected from the corrupting influence of urban culture:

> [E]n ce Royaume de demie lieuë on ne sçait que c'est de tromper que les oyseaux & les bestes, & le style du Palais est une langue aussi inconnuë que celle de l'Amerique. (1:133)

> [In this half-league wide kingdom, the only deception that is practiced is for the purpose of catching birds and animals, and the language of the Palace is as foreign as that of America.]

The mention of the New World evokes the contemporary fascination with American Indians as a natural people, most famously developed by Montaigne in his *Des cannibales*. Like the Indians, the peasants obey no other law than their generous nature and speak a language that has not yet been tainted by deception. Here, Balzac takes direct aim at the Parisian law-courts (the "Palace"), one of the most prestigious sites of French rhetorical culture.[15] Whereas the parliamentary style is corrupt and outdated, the language associated with Balzac's estate is paradoxically both new (a departure from tradition) and old (prelapsarian)—like the New World itself. The geographical setting, in other words, serves as an allegory for Balzac's renewal of eloquence, which is simultaneously a return to the past and a new beginning.

Continuing with the pastoral theme of the Golden Age, Balzac describes the amorous pursuits of his peasants:

> [P]artout où je commande, il n'y a personne qui ne face l'amour librement; & quand je voy d'un costé de l'herbe couchée par terre, & de l'au-

tre des espics renversez, je suis asseuré que ce n'est ny le vent ny la gresle qui ont fait cela, mais que c'est un berger & une bergere. (Balzac, 1:134–35)

Throughout my dominion, there is no one who does not make love freely, and when I see the grass matted down on one side and bent stalks on the other, I am sure that it is not the wind or the hail that are to blame, but a shepherd and a shepherdess.

Here, the pastoral landscape becomes an explicit figure for the text itself. Just as the matted grass has a clear meaning, marking the place of perfect communion where a shepherd and shepherdess have expressed their love, the text does not suffer from the ambivalence of signs characteristic of cities and courts. In semiotic parlance, we might refer to the pastoral sign as both an icon and an index. Because it bears the imprint of what it signifies, it both resembles the referent and furnishes positive assurance of its material reality. To put it another way, the pastoral sign partakes both of the permanence of writing and the innocence of spoken language. If, as Christian Jouhaud has argued, the preface *delocalizes* Balzac's eloquence, the pastoral serves inversely to *relocalize* it, providing a literary place that legitimizes his letters by placing them within a framework of transparency.[16]

In the later years of his career, when he withdrew entirely from public affairs, the pastoral would become a figure for Balzac's unique position within the Republic of Letters.[17] He gradually crafted a persona whose literary authority was enhanced by its distance from the commerce of the world. Known as the "Hermit of the Charente," he positioned himself as an objective arbiter in the great literary quarrels of his time, including the *querelle du Cid* and the battle over the Uranie and Job sonnets.[18] By remaining above the fray and asserting his singularity, he was able to participate in the literary and social life of his time without being implicated in the petty jealousies and rivalries of the Republic of Letters. Already, in this early letter, the use of the expression *Royaume de demie lieue* (half-league wide kingdom) assimilates the estate to the *state*, evoking the ideal of a sovereign, autonomous self. Given that aristocratic identity was closely tied to landed property, Balzac's literary discourse of place can be understood as an affirmation of his identity as an aristocrat-writer. Although his father (Guillaume Guez) did not use a noble title, Jean-Louis Guez *de* Balzac had pretensions to noble birth through his mother and sought to project an aristocratic persona. By associating his name with a place that was largely a literary construct, he was engaging in an assertive strategy of self-fashioning.

History and patronage intrude into the pastoral at the end of the letter, when Balzac describes the visits that Cardinal Richelieu and the duc d'Épernon paid to his estate over the years to relieve themselves temporarily of the burdens of politics, war, and personal grief:

> Le grand Duc d'Espernon est venu icy changer de felicité, & laisser cette vertu severe, & cét esclat qui esbloüit tout le monde, pour prendre des qualitez plus douces & une Majesté plus tranquille. Ce Cardinal, dont le Ciel veut faire de si grandes choses, & de qui je vous parle tous les jours . . . vint icy chercher du soulagement, & recevoir des propres mains de Dieu, qui ayme le silence, & qui habite la solitude, ce qui ne se trouve point dans les discours de la Philosophie, ny dans la foule du monde. (Balzac, 1:135–36)

> [The great duc d'Épernon came here for a change of pace, and to leave behind the severe virtue and reputation so admired by everyone, in order to adopt milder qualities and a calmer majesty. The cardinal whom heaven has destined for such great things, and whom I cannot refrain from mentioning in my letters to you . . . came here seeking solace, and to receive from God (who loves silence and inhabits solitary places) the things that cannot be found in the discourses of philosophy or in the agitation of worldly affairs.]

Within the boundaries of Balzac's estate, the great Épernon sheds his offical persona, assuming a more tranquil majesty while Richelieu, as befits his ecclesiastical station, seeks consolation for the death of his brother in prayer and silent meditation. In its final incarnation, the pastoral thus becomes a space of authenticity where aristocratic greatness and literature meet away from the bustle of the court. Like the form of the letter itself, Balzac's estate provides a human context for heroism, softening its edges. Simultaneously and inversely, the presence of these great men serves to consecrate both the landscape and the writer. At the end of the letter, alluding to the significant role that his estate played in the negotiations between the king and the queen mother in 1619, Balzac writes that the traces of princes and great lords are still fresh in the alleys of his garden ("les traces des Princes & des grands Seigneurs sont encore fresches dans mes allées" [Balzac, 1:136]). Through a kind of chiasmus, the writer takes on some of the "publicness" of his patrons, while the latter appear, if only momentarily, as private persons.

Writing the Gift: Balzac to La Valette (July 15, 1621)

Balzac's idealized relationship with his patrons is a precarious construct, constantly threatened by the realities of self-interest and social hierarchy. The unwritten rules of patronage, for instance, require that clients periodically recognize the asymmetry of the relationship. Balzac's July 15, 1621, letter to Cardinal La Valette thus begins with the acknowledgment of a favor:

> Vostre banquier me vient d'apporter la somme que vous lui avez commandé de me donner. (Balzac, 92)
>
> [Your banker has just delivered the sum that you ordered him to give me.]

This brief sentence captures the essence of the economic relation between the writer and his protector. The syntax brings out the contrast between the roles of giver (grammatical subject) and receiver (grammatical object), while the term "sum" and the mention of the banker as intermediary highlight the impersonal and abstract nature of the monetary gift. Faithful to his role as dependent, Balzac protests that he can never fully repay his debt:

> Je voudrois bien vous pouvoir remercier assez dignement de cette faveur, mais outre que vos bien-faicts sont trop grands, & que vous obligez de si bonne grace, qu'elle en augmente encore la valeur, je serois presomptueux si je croyois que les paroles que je vous pourrois dire fussent du prix des actions que vous faictes. (Balzac, 1:92)
>
> [I would like to be able to thank you in an appropriate manner for this favor, but besides the fact that your generosity is too great and that you give so gracefully that you further enhance the value of your gifts, I would be presumptuous if I believed that any words I might say could match your actions.]

At the same time that he acknowledges the gift and his inability to pay, Balzac subtly displaces its meaning. Here, it is the manner (*de si bonne grace*), rather than the matter, of the gift that is emphasized.

Since it derives in part from La Valette's graceful art of giving rather than from the exchange value of what he gives, value cannot simply be reduced to the "sum" evoked at the beginning of the letter.

Grace, of course, is an ambiguous term, for it describes both the gift itself (*gratia* means favor in Latin) and the manner of giving. Balzac plays off this ambiguity, suggesting that the essence of the gift is a matter of style—symbolic, rather than material or tangible:

> [J]e puis dire neantmoins sans vanité, que je n'ay jamais eu de si basse tentation que celle du gain. Je regarde donc vos bonnes graces toutes nues; & l'estime que vous faictes de moy, m'est une obligation d'autant plus chere que les autres, qu'elle considere mon merite, & non pas ma pauvreté, & qu'elle vient de vostre jugement, qui est plus parfaict que vostre fortune n'est relevée. (Balzac, 1:92–93)
>
> [I can say nevertheless without vanity that I have never been tempted by anything so base as a desire for material gain. I thus consider your generosity stripped down to its essence, and I cherish your esteem for me more than anything else, since it is a token of my merit, not my lack of means, and it comes from your judgment, which is greater than your fortune.]

Balzac structures his sentence around oppositions, contrasting "merit" with "poverty" and "judgment" with "fortune." Placing the emphasis on merit and judgment, he downplays the fortune, both material and providential, that separates him from his patron. With the patron and writer on the same footing, the gift ceases to be something calculable that can be measured in term of loss and gain; its value, rather, is a function of an intention that is expressed through the graceful performance of the giver. Manner and matter are thus paradoxically reversed. It is only by stripping away the material trappings of the gift that we can apprehend its symbolic truth, which lies in gesture. Divorced from circumstances of means and needs, the gift becomes a symbolic recognition of the inner worth of the recipient.

Balzac's letter to La Valette raises the larger question of the gift and its relation to literary patronage. The broad theoretical interest of the gift derives from the way in which it challenges and questions the premises of an economy based on calculation and self-interest. By their very nature, gifts have their own economy, distinct from (and opposed to) the abstract, impersonal logic of the market. Natalie Davis's study of the gift in sixteenth-century France, for example, stresses the role of the gift in opening "channels of communication . . . across boundaries of status and literacy" and giving "expression to the highly strained but genuine reciprocity between unequals in the social and economic order." Gifts, thus understood, are not discrete transactions; they serve, rather, to establish and maintain relationships between individuals occupying different places in a social hierarchy. When Marcel Mauss famously observed that the gift blurs the distinctions between persons and things, his larger point was that gifts lie at the intersection of the economic and the social.[19] What distinguishes a gift economy from the modern market is precisely this ethical emphasis placed on durable human relations.

According to Pierre Bourdieu, it is difficult for us to appreciate the way in which gifts function because we live in a society where the taboos against self-interest have gradually been eroded away. In our society, the denial of economic interest survives only in the narrow sphere of culture and more specifically art, which has become "a sacred island systematically and ostentatiously opposed to the profane, everyday world of production, a sanctuary for gratuitous, disinterested activity in a universe given over to money and self-interest."[20] He thus makes a suggestive link between the gift and the work of art. Both derive their specificity from a denial of calculated exchange and, consequently, a valorization of form over content. What connects the gift and the work of art, in other words, is that both are gratuitous.[21] They exist, at least ostensibly, for their own sake.

Balzac's letter to La Valette explores the relationships between gift giving, conspicuous consumption, and art:

> Car ne m'estimant ny pour entendre l'œconomie, ny pour estre propre à solliciter des affaires au Conseil, ny pour savoir bien courre la poste, vous faictes paroistre que vous estes veritablement du Sang des roys, qui ne sont riches que des choses inutiles. En effet il seroit difficile de deviner quel est en ceste vie l'usage des diamans, & des perles, & pourquoy un tableau couste davantage qu'une maison, si ce n'est que le plaisir . . . est une chose plus noble que la necessité. (Balzac, 1:93)

> [Since you do not hold me in high regard for my aptitude for managing money, or because I can plead your affairs in front of the Council, or because I can ride a horse at a gallop, you demonstrate that you are truly descended from the blood of kings, whose true wealth consists in superfluous things. Indeed, it would be hard to say what use diamonds and

pearls are in this life, and why a painting is worth more than a house, if pleasure . . . were not something more noble than necessity.]

Balzac's value to La Valette is independent of any practical competence he may possess, whether in the domestic or political spheres—*l'œconomie* and *des affaires au Conseil,* respectively. These formulations are well chosen, for Balzac's larger goal is quite simply to place himself and his artistic efforts outside the realm of "political affairs" and "economy." To the extent that value is a function of scarcity and pleasure, rather than utility, it follows that the most valuable commodities are those that do not circulate within the productive economy, that is, those things that are not in fact commodities at all. Like the nobleman himself, such superfluities remain noble only to the extent that they maintain their distance from the world of commerce and business. Otherwise, they derogate from their status as art, like the gentleman who practices a profession.

Balzac's description of the uses to which he has put La Valette's money provides a demonstration of this rarified anti-economy at work:

> Mais encore vous veux-je informer de quelle façon j'employe vostre argent, & vous rendre conte plus particulierement des affaires que je fais pour vous à Rome. Premierement au mois où nous sommes je cherche tous les remedes imaginables contre la violence de la chaleur. J'ay un esventail qui lasse les mains de quatre valets, & qui fait un vent en ma chambre, qui feroit des naufrages en pleine Mer. Je ne disne point que je ne noircisse de la neige dans du vin de Naples, & que je ne la face fondre sous des melons. Je vis la moitié du temps dans l'eau, & l'autre sur terre; Je me leve tous les jours deux fois, & quand je sors du lict, c'est pour entrer dans un bois d'orangers, où je resve au bruit de douze fontaines: Que si un jour de la semaine je suis obligé d'aller plus loin, je ne traverserois pas la ruë sans monter en carrosse, & marcher tousjours à couvert entre le ciel & la terre. Je laisse au vulgaire à sentir les fleurs, j'ay trouvé le moyen de les manger & de les boire . . . Outre cela en qualité de Monsieur vostre Agent je suis presque tousjours en festin; & là cependant que les autres se chargent de matiere, & de ce qui pese le plus, moy qui n'ay gueres d'appetit, je choisis les oyseaux qui sont engraissez de sucre, & je me nourris de l'ame du fruit & de la viande, qu'on appelle la gelée. (Balzac, 1:93–94)

[Let me tell how I am spending your money, and account more specifically for how I am advancing your affairs in Rome. This month, to begin with, I am looking for every conceivable remedy against the dreadful heat. I have a fan that exhausts the arms of four valets and produces a wind in my bedroom that would cause shipwrecks in the middle of the sea. I do not dine without pouring wine from Naples over snow, which I leave to melt under melons. I spend half of the time in the water and the other half on land. I get up twice a day, and when I am out of bed, I go straight into an orange grove where I daydream to the sound of twelve fountains. If once a day I am forced to go further, even if it is just across the street, I get into a carriage so as to remain protected from the sky and the earth. I let the common herd smell the flowers; I have found a way of eating and drinking them . . . Otherwise, as your agent, I am always feasting. Others fill themselves up on heavy food; since I hardly have any appetite, I pick birds that are fattened with sugar, and nourish myself with the essences of fruits and meats, which are called jelly.]

The term "affairs" is of course wholly ironic, since Balzac's self-described activities in Rome are anything but business. Rather than an accounting of his service as La Valette's agent, we are instead offered a comic Epicurean orgy. Balzac pushes the idea of refinement to its hyperbolic limits, imagining himself cooled by an enormous fan, crossing the street in a carriage, and concocting new forms of sensuous pleasure. To a large extent, this is a game of the imagination in which each sentence is more outrageous than the previous one. Balzac's style is not, however, without a certain grace. There is an elegance to his indulgence, exemplified by his manner of eating. Rather than allowing himself to be weighed down by heavy foods, Balzac nourishes himself on the distilled essences ("jelly") of meats. In this *nouvelle cuisine avant la lettre*, food becomes art by virtue of being dissociated from physical need, by denying its status as food. It is boiled down to the point at which it becomes a sign.

As with La Valette's gift, everything here is ultimately a matter of style—a self-consciously flowery style of writing, a stylized manner of eating, and so on. By transforming his own private pleasures into equally superfluous pleasures of language, Balzac's receiving becomes a literary gift, offered as entertainment to the patron. His theatrical consumption thus shows (but does not exactly say) that he can repay La Valette's generosity. The paradox, here, is that Balzac reciprocates without really reciprocating. From the perspective of economic exchange, after all, a gift of style is really a gift of nothing. Since it cannot be converted into material goods, it cannot be measured against La Valette's money. Nor, for that matter, can it be measured against the latter's stylized grace, as superfluities are by definition incommensurate with each other.

This brings us back to the question of the value of art. In the passages analyzed above, this value is a function of the rejection of a certain mode of exchange, namely the financial-support-for-service model of clientelist patronage. This anti-economic impulse recalls Bourdieu's famous characterization of the nineteenth-century autonomous literary field as an alternative value system that rejected the calculating economy of the market in favor of a "religion" of art.[22] Rather than posit artistic value in total opposition to patronage, however, Balzac imagines a rarified mode of (non-)exchange between patron and client, based on a logic that equates superfluity, aesthetic pleasure, and nobility. The discourse of the gift thus allows Balzac to sublimate his real (material) relationship with his patron. Because it still draws part of its energy from the social mystique of nobility, however, this art is not really autonomous in Bourdieu's sense. Indeed, to the extent that it is motivated by social desire and thus reinforces existing hierarchies, the rejection of the logic of exchange is not so much revolutionary as reactionary. Rather than carve out an autonomous literary field, it attempts to annex literature and its practitioners to the canons of aristocratic taste. At the same time, one paradoxical consequence of this annexation is to aestheticize nobility by reducing it to criteria of taste and style (rather than birth and military prowess). This is arguably a progressive effect, in that it tends to make nobility performative. Patronage does not merely draw writers into the world of nobility, it also draws the nobility into the world of letters, a point to which we will return in chapter 6.

The Battle Over Eloquence

A basic hesitation emerges in these letters. On the one hand, most notably in the letter to Épernon, Balzac aspires to a public role. On the other hand, in the letter to La Valette and, to a lesser extent, in the letter to La Motte-Aigron, he seems to retreat into a space of particularity and literary irony. Balzac's ambivalent position with respect to eloquence thus reproduces the indeterminacy of patronage—an institution that straddles the public-private/rhetoric-literature divide. The following pages will explore this and other inherent tensions and contradictions in his stance by examining the responses of his contemporaries to the *Lettres*.

Balzac's attempt to redefine eloquence met with considerable contemporary resistance, particularly during the lively quarrel that followed the publication of the *Lettres*. A major event in literary history, the *querelle des Premières Lettres* lasted over five years and helped set the terms for the great literary debates of the seventeenth century, including the *querelle des Anciens et des Modernes*.[23] The combative tone of the *Lettres* helped ignite the flames of the controversy. Placing himself apart from the competing *milieux* of literary society, Balzac launched an attack on two fronts: against the erudite *savants* (such as Father Garasse) and against the libertines (in the person of Balzac's childhood friend, Théophile de Viau). Against the *savants,* Balzac leveled the charges of pedantry and a servile respect for the Ancients, while Théophile and the libertines were taken to task for their disrespect for religious and political authority. Both camps responded to the call to battle, Garasse (*La Response du Sieur Hydaspe* [1624]) and Frère André (*La Conformité de l'eloquence de Mr de Balzac avec celle des plus grand personnages du temps present et passé* [1627]) on behalf of the *savants,* and Charles Sorel (in the eleventh book of *Francion* [1626]) for the libertines.[24]

Whereas the first stage of the quarrel was defined by the attacks in the *Lettres* against Garasse and Théophile and the various responses that they elicited, the second stage centered around Balzac's polemic with Dom Goulu, a *Feuillant* monk. The year 1627, which saw the publication of Balzac's *Œuvres* (the sixth edition of the *Lettres*), an *Apologie pour Monsieur de Balzac,* and the first volume of Goulu's *Lettres de Phyllarque à Ariste,* was the fiercest and most animated period of the quarrel. In this second stage, the terms of the debate became both more explicit and more theoretical. While the earlier attacks had been relatively brief, the *Apologie* and the *Lettres de Phyllarque* were longer works that made frequent use of citation and commentary. The *Apologie,* written by François Ogier with probable help from Balzac himself,[25] is three hundred pages long, and Goulu's remarkable commentary stacks up at more than one thousand pages, including a summary of Pliny's *Panegyric* to Trajan and a complete translation of Plato's *Apology*. Putting aside some important issues, we will concentrate primarily on a series of related questions raised in this second stage of the quarrel:

1) The possibility and implications of modernizing eloquence
2) The appropriateness of Balzac's tone with his patrons
3) His use of hyperbole

Responding to Balzac's early critics, the *Apologie* continues the defense of epistolary eloquence inaugurated in the preface to the *Lettres*, insisting on the noble history of the genre. Letter writing, Ogier explains, was valued by the Roman emperors because it allowed them to govern at a distance by sending decrees to far-flung outposts. Because they were extensions of imperial power and the depositories of its secrets (*arcana imperii*), secretaries were chosen with great care.[26] Like the preface to the *Lettres*, moreover, the *Apologie* insists on the suitability of the letter for monarchical culture. Since it is no longer possible for eloquence to appear before a Senate, it must confine itself to a tiny space (*petit espace*). At the court, moreover, persuasion is a matter of using *compliments* and *civilités* to put the listener/reader in the proper frame of mind—a task to which the letter, with its rituals of *politesse* and *flatterie*, is uniquely suited.[27] The *Apologie*, finally, situates Balzac's letters within the venerable tradition of panegyric, "since we could hardly call the letters he wrote to important persons anything other than panegyrics."[28] Panegyric, which flourished in the later years of the Roman Empire among the practitioners of the "Second Sophistics," is the rhetorical form most suitable to aristocratic or monarchical societies. A branch of epideictic rhetoric, it focuses on subjects of public praise and celebration, rather than politics or the law, the areas covered by deliberative and forensic rhetoric, respectively. To put it another way, it is less concerned with the struggle for power than with its spectacle. The *Apologie*, here, anticipates the broad trend in seventeenth-century France toward the restriction of rhetoric to ceremonial functions. Panegyric increasingly became a staple of literary life, especially in the nascent academies, where members were expected to praise the leading figures of their time.[29]

In nearly every respect, Goulu takes a position opposite to that outlined in the *Apologie*. Whereas the latter boldly embraces the principles of originality and modernity, Goulu advocates a respect for tradition and a strict doctrine of imitation. Eloquence, he contends, is a precious heritage that we must treasure and protect, not tamper with. "It is important for the welfare of mankind not to let this rich legacy be sullied or polluted."[30] He especially deplores the misuses of eloquence in court society, where this noble art is put to amoral, if not immoral, ends. In a chapter entitled "Description de l'orateur de Court," for example, he directly assimilates the decline of eloquence to its use in the court. The courtier, he claims, diverts eloquence from its true function by using it to assert his own superiority and individuality (*se retirer du commun*).³¹ Because of his sophistic concern for form over content, he becomes a declaimer (*déclamateur*) rather than an orator. What makes the diatribe particularly significant is the notion that eloquence should be impersonal—that it should never be used in the service of particular interests. For Goulu, as we will see, an "eloquence of patronage" is an impossibility.

Goulu takes direct aim at the form of the letter, mocking the presumption of those who would prefer a lousy bundle of letters (*un paquet de méchantes lettres*) to the majestic speeches of Demosthenes.³² Because it is a short, fragmentary form, the letter does not permit the fullness and dignity of great eloquence. For Goulu, consequently, Balzac's choice of a genre belonging to the competence of secretaries and notaries is a symptom of his inability to master the subtleties and complexities of longer pieces.³³ A second, more profound, criticism of the letter derives from the notion, inherited from Roman and Greek antiquity, that eloquence was primarily oral and public, intimately connected to specific oratorical places such as the forum, the pulpit, or the courts of law. In a direct rebuke to the preface to the *Lettres,* Goulu rejects Balzac's attempted respatialization of the letter. "It is very presumptuous for someone who has only spoken with women in a *cabinet* and with servants in a bedroom to presume to call himself eloquent or an orator. This so-called orator should content himself with being a 'mere writer' [*simple écrivain*]."³⁴ Stressing the domesticity of the places of Balzac's eloquence (*cabinet,* bedroom), he implicitly contrasts them with more dignified places, such as the courts or the forum. Goulu thus summarizes the fundamental question of the quarrel: could the ancient ideal of the orator be adapted and modified so as to accommodate new circumstances, or did the modern man of letters have to resign himself to being a mere "writer"?

Behind the debate between Balzac and Goulu (and indeed behind much seventeenth-century thinking about eloquence) lurks the specter of Tacitus's *Dialogue on Orators*. In this dialogue, Tacitus, through the character of Maternus, reflects on the causes of the decline of eloquence under the empire. Like fire, he reasons, great eloquence requires combustible material in the form of political conflict: "strife between the Senate and the people," "prosecutions of influential citizens," and so on.³⁵ Just as war produces good soldiers, political conflict produces great orators by raising the stakes of public debate. The more fragmented the *res publica* and the more urgent the dangers that confront it, the greater the role played by orators, who mobilize social and political energies. With the peace and prosperity of the *Pax Romana*, however, eloquence has been forced to forsake the great stage of history for lesser venues. "What contempt (so I think at least) has been brought on eloquence by those little overcoats into which we squeeze, and, so to say, box ourselves up, when we chat with the judges! How much force may we suppose has been taken from our speeches by the little rooms and offices in which nearly all cases have to be set forth. Just as a spacious course tests a fine horse, so the orator has his field, and unless he can move in it freely and at ease, his eloquence grows feeble and breaks down."[36] Everything in Maternus's description speaks of physical constraint, from "the little overcoats" into which the lawyers squeeze themselves to the "little rooms and offices." When the great political problems have been resolved, eloquence has nowhere left to go but confined, private spaces, where it must necessarily wither and die for lack of material. The end of history, decidedly, does not make for good rhetoric.

But should we really deplore this loss? Maternus answers in the negative. Prosperity and peace are infinitely preferable to eloquence. "The great and famous eloquence of old is the nursling of the license which fools called freedom; it is the companion of sedition, the stimulant of an unruly people."[37] Of course, this is Maternus, and not Tacitus, speaking. The latter presumably shares not only Maternus's cynicism, but also the more idealized vision of eloquence offered by the other interlocutors in the dialogue. (See, for example, Marcus Aper's enthusiastic portrait of the orator.) Ultimately, Tacitus's narrative of the decline of eloquence is a tragedy in the deepest sense, in that it combines a genuine longing for the Golden Age of eloquence with a profound sense of the historical impossibility of a return to the past.

This is the basic framework which Balzac, Goulu, and their learned contemporaries share, although they draw dramatically different conclusions from it. Goulu, on the one hand, is squarely in the camp of the Ancients. Because he lacks a historical consciousness that can conceive of change without equating it with decadence, he affirms the nostalgia of origins without really acknowledging the tragedy of the present situation. Through diligent reading and imitation of Cicero and Isocrates, he believes, we can reconnect with the past. The Balzac of the *Lettres* and *Apologie,* on the other hand, seeks to rewrite Tacitus's tragic plot as *novel.* If eloquence cannot continue as it is, then it follows that it must change; if the great stage of public discourse is closed, then it must seek to thrive in the more confined spaces of the court; if these spaces do not allow for the sublime style of public oratory, then we must find a more moderate, conversational style; and so on. We may wonder, however, whether this position is any less shortsighted than Goulu's. Did the aristocratic/monarchical culture of seventeenth-century France really have a place for an ambitious pseudo-orator whose discursive practices blurred the boundaries between private and public discourse?

Balzac's relatively familiar stance with regard to his patrons is another *leitmotif* that runs through the quarrel. Early on, in his *Response du sieur Hydaspe au sieur de Balzac* (1624), Garasse admonished his former student to adopt a more deferential tone when dealing with his social superiors.[38] Goulu picks up this line of criticism, taking Balzac to task for bringing up especially inappropriate subjects, such as his mistresses and his health, with his patrons.[39] On the basis of the letters alone, he warns, a reader would form an inaccurate and unfavorable impression of many of Balzac's correspondents. "He has pushed his imprudence to the limit in the way he addresses certain prominent persons. Those who do not know the merit of the latter will undoubtedly judge them harshly for their actions."[40] Whereas Balzac tends to blur the line between patronage relationships and friendships, Goulu sees these two categories as distinct, if not exclusive.[41] Richelieu, Épernon, and La Valette are public figures. If these eminent persons have allowed Balzac to write to them on personal matters, Goulu suggests, it is under a seal of confidentiality.[42] By suggesting that certain aspects of Balzac's relationships with prominent persons are not suitable for publication, Goulu raises an interesting dilemma. How can a writer *advertise* an intimate relationship with a patron without *publicizing* indiscreet details? The very thing that makes publishing patronage letters attractive, in other words, makes it compromising as well.

Goulu isolates other similar instances of imprudence. The inclusion of letters to multiple patrons, for instance, is an important part of Balzac's authorial strategy. It allows him to mobilize the social energies of patronage while maintaining a margin of independence. On the one hand, his status is enhanced by these powerful connections; on the other hand, as long as he cultivates multiple relationships, he will never become Épernon's (or Richelieu's) "man." The potential cost of this strategy, as Goulu points out, is to dilute the effect of Balzac's praise: each letter presenting a particular patron as the greatest cancels out the others and compromises the possibility of any coherent, general message. Balzac, here, is not so much an orator as a con artist, selling the same fraudulent *marchandise* (merchandise) to multiple buyers.[43] If the *Lettres* are public, it is in the degraded sense of commercial objects that are offered for sale in the marketplace.

In none of these instances, it should be noted, does Goulu question the basic principles of patronage. Quite to the contrary, he repeatedly stresses the importance of discretion and personal loyalty. What he challenges, rather, is Balzac's use of patronage as a means for glorifying the status of the writer—his attempts to bask in the glory of the likes of Richelieu and Épernon. Patronage, for Goulu, is not a legitimate arena for eloquence, and it is certainly not a substitute for the traditional circumstances of public oratory.

Hyperbole: An Explosive Figure

The most prominent issue in the quarrel, however, was Balzac's use of hyperbole. One of Balzac's most often used figures, hyperbole is obviously well suited to the glorification of the patron. In contrast to other, more expansive stylistic devices, however, it is easily accommodated within the limiting confines of the letter. In fact, hyperbole is arguably most effective when it is expressed succinctly, that is, when its shock value is greatest. Not surprisingly, then, hyperbole is the aspect of Balzac's style that has received the most attention, not only among literary historians, but also among his contemporaries.[44] Indeed it was the most identifiable characteristic of the fashionable speaking style that Balzac popularized in his letters (known as *le parler Balzac*).[45]

In a passage from the opening letter to Épernon, we find a typical and revealing example of Balzac's use of hyperbole:

Toutesfois quand je considere les actions de vostre vie, qui sont telles, que nous avons de la peine à les croire apres les avoir veuës, & en tel nombre, qu'il semble aux estrangers que vous viviez dés le commencement de nostre Monarchie, je pense pouvoir dire avec verité, que s'il y a encore quelque chose de grand à faire dans le monde, il ne faut pas que ce soit un autre que vous qui l'entreprenne. (Balzac, 1:8)

[However, when I consider the actions of your life, which are such that we have difficulty believing them after we have witnessed them, and so numerous that it seems to foreigners that you have been alive since the origins of our Monarchy, I think I can truly say that if there is something left to be accomplished in the world, you are the only one worthy of undertaking it.]

This passage lays bare the basic mechanism of all hyperbole. Hyperbole expresses precisely that which we have difficulty believing. By going beyond the truth, it attempts to reproduce in language the sense of marvel that one experiences before the divine, the spectacular, and the unbelievable. Hyperbole, in other words, communicates the truth paradoxically—by lying. Balzac's use of hyperbole echoes Quintilian's theoretical discussion at the end of the eighth book of his *Institutio oratoria*. Beginning with a caveat—"I have kept hyperbole for last, on the grounds of its boldness"—Quintilian describes this figure as an "elegant straining of the truth" (*decens veri superiectio*),[46] and stresses that it "lies without any intention to deceive."[47] It is reserved, he insists, for exceptional circumstances, "when the magnitude of facts passes all words, and in such circumstances our language will be more effective if it goes beyond the truth than if it falls short of it."[48] Implicit in this theory is an assumption that ordinary language is flat and banal, and therefore inadequate to describe the abnormal, the unusual, and the marvelous. In order to overcome the shortcomings of language and to convey such qualities, the orator must exaggerate, preferably in as elegant a manner as possible.

The letter to La Valette, which we examined earlier in this chapter, reveals another, more properly literary, side of hyperbole. Because it is detached from ordinary reality, hyperbole offers a rich terrain for stylistic invention and play of the sort we found in Balzac's descriptions of his Epicurean indulgences. This emphasis on decor over function has led Jean Rousset to describe it as the baroque's quintessential figure, comparing it to the oversized façades on Jesuit churches. Gérard Genette makes a similar point, comparing the far-fetched comparisons of hyperbole to the technique of juxtaposition used by the surrealists. Liberated from the constraints of naturalism, language is free to become a pure object of the intellect.[49]

In a letter to Father Garasse published in the 1627 edition of the *Lettres,* Balzac himself suggested that his hyperbolic language might be no more than an exercise in stylistic bravado. Balzac and Garasse had fallen out over a long invective against humanist pedantry printed in the 1624 edition, in which the pupil had written that the only things more distasteful than his old schoolmaster's writings were "beer and medicine" (Balzac, 1:60). Seeking reconciliation, Balzac now insisted that the emotion in the letter had been feigned, rather than heartfelt, thus establishing a critical rupture between feeling and style. Rather than a genuine expression of his thoughts and affections, the letter to Hydaspe, with its hyperbolic tone, was no more than a game (*jeu*). His only desire, he explained, was to affirm his creativity through a *tour de force* of stylistic experimentation:

> J'ay seulement voulu faire voir que je pouvois estre plus fort que la verité. (Balzac, 2:29)

> [I only wanted to demonstrate that I could be more compelling than the truth.]

Balzac, here, situates himself within a long rhetorical tradition of *éloges paradoxaux*, exercises in verbal prowess often practiced by classical rhetoricians who wanted to show that they could create eloquent eulogies on insignificant or base subjects.[50] Indeed he cites the most famous example of this genre, the *Éloge de la fièvre quarte*.

The implication is that Balzac's motivations, in his attack against Garasse, were purely literary. His intention was to impress (*exciter plutost de l'admiration en l'esprit des hommes*) rather than actually convince anyone (*y gaigner de la creance*). Pushing the point even further, he adopts a position analogous to the age-old defense of fiction. Since fictional discourses do not make truth claims, the argument goes, they should not be judged on grounds of veracity. Instead, only aesthetic criteria, such as the internal coherence and beauty of the fictional universe, should apply:

> On ne peut pas convaincre de fausseté ceux qui font des miroirs qui representent un object pour un autre, & l'erreur est quelquefois plus belle que la verité. (Balzac, 2:30)

> [Those who create mirrors that represent one object as another cannot be accused of lying; sometimes error is more beautiful than the truth.]

An alternative conception of eloquence emerges in these passages. Rather than being a reflection of reality, the despicable as well as the praiseworthy, it is a kind of distorting mirror that no reasonable person should take seriously, except on purely stylistic grounds. The letter to Garasse thus redefines the status of hyperbole, which functions less as a descriptive or persuasive device than as a form of stylistic fireworks, establishing a fissure in the relationship between style and reality that his opponents would exploit during the quarrel.

Goulu first raises the question of hyperbole in a chapter entitled "Inepte et sotte manière que tient Narcisse à loüer les personnes illustres" during a general discussion of the appropriate uses of figurative language. "Those who have given us principles of good speech have written that the praise of great men should be treated differently by orators and poets. We allow the latter to use ornaments that are strictly forbidden to others. It is appropriate for poets . . . to depict those whom they wish to immortalize eating ambrosia and drinking nectar . . . They are allowed to explain this kind of thing with special words and to use hyperboles and metaphors to adorn and magnify things. But this sort of poetic license is forbidden to orators."[51] According to this ancient argument, which goes back at least to Horace's *Ars Poetica,* the criteria according to which we interpret and judge poetry and eloquence are entirely distinct. Poetic discourse is less consequential than eloquence and thus accommodates more freedom of expression. Eloquence, by contrast, is a sober matter of argument, reason, and truth, and thus admits of little ornamentation.[52] Goulu, indeed, seems to banish virtually all ornate and figurative language from the orator's repertoire, holding him to a standard of extreme austerity. He is only permitted to use common language (*les paroles usitées*) and must take care that his expressions conform to reality (*la verité de choses mêmes*). Style must never be allowed to take on a life of its own.

The *Apologie,* by contrast, insists that hyperbole be considered a legitimate weapon in the orator's arsenal, echoing Quintilian's definition of the figure as a necessary lie—a means for conveying extremes that ordinary language cannot express.[53] Certain passions, thoughts, even persons, belong to another, higher, order of existence. By exaggerating, the orator enhances effect, bringing the listener around to an idea of the sublimity of the object. "Just as there is a certain heroic virtue, according to philosophers, that soars above ordinary virtue [*va tout d'un autre vol que la Vertu commune*], and goes beyond laws and ordinary rules, similarly there is a certain style that seems to be expressly created for this extraordinary virtue and is not easily subjected to the tyranny of art or theoretical principles."[54] The autonomy of the hero and the autonomy of heroic discourse go hand in hand. Just as the hero cannot be held to the conventions of law, the language that expresses the hero's greatness does not follow the theoretical principles of rhetoric or the tyranny of artistic norms. Ordinary language is an imperfect medium that resists the expression of the sublime. When the orator attempts to convey an idea of greatness, he finds that the material is resistant and defective (*de la repugnance & du deffaut de la part de la matiere*).[55] Rather than simply persuading his audience, consequently, the orator must exalt it. "The sovereign orator does not merely lead his audience where he wishes; he actually ravishes it, transporting it outside of itself [*le ravit, & le transporte hors de soy-mesme*]."[56]

In sublime discourse, according the *Apologie*'s reasoning, effect and affect replace argumentation. The listener is not led through a chain of reasoning; rather, he is stunned to such an extent that he loses himself and is carried away by the orator. Such was the language used by the earliest prophets, legislators, and philosophers to communicate their great thoughts.[57] Such is also the language that the Holy Scriptures use to express divine truths in a form accessible to the minds of men.[58] The true test of the orator's prowess is his ability to contain and guide this excess. "Let him disappear from sight, as long as he does not wander. Let him walk over precipices, as long as he does not fall."[59] Hyperbole, in other words, is an exercise in retaining control while pushing the limits of enthusiasm. To be effective, it must be used judiciously, otherwise the faculty of reason rebels against the desired effect. This is why the orator must lie artfully, only abandoning the truth when appearance of truth is more seductive (*mentir subtilement, & ne quitter la verité que quand la vraysemblance est plus belle*).[60]

For Goulu, however, Balzac's hyperboles are anything but subtle. Indeed, he argues that Balzac uses hyperbole more like a comic actor (*plus comme farceur & Comédien*) than like an orator.[61] In the mouth of a flatterer or a parasite in a comedy, hyperbole has an effect opposite from that of the orator. Rather than persuading, the gap between expression and reason makes the spectator laugh. "Actors [*les Comediens*] also use hyperboles, but to an end entirely different from that of orators. For they only put them in the mouths of Rodomonts, Thrasons, and other flatterers and parasites in order to make people laugh."[62] This characterization of hyperbole as a potentially burlesque figure returns constantly in the quarrel. One of the interlocutors in Jean-Pierre Camus's *Conférence académique,* for instance, compares Balzac to the *capitan,* the ridiculous fanfaron of the *commedia dell'arte.*[63] Bernard de Javersac, who intervenes in the quarrel in 1628 with his *Discours d'Aristarque à Nicandre,* makes a similar point. "He has acquired such a propensity to mockery [*à railler*] that he is hardly ever serious except when he is praising himself and uses nothing but irony and hyperbole in his flattery of great lords."[64] And Charles Sorel constructs an entire episode of his comic novel *Histoire comique de Francion* around Hortensius, a pompous pedant with a penchant for pastiching Balzac's letters. In Hortensius's speech, Sorel strings together the most extreme of Balzac's hyperboles and comparisons, taking them out of their immediate context in order to highlight their absurdity. Hyperbole thus appears as a kind of burlesque parody of polite speech, the language of good society as only a pedant would imagine it.[65]

This notion of the burlesque and the comic brings us back to the fundamental problem of hyperbole—that it always risks the possibility of not being taken seriously in both senses of the expression: a hyperbole can have comic effect or simply not be believed.[66] The claim that Balzac is unaware of this danger is not justified, however. The question of the relationship between hyperbole and the comic comes up explicitly in the *Apologie,* where the author defends Balzac's use of this figure by suggesting that many of his hyperboles are in fact not intended to be serious. "Most of M. B.'s hyperboles are intended to be funny."[67] In the context of the comic possibilities of hyperbole, the *Apologie* even mentions the *capitan* figure, perhaps inspiring Goulu. "When Pompey boasted that he could bring legions of soldiers out of the earth by stomping it with his foot, he was doing a *rodomontade* long before the poets had invented Rodomont and playing the role of the *capitan* in a comedy."[68] The author of the *Apologie* is aware, then, that heroic, hyperbolic language can lend itself to humorous, theatrical use. At the same time, however, he claims that Balzac's use of humorous hyperbole is not abusive, but rather sober and reasonable. Unlike the burlesque figure of the *capitan,* his mockery is philosophical and moral. "He laughs in the manner of a Roman censor or an Athenian philosopher."[69] When he decides to praise someone's merits, by contrast, he adopts a dignified, serious tone.

Do we always know, however, whether Balzac is being serious or not? In spoken discourse, certain contextual signs—tone of voice or physical behavior, for example—may indicate to a listener whether to interpret a hyperbole seriously or not. Written hyperbole, by contrast, is particularly difficult to decode. The context is a broad set of implicit ideas about the world and the types of characterizations that are adequate to describe it. This problem led Quintilian to assert that "as a rule" hyperbole was a trope rather than a figure. Figures, for the Latin rhetorician, are more extended than tropes. Whereas the latter are essentially ornamental, the former enter into the realm of discourse and thought. He distinguishes, for example, between a figurative form of irony, which he qualifies as "disguised," and the trope, which "is franker in its meaning."[70] The rationale for this distinction is obvious. On the basis of the immediate context, we can usually determine whether a single word or expression is ironic, in the classical sense of meaning the opposite of what it says. When an entire discourse is ironic, however, we need more sophisticated tools, such as tone of voice and/or demeanor, to determine its sincerity. If we do not heed these clues, we risk a total breakdown in communication. Quintilian's motivation for limiting hyperbole to "tropic" uses thus becomes evident. As long as this device is nothing but a single word or expression, its tendency toward excess and its potential ambiguity is contained; when it becomes a figure of thought, by contrast, the surrounding context is no longer useful to a listener or reader seeking to determine whether to take a hyperbole at face value or not.

Balzac's use of hyperbole is largely figurative, however. A linguistic reformer in the tradition of Malherbe, he generally avoids Italianate superlatives as incompatible with the genius of the French language. The *Apologie* proudly notes that even Balzac's detractors have generally acknowledged the purity of his diction. "As for the words, they do not touch them, acknowledging that they are the purest in our language [*les plus propres de nostre langue*]."[71] Because he uses the restrained diction of the court, he needs to compensate for the deficiency of words on the level of discourse. "That is why it has been necessary to use invention and the structure of the sentence to compensate for the lack of forcefulness in the words."[72] Because Balzac's style is *discursive*—because it depends on the semantic, as well as musical, effects of combining words—it is difficult to determine where style ends and thought begins.

This ambiguity is manifest in the *Apologie*'s long compilation of humorous *railleries* from Balzac's *Lettres*.[73] While many of these are clear examples of humor or stylistic play, others present problems of interpretation. When the author cites the following passage from a letter to Épernon, for example, it is far from clear what permits one to judge that it is mockery rather than serious:

> Lors que je pense combien de fois Dieu vous a tiré du peril contre toutes les apparences humaines, & la resistance que vous avez euë à venir jusques icy, par des escueils & des precipices, je croy tout de bon que vous avez passé le temps de mourir.[74]

> [When I think about how many times God has saved you from misfortune against all human expectation, and the obstacles that you have encountered along the way, in the form of perils and precipices, I really think that you are past dying.]

This passage could be understood as an innocent form of polite humor, an expression of the author's bemused bewilderment at the luck and good fortune of his benefactor. Or it could be taken as a sincere form of praise, an expression of Épernon's divine election and grandeur. Without actually affirming Épernon's immortality, Balzac could be using a hyperbolic expression for effect to convey an impression of his patron's long and distinguished life. The matter is complicated by the fact that most of Balzac's hyperboles, as Goulu points out, use expressions (such as *tout de bon* meaning "really") that would suggest that he intends to be taken seriously.[75]

We are thus led to an impasse. The more affirmative the hyperbole is, the more potentially comic it becomes, and the less persuasive it is. In the final analysis, it is an evanescent figure, apt to evaporate, explode, or deflate at any moment. Indeed, the *Apologie* implicitly acknowledges this point when it places the burden of sorting out mockery from serious praise on the reader. "M. Balzac cannot prevent others from taking literally [*au pied de la lettre*] what was said in jest [*en riant*]."[76] Instead of establishing clear criteria for judging the sincerity of hyperbole, the author throws up his hands.

Alain Viala has argued that rhetorical ambivalence—or "duplicity," as he calls it—is one of the defining characteristics of seventeenth-century patronage discourse, indeed of all literary production of the period. It is a sign, he argues, of the instability of the writer's social position, of the multiple ideological demands that are placed on him.[77] Balzac, we have seen, is caught between two conflicting aspirations. On the one side is his desire to preserve the efficacy of eloquence to represent and act on the world, but at the risk of implicating the writer in the sordid business of flattery. On the other side is the temptation to preserve the integrity of eloquence by detaching it from reality and retreating into stylistic virtuosity, which amounts to putting eloquence aside in favor of literature.[78] This ambivalence was latent in our readings of Balzac's patronage letters in the first part of this chapter. In the grand, heroic style of the letter to Épernon, we identified a desire to make language adequate to the representation of contemporary heroism. By contrast, the language of Epicurean gratuitousness, which we analyzed in the letter to La Valette, tends to undermine the referential function of discourse, reducing it to questions of taste and pleasure. This aestheticizing of the patronage relationship moves away from the ideal of transparency, weakening the relationship between words and reality and rendering the terms of discourse, which are intended to be appreciated rather than understood, semantically opaque. Hyperbole, in conclusion, is a symptom of a hesitation *vis-à-vis* the dilemma of how to modernize eloquence. Balzac himself was aware of his inability to satisfactorily resolve the question. Indeed in later years, as his patronage aspirations failed and as he internalized the criticisms of his detractors, he would repeatedly declare that he had abandoned hyperbole.

Epilogue

In 1631, Balzac published the *Prince*, a hybrid of princely mirror and panegyric of Louis XIII.[79] This text offered Balzac the opportunity to gain favor with the crown and prove that he was capable of a more sustained eloquence than he had demonstrated in the *Lettres*. The reception did not live up to his expectations, however. The Sorbonne censors expressed concern over a number of theological points. In their eyes, Balzac's celebration of absolute power went too far, placing the monarch above the constraints of Christian piety. Then, on the political front, enemies of Richelieu's politics, such as Matthieu de Morgues (Marie de' Medici's polemicist), entered the fray and the *Prince* became entangled in the debate over Richelieu's politics. Most serious, however, was the cold shoulder that the *Prince* received from the royal administration, in general, and Richelieu, in particular. Although this official rebuff may seem surprising, given the *Prince*'s apparently sympathetic portrait of royal authority, critics and historians have proposed a number of plausible explanations. In a letter accompanying the *Prince*, Balzac had alluded to the fallout between Richelieu and Marie de' Medici after the *journée des dupes* (when Richelieu weathered an attempted *coup* by Marie's allies) and sought to reconcile them. By representing his patrons in conflict, Christian Jouhaud has suggested, Balzac committed the sin of mentioning that there was a conflict. Such a display of the inner workings of the court and the cabinet could only displease the cardinal.[80] Another possibility is that Balzac was so extreme in his defense of royal authority and reason of state that he compromised Richelieu's public relations efforts. The *Prince,* notoriously, had suggested that the king should be able, on the basis of mere instinct or suspicion, to punish plots against his authority before they were hatched.[81] A third possible explanation is that the *Prince,* in its apotheosis of the person of the monarch, tended to downplay the role played by important ministers such as Richelieu. In his *Historiettes,* Tallemant des Réaux relates that the cardinal was bitter that Balzac had not dedicated the text to him. "Does he think himself such a great lord that he does not have to dedicate his books?"[82] My point, here, is not to weigh the relative merits of these interpretations, but rather to point out that in each instance, Bazac's failure is attributed to a sin of excess: saying too much; going too far in his defense of reason of state; praising the king too enthusiastically. The *Prince,* like the *Lettres,* is a hyperbolic text.

The failure of the *Prince* appears to have had direct, practical implications for Balzac, interrupting the payment of his pensions.[83] This autobiographical detail would be of little interest were it not for the fact that Balzac himself linked his career failures to a crisis of language. Searching, in 1644, for words adequate to describe Mme de Rambouillet, Balzac writes:

> Et en conscience je n'eus jamais tant de besoin de cette officieuse figure, qui aide les bonnes intentions; qui acquite les debtes des pauvres; qui non seulement esgale les choses par les paroles, mais qui les sçait aggrandir jusqu'à l'infini. Vous la connoissez, MADAME, sous le celebre nom d'Hyperbole; & je vous advouë que je l'abandonnay laschement, il y a pres de dix-huit ans.[84]

> [I can say in good conscience that I have never had so much call for that officious figure that is so helpful in aiding good intentions, that settles the debts of paupers, that not only equalizes things with words, but can enlarge them infinitely. Madame, you know it under the famous name of "hyperbole," and I confess that I abandoned it cowardly eighteen years ago.]

By a subtraction of dates (1644 −18 = 1626), we can suppose that Balzac is alluding to the quarrel in this passage. Hyperbole is presented in a positive and nostalgic retrospective light, as the means by which language rectifies the inequalities of favor and fortune (*esgale les choses par les paroles*). But the quarrel forced Balzac to abandon this equalizing tool and to content himself with the "simplicity of my native tongue . . . like another man."[85] Writing to Monsieur de Brye in 1635, Balzac identifies the failure of the *Prince* as a second moment of rupture:

> Et quoy qu'il y ait plus de quatre ans que j'ay quitté le monde & perdu l'usage de la parole, la Haine & l'Envie viennent troubler le silence de mes bois.[86]

[And although I abandoned the world and lost the faculty of speech four years ago, hate and envy still find me in the silence of my woods.]

The crisis of 1631, like the crisis of the quarrel, is portrayed as more than a professional failure. It marks the moment, rather, when he was forced into silence, when he had to forsake his vocation of eloquence.

What makes Balzac's story important is the scale of his ambitions and the extent of his failure. As we have seen, his program was no less than a wholesale revamping of eloquence to adapt it to the aristocratic and monarchical culture in which he lived. To this end, he focused his attention on the letter—a form that was well suited for expressing the relationships between the writer and his patrons. Like patronage itself, the published letter straddled the public and private spheres, rhetoric and literature. Because of its liminality, this form allowed Balzac to play at being an orator in a political context where public oratory was highly suspect. (When controversy reared its ugly head, he could always retreat into irony.) The instability of this position, however, was ultimately as much a curse as a blessing. Balzac's critics, we have seen, called him on his equivocations, variously characterizing him as bombastic, superficial, and obsequious—judgments that eventually became commonplaces of literary history. If Balzac plays such a central role in my argument, making several appearances in the pages that follow, it is not despite but rather *because of* his bombast, superficiality, and obsequiousness—failings that are symptomatic of the tensions inherent in patronage culture.

3
His Master's Voice: Poetry in an Age of Collective Authorship

Qu'importe qui parle?

[What matters who is speaking?]

—Samuel Beckett, *Fin de partie*

WHEREAS THE PRECEDING CHAPTER FOCUSED ON THE COMPLEX RELAtionship of patronage discourse to its object, we shall now turn to the question of authorship. Authorship is a tricky matter in seventeenth-century France. Did Louis XIV, for instance, actually write "his" memoirs? In what sense? Did he actually put pen to paper? Did he dictate?[1] If he did not, does that make him any less of an author? Is the author (the authority behind a discourse) necessarily the same as the "writer" (the person who gives it form)? Who is really speaking in a text written on behalf of a patron? The next two chapters will examine these questions as they pertain to the creation of literary texts and, more specifically, lyric poetry. First, however, we will take a detour through art history.

HIRED HANDS: POLITICAL ART AND ARTFUL POLITICS

Commissioned for the Luxembourg Palace and depicting the life of Marie de' Medici, the 24 paintings of Rubens's Medici cycle are a remarkable example of art patronage, perhaps the most remarkable in seventeenth-century France prior to Le Brun's work at Versailles. The contract for the commission reveals the extent of the role of the patron in the artistic process.[2] Rubens agrees to represent a set of specified episodes that are "conveyed and described in extensive detail in writing according to the wishes of Her Majesty, who gave a

Fig. 2. Rubens, Peter Paul (1577–1640). *The Treaty of Angouleme, April 30, 1619*. Oil on Canvas, 12.9 × 2.9 ft. INV1786. Photo: Ojéda/Le Mage. Louvre, Paris, France. Courtesy of the Réunion des Musées Nationaux / Art Resource, NY.

copy to the aforementioned Rubens through her secretary, the aforementioned Bouthillier."[3] Marie, moreover, reserves the right to modify the content by "adding or subtracting from the aforementioned paintings before they are begun and having figures that do not please her touched up or changed."[4] The terms of the agreement contain a valuable lesson for the modern-day viewer, who is accustomed to evaluating artistic creation in terms of creativity and personal inspiration. The decisive role of the patron in determining both the basic iconography and the final form of the Medici cycle forces us to forgo these criteria and to apprehend artistic creation as a collaborative, rather than purely individualistic, undertaking.

Most scholars agree that the subjects and much of the iconography of the Medici cycle were chosen with a specific political intent, although interpretations of the precise meaning vary. Jacques Thuillier has advanced an interpretation based on the depiction of Marie as Bellona, the Roman goddess of war. Following his reading, each painting fits into a larger framework of conquest: military conquest, conquest of a husband (Henry IV), defeat of Marie's personal enemies, and so on. On the basis of minute iconographical analysis, Ronald Millen and Robert Wolf have advanced an alternative interpretation. The hidden subtext of the cycle, intelligible only when the various emblems and other "mystic figures" are deciphered, is the military and political conflict between Marie and her young son, Louis XIII.[5]

The "Treaty of Angoulême," an allegorized depiction of the negotiations between queen and son in 1619, plays a central role in Millen and Wolf's argument (figure 2). This painting depicts Mercury (on the right) accompanied by Cardinal La Rochefoucauld, offering an olive branch to the queen (on the left, framed by the figures of an attendant and Cardinal Richelieu) on behalf of the king. As Millen and Wolf point out, the entire scene is marked by ambivalence and ambiguity. It is not clear whether the setting is indoors or outdoors, nor do we know, on the basis of the painting itself, whether the offer of peace will be accepted. Marie's hand is extended in a gesture of reconciliation, but Richelieu's restraining hand on her arm suggests caution. Most important, perhaps, Mercury is holding a caduceus, a traditional symbol of *concordia discors*, in his other hand. The serpents wrapped around the staff are writhing, suggesting "unappeased conflict." Perhaps, speculate Millen and Wolf, the treaty has resolved nothing.[6]

A number of elements in the painting suggest a mute rhetorical allegory. Millen and Wolf observe, for instance, that the caduceus is not merely an emblem for *concordia discors,* but also the symbol of silver-tongued eloquence. They furthermore note that the "swirling eloquence" of the right-hand side of the painting contrasts sharply with the sobriety of the "tight group" on the left.[7] This is suggestive (although Millen and Wolf do not go this far) of the traditional opposition between Asiatic and Attic rhetoric. Whereas the former is characterized by flourish and ornamentation, the latter is typically defined by caution and restraint. This contrast between two styles of rhetoric is paralleled by the opposition between public display (on the right) and private counsel (on the left). As they offer the olive branch, the bodies of Mercury and La Rochefoucauld are turned both toward the queen (in the case of Mercury) and the viewer (in the case of La Rochefoucauld). Richelieu, by contrast, is in the shadows, turned away from the viewer as if in private consultation with Marie. The positioning of the hands reinforces this general impression. La Rochefoucauld's hand is turned up beneath the hand of Mercury, as if to highlight and repeat the latter's gesture of offering. Richelieu's is turned down, in caution, as if to prevent the queen from precipitously accepting the offer of peace.

The positioning of the hands invites a reading of the painting in terms of displacement, delegation, and deflection. The primary displacement is the exclusion of the king, who is entirely absent from the painting. This omission has a number of consequences. First and foremost, it reminds us that this is Marie's story, not Louis's. Second, it highlights the manner in which power is exercised indirectly, by delegation. Louis has delegated his word (his action, his power) to the allegorical Mercury, god of eloquence, whose rhetorical performance—reduced to gesture in the visual language of the painting—is framed and (re)directed by La Rochefoucauld's gesture of presentation. Marie's hand is extended as if to accept the offer, but the hand of her advisor, Richelieu, deflects the gesture. Meanwhile, lest we forget, the entire scene, with its enigmatic message, has been staged for the viewer by the hand of Rubens, himself an experienced ambassador, trained in rhetoric. The theatrical, "stagy" atmosphere of the painting contributes to this sense of artful display. The figures occupy the foreground, in front of an assemblage of architectural fragments, much as actors appeared on the seventeenth-century stage. From the historical record, finally, we know that Rubens's hand was guided by the will of the patron-queen and her minister, who dictated the content of the painting, its political message(s).

Power, in sum, does not appear as monolithic or totalizing; if anything, it is local, the product of a series of rhetorical displacements, redirections, deflections, and interpretations in which ruler, counselor, and artist all participate. Although it emanates from the sovereign subjects, its exercise is ultimately delegated to proxies.

A similar series of displacements can be observed in a grouping of letters published in the 1624 collection of Guez de Balzac's *Lettres*. A client of the duc d'Épernon, Balzac was present along with Richelieu at the negotiations between Marie de' Medici and Louis XIII, which took place in and around his ancestral home in Angoulême. Earlier in 1619, moreover, Balzac had participated in another episode depicted in Rubens's Medici cycle: Épernon's daring mission to liberate the queen mother from Blois, where she had been held in captivity by order of the king. The young Balzac's contribution to Marie's escape was essentially literary, consisting of three letters to the king on behalf of Épernon. In the first letter (January 17, 1619), Épernon asked to be relieved of his command at Metz, where the king had posted him, and to return to his *gouvernement* in the west. This letter, we learn from Girard's *Histoire de la vie du duc d'Épernon*, was a diversionary tactic, a ploy to cover his intentions (*couvrir son dessein*) to depart immediately to liberate the queen. If we are to believe Girard, only Richelieu, Rucellai, and Épernon's children were privy to the duke's intentions; Balzac was unaware of the intended deception.[8] It is only in a limited sense, therefore, that we can talk about Balzac as the "author" of the letter. His role, rather, is that of Épernon's hired hand (in a similar context, Girard uses the expression *écrire d'une main empruntée* [to write with a borrowed hand]).[9] Balzac himself characterized the collaboration with Épernon in terms that acknowledge his subordinate role as secretary. Conceding the initiative to the duke, he described his own contribution as providing the words (*verba*) to express the latter's conceptions (*res*):

[M]es *paroles,* que vous avez choisies autrefois pour recevoir vos grandes *pensées.*[10]

[My words, which you formerly chose to express your great thoughts.]

After liberating Marie from Blois, Épernon again borrowed Balzac's hand to write to the king. In this second letter, Épernon resorted to a favorite tactic of treasonous subjects in this period: reinterpreting the royal will in accordance with their own agendas.

Justifying his disregard for the king's order to remain in Metz, Épernon asserted a paradoxical loyalty:

> [E]n cela je ne desobey point aux commandemens de vostre Majesté; mais au contraire je les explique selon leur vray sens, & leur donne la meilleure interpretation, puis que c'est celle qui est la plus utile à vostre service.[11]

> [In this, I do not disobey your Majesty's commands; rather I explain them according to their true meaning and give them the best possible interpretation, because it best serves your interests.]

If the king's will is synonymous with the preservation of his authority and the well-being of the kingdom, it follows that one can reinterpret his decrees by arguing that they cannot mean what they appear to mean, since their ostensible meaning would be contrary to the interests of the kingdom (and thus the king himself).[12] According to Épernon (speaking through Balzac), the best interpretation of the king's intentions—the interpretation most compatible with the need to maintain harmony in France—was that the duke return to the western provinces where he could be effective in containing religious strife. Épernon thus *deflected* the king's sovereign authority, invoking and subverting it for his own purposes.

In writing these letters for Épernon, and in later discovering the disguised motivations behind them, Balzac must have learned an important lesson about the relationships between underlings and their masters and, by extension, between writers and their patrons. Indeed, Balzac later performed a different sort of deflection when he included the Épernon letters in the first edition of his *Lettres*.[13] Balzac's enemies were quick to jump on this potentially transgressive claim to authorship on the part of a secretary. Dom Goulu, for instance, marveled at Balzac's presumption. How could he publish, as his own, letters that dealt with Épernon's business and that were written at the latter's behest? How could he claim, while the duke was still alive, that he, and not his master, had written them?[14] Although it was well known that grandees such as Épernon used secretaries, the latter were expected to quietly efface themselves behind their masters. As Christian Jouhaud has put it, "When he put his name on a pamphlet, a grandee assumed authorship of the action, the commission, and the strategy behind it, but not the actual words. By his gesture of publication, by appropriating as an author the work that he had produced as a secretary, Balzac seemed to subvert this self-evident hierarchy."[15] If Épernon had borrowed Balzac's hand, Balzac was now returning the favor. By publishing the letters under his own name, he appropriated the duke's defiant individualism—the heroic actions of his sword. Much as the letters themselves raise questions about the relationship between noble and monarch, their inclusion in the published editions of Balzac's works blurs the relative roles of patron and writer as *authors*.

As Jouhaud has noted, the version of the text reproduced in the 1624 *Lettres* differs significantly from the 1619 version printed in the *Mercure français*, most notably by the omission of a number of contextual details, including dates, financial details, and references to Épernon's personal affairs and petty resentments.[16] This decontextualization, he points out, may well have suited Épernon, who undoubtedly wished to put his conflicts with the king in a more dignified, less selfish light. I would like to insist, however, on another effect of Balzac's rewriting. By removing a certain amount of detail, Balzac makes Épernon's discourse more susceptible to literary appropriation. No longer narrowly inscribed within the contingencies of the duke's biography, the letters acquire the more general character of a literary drama. Indeed, in their treatment of the confrontation between a rebellious subject and his sovereign, they anticipate the political theater that would appear on the French stage a decade later in the tragedies of Pierre Corneille, Jean de Rotrou, Jean Mairet, and Pierre Du Ryer. This generality, however, is limited by the fact that the "I" of the letter remains referentially attached to the duke, whose name appears in the heading to the letters (*Pour Monseigneur le Duc d'Espernon au Roy*).[17] The published letter thus maintains a connection with a specific historical moment, which gives it what Jouhaud calls "a rhetorical energy linked to a written discourse conceived at a particular stage of a political action."[18] The Épernon letters ultimately occupy an ambivalent, intermediate zone between history and literature.

Authorship in a Culture of Patronage

These examples illustrate the difficulty of applying modern notions of authorship to objects such as commissioned paintings or letters composed by secretaries, where collaboration and appropriation, rather than originality, were the rule. Literary creation in seventeenth-century France is perhaps best understood as a series of interventions by different actors. In the rhetorical mind-set of the time, invention (the selection and/or creation of ideas and arguments) was clearly distinct from disposition (the ordering of arguments) and elocution (the arrangement of words into figures, sentences, and other forms). These functions, which we tend to assign to a single creator, were often fulfilled by different persons. This meant that originality was less important than it is today. In many cases, of course, the content (plot, metaphors, and other elements) of literary discourse was imitated from ancient, or occasionally modern, authors (Virgil, Ovid, Seneca, Marino, and so on). The work of writing, from the Middle Ages through much of the eighteenth century, was largely a matter of reworking or putting a stylistic twist on an old idea, rather than novelty.

In patronage writing, similarly, the authority/authorship of a literary work was shared. Commenting on Richelieu's writings, Tallemant des Réaux claimed that Richelieu himself had written only one work (*L'Instruction du chrétien*); for the rest, the content was due to Lescot and the form to Desmarets de Saint-Sorlin.[19] Although Tallemant is hardly a reliable source, especially when it comes to Richelieu, his comments testify to the workshop atmosphere that characterized seventeenth-century writing in general and secretarial practice in particular. By definition, secretaries wrote on behalf of others. As one historian has put it, "it was not his 'I' that spoke in correspondence but the person of the patron."[20] As his name—derived from the Latin *secretum*—suggested, the secretary exercised his art in *secret*. This was both his curse and his privilege. It meant that he was denied recognition, but it carried certain advantages as well. His position behind the scenes and his mastery of rhetorical illusion gave the secretary a broad perspective, critical distance, and a deep insight into the functioning of power and its legitimation.[21]

The phenomenon I am describing was hardly limited to secretaries. It was not unusual for literary authors, for example, to designate their patrons as the true authors of their literary works. Chapelain's dedication of his *Pucelle*, based on the life of Joan of Arc, to the duc de Longueville is typical. After invoking the duke's fine taste, his material generosity, his ancestral link to Dunois, one of the poem's heroes, and his heroic achievements, Chapelain concludes that "this is your work, not mine," a message that was reinforced by the inclusion of an engraved portrait of Longueville in the first edition.[22] Such declarations cannot be attributed to mere flattery, either, as they reflect the concrete reality of many writers' situations. Poets who served in the households of aristocrats were often called on not only to perform secretarial duties but also, for example, to write love poems and amorous letters for their masters.[23]

The most revealing example, perhaps, of collaborative authorship during this period is court ballet.[24] Typically, the broad outline of a ballet (themes and characters, such as they were) was determined by a member of the court and/or a court poet—such as René Bordier, Étienne Durand, Desmarets de Saint-Sorlin, or Guillaume Colletet—working on commission. In the dedication to the libretto for the *Délivrance de Renaud* (1617), Durand describes the process of selecting a subject as a collaboration between writer and patron. "Your Majesty [Louis XIII] (who is fond of great actions) had chosen the *Délivrance de Renault* from the many subjects that I had presented to him."[25] Although the poet presumably possesses the greater knowledge of classical mythology and allegory, the final choice lies with the king, who chooses a subject from among those proposed to him. Explaining his decision to publish a description and partial libretto, Durand reiterates that the ballet belongs to the king. "Since Your Majesty used me in the invention and disposition of *your* play, you will not be offended if I advertise its beauty."[26] Just as the Louvre is the property of the king and not his architects, so are *his* ballets. This intellectual ownership is reflected in titles such as: *Ballet comique de la reine, Ballet de Madame,* and *Ballet du Dauphin.* The *de,* in these instances, does not merely identify; it carries a possessive weight, as in *les violons du Roy.*

The actual verses recited by the courtiers who performed in the court ballets were not necessarily written by the principal poet who had drafted the broad outline of the performance, either. More typically, one or more other poets would contribute verses. In the case of the *Délivrance de Renaud,* for instance, the majority of verses were written by Bordier (rather than Durand). The notorious *Ballet des bacchanales* (1623) includes contributions from a virtual army of poets, including Théophile de Viau, who wrote verses for his patron the duc de Montmorency in which the latter brazenly avowed his affections for Anne of Austria, the queen. Behind the mask of his character, Montmorency imagined himself taking the king's place next to Anne:

> Plust au Ciel qu'un jour seulement
> Jupiter m'eust donné sa face,

> Et qu'il voulust pour un moment
> Me laisser régner en sa place.²⁷
>
> [Would that it pleased God that for just one day
> Jupiter would lend me his countenance
> And let me, if only for a moment,
> Rule in his stead.]

Who is the author of these words: Théophile, who gave them poetic form, or the duke, who speaks them and whose poetic desire they speak?

In a suggestive essay, Marie-Claude Canova-Green has described the mechanism of ballet authorship in terms of the interchangeable roles of creator and creature—*créateur* and *créature*.²⁸ On a primary level, as we have seen, the courtier-patron was the *créateur* and the poet a mere *créature*, alienated from his own poetry. The irony, as she points out, is that within the actual performance of the ballet, the patron followed the poet's script, becoming a *créature* of the latter's creation. Ultimately, however, the authorship of the verses probably mattered little. Although published librettos sometimes provided attributions of authorship, the primary focus was on the aristocratic actors and their *performances* in their roles. Dancing was above all a medium for displaying the grace and self-control expected of well-behaved courtiers. The following description, from an unspecified ballet, is typical in its emphasis on corporal grace over words: "The page was played by M. Payenne, who won the prize for poise [*disposition*]. The Hermaphrodite was played by M. Montaigu, who appeared to partake of both natures as he fluttered in the air."²⁹ The author of the text, a mere poet, remains anonymous.

What Is an Author?

Michel Foucault, in his essay "What Is an Author?", attributes the conceptual power of authorship to its capacity for classifying and suppressing discourses. First and foremost, the author's name "permits one to group together a certain number of texts, define them, differentiate them from and contrast them to others."³⁰ It is a mechanism for containing the potentially infinite proliferation of meaning by positing an external principle of coherence. Classification and containment, in turn, create the possibility of various sorts of appropriation, including intellectual property and, most important, "penal appropriation."[31] According to Foucault, "Texts, books, and discourses only began to have authors to the extent that authors became subject to punishment."[32] The writer, in other words, only became an author to the extent that potentially transgressive discourses could be attributed to him or her. By focusing on this penal responsibility, Foucault challenges the familiar association between authorship and creativity. For him, authorship and, more generally, subjectivity ultimately have more to do with social control than with freedom.

We have already examined some of the complexities of intellectual property in a culture of patronage. Anecdotal evidence suggests that patronage played a role in both the classification and penal appropriation of texts in the early modern period as well. François de La Croix du Maine's proposed, but never completed, bibliographic project the *Grande bibliothèque française* (1579) was to include information regarding patron-dedicatees as well as authors, printers, formats, and dates.[33] This reflected a concrete reality, namely that lavishly bound books dedicated and offered to patrons were among the most highly prized pieces in the latters' libraries. It also illustrates the degree to which the dedication was part of a book's social profile.

The degree of penal appropriation of texts seems to have been highly variable depending on a writer's position within the patronage system. In his study of seventeenth-century libertines, René Pintard has observed that well-connected writers were less likely to suffer punishment for transgressive writings.[34] For instance, although the poet Théophile de Viau was incarcerated between 1623 and 1625 for his blasphemous and obscene writings (see the following chapter), his political connections appear to have saved him from being burned at the stake like Giulio Cesare Vanini, another freethinker. Indeed Théophile's nemesis, Father Garasse, complained about the efforts made on the poet's behalf by one of his protectors—the duc de Liancourt—during his captivity. "Every day, it was insinuated to the king that we were lobbying against the criminal, and those who were trying to save his life, namely M. de Liancourt et de La Roche-Guyon, publicly implored the judges not to heed the calumnies of Father Voisin, who had adopted the cause as his own."[35] Liancourt's role is further confirmed by Théophile himself in a letter to his friend Jacques Vallée Des Barreaux.[36] Théophile may have only been slightly exaggerating, moreover, when he wrote to another of his protectors, the duc de Montmorency that "those whom you deign to acknowledge [as your servants] are protected from all sorts of disgrace."³⁷ Before the poet's arrest in 1623, Montmorency had intervened with the *procureur général* Mathieu Molé to head off the impending crisis. Although this intervention did not save Théophile from being arrested, his support may well have helped spare Théophile's life. The poet's letters after his release from prison, finally, clearly show his continuing efforts to shore up the support from Montmorency and his entourage.³⁸

THE SPECTER OF THE "OTHER"

If we use Foucault's criteria (classification, intellectual property, and penal appropriation), it is clearly not possible to consider the writer in isolation from the patron. Patronage texts, rather, would seem to call for some kind of *corporate* model of authorship. We should be cautious, however, about exaggerating the harmony between collaborators. The problem of patronage authorship was a central theme of contemporary literary satire. In Marc-Antoine Girard de Saint-Amant's "Poëte crotté," for example, the poem's eponymous antihero describes the role of a poet at court:

> S'il se faisoit Galanterie,
> Course, Carrouzel, Mommerie,
> Combat de barrière, Ballet;
> S'il falloit chanson ou poulet,
> J'étois leur mon-Coeur, leur mon-Maistre,
> Leur Ame m'ouvroit la fenestre
> Pour m'exhiber tous ses regrets,
> C'est à dire mille sottises;
> Je leur fournissois de devises,
> De beaux couplets, de hauts discours.
> O faux Galands! ô Hapelourdes!
> Que vous avez les testes lourdes.³⁹

> [If there was some kind of Gallantry,
> Joust, Carousel, Mascarade,
> Tournament or Ballet,
> If a song or a love letter were needed,
> I was their "My Dear," their "My Master,"
> Their souls opened their windows to me

> To show me all of their regrets,
> A thousand idiocies, that is.
> I furnished them with mottos,
> With fine verses and pompous speeches.
> Oh false wits! Oh handsome fools!
> You are so slow-witted.]

Saint-Amant's convoluted syntax, with its confusing proliferation of pronouns ("*J*'étais *leur mon*-coeur, *leur mon*-Maistre"), captures the complex relationship between discourse and identity at court, with its alienating effects for both writer and patron. The writer never expresses himself in his own voice; he merely contributes to the pleasures (ballets, tournaments, gallantry) of another. The courtier, on the other hand, appears as a mere puppet, animated by the words of the poet: "Oh false wits! Oh handsome fools [*Hapelourdes*]!"[40] According to the *Dictionnaire de l'Académie*, *happelourdes* (literally false precious stones) are persons who have an attractive outward appearance, but are completely lacking in intelligence.[41] At court, language is disconnected from identity, with the gap between the author and his words mirroring the more general discrepancy between appearances and reality (*être* and *paraître*).[42]

In his third *Satire*, similarly, Mathurin Régnier rails against those poets who prostitute their Muse for their patrons:

> De porter un poulet je n'ai pas la suffisance:
> Je ne suis point adroit, je n'ai point d'éloquence
> Pour colorer un fait, ou détourner la foi;
> Prouver qu'un grand amour n'est sujet à la loi;
> Suborner par discours une femme coquette,
> Lui contant des chansons de Jeanne et de Paquette,
> Débaucher une fille, et par vives raisons
> Lui montrer comme Amour fait de bonnes maisons,
> Les maintient, les élève, et, propice aux plus belles,
> En honneur les avance, et les fait demoiselles; . . .
> Or, pour dire ceci il faut force mystère;
> Et de mal discourir il vaut bien mieux se taire.
> Il est vrai que ceux-là qui n'ont pas tant d'esprit
> Peuvent mettre en papier leur dire par écrit,
> Et rendre par leurs vers leur muse maquerelle;
> Mais pour dire le vrai, je n'en ai la cervelle.
> Il faut être trop prompt, écrire à tous propos,
> Perdre pour un sonnet et sommeil et repos.

Puis, ma muse est trop chaste, et j'ai trop de courage,
Et ne puis pour autrui façonner un ouvrage.[43]

[I don't have it in me to deliver a love letter:
I'm not nimble, I don't have the eloquence
To twist a fact or corrupt someone's faith,
Prove that a great love is not subject to the law,
Lead a coquettish woman astray with flattery,
Telling her stories about Jeanne and Paquette,
Debauch a girl, and with subtle arguments
Show her how love creates dynasties,
Maintains them, elevates them, and how it raises the social station
Of beautiful women, making them ladies . . .
This takes a great deal of subtlety,
And it would be wiser to be silent than to stumble.
It is true those who are not so quick on their feet
Can put their speeches on paper,
And prostitute their muses in their verses.
But, to tell the truth, I don't have the brain for it.
You need to be quick-witted and write on the spot,
Lose both sleep and rest for a sonnet.
And then, my muse is too chaste, and I am too proud
To compose a work for someone else.]

Régnier begins by describing a role that is essentially nonliterary—that of the go-between (*entremetteur*) who assists his master in a kind of seduction by proxy. As an advocate for his patron, the go-between cynically dismisses the lady's scruples, appealing instead to her vanity, material greed, and social ambition. He is a crafty rhetorician, using a wide range of arguments, but he is hardly a writer. The literary implications arise when the poet-servant, perhaps because he is tongue-tied, commits these arguments to paper. When the poet puts his verse at the service of his master's passion, he is no longer in the realm of ephemeral spoken words, but rather works (*ouvrages*) that are passed on to posterity. He must compose on demand, adapting his verse to the circumstances of the moment. His role as *serviteur* within the patron's household thus contaminates his poetic spontaneity and integrity. Régnier takes a hard line against this literary promiscuity, insisting that he cannot write on behalf of another.

Authorship, in sum, was highly contested. By its very nature, the patronage relationship entailed the appropriation of the writer's creative labor by the patron. Inversely, as we saw with Balzac, a writer could reappropriate a patronage text by publishing it, an act that invested the text with new meaning. This was especially true of texts in verse. As the examples of poets such as Saint-Amant, Théophile, François Malherbe, François Tristan L'Hermite, and others show, love poems and ballet verses were often (re)published, with attributions, during authors' lifetimes. They appear both in volumes intended to consecrate a single author's *œuvre* and in multiauthor anthologies (*recueils collectifs*), such as the famous *Recueil des plus beaux vers* (1627), which sought to publicize and consolidate Malherbe's poetic reforms.[44]

The Poetics of the Occasion

The republication of occasional verse in collective volumes provides a clue to the status of such poetry in early modern culture. After all, if occasional material were considered to have no merit, it would hardly have been published in major poetic manifestos such as the *Recueil des plus beaux vers*. One of the goals of this chapter is to make the case for the literary study of occasional poetry. In arguing that patronage raises properly poetic issues, I am departing from the critical habit of taking individualistic texts as authentic, or at least deserving of our interest, and dismissing patronage poetry as insincere and/or conventional.[45] In doing so, we miss the possibility that the poet's assertions of independence might themselves be conventional. As a matter of fact, the notion of the poet seeking his freedom has its own literary tradition. In particular, Horace's declarations of independence to Maecenas provided a model that found its way into many poets' verses. Another convention was the *adieu à la cour*, in which the poet decried the corruption of the court and sought his freedom in a country retreat. By affirming their independence, poets not only obeyed literary convention; they also lent credence to their praise of actual and potential protectors. Independence, in other words, could easily be just another pose.

Still confined within a post-romantic perspective, we tend to conceive of poetry in terms opposite to those that predominate in the occasional verse (*vers de circonstance*) of the seventeenth century.[46] We take it for granted that poetry is shaped by the individuality of a particular consciousness, yet we tend to feel that serious poetry is compromised when it is placed at the service of a specific, external occasion. Because it is too close to a particular moment in time, occasional verse is vulnerable to becoming dated as events come to be viewed with greater historical distance, or even forgotten. At the same time, the emotions expressed in occasional verse (such as gratitude and admiration) often seem excessively conventional, too general to be worthy of poetic expression.[47] We are wary, in sum, of what Hegel called occasional verse's "entanglement with life," by virtue of which it "seems . . . to fall into a position of dependence." Hegel concluded that the poet should not devote himself to the "exaltation, embellishment, [or] commemoration" of external circumstances, but rather that he should internalize such circumstances, creating "from his own resources what without his aid we would not have become conscious of previously." Poetry thus emerges as an "inherently infinite [i.e. self-bounded] organism."[48]

This separation of poetry and circumstance is a relatively recent phenomenon. In the eighteenth and nineteenth centuries, the evolution of aesthetic thought (Kant, Hegel, and Schiller) and a growing divide between art and the social establishment conspired with the decline of the aristocracy, which had provided many of the occasions for earlier poetry, to create a new poetic ideal.[49] As one scholar has put it, "The most profound wish of the German romantic poet was to protect his song from any direct or indirect contact with the circumstantial."[50] By circumstantial, we should understand external circumstances/occasions, for which the romantics substituted internal (that is, subjective) ones. This trend continued throughout the nineteenth century and is particularly strong in movements such as *L'Art pour l'art* and symbolism. Indeed the symbolist focus on music is probably the most obvious and far-reaching of the various attempts to divorce poetry from the referential function of language and, consequently, the specter of external circumstance/occasion.

None of the factors described above were present in significant force in the seventeenth century. Art was still closely tied to a flourishing aristocratic culture, and utility was still accepted as its guiding principle ("pleasing" and "instructing" were still the order of the day). It was still possible, in other words, to imagine an art of the circumstantial focused on "exaltation, embellishment, [and] commemoration" and in which it hardly mattered whether the poet was speaking in his own voice. Indeed, when the French Academy was founded in 1635, one of the primary functions of this consummately literary institution was to develop a ceremonial oratory for celebrating the triumphs of the French crown.[51] At the same time, however, Régnier's and Saint-Amant's reservations regarding the practice of writing love poems for a patron suggest that early seventeenth-century writers already perceived a potential conflict between poetry and circumstance.

Writing in another's voice, of course, is the ultimate dependence on external circumstance. A historical event readily lends itself to the kind of "internalization" that Hegel proposes, in which the objective world is filtered through a subjective consciousness—witness the poetry of Victor Hugo, for instance. Another person's emotions, by contrast, are more intractably "other." They already bear the stamp of subjectivity; the problem is that this subjectivity belongs to someone else. Writing for another thus raises two problems:

1) The relative autonomy of the poetic work with respect to the external world
2) The subjective relationship of a poet to his work

To the extent that a poet struggles with these issues, we can speak of a special kind of "anxiety of influence."[52]

In the remainder of this chapter and in the next, I will examine these questions in relation to five authors who occupy a range of positions within the seventeenth-century literary field: Saint-Amant, François Malherbe, François Tristan L'Hermite, Théophile de Viau, and Charles Sorel. Malherbe is typically considered the most orthodox of the five writers under consideration, both for his enthusiastic support of political and religious order and his insistence on respecting poetic rules. The four remaining writers, whom I examine in the following chapter, have traditionally been assigned to the loose-fitting category of *irréguliers*—that is to say, nonconformists and individualists. As such, their responses to the problems of patronage writing are particularly provocative. We will identify a wide range of strategies and attitudes, from identification and fusion with the patron to alienation and subversion.

POMP AND CIRCUMSTANCE:
PONGE ON MALHERBE AND SIGOGNE

Francis Ponge, with his poetics of the commonplace, represents a notable twentieth-century rejection of the divorce between poetry and circumstance.[53] He has particular relevance to the study of seventeenth-century occasional verse, moreover, because of his extensive reflections on François Malherbe (1555–1628) in *Pour un*

Malherbe. In the following pages, I will read Malherbe's circumstantial patronage poetry through Ponge, who remains one of his best commentators.

In Malherbe, Ponge found a refreshing antidote to the romantics and post-romantics, who poured out their "sensitive souls" on paper. "It is not really our style to look for a personality, and we could not care less about finding one in a book. We are seeking something else, which feeble minds cannot understand: that 'indefinable quality' [*je ne sais quoi*], for example, 'that can be found on the face of a beautiful woman and one sees but cannot express' that Godeau, commenting on Malherbe, claimed could be found 'in all of his periods, as if the muses themselves had measured them out'."[54] For Ponge, Malherbe's interest does not lie in facile subjectivity. Instead, he embraces the poet's circumstantial verse precisely because it is not only relatively impersonal, but also free of metaphysical pretensions. "Malherbe, like us, was indifferent to abstract problems. He wanted to live in society at the only level that suited him, as a superior intellect. If we consider him in Aix, it is obvious that he is already looking toward the Louvre. Once he was received at the Louvre, he praised the king so that he could bestow even greater praise upon himself. This is how he maintained his rank while simultaneously preserving the prestige of poetry. But this required a kind of *tour de force*. Every day he had to draw the strings of his lyre more taut so that its sound would be true and would add to his own glory (the glory of a well-strung instrument [*un instrument bien tendu*])."[55]

The social context of the court does not interest Ponge *per se;* rather he takes it as the ideal pretext for a quasimystical elevation of language (*la parole*).[56] He views ambition as a positive force that drove Malherbe to raise his art to another level, to perfect a form of language that would capture the Bourbon monarchy's aspirations for itself and the French nation while elevating his own glory, as high priest of the poetic word. Departing from a conception of poetry as the free expression of interiority, he thus sees the social constraint and the rigid hierarchies of *ancien régime* society as the conditions of, rather than hindrances to, great poetry, for it is under their influence and pressure that the poet draws the strings of his lyre tightly. And the more taut the lyre, the more clearly and sonorously it rings. Trite subjectivity and metaphysical abstraction, by contrast, slacken the lyre by providing cheap substitutes for the expressive purity of disciplined poetic language.

Since poetry is not a matter of individual subjectivity, it does not bother Ponge in the slightest that Malherbe lent his lyre ("prostituted his muse," Régnier would say) to the expression of Henry IV's adulterous love affairs. Indeed, the radio play that Ponge devoted to the poet's life includes one such episode:

(*Comings and goings. Young people laughing. The faint sound of running in the corridors.*)

HENRY IV: Ah! Malherbe. Listen. You see that little . . .

MALHERBE: Of course I see her. It is Mademoiselle de Montmorency.

(*The king grabs one of the young women who is running by. A cry.*)

CHARLOTTE DE MONTMORENCY: Ah! Sire! You're mad!

(*She runs away*)

HENRY IV: Did you ever see anything so beautiful and spirited? . . .

MALHERBE: Sire, I understand your Majesty's meaning. Hasten her marriage, and then we will sing your love to her."[57]

No sooner has the king noticed a "young person" than Malherbe is already thinking about the poetic opportunity that the situation offers. The poet, here, does not so much guess at the king's meaning as anticipate it, encouraging the latter's desire for his own (poetic) purposes.

The historical events referred to here bear closer examination. In January 1609, the fifty-five-year-old Henry IV fell in love with Charlotte de Montmorency, a sixteen-year-old.[58] For the sake of appearances, Charlotte was married off to the Prince of Condé who, despite his general lack of interest in women, quickly became jealous of the king. Condé fled with his young bride, first to Vallery, then (after a brief return to the court) to Muret, and finally, at the end of November, to Brussels where the couple established itself in exile. During the course of these events, Malherbe wrote four poems in which Henry IV, under the name of "Alcandre" described his various emotions at different moments of the affair: "Pour Alcandre, au retour d'Oranthe à Fontainebleau" (For Alcandre, on the Return of Oranthe to Fontainebleau), "Pour Alcandre" (For Alcandre), "Il plaint la Captivité de sa maîtresse, pour Alcandre" (He Complains about his Mistress's Captivity, for Alcandre), and "Sur le même sujet" (On the Same Subject). Unfortunately, Ponge never finished his work on Malherbe, and his notes contain no extended discussion of this episode. Some of his notations are intriguing, however, and suggest the direction he might have gone. One such notation seems to contrast Malherbe's activities at court with those of his contemporaries. "Note the difference with other servants. Example from the Charlotte affair. Malherbe's behavior/Segogne's behavior."[59]

"Segogne," in Ponge's notation, refers to Charles Timoléon de Beauxoncles, seigneur de Sigogne (1560–1611), a courtier and satirical poet of Malherbe's generation.[60] In 1604, Sigogne was implicated in an affair that presents an interesting parallel to the Charlotte affair, and which presumably inspired Ponge's comparison. Sigogne was close to both Henry and his mistress, Henriette d'Entragues. Indeed, it was he who revealed that Henriette was conspiring with Bouillon, Charles of Valois, and the Spanish ambassador Balthazar de Zuniga to put her illegitimate son by the king on the throne after Henry's death. Sully reports that Sigogne was assigned the task of reassuring Henriette of the king's continuing affections during her disgrace. "He could not bring himself to leave her in doubt for one minute regarding her pardon. He barely saved appearances by telling the marquise, through different messengers, that she would have to earn her pardon by completely submitting to his conditions. La Varenne, Sigogne, and the entire court were entrusted with these messages, which (considering the way they were written) really amounted to advances from a lover who, despite his anger, was afraid of creating insurmountable obstacles to his reconciliation with his mistress."[61] On November 11, love letters from Sigogne to Henriette were discovered among the latter's affairs, leading to the poet's disgrace. Claude Groulart describes this *rocambolesque* turn of events in his *Mémoires*. "During this domestic drama, it happened that His Majesty discovered that Sigogne, who was the go-between between the lovers, had fallen in love himself. He was shameless enough to write several letters to the marquise, beseeching her to give him her love. These letters were full of intolerable impertinence and contempt for the king, who was indulgent enough to content himself with banishing Sigogne from his presence."[62] In Groulart's version, Sigogne was the victim of real-life mimetic desire.[63] In the course of courting Henriette on the king's behalf, he had taken over his master's role, substituting his "I" for Henry's and writing letters that expressed his own desires.

Sigogne, in a letter to the king, offers a different version of the events. Specifically, he suggests that Henriette had commanded him to write the *poulets* to arouse the king's jealousy. "She wanted extraordinary services, complete submission to her wishes, and demonstrations of great concern for her welfare. Seeing that you had fallen under her spell despite a long struggle, I thought that I could use all sorts of devices [*toutes sortes d'inventions*] to serve you in your pleasures, and that this was the only way I could help you."[64] Sigogne thus argues that he wrote the letters with the paradoxical intent of serving the king: by making his master jealous, he was helping to reunite him with his mistress. In assessing this episode, it is not particularly important to determine which version of the events is more accurate. What is important, rather, is the ambiguous landscape of authorship suggested by the conflicting accounts. Was Sigogne working on behalf of the king, himself, Henriette, or more than one at the same time? It is hard to say, and indeed it is possible that even he did not know anymore.

Sigogne provides an example of a courtier-poet caught up in the shifting sands of court culture. As such, he may have provided Ponge with a particularly striking contrast to Malherbe. Malherbe, as described by Ponge, is not an *intrigueur*, nor does he participate in the theater of court life. "No actor in him. None of the traits of a court abbot, like Desportes or Bertaut. Nothing of the confessor. Nothing overly sweet [*rien de douceureux*] or hypocritical."[65] One is tempted to take Ponge's account, which borders on the hagiographic, with a grain of salt. And yet the contrast between Malherbe and Sigogne is not without interest. Each chose a different genre and social strategy. Sigogne, as we have seen, threw himself into the intrigue of the court. His *poulets* (love letters) were real utterances with real consequences, most notably exile. Malherbe's lyric "Charlotte" poems, by contrast, have a strong literary, even fictional, dimension. Indeed, three of the four poems include fictional frames that shape the reader's response to the lover's complaint. These include not merely the transparent substitution of "Alcandre" for "Henry" but also a geographical setting and description of the lover. "Il plaint la captivité de sa maîtresse," for instance, ends with the following lines:

> Ainsi le grand Alcandre aux campagnes de Seine
> Faisait, loin des témoins, le récit de sa peine,
>   Et se fondit en pleurs:

> Le fleuve en fut ému: ses Nymphes se cachèrent
> Et l'herbe du rivage, où ses larmes touchèrent,
>   Perdit toutes ses fleurs.[66]

[Thus the great Alcandre, along the banks of the Seine,
Far from witnesses, told the tale of his suffering
    And burst into tears:
The river was moved: the Nymphs hid
And the grass of the banks, touched by his tears,
    Lost all of its flowers.]

Alcandre's words come to the reader explicitly filtered by the voice of the narrator/poet. Although this narrating voice never speaks in the first person, its presence profoundly alters the reader's experience of the text, putting the remainder of the poem (Henry's complaint) inside implied quotes. Much as a "play within a play" highlights the artifice of theatrical representation, the presence of a "poem within a poem" draws the reader's attention to the role of poetic artifice in mediating the lover's sensibility. This impression is further enhanced by the fact that the complaint is uttered "far from witnesses." Strictly speaking, of course, this is impossible. If there was no one there to see or hear the lover, there can be no one to describe and pass on his lament. It might be objected, of course, that the solitary lover is a conventional device in both lyric poetry and the novel. This, however, only serves to enhance my point. Within the context of a poem written for a real lover, such a device has the effect of enhancing the general effect of artificiality and fictionality.

Unlike Sigogne's *poulets,* Malherbe's patronage poems do not carry the risks (or advantages, for that matter) that real utterances necessarily entail. By presenting his poems within fictional frames, he partially detaches them from the ephemeral world of court intrigue and appropriates them as literary objects. He does not, however, attempt to make Alcandre's voice his own. Indeed, the question of voice may be entirely beside the point here. What matters for Malherbe is what Ponge calls *la parole*—the relatively impersonal deployment of the expressive powers of language. Poetry is not about communicating a message or a subjective experience, but rather about demonstrating what language can do. In this sense, we can say that *poetry creates its own circumstance/occasion,* lending it dignity, grandeur, or pathos (depending on the situation), rather than vice versa. In the last lines of the poem, the natural world is transformed by Alcandre's complaint (*le récit de sa peine*): the river is "moved", the nymphs hide, and the flowers lose their bloom. This is not so much the familiar "pathetic fallacy" as a demonstration of the power of the word to give form to the world: it is not the lover's emotions that affect the landscape, but rather their expression. Commenting on the "Stances pour Alcandre," Ponge has noted what can only be described as an irony of history: the death lament contained in the last of the Alcandre poems preceded Henry's actual death by only a few months.[67] For once, historical circumstance appeared to have actually taken its cue from poetry.

For a self-effacing artisan such as Malherbe, for whom lyrical authenticity is beside the point, writing for another is relatively unproblematic. Indeed it can be viewed as a kind of opportunity, in that it provides a pretext for experimenting with the expressive powers of language while keeping a healthy distance from subjective content. For the poets treated in the next chapter, all of whom put something of *themselves* in their poetry, matters are not so simple.

4

The Anxiety of Influence: *Irréguliers,* Libertines, and Their Patrons

Escrivant pour autruy, je me sens tout de glace.

[Writing for another, I am all ice.]
—Théophile de Viau, "À Monsieur de Fargis"

THE *IRRÉGULIERS*—SEVENTEENTH-CENTURY WRITERS WHO DO NOT conform the norms of classicism as formulated by Nicolas Boileau in his *Art poétique* (1674)—have long fascinated literary critics and historians. One landmark in their critical rehabilitation is Théophile Gautier's *Grotesques* (1844), a polemical attack on the monotonous good taste of Ludovican classicism.[1] By rehabilitating forgotten writers, Gautier sought to recover some of the flavor (*saveur*) of seventeenth-century literary culture before it had been sanitized by Boileau, the "Legislator of Parnassus." His greatest legacy has been to create a sort of anticanon of outsiders and nonconformists—writers such as Théophile, Tristan, Sorel, Saint-Amant, and Cyrano de Bergerac—thus anticipating the twentieth-century fascination with both *libertinage* and the baroque.[2]

Although Gautier acknowledged that some of his subjects—most notably Théophile and Saint-Amant—were great writers, this was not the principal criterion for their inclusion in the *Grotesques*. Instead, they were of interest to him primarily by virtue of their deviation from the norm, their particularity or singularity. As Gautier put it in his preface, "I have chosen, here and there, on various occasions and as I happened across them in my readings, several characters whom I found amusing or singular."[3] This anecdotal approach is apparent in his physical description of his authors. The portrait of the crippled Scarron, for example, begins as follows: "The deviations in his verse are mirrored in the deviations of his backbone and his limbs."[4] Gautier's *irréguliers* are above all individuals, and this individuality expresses itself in both their deviant style and their unusual physiognomy.[5]

Gautier's account has had an enormous influence on subsequent generations of literary historians. Joan DeJean, for instance, has stressed the non-conformity of many of the same writers, emphasizing their status as self-elected outsiders. This status, she argues, is reflected in the ways in which the libertines truncated their names: "They revealed themselves to be subversive individuals by destroying the importance of a possession treasured by a society where it could open or close doors, the name. They rejected the name and all it stands for: paternal authority, family obligations, a fixed social status. As a replacement for the name, they adopted onomastic masks that give none of the information normally conveyed by names."[6]

In placing emphasis on names and downplaying the libertines' actual ties to established social hierarchies, DeJean's study betrays the strong influence of the poststructuralist "linguistic turn" that was in vogue when it was published. As we have seen in the previous chapter, however, libertines such as Théophile were able to advance radical ideas in part because of the protection extended to them by patrons. It is all too often forgotten that not only Montmorency, but also Gaston d'Orléans and even Richelieu surrounded themselves with writers of dubious morals. We need to be careful, in other words, not to draw too sharp a line between the libertines and the social and political establishment. Aristocratic culture had a deviant streak that was far from incompatible with its political power and social influence.

The strength of DeJean's argument lies in her analysis of the paradoxical nature of libertine identity. Whereas Gautier's *irréguliers* assert their uniqueness through idiosyncratic and transgressive forms of language, her libertines are self-conscious skeptics, aware of the impossibility of a fully autonomous subject. Language, to borrow a poststructuralist *cliché*, speaks through them. "Writers constantly aware of the slippage between discourses, of the impossibility of staking a claim and policing it in the territory of language, know that they can have no voice of their own."[7] This is illustrated, according to DeJean, by the libertines' ambivalent relationship with citation. On the one hand, in the hands of a Cyrano de Bergerac or Charles d'Assoucy, the presence of multiple voices within the text could be a powerful subversive tool for breaking down epistemological and social hierarchies. Following Mikhail Bakhtin, DeJean insists on the dialogical power of citation, its capacity to decenter the text, opening it up to a plurality of meanings and returning it to a "context of relativism."[8] On the other hand, citation could lead to alienation, to the invasion and colonization of the self by the voices of others. As she eloquently puts it, "[I]f the same thing can be said by two speakers, then the speaker's *identity* is no longer important."[9]

Despite her poststructuralist baggage, DeJean's analysis of the libertine subjects' ambivalent feelings toward the "other" provides a useful framework for thinking about the relationship between literary practice and authorial strategy in the early seventeenth century. In the following pages, I will tackle this question from a similar angle, using seventeenth-century "ghostwriting" as the point of departure for close readings of Saint-Amant, François Tristan L'Hermite, Théophile de Viau, and Charles Sorel. While benefiting from DeJean's insights, this approach has the virtue of reinscribing the *irréguliers* within their social context.[10] These writers' responses to the demands of patronage, we will see, ranged widely, from the playful integration of the voice of the patron-other (Saint-Amant) to transgressive fantasies of usurping the patron's powerful position (Sorel).

JE EST UN AUTRE: POETIC VOICE IN SAINT-AMANT AND TRISTAN

Although Marc-Antoine Girard de Saint-Amant (1594–1661) satirized patronage writing in "Le Poëte crotté" (see chapter 3), he was not above writing a love poem for a protector. Indeed the "Élégie à Damon," first published in the 1629 *Œuvres,* is a reflection on this very practice. This poem, possibly written for the duc de Retz,[11] opens with the staging of two parallel awakenings—the erotic awakening of the lover and the inspiration of the poet:

> Damon, je languissois dans un sombre silence,
> Suivant de mon humeur la froide nonchalance,
> Quand cét Œil gracieux, dont tu te sens espris,
> En te bruslant le cœur éclaira mes esprits:
> Lors mille hauts sujets réveillerent ma veine,
> Et publiant sa gloire en dépeignant ta peine,
> Je mis la Muse en œuvre, et taschay par mes Vers
> De le faire briller aux bouts de l'Univers. (Saint-Amant, 1:154)

> [Damon, I was languishing in an obscure silence,
> Indulging the cold indifference of my humor,
> When that graceful eye, with which you are enamored,
> Illumin'd my mind as it burned your heart.
> In that moment, I was inspired by a thousand subjects,
> And publishing its (the eye's) glory while depicting your misery,
> I put my Muse to work, and set out to use my verse
> To make it (the eye) shine across the universe.]

Saint-Amant invokes and combines two separate traditions here. The motif of the lady's burning eyes (*te bruslant le cœur*) is a commonplace of the Petrarchan tradition. This erotic metaphor is coupled with an age-old *topos* that links poetic inspiration to luminosity (*éclaira mes esprits*). Orante is thus both seductress and muse, lighting the way for the poet as she burns Damon's heart. From the description of the narrator's poetic activity in terms that suggest a flagging libido (*la froide nonchalance*) to the "shining" poetry that goes to the ends of the universe, the entire passage revolves around this interplay between eroticism and creation, heat and light.

John D. Lyons cautions against conflating Saint-Amant, the poet, with the various voices that speak in his poems. Rather than attempt a referential reading, he suggests, we would do better to examine the theatrical and ironic ways in which the poet distances himself from such personae and experiences.[12] With its peculiar triangular lyric (lover/lady/poet), the "Élégie à Damon" seems to enact precisely such a separation of inspiration from experience. The roles of lover and poet are split, assigned to Damon and the narrator, respectively. Whereas Damon experiences the burning gaze of Orante directly, the poet perceives it obliquely, through its effects on his friend/protector, which he reads and then reencodes in verse as poetry (*dépeignant ta peine*). The poet's role is not merely one of composition, however; he actually publishes both Damon's suffering and, by extension, Orante's devastating beauty.

A few lines later, Saint-Amant expands on this arrangement, explicitly assigning separate duties to poet and lover:

> moy de la *loüer*. et toy de la *servir*. (Saint-Amant, 1:154, emphasis added)

> [I, to *praise* her, and you to *serve* her.]

The knight and the bard relate to Orante in distinct ways. Damon experiences his lady in highly sensual terms, through sight (in the opening lines of the poem), smell (her sweet-smelling mouth), taste, and touch (her kiss). His service to her is physical, consisting of participation in various chivalric contests. He must defend by his valor the words that the poet has written about Orante:

> Deffiant au combat, d'une ardente menace,
> Quiconque osera dire enflé de vaine audace,
> Que la Beauté qu'il sert s'égale au moindre trait [de son portrait].
>   (Saint-Amant, 1:154)

> [Daring to combat, with a bold challenge,
> Whomsoever is so foolhardy as to claim,
> That the Beauty he serves is equal to the slightest detail (of her
>   portrait).]

Sound and language are left to the poet, who is above all a manipulator of signs. As we have seen, his task is to translate the symptoms of the lover's torment into verses suitable for disseminating/publicizing his mistress's beauty. The measure of his success is the extent to which his poetry produces an aesthetic effect that simulates the rapture produced by Orante herself:

> J'ay fait dire à mon Lut qu'Orante seulement
> Élève tous les cœurs dans le ravissement.
> Et lors, sans vanité, qu'il *chante* ses merveilles,
> Il ne transporte pas possible moins d'*oreilles*. (Saint-Amant, 1:154–55;
>   emphasis added)

> [I have had my Lute declare that Orante alone
> Lifts all hearts into rapture,
> And, all vanity aside, when it sings her marvels,
> It (the lute) ravishes just as many ears.]

The poet's verbal monopoly is such that he puts words in the lover's mouth at the end of the poem:

> Je croy que tu diras qu'apres un tel plaisir
> Tu ne sçaurois trouver dequoy faire un desir. (Saint-Amant, 1:159)

> [I think that you will admit, after such a pleasure (receiving your
>   mistress's favors),
> That you will no longer be able to form the slightest desire.]

It is significant that Saint-Amant uses the future tense here. Whereas the lover is trapped in the sensual experience of the moment, the poet enjoys the advantage of a temporal distance that permits him both to record the past for posterity and anticipate the future.

This idea of "giving voice" provides a powerful poetic rationale for the kind of ventriloquism we often find in Saint-Amant's patronage poetry. In poems such as these, it is not so much the poet's individuality that matters, but rather his protean ability to adapt to circumstance, to give voice to the other. Indeed, to the extent that the poet's individual personality would tie him down to single voice, it becomes a liability, a limitation on his poetic freedom. Rather than merely focusing on how writing for others constrains artistic expression, we would do well to consider its emancipatory effects as well. The imperative to speak one's own heart can be an onerous burden rather than a privilege.

Nowhere is Saint-Amant's poetics of ventriloquism better illustrated than in "L'Épître Heroïcomique À Monseigneur le Duc d'Orléans," addressed to Gaston d'Orléans, the brother of the king, during the siege of Gravelines (1644). As in the "Élégie à Damon," Saint-Amant uses his stylistic virtuosity to practical effect. Here, however, it is not the patron who speaks through the poet; rather, a whole concert of voices invade the poem to alternately praise and entertain Gaston. By combining a wide variety of registers and tones, the poem evokes a mood of public acclamation and celebration. The result is a poetic *tour de force* that is also an extremely effective *pièce de circonstance.*

From the outset, the poem's description as *héroïcomique,* or mock heroic, suggests a mixture of high and low poetic registers. The opening of the poem thus combines elements of a popular drinking song with aspects of epic poetry, comparing the barrels of the canons at the siege of Gravelines with oak wine barrels:

> Gaston . . . un beau desir de gloire
> Te porte aux Coups, t'anime et te fait boire . . .
> D'un noir breuvage enclos dans les barils
> Non de Merrain, mais d'un métal qui tonne. (Saint-Amant, 3:93)

> [Gaston . . . a praiseworthy thirst for glory
> Drives you to shots, animates you, and urges you drink . . .
> From a black brew that is kept not in barrels
> Of oak, but of thundering metal.]

4: THE ANXIETY OF INFLUENCE

Here, the heroicomical mode allows Saint-Amant to give Gaston the praise that is his due while avoiding the humorless monotony of traditional panegyric. In another passage, similarly, the poet pastiches the style of a pair of Pont-Neuf entertainers:

> Bref ce beau Couple en rimant Sainte-Barbe,
> Dit que dans peu tu prendras à la barbe
> De l'Espagnol, et du brave Sienois,
> Ce qui t'oblige à porter le harnois. (Saint-Amant, 3:103–4)

> [So this handsome couple rhymes "Sainte-Barbe"
> And says that soon you will take from under the noses
> Of the Spaniard and the Brave Sienese
> That which forces you to take up arms.]

Although the words of the singers are conveyed through indirect discourse, Saint-Amant manages to capture the stylistic nuances of their song in his own verse. *Rimer Sainte Barbe* means to rhyme haphazardly, and that is precisely what he does here, pairing the phonetically identical *Barbe* and *barbe* (beard). This sense of vernacular poetic license, characteristic of popular song, is reinforced by the enjambment at the end of the second verse: "à la barbe / De l'Espagnol."

Other examples of voices that praise Gaston from within the poem include a company of sententious magistrates, a "wise soul" who reflects on the vanity of human existence, and a talking statue of the late Henry IV (also on the Pont Neuf). The example of the statue is particularly revealing, as it suggests the poet's ability to give voice to anything, even the inanimate. This crescendo of voices reaches a climax toward the end of the poem, when Saint-Amant imagines the popular acclaim that will greet Gaston after his triumph at Gravelines:

> De tous costez les Masses retentissent;
> De tous costez les Verres engloutissent;
> Gaston resonne, et ce Nom entonné,
> Rend par son ton maint Flacon estonné. (Saint-Amant, 3:114)

> [On all sides, the toasts ring out;
> On all sides, the glasses are emptied
> "Gaston" resonates, and the intoning of this name
> Rattles many a bottle with its sound.]

Here, the words of the poem echo the sounds of the people shouting Gaston's name and the bottles' rattling: "Gast*on*," "n*om*," "en-t*onn*é," "s*on*," "t*on*," "Flac*on*," "est*onn*é." The chanting/echoing/rattling effect is reinforced by various repetitions and internal rhymes (*De tous costez/De tous costez; nom/flacon*).

Saint-Amant's poetic practice, in conclusion, is characterized by a strong imitative dimension that allows him to integrate other voices into his poem. In his preface to "Les Nobles triolets," a poem about the *Fronde* with close affinities to the "Épistre Héroïcomique," he neatly summarizes this polyvocality of his poetry in his own words:

> [T]antost c'est moy qui parle: tantost c'est le tiers & le quart. (Saint-Amant, 3:225–26)
>
> [Sometimes it is me speaking; sometimes a third or fourth party.]

This quality, along with the relatively familiar, heroicomical tone, make it possible to sing the praises of Gaston without degenerating into the repetitive *clichés* of panegyric. No longer an individual witnessing, the patronage poem becomes a rich, varied compendium of various forms of praise and acclaim, representative of the different segments of society. Saint-Amant, in turn, becomes the spokesman (or ventriloquist, perhaps) of the French people.

A related poetic sensibility can be found in François Tristan L'Hermite's ode to "Monsieur l'Ab[b]é de la Rivière," published in his *Vers héroïques*.[13] The poem describes the harmonious relationship between La Rivière, a chaplain to Gaston d'Orléans, and his master:

> Les Destins qui te firent naistre
> Pour adorer jusqu'à la mort
> Un si grand & si digne Maistre
> Ont mis tous vos pensers d'acord.
> Il paroist qu'en chaque ocurrence,
> Ou ta crainte ou ton esperance,
> Respond à celle de GASTON,
> Comme font en chaque partie
> Deux luts montez sur mesme ton,
> Qui resonnent par sympathie.[14]
>
> [Destiny, who chose you
> To adore until death
> Such a great and worthy master,

Has harmonized your thoughts.
It would appear that in every instance
Your fear or your hope
Echoes Gaston's,
Just as in music
Two lutes tuned to the same note
Resonate by sympathy.]

Tristan uses the Renaissance discourse on music to characterize the almost mystical affinity between patron and client. Because La Rivière and his master are in perfect harmony (*accord*), each of the master's emotions elicits an identical response from his servant. Elsewhere, Tristan uses this same notion of sympathy (literally, the shared experience of the same feeling) to express his own relationship with one of his protectors (Saint-Aignan):

C'est avec tant de sympathie
Que mon ame est assujetie
Au Sort de ce digne Heros. (Tristan, 260)

[It is with much sympathy
That my soul is attached
To the destiny of this worthy Hero.]

The analogy of the sympathetic vibration between two lutes provides an apt metaphor for the patronage poet, whose poetry does not depend on the expression of his own individuality, but rather on providing the perfect medium for artistically expressing the subjectivity of another. This does not imply that the poet's vocation is any less noble; quite to the contrary, only the most finely tuned instrument constructed of the most resonant materials is suited to the task.

As in Saint-Amant, this ideal results in a poetic practice that depends heavily on imitative effects. Indeed Tristan himself, in his ode "À Monseigneur le Mareschal de Schomberg, sur le combat de Locate," posits imitation of Schomberg's heroic deeds as his primary poetic aspiration:

Je veux imiter le Tonnerre,
Qu'on a veu partir de tes mains. (Tristan, 99)

[I want to imitate the thunder (lightning)
That was seen surging from your hands.]

Later in the same stanza, he uses musical effects to this very end:

> J'oy déja le Canon qui tonne,
> Et toute la Coste resonne
> De Trompettes & de tambours.
>
> [I already hear the cannon that thunders,
> And the entire hill reverberates
> With trumpets and drums.]

Like the landscape, the poem resonates with the sounds of war, captured in French by the hard consonants (d, t, p, b, c) that effectively convey the firing of cannons, the playing of trumpets and drums, and other sounds. Tristan, like Saint-Amant, pursues what we might call an "occasional aesthetic," in which poetic artifice is placed at the service not of the self, but of the other and of the historical circumstance. The poet, paradoxically, is never more of a poet than when he embraces this otherness.

And yet a certain discordant tension can be detected not so much at the level of the poem, but rather at the level of the collection. Within the *Vers héroïques*, Tristan's ode to La Rivière, with its idealized description of the client as resonating with his patron, is followed by two poems that undermine this notion of perfect harmony. The first is "À Monsieur L'Ab[b]é de la Rivière, Stances," in which Tristan asks La Rivière for his support (*appui*) in obtaining favors from Gaston:

> Si vous n'apuyez mon bon droit,
> J'ay perdu mon temps & mes peines. (Tristan, 61)
>
> [If you do not press my just cause.
> I will have lost my time and my effort.]

The second, entitled "À Monsieur de Patris, Luy faisant voir l'ode que j'ay composée à la gloire de Monsieur l'Abbé de la Riviere" ("To M. de Patris, showing him the ode that I composed for the glory of M. l'Abbé de La Rivière") explicitly refers back to the earlier poem in its title. Here, Tristan is blunt regarding his patron's lack of generosity:

> [T]ous les Fruits de mon estude
> N'ont esté payez jusqu'icy
> Qu'en especes d'ingratitude. (Tristan, 62)

[All the fruits of my study
Have earned me little until now
Other than the currency of ingratitude.]

The inclusion of these two poems alongside the ode to La Rivière introduces a dissonance that retrospectively reshapes our experience of the earlier poem. Since Tristan's services have gone unrecognized, we can only conclude that somewhere between Tristan, La Rivière, and Gaston, the harmony is less than perfect.[15]

Tristan's poems operate on two levels. On a primary level, they are artifacts of the life of the court, where they probably circulated individually in manuscript form. Within such a context, a poem such as the ode to "Monsieur l'Ab[b]é de la Rivière" would seem to posit an ideal of harmony between protector and client, between social hierarchy and poetic expression. On a secondary level, publication reframes and juxtaposes the poems/occasions in a manner that suggests tension and conflict, implicitly undermining this harmonious vision. This critical effect is enhanced by temporal distance. With the benefit of cynical hindsight, the ideal expressed in the poem appears to both poet and reader as a fruitless strategy for obtaining favor. The *Vers héroïques* thus illustrate how the publication of a patronage text can be a critical act that questions the official version of the patron-poet relationship.[16] Within the confines of the book, the echoes of the patron's heroism become a discordant clamor.

UN SERF SI LIBERTIN: THÉOPHILE DE VIAU

Tension and conflict between self and other are a hallmark of another poet of this era, Théophile de Viau. Paradoxically, Théophile was both the consummate seventeenth-century libertine and the paragon of a court poet.[17] Pursued for obscenity and freethinking, he was protected successively by the comte de Candale, the duc de Liancourt, the duc de Montmorency, and the comte de Béthune. During his periods of favor at the court, he wrote numerous occasional pieces, including verses for court ballets (notably the famous *Ballet des Bacchanales* [see chapter 3]), semipolitical poetry celebrating the duc de Luynes (Louis XIII's then favorite), and ghostwritten love poems.[18] To a modern reader, he thus appears as somewhat of a contradiction: an independent thinker who was nonetheless dependent on the protection of aristocrats to whom he lent out his pen.

Théophile himself was well aware of the irony of his situation. Indeed, in many of his poems and letters, he reflected explicitly on the costs and benefits of his service to his patrons. "Desja trop longuement la paresse me flatte" ("I have been indolent for too long"), for instance, is an extended meditation on various kinds of *servitude*, including the physical bondage of the galley slave, the intellectual constraints imposed by custom, and the relationships between masters and servants. Grandees impose various degrees and kinds of servitude on those below them, ranging from the yoke (*joug*) imposed by crass and ignorant masters to the less heavy-handed authority of more enlightened patrons (Théophile, 1:137). The authority of a gentlemanly (*honnête*) master depends less on coercion, however, than persuasion, "ceste douceur d'esprit, / Qui si facilement par l'oreille me prit" (that sweetness of mind, / That so easily ensnared my ears) (Théophile, 1:382). This distinction makes it possible for Théophile to characterize his own submission to Candale as voluntary ("Je dois aymer mon joug, m'y rendre volontaire") and himself, paradoxically, as a *un serf si libertin* (free serf) (Théophile, 1:375).

Such a relationship is closer to friendship than traditional forms of patronage, and indeed Théophile refers to the *juste amitié* (true friendship) that incites him to write on behalf of his master. In one remarkable passage, he imagines a mode of writing where the bond of friendship between patron and writer would render the attribution of a text to a single author impossible:

> Ta vertu me ravit et fait que mon poëme
> Servant à ton plaisir m'obligera moy-mesme.
> Or pour le grand dessein où j'engage mes vers,
> Il faut que tes destins me soient mieux descouverts,
> Que j'entre dans ton ame, et que de là je tire
> La matiere du livre où je te veux descrire:
> Mon travail sera long, et depuis ton berceau
> Possible durera jusques à mon tombeau. (Theophile, 1:384)

> [Your virtue delights me, and thus my poem,
> Although it serves your pleasure, will gratify me as well.
> Now, as for the great project to which I consign my verse,
> Your destiny must be better revealed to my eyes,
> I must enter your soul, and from there draw
> The matter of the book in which I intend to describe you:

My labor will be lengthy, and from your cradle
Will perhaps last until my grave.]

The proliferation and confusion of pronouns recalls Saint-Amant's "Poëte crotté" (chapter 3). Théophile, however, pushes the technique further, using the alternation between first and second person possessive adjectives to subvert the notion of ownership:

> [M]on poëme
> Servant à *ton* plaisir *m*'obligera moy-mesme . . .
> *Mon* travail sera long, et depuis *ton* berceau
> Possible durera jusques à *mon* tombeau."
>
> [*My* poem,
> Although it serves *your* pleasure, will gratify *me* as well . . .
> *My* labor will be lengthy, and from *your* cradle
> Will perhaps last until *my* grave.]

In the first two lines, moreover, the poet plays with the notion of agency by twice making the grammatical subject of one clause the object of another. The first person pronoun moves from object position (*me ravit*), to subject position (*mon poëme/Servant*), and then back to object position (*m'obligera*). The most important difference with respect to Saint-Amant, however, is the shift from alienation to fusion, placed under the banner of friendship. The poet penetrates (or rather is admitted) *into* the patron's soul, where he finds the matter of a book that ultimately belongs to both (and neither) of them. If, as Montaigne famously put it, true friends are "a single soul in two bodies," all exchange becomes impossible, since you cannot give something to yourself. Taken to the extreme, the logic of friendship abolishes the boundaries between persons and undermines any univocal notion of the author.

Other passages in Théophile's writings, by contrast, would seem to posit the radical impossibility of writing for another. In the autobiographical "Première journée," the narrator (Théophile's fictional alter ego) admonishes a friend who would have him write a love poem for him:

> Et comment, luy dis-je, voudriez vous emprunter les habits d'un autre pour vous parer devant vostre Maistresse et vous farder le visage pour luy plaire? Cela est encore plus estrange d'avoir des imaginations empruntées pour luy discourir; et sçachez, je vous prie, que les pensées d'un autre ne se rapportent jamais si bien à nos sentimens et qu'il faut estre Amoureux pour les sçavoir dire. (Théophile, 2:252)

[And so, I asked, would you want to borrow someone else's clothes to adorn yourself for your Mistress and cover your face in makeup in order to please her? It is stranger still to use borrowed ideas to speak to her. You should know that the thoughts of another never fit our feelings very well; you must be in love to communicate them.]

This passage, similar to many others in Théophile's writing, raises the issue of *ethos*—the relationship, in rhetoric, between a speaker and his or her discourse.[19] Like Plato in the *Phaedrus* and the *Gorgias*, Théophile argues for the inseparability of speaker and speech. For Plato, this inseparability guaranteed the integrity of philosophical truths. Only someone who had prior knowledge of the forms was in a position to describe them. For Théophile, the truths in question are subjective, but the logic is the same. Only the person who experiences them is competent to express them; anyone else can only imagine them. First imagined by another, and then transferred to language, such secondhand emotions would be twice removed from the immediacy of feeling. To use an analogy common to both Plato and Théophile, they would be cosmetic rather than authentic.[20]

The beginning of Théophile's "À M. de Fargis" echoes this position within a patronage context:

> Je ne m'y puis resoudre, excuse moy de grace
> Escrivant pour autruy, je me sens tout de glace;
> Je te promis chez toy des vers pour un amant,
> Qui se veut faire ayder à paindre son tourment:
> Mais pour luy satisfaire, et bien paindre sa flamme,
> Je voudrois par avant avoir cogneu son ame. (Théophile, 1:386)

> [I cannot bring myself to do it, please excuse me
> Writing for another, I am all ice;
> I promised you verses for a lover
> Who needs help in describing his torment
> But in order to satisfy him, and paint his flame,
> I would first have to know his soul.]

Unlike Saint-Amant, Théophile is cold and impotent (*de glace*) before a fiery passion (*flamme*) that is not his own. He had promised "verses for a lover," but it is not possible to write for a generic other. To compose for another, it is necessary to know his soul, for no two lovers are the same:

> Tu sçais bien que chacun a des gousts tout divers,
> Qu'il faut à chaque esprit une sorte de vers. (Théophile, 1:387)
>
> [You know that everyone has different tastes,
> And that each mind requires a different kind of verse.]

The subtext of this poem, as Adam has observed, is Théophile's strong claim to individuality and particularity. As long as verse is an expression of diversity and particularity, writing for someone else—particularly a patron—raises the specter of the absorption of the self by the "other."[21] Théophile returns to this theme at the end of the poem:

> Penses tu quand j'aurois employé tout un jour
> A bien imaginer des passions d'Amour,
> Que mes conceptions seroient bien exprimées
> En paroles de choix, bien mises, bien rimées:
> L'autre n'y trouveroit possible rien pour luy,
> Tant il est malaisé d'escrire pour autruy. (Théophile, 1:389–90)
>
> [You should consider that if I were to spend an entire day
> Imagining all of the passions of love,
> And if my ideas were well expressed
> In choice words, carefully arranged, in good rhyme,
> Still the other might not find anything for him
> So hard it is to write for someone else.]

Here the perfection of form is contrasted with the authenticity of sentiment.[22] However pure the diction and the rhyme, the lover will always feel that the poet has not done justice to his passion:

> Il voudroit que son front fust aux astres pareil,
> Que je la fisse ensemble et l'Aube, et le Soleil,
> Que j'escrive comment ses regards sont des armes,
> Comme il verse pour elle un ocean de larmes. (Théophile, 1:390)
>
> [He wants me to compare her forehead to the stars,
> To make her both the Dawn and the Sun,
> To write about how her glances are weapons,
> And how he sheds an ocean of tears for her.]

Behind the "other" lurks the equally, if not more, formidable specter of the already said (*déjà dit*). What appears to belong to the other person—his emotions, the traits he especially admires in his beloved—turn out to be poetic platitudes, such as the lady's arrowlike glances and *la belle matineuse* (the lady compared to the dawn). The poet's identity is thus not merely threatened by the presence of a specific "other," but rather by a kind of banal, generic otherness. Writing for others, in other words, ultimately implies submission to convention. With this notion of language as an expression of personality and particularity, we are close to Gautier and his notion of the *irrégulier*-as-stylistic-deviant.

Théophile, in sum, seems to alternate between two visions of poetry and identity. In the first, poetry overflows the limits of individual subjectivity, blurring the limits between self and other. In the second, poetry is above all the signature of the individual, and thus fundamentally inalienable and irreproducible. A number of Théophile's poetic texts can be seen as attempts to work out a solution to this apparent tension. His "À M. le marquis de Boquingant," for instance, develops a gift economy that reconciles self and other within the broader framework of nature.[23] After complimenting the English Marquis of Buckingham on his generosity, he launches on an extended digression that traces the history of gifts back to the creation of the universe out of chaos:

> Personne n'est fasché du bien
> Dont vostre sort heureux abonde,
> D'autant qu'il ne vous sert de rien
> Qu'à faire du plaisir au monde.
> Ainsi le celeste flambeau
> Qui fut l'ornement le plus beau
> Qu'enfanta la masse premiere,
> N'a jamais eu des envieux,
> Car il n'use de sa lumiere
> Que pour en esclairer nos yeux. (Théophile, 1:229)

> [No one is angered by the good fortune
> You have enjoyed over the course of your life,
> Especially since you use it
> Solely to please others.
> Thus the celestial torch,
> Which was the fairest ornament
> To be engendered by the primal mass,
> Has never attracted envy
> For it uses its light solely in order to
> To illuminate our eyes.]

The notion of creation as a gift from God to man goes back to Genesis, if not before. As Natalie Davis has shown, the early modern understanding of the gift was rooted in the principle that "everything we have is a gift of God, and what comes in as a gift has some claim to go out as a gift."[24] Gifts, in other words, were not merely a human affair; they were part of a larger economy, and men were expected to show their thanks to the Creator by recirculating them, an idea echoed in the ode to Buckingham. Inspired, perhaps, by the materialism of Giordano Bruno and the Paduan neo-Aristotelians, Théophile diverges from this tradition, however, by leaving God out of the picture. His creation is a spontaneous and natural birthing (note the verb *enfanter*), in some ways more evocative of our Big Bang than the first chapter of Genesis. When God is finally mentioned later in the poem, Théophile puts a distinctly deistic spin on his influence. Although created by God, the world was not created *for* God, but for mankind:

> Ce monde, ouvrage de ses mains,
> N'est point basty pour son usage,
> Car il l'a fait pour les humains. (Théophile, 1:232)

> [This Earth, the work of His hands,
> Was not built for His use,
> For He made it for men.]

The verb *donner* (to give) occurs no fewer than twenty-one times in this 100-line poem, reinforcing Théophile's central theme that "tout donne" (everything gives).[25] Nature, for Théophile, is endowed with innate procreative powers. Out of chaos emerges the sun, which gives the seasons. The seasons, in turn, bestow their gifts on men: with autumn come apples; with winter, night and rest for weary laborers; with spring, colorful flowers; and with summer, finally, the grain that provides human sustenance. Using terms (*ventre* meaning womb, *sein* meaning breast) that recall the description of creation as a birth, Théophile characterizes both the earth and its oceans as generous. In nature, every taking is also giving:

> L'Abeille ne *prend* point du Ciel
> Les doux *presens* de la rosée,
> Que pour nous en *donner* le miel. (Théophile, 1:231; emphasis added)

> [The bee only *takes* from the sky
> The sweet *offerings* of the dew
> In order to *give* us honey.]

Théophile uses poetic form to evoke this cyclical dynamic of giving:

> Les Zephirs se donnent aux flots.
> Les flots se donnent à la Lune,
> Les Navires aux Matelots,
> Les Matelots à la fortune. (Théophile, 1:231)
>
> [The Zephyrs give themselves to waves,
> The waves give themselves to the moon,
> The ships to the sailors,
> And the sailors to fortune.]

Each line in this passage represents a link in a chain of giving, connected to the previous and subsequent lines by the repetition of words ("Les Zephirs se donnent aux *flots* / Les *flots* se donnent à la Lune") and sounds (*Zephirs/Navires, flots/Matelots, Lune/fortune*). The repetition of the same sound sequence "ir-ot-ot-une" in the first and second halves of the stanza contributes to a strong sense of cyclical movement, evocative both of the tides and of the circulation/cycle of nature's gifts to man. The sailors giving themselves over to fortune, finally, evokes the ultimate natural rhythm—the inevitable cycle of life and death. According to Théophile's deistic determinism, our fates are decided neither by ourselves nor by a benign deity, but rather by an implacable law of nature to which we must give ourselves.[26]

On the one hand, through its thematic content and verbal form, Théophile's poetic creation is a mirror of natural creation. On the other hand, as the poet's gift of the poem to Buckingham suggests ("Je veux que tout le monde sçache / Que je vous ay donné des vers" [I want everyone to know / That I have given you my verses]), it is itself deeply implicated in the global cycle of giving (Théophile, 1:232). Like all gifts, the poem is part of the ebb and flow that characterize the natural order. In Théophile's poetry, gift giving is transformed into a global, generalized economy that both subsumes and transcends the exchanges between patron and poet. All-inclusive, nature is both universal and diverse, reconciling individual identities without effacing their specificity. Each individual is at the same time part of nature and a reflection of its infinite diversity (he or she has his or her own nature).

Théophile further develops this relationship between nature, gift giving, and patronage in *La Maison de Silvie*. Directly inspired by Théophile's biography, this poem belies Henri Lafay's contention that Théophile's richest poetry is divorced from his social situation. More than 1,000 lines long, it is one of his most ambitious and, by general consensus, most successful efforts. And yet its poetic success is not merely a function of the expression of "individual values."[27] To pay tribute to the patrons who protected him in his darkest hour, Théophile weaves "other" voices into a compelling story of personal redemption.[28]

Before examining this poem in detail, it is necessary to briefly review the events surrounding the poet's arrest and imprisonment in 1623.[29] In November 1622, "Phylis, tout est . . . outu," a scandalous poem "Par le sieur Theophile," appeared in front of a collection of satirical works entitled *Le Parnasse satyrique*. Although such works had appeared before without much fanfare, France was in the grip of Counter-Reformation fervor and the collection caught the attention of the Jesuits, including Father Garasse, who published a long vituperative pamphlet entitled *La Doctrine curieuse des beaux esprits de ce temps, ou prétendus tels* (1623) that attacked Théophile and other libertines for their irreligiosity and debauchery. Garasse was particularly concerned about the influence of libertine writers on young nobles. Addressing the latter, he warned them that protecting a debauched writer could lead to their moral and social downfall, filling their households with impieties and filth (*ordures*).[30] The scandal reached the Paris *parlement*, which ordered the arrest of Théophile and the other authors of the *Parnasse satyrique*, including Théophile's friend Guillaume Colletet, on July 11, 1623. Théophile went into hiding, spending part of the month of August at the duc de Montmorency's château at Chantilly. Meanwhile, he was condemned to death *in absentia* and burned in effigy on the Place de Grève in Paris on August 18. On August 26, he left Chantilly, heading north toward Picardy and the border with Flanders. He was arrested on September 17 at the fortress of Catelet in Picardy, from where he was brought back to Paris. During his trial, he was imprisoned in the Conciergerie, in the same cell that had been occupied by Ravaillac, Henry IV's assassin. After a long series of legal and political maneuvers, Théophile's sentence was commuted to perpetual banishment, and he was released from prison on September 1, 1625.

Published during Théophile's imprisonment in 1624, *La Maison de Silvie* is part *apologia*, dealing with the poet's condemnation and arrest, and part tribute to Montmorency and his wife Maria-Felicia Orsini (as Silvie), who protected him during his flight, with a healthy dose of mythology and some natural descriptions of Chantilly mixed in. Critics have commended Théophile for focusing his praise on the natural wonders of Chantilly, thereby avoiding many of the clichés and conventions of panegyric and giving full range to his talent for descriptive and personal poetry.[31] As in the ode to Buckingham, this praise of nature reflects back on the duke and the duchess:

> Elle [la nature] a mis toute sa bonté,
> Et son sçavoir et sa richesse,
> Et les thresors de sa beauté
> Sur le Duc et sur la Duchesse. (Théophile, 3:168)
>
> [She (nature) has bestowed all of her goodness
> And her knowledge and her riches,
> And the treasures of her beauty,
> Upon the duke and the duchess.]

This formula of praising a patron through his château and/or gardens would prove popular later in the seventeenth century, most notably in the hands of Tristan ("La Maison d'Astrée"), Saint-Amant ("Le Palais de la Volupté"), Jean Desmarets de Saint-Sorlin ("La Promenade de Richelieu"), and Jean de La Fontaine ("Le Songe de Vaux").

The eponymous "maison de Silvie," where Théophile stayed during his visit was a hunting pavilion built in the park at Chantilly for the purpose of receiving Henry IV. In Ode X, Théophile alludes to the late monarch's visits:

> Sous ce toict loing des Courtisans
> De qui les soupçons mesdisans
> N'ont jamais appris à se taire,
> Alcandre a mille fois gousté
> Ce qu'un Prince a de volupté
> Quand il trouve un lieu solitaire. (Théophile 3:184)
>
> [Under this roof, far from the courtiers
> Whose slanderous suspicions
> Have never learned to hold their tongues,
> Alcandre tasted a thousand times
> The pleasures that a Prince can enjoy
> When he finds a solitary place.]

The mention of Alcandre's loves is arguably as much a literary allusion as a historical one. The duc de Montmorency's sister was Charlotte de Montmorency, the same "Oranthe" whom we encountered in Malherbe's Alcandre poems (see chapter 3). This historical link to Malherbe is reinforced by thematic echoes such as the "solitary place" described by Théophile, which evokes the natural, solitary settings of the Alcandre cycle. By alluding to the history of the *maison*, Théophile invokes a poetic tradition associated with Malherbe—a tradition of poets' complicity in their protectors' amorous affairs and, inversely, patrons' appropriation of their poetry. Théophile, however, remains at the level of evocation, carefully avoiding any details regarding the nature of the pleasures enjoyed by the late king within the walls of the pavilion:

> Je dirois les secrets moments
> Des faveurs, des feintes malices,
> Dont le caprice des Amants
> Forme leur plainte et leur[s] delices:
> Mais si l'œil de Silvie un jour
> De ceste lecture d'Amour
> Avoit surpris son innocence,
> Ma prison me seroit trop peu,
> Lors faudroit-il dresser le feu
> Dont on veut punir ma licence. (Théophile, 3:184–85)

> [I could tell of the intimate moments,
> The favors, the feigned spite,
> From which capricious lovers,
> Form their complaints and delights:
> But if Silvie's eyes were ever
> To have their innocence shocked
> By this licentious reading,
> My prison would not be enough.
> It would be necessary to erect the pyre
> With which they seek to punish my license.]

The chaste Silvie, associated with purity throughout the poem, exerts a restraining influence on the poet. Indeed, her censure is described as worse than anything that the Conciergerie can threaten. Instead of lingering, Théophile thus abandons this area of the park to the "Fauns and the Satyrs," and takes the more virtuous path (*vertueux sentier*) that leads to the park's chapel (Théophile, 3:185). The setting of the chapel, in turn, sets the scene for the religious tone of the end of the poem, where Théophile predicts that Montmorency will lead a holy crusade to defeat the Turks.

The allusion to Alcandre and Oranthe fits into a larger contrast, within the poem, between poetic propriety and verbal transgression. In Ode VII, for instance, the poet uses suggestive language to describe the singing birds that flutter around Silvie as she sits in the park:

> Leurs cœurs se laissent desrober
> Insensiblement ils s'oublient,
> Et des rameaux qu'ils font courber
> Quelquesfois leurs pieds se deslient. (Théophile, 3:169)
>
> [They let their hearts be stolen away,
> Insensibly they forget themselves
> And sometimes their feet slip
> From the branches that bow under their weight.]

Despite the description of their desire as "holy" and the characterization of their "liberties" as "innocent," the birds' physical proximity to Silvie along with the description of their ecstasy suggest an animalistic, erotic subtext. This subtext comes to the fore as their song becomes a nuisance, degenerating into a flattering, but unpleasant din reminiscent of the popular acclamation of the king in the Paris streets. Throughout the poem, birds stand in for the figure of the poet, and this passage is no exception:

> Ainsi l'entretien d'un rimeur,
> Enflé des arts et des sciences,
> Lors qu'il se trouve en bonne humeur
> Vient à bout de nos patiences. (Théophile, 3:170–71)
>
> [Thus the conversation of a rhymer,
> Puffed up with knowledge of the arts and sciences
> When he is in good humor,
> Tries our patience.]

Like the birds, the rhymer is so caught up in his virtuoso poetic performance that he overwhelms his audience. The explicit analogy between the birds and poets thus suggests a code of poetic decorum that must not be transgressed, personified by the virtuous Silvie. A similar passage can be found in Ode II, in which the fish in the pond at Chantilly make a racket as they compete to get hooked on the duchess's fishing line, while she waves away the disorder with her hand (Théophile, 3:136). Throughout the poem, Silvie puts limits on poetic expression, preserving harmony (both literally and metaphorically) and keeping noise and bestial vulgarity at bay.

The theme of transgression is echoed in a number of the mythological references in the poem. Odes II and III deal with the myth of Phaeton, who had the temerity to attempt to drive Apollo's chariot of the sun and whose death was lamented by his friend Cycnus, who was transformed into a swan. Within the larger arc of the poem, this myth provides the transition between the description of Chantilly, with its swan-covered pond, and the narrative of Théophile's personal tribulations. The poet is compared to the transgressive Phaeton, while Cycnus represents his friend Tyrsis (possibly Jacques Vallée Des Barreaux), whose dreams presage the poet's misfortunes. Théophile alludes to another fable of transgression in Ode II, when Silvie magically transforms sea tritons into deer, a metamorphosis that is compared to Diana's punishment of Actaeon (Théophile, 3:138). The Diana/Actaeon myth, finally, returns in Ode IX in the song of the nightingale, who claims to be the only creature to have enjoyed the privilege of seeing "the queen of the wood" (that is, Diana) bathe nude, the precise crime for which Actaeon was punished. Silvie's chastity, however, triumphs yet again over sexual license. A chaste gaze from Silvie replaces the voyeuristic pleasures of watching Diana bathe (Théophile, 3:178–79).

These examples reveal a cluster of related poetic motifs in the poem: sexual transgression, poetic excess, and censure (both by the authorities and by the patroness), on the one hand; self restraint and poetic propriety, on the other. The Théophile of *La Maison de Silvie* is clearly a chastened poet, careful to respect limits of decorum. The allusion to Malherbe's Alcandre cycle, moreover, suggests a desire on the part of the poet to distance himself from court poetry as practiced by Malherbe, and as he himself had practiced it earlier in his career. Gone is promiscuous *privauté*, or compromising familiarity between poet and patron/patroness. Instead, the patroness, by virtue of her moral authority, holds sexual and poetic license in check. This aura of discipline and order is reinforced by the setting of the poem in a park, where nature is kept under control:

> Ils [les animaux] y trouvent tousjours du vert,
> Qu'un peu de soin met à couvert
> Des outrages de la Nature. (3:141)

> [They (the animals) always find greenery there,
> That a little care shelters
> From the violence of Nature.]

David Michael Roberts has rightly insisted on the latent violence lurking behind the landscape of Chantilly.[32] As we have seen, the poem is filled with constant reminders of the imprisoned poet's vulnerability and impending death (for example, Actaeon and Phaeton). Rather than seeing the idyllic description of Chantilly as undermined by these suggestions of violence, however, I would argue that it is an attempt to keep violence and sexuality in check by containing them within the geometrical framework of the baroque park. Brute nature is not in itself restorative for Théophile; it needs to be ordered by *un peu de soin* (a little care).

More generally, *La Maison de Silvie* can be read as an attempt by the persecuted Théophile to master his situation in 1624. The nightingale—a reference to the Ovidian myth of Philomela—is the primary figure for this aspiration. The story of Philomela, who lost her voice when her tongue was cut off by her brother-in-law only to regain it when she was transformed into a bird, clearly evokes Théophile's own situation.[33] The decrees of the *parlement de Paris* have attempted to silence him, but song and poetry offer a path to redemption. Numerous passages highlight the therapeutic role of the poetic word in overcoming loss and suffering:

> Dieux que c'est un contentement
> Bien doux à la raison humaine,
> Que d'exhaler si doucement
> La douleur que nous fait la haine. (Théophile, 3:174)
>
> [Heavens, it is a sweet satisfaction
> For human reason
> To exhale so gently
> The pain inflicted upon us by hate.]

Singing one's pain is a way of externalizing it, of distancing it, almost as if suffering were expelled in the same breath as song. On another level, moreover, the nightingale functions as a figure of the poet's affinity with nature:

> Comme en la terre et par le Ciel
> Des petites mouches errantes

4: THE ANXIETY OF INFLUENCE

> Meslent pour composer leur miel
> Mille matieres differentes,
> Formant ses airs qui sont ses fruicts
> L'oyseau digere mille bruicts
> En une seule melodie. (Théophile, 3:181–182)

> [Just as, on land and in the sky,
> Little wandering flies
> Mix a thousand different substances
> To make their honey,
> The bird, creating the songs that are its fruits,
> Digests a thousand sounds
> Into a single melody.]

The comparison of the poet to the honeybee flitting from flower to flower to gather pollen so as to make honey is a commonplace image that goes back to Horace, where it is a figure of poetic variety. The poet does not create *ex nihilo;* rather he is a gatherer, who remixes the world (to borrow a modern metaphor) into something new. Like the bee, the nightingale combines other voices:

> Le doux charme des voix humaines,
> La musique des instrumens
> Et les paysibles roulemens
> Du beau cristal de nos fontaines. (Théophile, 3:181)

> [The sweet charm of human voices,
> The music of instruments,
> And the peaceful rumble
> Of the fine crystal of our fountains.]

Poetry, Théophile would seem to be saying, is all about lending one's voice to the diverse marvels of the world. As with Saint-Amant and Tristan, the poet only fully becomes himself, paradoxically, when he is other. His ultimate ambition is to gather the variety of nature within his poem, much as the migrating birds bring objects to Chantilly from faraway places:

> Avec elles voit-on manger
> Ce que l'air le plus estranger
> Nous peut faire venir de rare,
> Des oyseaux venus de si loing
> Qu'on y voit imiter le soing
> D'un grand Roy qui n'est pas avare. (Théophile, 3:141–42)

[We see them eat
All of the finest products
Of foreign climes,
Delivered by birds from afar,
And it reminds us of the efforts
Of a magnanimous king.]

There are echoes, here, of Théophile's ode to Buckingham and its celebration of liberality. By encompassing diversity, Chantilly and the poem both become mirrors of the bounty of nature and gifts in their own right. They represent a tolerant, generous, and regenerative spirit that contrasts sharply with the conduct of the religious and social authorities who were pursuing the poet.

The success of *La Maison de Silvie* as a patronage poem can in part be attributed to the manner in which Théophile keeps the specter of otherness and alienation at bay by embracing a more all-encompassing otherness. For Théophile, as we have seen, man does not exist apart from nature; he is part of it and it is part of him. This nature is humanized and moralized by the presence of his patroness Silvie, who both restrains and protects him. The exile's new voice thus emerges from the conjunction and synthesis of two external influences: the beneficent abundance and variety of nature; and the restraining, civilizing influence of the patroness, who keeps disorder and sexual transgression in check. Although aspects of Théophile's libertine philosophy are left intact, we are far from the philosophical and sexual provocations of his earlier poetry. Instead, we are closer to the natural wisdom of Montaigne, which is combined with the poet's life experience.

Performing Authorship: Sorel's *Francion*

The examples analyzed to this point illustrate the poetic possibilities of writing on behalf of a patron. I have tried to show that the constraints of circumstantial poetry were not incompatible with expressive poetry, or even (in the case of Théophile) libertine wisdom. At the same time that patronage closed certain doors, it opened others. Nevertheless, the ambivalence expressed by both Tristan and Théophile points to an undeniable tension between deference to the other and self-expression. This tension explodes in Sorel's *L'Histoire comique de Francion* (1623–33), revealing a new and radical vision of authorship.

L'Histoire comique de Francion recounts the adventures of a young libertine who in many respects recalls Théophile.[34] After finishing his studies in a Parisian *collège*, Francion ventures out into the world, looking for a career where he can pursue his literary interests. This offers Sorel an opportunity to paint a satirical portrait of contemporary literary life, including the habits and vices of authors, their relationships with publishers and patrons, and their abject poverty. We learn that most authors, banking on the fruits of patronage, are biding their time waiting to meet a protector who can take them into his personal service or recommend them to the king.[35] Francion is no exception; because he is of noble lineage, however, his goal is not so much to obtain a *gratification* or a position as a secretary as it is to pursue a career at court.

Seeking to acquire a reputation at court, Francion inquires into the distribution of roles for the latest court ballet and composes verses for the queen. Looking back in retrospect, Francion laughs at his *naïveté:*

> Or, il faut que vous sachiez que j'en étais si glorieux qu'il me semblait que j'étais une personne fort nécessaire à l'État et que de servir le roi en son ballet comme je faisais, c'était le servir en une chose très importante. (Sorel, *Francion,* 1633 ed., 257)

> [You are to understand that I was so glorious in my own conceit, that I seemed to be a person very necessary to the State, and to serve the King, as I did in the Mask, was to serve him in a businesse of the greatest importance.][36]

Francion's verses do gain him entrance to the ballet, but his role is an extremely limited one: after crossing the long galleries that lead to the Salle de Bourbon, he ends up serving as a comical human music stand and, for lack of anywhere to sit, using his papers as a makeshift bench. He complains bitterly that the only fruit of his efforts was an opportunity to see the ballet:

> Car, de profit ni d'honneur, il n'en faut espérer par un tel moyen. (Sorel, *Francion,* 1633 ed., 257)

> [For in that way I hoped neither for profit nor honour. (Sorel, *Francion,* 1655 ed., 5:13)]

Here, Sorel (through Francion) seems to deride the notion that literary service can provide a career pathway to political appointments.

Again and again over the course of the novel, Sorel points out the futility of using a literary career as a stepladder to social advancement. Francion's dedication of a book to an influential grandee, for instance, proves to be equally fruitless. At this juncture, he resolves that henceforth he will only write for himself, recalling Théophile's early professions of independence:

> Depuis cela, je me délibérai de n'écrire plus que pour moi. (Sorel, *Francion*, 1633 ed., 268)

> [After that, I determined with my self to write no more books, but for myself only. (Sorel, *Francion*, 1633 ed., 5:15)]

Sorel's own misgivings regarding dedication are manifest in the pseudo-dedication "Aux Grands" ("To the Grandees") in the 1626 edition:

> Ce n'est point pour vous dedier ce Livre que je fais cette Epistre, mais pour vous apprendre que je ne vous le dedie point.[37]

> [It is not in order to dedicate this book to you that I write this epistle, but rather to notify you that I do not dedicate it to you at all.]

Sorel further subverted the conventions and functions of dedication by publishing *Francion* anonymously. What is the point of dedicating a work, after all, if you do not sign it?

The 1626 edition also gives a hint as to why Sorel might have chosen to maintain his anonymity:

> [J]e tiens pour maxime, Qu'il se faut taire quelquefois afin de parler plus long temps, c'est à dire qu'il est bon de moderer sa mesdisance en de certaines saisons, de peur que les Grands ne vous mettent en peine et ne vous fassent condamner à un eternel silence.[38]

> [I take it as a maxim that it is sometimes necessary to be silent in order to continue to speak—that is to say, it is a good idea to hold one's tongue at certain times, for fear that the powerful will punish you and have you condemned to an eternal silence.]

The prudent satirist knows when to hold his tongue so as not to offend the *grands,* who are a fickle and sensitive bunch. Théophile de Viau has often been suggested as a model for Francion, and his various exiles and long imprisonment may well have inspired this passage.[39] Other writers also come to mind, however, most notably Sigogne and the poet Étienne Durand, who was "eternally silenced" (executed) in 1618 for participating in a conspiracy against Luynes, Louis XIII's then favorite.[40]

These episodes reflect Sorel's uneasiness with regard to the traditional forms of literary patronage. It is thus both paradoxical and significant that a substantial portion of the novel revolves around the protagonist's relationship with a noble protector.[41] In a salon, Francion meets the aristocratic Clérante, who has heard of his reputation as a poet and all-around *honnête homme* and who is duly impressed when he is shown samples of his verse. Clérante's interest in Francion is not purely literary, however. He is preoccupied by an anonymous satire that pokes fun at many of the leading figures of the court, including himself, and he seeks the young poet's advice in identifying the source and fashioning an appropriate response. Francion quickly determines that Alcimidor is behind the slanderous text, since he is the only courtier deserving of ridicule who is not satirized therein:

> Or ceux qui ne sont point en cette Satyre cy, se sont exemptez d'y estre par leur vertu signalée, mais luy je ne sçay pas à quel subject le Poëte ne l'a mis sur les rangs, si ce n'est à cause qu'il n'a composé cecy qu'à sa persuasion. (Sorel, *Francion*, 1633 ed., 259)

> [Now, those who are not named in this Satyre are exempted by their remarkable Vertue, but as for him, I know not for what reason the Poet left him out, but only for this, that by his perswasion (sic) he did write it. (Sorel, *Francion*, 1655 ed., 6:6)]

Francion applies a kind of literary expertise here—not so much the specialized knowledge of mythology or literary forms, but rather a broad theoretical understanding of the social uses of literary texts. The literary (and moral) efficacy of satire depends on the illusion that it emanates from a neutral vantage point, outside the court. Francion shatters this illusion by showing the satire's blind spot— the fact that the satirist's own benefactor (Alcimidor) is excluded. Francion solves another literary mystery regarding a second defamatory poem in similar fashion. This time, the grievance turns out to be the poet's. Years earlier, Clérante had refused him his protection. Satire of the court is thus ultimately shown to be bound up with the networks of self-interest that it claims to satirize. On one level, the *grands* are at war with each other, using their poets as surrogates. On a second level, the poets are revealed to have their own program, avenging themselves on ungrateful patrons. (Since *Francion* is itself a satirical text, the reader is left wondering what *Sorel*'s agenda is.)

Once the diagnosis has been made, Francion shows Clérante the poetic faults in the satire and offers to help craft a response:

> [A]fin d'effacer les mauvaises impressions, que les Courtisans pourroient avoir à son deshonneur. (Sorel, *Francion*, 1633 ed., 260)

> [To take away the evil impressions which the Courtiers might have received of him. (Sorel, *Francion*, 1655 ed., 6:7)]

The situation recalls the example of the duc de Montmorency, mentioned in chapter 1, who reputedly surrounded himself with "men of learning whom he employed to write verses for him, to discuss a thousand matters with him, and to tell him what to think about things that were being published at the time."[42] Francion becomes Clérante's literary advisor/publicist/image consultant, helping him refine his manners and learn the rules of polite conversation so that he will no longer be vulnerable to accusations of ignorance. In order to put his master on the right path, he must first disabuse him of his prejudices against letters, typical of the aristocracy of the period. If one wants to command men, he explains, it is necessary to excel in intelligence as well as bodily strength:

> [C]eux qui veulent commander aux autres doivent avoir plus d'esprit, non pas plus de force, ainsi qu'entre les bestes brutes. (Sorel, *Francion*, 1633 ed., 261)

> [Those who would command others ought to have more strength of Spirit (mind) than of Body, as it is seen amongst brute Beasts. (Sorel, *Francion*, 1655 ed., 6:7)]

Francion's education of Clérante gives a sense of the ongoing transformation of the nobility from a warrior class into a social elite distinguished by fine taste and a refined style of living.[43] Indeed, obtaining a veneer of politeness seems to be among Clérante's primary motivations in seeking out Francion. One of the first subjects that he broaches in his conversations with Francion is Luce, the *salonnière*/courtesan, with whom he is in love and whom he desperately wants to impress.

4: THE ANXIETY OF INFLUENCE

Francion's relationship with Clérante is an ambivalent one. Although the latter possesses political influence at court, the former has the social and cultural skill that are valued by polite society. It is thus Clérante, ultimately, who is the most transformed by the interaction, as he is reinvented in Francion's image. Both his public persona and his private conversation are scripted and crafted by Francion to such an extent that it is questionable whether there is much of the original, authentic Clérante left. If Clérante is the nominal master in the master-servant relationship, Francion is clearly the master in the equally, if not more, important master-pupil relationship, a fact that he is eager to bring to the attention of his listener/reader:

> L'on dit que Diogène estant mis en vente, avec des autres esclaves, fit crier s'il y avoit quelqu'un qui voulust achepter un Maistre, et que de fait, celuy qui l'achepta, souffroit d'estre maitrisé de luy, recevant les enseignemens de Philosophie qu'il luy donnoit; ainsi j'estois au service d'un maistre qui me nourrissoit, et me bailloit bon appointment, et si je prenois de l'authorité sur luy, et luy commandois qu'il s'abstint de beaucoup de choses. (Sorel, *Francion,* 1633 ed., 262)
>
> [It is said, that when Diogenes was to be sold amongst the other Slaves, he caused the Cryer to Cry, Is there any one who would buy a Master? whereupon he who bought him, suffered himself to be governed by him, receiving those Instructions of Philosophy which he gave him. In the same manner I was in the service of a Master, who nourished me, and gave me a good allowance, and I did exercise authority over him, and commanded him to abstain from many things. (Sorel, *Francion,* 1655 ed., 6:8)]

Here Sorel explores how a servant can become so essential to his master's sense of identity that he paradoxically holds the real power. Francion becomes a seventeenth-century Diogenes, not so much looking for a honest man as an *honnête homme* (a true gentleman). This special relationship gives a distinct flavor to Francion's otherwise rather banal claims to independence:

> Il m'offroit un appointement honneste que j'acceptay, pourveu que j'eusse tousjours ma franchise, et qu'encore que je luy rendisse des services, que malaisement pouvoit il esperer d'un autre, je n'eusse point la qualité de serviteur. Il me promit qu'il ne me tiendroit jamais que comme son amy. Je me mets donc en sa maison. (Sorel, *Francion,* 1633 ed., 261)

> [He offered an honest exhibition (appointment), which I accepted, because I had my liberty entire; and although I did him services, and such peradventure that he could not expect from any other, yet I was not in the quality of a servant. He promised that he would always esteem me as a friend, wherefore I did put my self into his house. (Sorel, *Francion*, 1655 ed., 6:7)]

The allusions to freedom (*franchise*), equality, and friendship hide a more subversive truth. Because he can provide services to Clérante that few others could, the young poet ends up as the real master.

The most revealing episode in the dealings between the two characters occurs when Clérante recruits Francion to help him seduce Luce. When he is not able to see his beloved in person, he is forced to resort to letters and verse written by Francion. The latter proposes a letter that would permit Clérante to seduce Luce without compromising himself:

> Je luy dis que je ferois ce poulet d'une telle façon qu'en l'adressant à sa Maistresse, sa grandeur ne recevroit point de taches, qu'il tesmoignerait une affection plus gaillarde que serieuse. (Sorel, *Francion*, 1633 ed., 277)

> [I told him that I would draw up his Letter in such a fashion, that in addressing himself to his Mistresse, his greatnesse should receive no blemish, for he should shew a Spirit more frolick than serious. (Sorel, *Francion*, 1655 ed., 6:16)]

The key to this kind of *galanterie* is to *play at playing* a lover, to adopt the kind of amorous language that noblemen of the period used indiscriminately with ladies as a way of passing the time, but without any real intent to seduce them. This playful mask hides a real desire for sexual possession, offering the opportunity for pleasure at minimum risk.

The recourse to letters and verses—to a *written* form, that is—makes Clérante's rhetorical performance purely verbal. Without a corporeal support, he becomes a disembodied first person pronoun, detached from any physical person—a "virtual person," we might say today.[44] Clérante's eventual goal, of course, is physical enjoyment, which obviously requires bodies, but who is to say that the body that receives this enjoyment will necessarily be his? As a matter of fact, Luce immediately recognizes Francion's hand in the letters and love verses, and draws her own conclusion:

> [E]lle prisa grandement ce qu'il luy avoit *envoyé,* comme une piece très bien faite, et cognoissant au *style* qui ne luy estoit pas nouveau, et par beaucoup de conjectures, que j'en estois l'Autheur, elle m'affectionna au lieu d'affectionner celuy qui souspiroit pour elle. (Sorel, *Francion,* 1633 ed., 278; emphasis added)
>
> [She greatly esteemed what he had *sent* her, and did commend it for a very good piece, and knowing by the *style* that it was none of his own, she strongly conjectured that I was the Author, and loved me instead of loving him who breathed forth so many sighs for her. (Sorel, *Francion,* 1655 ed., 6:17; emphasis added)]

The key criterion in attributing authorship to a text is no longer the originating intent (on the part of the protector) or sincerity (*à la* Théophile), but rather *style* as recognized by a reader. Ideas and referential content are impersonal, subject to infinite reappropriation; style, by contrast, is a manifestation of personality, an unmistakable mark of the creative powers of an individual. If Luce is won over by Francion, it is because he has shown himself, through his words, capable of providing pleasure. If Clérante cannot perform verbally, she reflects, why should she expect him to perform physically? Francion's stylistic triumph over his master thus anticipates a much more savory *sexual* triumph.

Although capitalization practices in the seventeenth century are highly variable, it is tempting to take the fact that *Autheur* is capitalized in the text as an indication that more than the attribution of a couple of poems and letters is at stake here. Indeed Sorel, through Francion, has effectively reversed the traditional hierarchy of invention and elocution, thus redefining the very nature of authorship. As Roger Chartier has shown, this association between personality, form, and aesthetic pleasure provided the rationale for the emerging notion of authorial intellectual property in the eighteenth century. "They [defenders of literary property rights] argued that although ideas could be held in common and shared widely, the same was not true of the form in which the irreducible singularity of style and sentiment was expressed."[45] Luce's position would seem to anticipate a new understanding of authorial prerogative:

> [A]vez vous fait quelque vœu au Ciel, de ne parler jamais pour vous, et de ne procurer que le bien d'autruy? (Sorel, *Francion,* 1633 ed., 279)
>
> [Have you made a vow to Heaven to speak never for your self, but to procure good to others altogether? (Sorel, *Francion,* 1655 ed., 6:17)]

By sleeping with Luce, Francion takes this advice to heart and profits materially from his work, so to speak. Abandoning all pretext of loyalty to his protector, he concentrates on his own welfare.

[M]on plaisir ne me devoit-il pas toucher de plus près que celuy d'un autre? (Sorel, *Francion,* 1633 ed., 280)

[My own pleasure ought to be more near unto me, and I am to be more sensible of it, than of the pleasures of another. (Sorel, *Francion,* 1655 ed., 6:18)]

Over the last twenty-five years, the history of the emergence of a literary field in France has become a central preoccupation of literary historians and sociologists, including Pierre Bourdieu, Alain Viala, Daniel Roche, and Christian Jouhaud.[46] We have seen that Sorel, by suggesting that the writer can stand on his own outside of the traditional structures of patronage, anticipates this "autonomous" field. In *Francion,* however, the possibility of a new mode of authorship, like many other of Sorel's more daring ideas, remains at the level of pure fantasy. In a farcelike moment of implausibility reminiscent of Beaumarchais or Feydeau, the servant assumes the role of the master and insinuates himself into the latter's bed. Any substantive subversion that the figure of Francion embodies is tempered by the fact that his story is fictional and his pleasure must be enjoyed secretly: it is not Sorel who takes the risk of offending his patron, but Francion. Sorel's radical vision of authorship is couched in layers of satire, fiction, and irony.

Beyond the pleasure principle, moreover, there is no broader justification for his betrayal. Much later, in his *De la connoissance des bons livres* (1671), Sorel would couple disdain for those who seek to please grandees, with a more serious justification of writing for profit. "Those who disapprove of men of letters who write for profit, and who hold such a custom responsible for the proliferation of bad writers during the last century, should remember that we have also gained good ones, who would never have written if they had not been forced to do so by financial constraint."[47] In this more mature and serious work, the foundation for the claim to authorial legitimacy is not pleasure, but rather expertise and hard work. By manifesting these professional qualities, which Sorel's successors would repeatedly invoke in the eighteenth century, writers-for-profit distinguish themselves from the rich, who "needing nothing . . . put less care and investment into their work."[48] This notion of the dignity of literary labor is completely absent in *Francion*. As we have seen, the title character is reduced to the ambivalent gesture of secretly stealing from his master. This episode thus confirms Martine Debaisieux's astute observation that literature, in *Francion*, is consistently assimilated to theft and lawlessness. Without an institutional framework that recognizes his claims as legitimate, Francion is doomed to operate outside of the law, on the margins of society.[49]

The four authors analyzed in this chapter illustrate a wide range of responses to the problem of writing for others. Saint-Amant, Tristan, and Théophile all make a virtue of necessity, exploring the poet's protean ability to assimilate and integrate other voices. This solution does not come easily to everyone, however. Tristan's aesthetic of resonance, for example, is undermined by a practice of publication that introduces a note of dissonance into his poetry. And Théophile, we have seen, makes the uneasy dialectic between self-expression and the voice of the other one the central preoccupations of his late poetry. Sorel, finally, goes beyond the aesthetic appropriation of otherness, exploring the radical possibility of a writer-centered model of intellectual property, based on the criterion of style. While illustrating the collaborative nature of authorship in the early seventeenth century, these texts thus illustrate the tensions present in the literary field and look forward to new models of literature and authorship. It is important, however, to distinguish the tentative aspirations of the early seventeenth century from the confident self-assertions of Enlightenment and romantic writers.[50] Patronage culture weighs heavily on Saint-Amant, Tristan, Théophile, and Sorel, shaping and placing limits upon their authorial and poetic strategies.

5
The Public and Private Lives of the Theater

> Tous ceux qui se sentoient quelque génie, ne manquoient pas de travailler pour le Théatre: c'étoit le moyen d'approcher des Grands, & d'être favorisé du premier Ministre.
>
> [All those who thought they had a little talent did not fail to try their hands at the theater: it was the way to meet the powerful and curry favor with the prime minister.]
> —Paul Pellisson, *Histoire de l'Académie*

THE ROLE OF PATRONAGE IN THE DEVELOPMENT OF THE FRENCH CLASSI-cal stage is well documented. Every student of the period is at least dimly aware of Richelieu's personal involvement with the theater. Specialists in dramatic literature will know something of the contributions of other patrons, most notably the duc de Montmorency and the comte de Belin, as well. This notoriety of dramatic patronage should not, however, obscure what I would call the paradox of theatrical patronage. The theater is dominated by the public exchange between actors and audiences. Patronage, by contrast, is built on networks of particularistic, often private, relationships between patrons, brokers, and clients. It depends on personal favors, an awareness of individual temperament and taste, and a fine sense of tact. This is not to suggest, of course, that the publicity value of dramatic spectacle did not attract patrons to the stage. Richelieu, for one, recognized both the pedagogical and propagandistic function of theater—how it could be used to affirm political values such as royal authority and obedience while lending an aura of cultural prestige to the French monarchy.[1] My point, rather, is that this program depends on a public intelligibility. What about the patronage relationship itself, the particularistic bond between *protecteur* and *créature?* How was this relationship embedded in dramatic practice, if at all? Did patrons have a special relationship, as spectators and readers, with the plays they sponsored? This chapter seeks to examine the exchanges between the public and private lives of the French stage during its formative period. The first half will situate dramatic authors and patrons among the other players in seventeenth-century theatrical culture: actors, spectators, publishers, and readers. We will examine a range of authorial strategies, from the complete rejection of the theater (Maynard), to the fantasy of an exchange between poet and audience untainted by actors and patrons (Corneille), to a dramatic practice deeply implicated in patronage (Mairet). The second half will focus closely on two examples that illustrate how theatrical patronage was reconfigured and reimagined in the seventeenth century: Pierre Du Ryer's pastoral *Vendanges de Suresnes*, an allegory of authorship that pits the dramatic author (and his patron) against the vested interests of actors; and Richelieu's theatrical patronage, which anticipates a new, more bureaucratic model.

THE PARADOXES OF DRAMATIC AUTHORSHIP

In chapter 3, we saw how performance trumped authorship in court ballet. It mattered little who wrote the verses, which were often not even recited in the course of the ballet; the bulk of the attention of the spectators was turned, instead, to elements of spectacle (music, decor, and costumes) and the corporeal grace of the dancers. Public spectacle, of course, was central to the life of the *ancien régime* society, in general, and the royal court, in particular. It was through spectacle that kings, princes, cities, religious orders, guilds, and other individuals and corporations maintained their social rank and asserted symbolic power.[2] While writers might well play a role in such symbolic displays, by writing inscriptions or suggesting iconographic programs, their role was necessarily a secondary one. Center stage was occupied by the patron, whether a person or a corporation, and the trappings of spectacle. Accepting a commission of this sort might prove profitable for a writer (in terms of pensions and *gratifications*), but it offered little literary prestige.

Performance, moreover, significantly complicates our picture of collective authorship. In addition to *inventio* (the creation or selection of arguments), *dispositio* (organization), and *elocutio* (stylistic embellishment), each of which can be assigned to a different author, we must consider the aspects of rhetoric concerned with performance, namely *memoria* and *actio*. *Memoria* is exactly what the name suggests—the art of committing arguments and embellishments to memory so that they can be deployed in performance.[3] *Actio* consists primarily of vocal techniques and gesture. In rhetorical treatises, it is often considered the most difficult and challenging aspect of eloquence, and thus the mark of a true orator. Jean-Pierre Camus, for instance, refers to delivery as "the touchstone of the true and perfect orator" (*la pierre de touche du vray et parfaict Orateur*).[4] By handing their texts over to actors, whether amateur or professional, dramatic poets surrendered some of the most prestigious aspects of their verbal art.

It is thus not entirely surprising that we find voices of dissent amid the renewed interest in—and prestige of—the theater between 1625 and 1635. François Maynard, for instance, rejects a friend's advice that he write "comedies" (that is, dramatic works):

> Mon cher FLOTE, depuis deux ans
> Il n'est jour que tu ne me dies,
> Que je seray sans partisans,
> Si je ne fais des Comedies.
>
> Et que des Vers de moindre pris
> Que ceux que Neuf-germain compose,
> Sont admirez des bons Esprits,
> Dans la bouche de Belle-Rose.
>
> Ton sentiment choque le mien.
> Sçache que je n'en feray rien.
> Tes raisons ont beau me combatre.
>
> Ma Muse se voit de si loin,
> Que je diroy qu'il n'est pas besoin
> De la monter sur un Theatre.[5]
>
> [My dear Flote, for two years now,
> There has hardly been a day when you haven't told me
> That I will have no supporters,
> Unless I write comedies.
>
> And that verses of lesser worth
> Than those composed by Neufgermain,
> Are admired by connoisseurs,
> In Bellerose's mouth.
>
> Your sentiment shocks mine.
> Know that I have no intention of following your advice.
> And that it is no use to reason with me.

My muse is visible from so far away
That I can say that there is no need
To put it on a stage.]

Maynard's reasons for repudiating the theater seem to derive from the latter's spectacular/performative nature. By inserting himself or herself between the writer and the audience, the actor distorts the poetic text to such an extent that it becomes unrecognizable. Even the verse of a hack like Neufgermain can be made palatable if it is recited by Bellerose, the great leader of the *comédiens du roi* of the Hôtel de Bourgogne. Implicit in this critique is the notion of the theater as a form of mass entertainment that appeals to the senses, rather than to rational judgment. On the stage, the poetic text is little more than a *pretext* for an experience that is eminently popular and sensual. When Maynard boasts that his muse is visible from afar, the clear implication is that it does not require the physical immediacy on which the theater relies for its effects. Like his friend Guez de Balzac, Maynard opts for a strategy of distance rather than proximity, presenting himself as a gentleman-author, an outsider who forsakes the rewards and compromises inherent in literary self-promotion.

In an epistle to Balzac, he reiterates his rejection of the theater and its ostentation:

> Je n'écris que pour trois ou quatre
> Et suis un Modeste caché
> Qui fuit la pompe du Theatre.[6]
>
> [I write for only three or four persons,
> And am a humble, private person
> Who avoids the pomp of the stage.]

The choice is clear: on the one hand, an elite audience; on the other, the masses that patronize the public playhouses. The latter offer authors material advantages—although these, as we will see, were limited as well—but little prestige. As Maynard puts it in another sonnet, addressed to the Muses from atop Mount Parnassus,

> Je hay ce Mont. J'en veux descendre.
> Vous n'avez point de Favory,
> Que la faim ne force de vendre
> Ses Ouvrages à Mondory.[7]

[I hate this Mountain. I want to get down off it.
You have no Favorite,
Whom hunger does not force to peddle
His works to Mondory (leader of the Theater of the Marais).]

The writer who composes for the theater might be compared to the aspiring novelist who slums as a television screenwriter in Hollywood. His decision is comprehensible in commercial, but not artistic, terms.

As we have seen, Maynard spurned the commercial world of the theater. Those authors who opted to write for the stage found themselves negotiating a complex landscape of vested interests. First of all, they had to contend with the actors, who were both necessary partners and inevitable rivals. Then there was the theatergoing public, which was viewed variously as an arbiter of literary glory and a mob. A second public consisted of readers, including erudite literary critics, who necessarily applied a different set of criteria to the play. Finally Maynard, with his "three or four persons," hints at a third possible audience: the chosen few.

Discourses of Patronage in the *Querelle du Cid*

The most notorious statement on dramatic authorship during this period is Pierre Corneille's *Excuse à Ariste:*

> Je sçay ce que je vaux, et croy ce qu'on m'en dit:
> Pour me faire admirer je ne fais point de ligue,
> J'ay peu de voix pour moi, mais je les ay sans brigue,
> Et mon ambition, pour faire plus de bruit
> Ne les va point quester de Reduit en Reduit,
> Mon travail sans appuy monte sur le Theâtre,
> Chacun en liberté l'y blasme ou l'idolatre,
> Là sans que mes amis preschent leurs sentiments
> J'arrache quelque fois trop d'applaudissements,
> Là content du succès que le mérite donne
> Par d'illustres avis je n'éblouïs personne
> Je satisfaits ensemble et peuple et courtisans
> Et mes vers en tous lieux sont mes seuls partisans
> Par leur seule beauté ma plume est estimée
> Je ne dois qu'à moy seul toute ma Renommée,

Et pense toute fois, n'avoir point de rival
A qui je fasse tort en le traittant d'égal.⁸

[I know what I'm worth and believe what I'm told:
I don't need a faction to win acclaim,
I have few supporters, but they're not part of a cabal,
And my ambition, in order to create a buzz, does not go looking
For them from enclave to enclave.
My work appears on the stage without support,
Anyone can criticize or worship it.
There, without friends to exalt my work,
I sometimes receive too much applause.
There, satisfied with the fruits of merit,
I do not dazzle anyone with illustrious opinions.
I satisfy both the people and the courtiers
And everywhere my verses are my only partisans.
For their beauty alone my pen is admired.
I owe my fame to none but myself,
And nonetheless I believe that I have no rival,
Whom I cannot treat as a peer.]

Although Corneille situates his poetry within a theatrical context, alluding to the applause that it receives from theatergoers, his conception of dramatic practice is primarily textual. There is no mention of actors or of the spectacular elements of theatrical performance; instead, the dramatic text is the source of all value:

> Et mes vers *en tous lieux* sont mes *seuls* partisans
> Par leur *seule* beauté ma plume est estimée.
>
> [And *everywhere* my verses are my *only* partisans.
> For their beauty *alone* my pen is admired.]

The allusion to *ma plume* (my pen) suggests the priority of the written text over performance, while the *partout* (everywhere) serves a double purpose. It reinforces the point that Corneille's verses reign supreme even in the theater, on the actor's home turf, while at the same time serving notice that his poetry does not need the trappings of spectacle to be efficacious. This does not necessarily imply that Corneille's creation is purely textual; rather the text generates the theatrical effects that it needs, either on stage or in the imagination of a reader. Each spectator is thus able to apply his own critical reason:

> Chacun en liberté l'y blasme ou l'idolatre.
>
> [Anyone can criticize it or worship it.]

Without the interference of the actors, author and audience enter into a direct, unmediated relationship.[9]

If this unmediated relationship is possible, it is only in part because of the secondary role assigned to actors and spectacle. Corneille alludes to another potential source of interference:

> J'ay peu de voix pour moi, mais je les ay sans brigue,
> Et mon ambition, pour faire plus de bruit
> Ne les va point quester de Reduit en Reduit,
> Mon travail sans appuy monte sur le Theâtre.
>
> [I have few supporters, but they're not part of a cabal,
> And my ambition, in order to create a buzz, does not go looking
> For them from enclave to enclave.
> My work appears on the stage without support.]

Support (*appui*) could, and probably does, mean a number of things here: the backing of actors, salons, the Republic of Letters, and others. As we saw in chapter 1, however, *appui* is part of the vocabulary of patronage. It can refer either to an influential person, or to the influence and protection that such a person provides.[10] In addition to the specter of the seen (that is, spectacular), the dramatic author must also contend with the unseen. The reception of a dramatic text can be influenced by publicity campaigns that occur behind the scenes. In order to promote their plays, some writers are tempted to seek the support of prominent and influential figures. Rather than deferring to the critical judgment of the people and the courtiers, such dramatists deploy social and political pressure outside of their legitimate spheres so as to influence perceptions of aesthetic value.[11] Describing the effect of such a campaign, Corneille again uses the language of spectacle:

> Par d'illustres avis je n'éblouïs personne.
>
> [I do not dazzle anyone with illustrious opinions.]

Like the actors' performance, the intervention of powerful protectors can potentially dazzle public opinion, blinding it to the true merit of a dramatic poem. At stake, in sum, are the limits of writers' uses of social networks to promote their dramatic poems, and more generally the boundaries between social and literary practices.

There is reason to believe that Corneille was thinking specifically about the polite circles that heavily influenced public opinion during this period. For Furetière, *réduit* (cubbyhole, enclave) is a synonym of *salon*. "*Réduit*, is used to describe a place where several people get together to talk and entertain themselves. This lady's *ruelle*, her alcove is a pleasant *réduit* frequented by persons of good breeding." He goes on to quote Corneille's *Excuse*. "Corneille, discussing the solicitation of favorable reviews in his *Excuse à Ariste*, writes: 'And my ambition, in order to create a buzz, does not go looking/For them from enclave to enclave [*de réduit en réduit*]'." *Réduit*, like *ruelle* (a term closely associated with salons in the seventeenth-century spatial imagination), suggests a small or confined space, contrasted implicitly with the more open, public space of the theater.[12]

These observations fit into a larger critique of patronage within the *Excuse*. If Corneille has abandoned patronage, it is because patrons have abandoned poetry:

> La Parnasse autrefois dans la France adorée
> Faisoit pour ses mignons un autre aage doré . . .
> Mais elle est espuisée, et les vers à present
> Aux meilleurs du mestier n'apportent que du vent,
> Chacun s'en donne à l'aise et souvent se dispense
> A prendre par ses mains toute sa recompense.[13]

> [Once Parnassus, adored in France,
> Bestowed the favors of a Golden Age upon its favorites . . .
> But now it is spent and the best verses
> Earn poets nothing but hot air.
> Everyone gives himself a little and takes the liberty
> Of seizing his reward with his own hands.]

Here, Corneille picks up the familiar contrast between the Golden Age of patronage and the corrupt present. His nostalgia, however, is tempered with irony. While the term *mignon* suggests a certain material comfort, it also carries pejorative connotations of submissiveness and effeminacy. If the Golden Age of patronage is over, Corneille seems to be saying, then so be it. The assertive, virile figure of the autonomous writer, who boldly takes his reward "with his own hands," will fill the power vacuum nicely.

The *Excuse*'s claim to fame derives from its position as the inaugural document in the famous *querelle du Cid*, the defining literary event of the 1630s, if not the first half of the seventeenth century. Indeed, the quarrel had as much to do with the *Excuse*, and the attitude that Corneille assumed there, as with his famous tragicomedy. His bold attempt to carve out an authorial position that dispensed with both the intellectual authority of erudite critics and the social authority of prominent patrons set into motion a flurry of attacks and counterattacks that culminated with the *Sentiments de l'Académie française sur la tragédie du Cid*. Over the course of the polemic, Corneille and his critics would return repeatedly to his assertion that his work appeared on the stage "without support." In the critics' minds, this claim captured Corneille's presumptuous rejection of the traditional channels of cultural authority. As Georges de Scudéry famously put it, Corneille had deified himself on his own authority (*se Deifioit d'authorité privée*).[14]

Corneille's rival Jean Mairet appears to have taken Corneille's verses as a personal slight. In his *Épître familière*, he writes:

> You know that I am one of those people who are admitted into these honorable places to which you give such a funny name when you make fun of those who are received there:
>
> > And my ambition, in order to create a buzz, does not go looking
> > For them from enclave to enclave.
>
> You know, moreover, that the obliging curiosity that persons of intelligence and condition have expressed for our work sometimes gives me call, like many others, to enter the most dignified cabinets of Paris, which are the real schools where you and I could learn courtesy of manner and language, along with the propriety of content and form that we so often forget in our masterpieces. It is there, my good friend, that you are generally blamed [for not having corrected your play].[15]

Mairet reintroduces the social component of aesthetic judgment, implicitly set aside by Corneille. The relationships that a writer cultivates with aristocrats are valuable in that they give him access to "the most dignified cabinets of Paris"—the schools of politeness where taste and purity of language are acquired. Alluding to the criticism that *Le Cid* was disrespectful of the canons of moral propriety (*bienséance*), Mairet invokes the moral authority of those "persons of intelligence and condition" who blame Corneille for not expunging offensive material from his play. For Mairet, all audiences are not equal, nor are all judgments equivalent. Since good taste is the prerogative of the aristocratic elite, aesthetic hierarchies cannot be divorced from moral and social authority.

As the polemic degenerated, the problem of patronage and social influence continued to play a central role in the *ad hominem* attacks exchanged between the adversaries. The anonymous author of the *Lettre du Des-interessé* tried to put Mairet in his place by reminding him of his debt to the comte de Belin, who had received the poet in his household after the execution of his first benefactor, the duc de Montmorency. "But if the Parnassus is like paradise, where you cannot gain entry with ill-gotten gains, you must agree with everyone else that you will be excluded unless you make restitution of a large part of your reputation to a master whose excessive kindness was not limited to welcoming you into his house during the worst of your misery, but who also encouraged his friends to speak favorably about your works. It is him alone, and not the merit of your works, that you have to thank for the little esteem that you possess."[16] Like heaven, the Parnassus (the literary field) is set apart from the world of human competition. The anonymous author highlights this point by playing on the double signification of works (*œuvres*), which could be taken to mean both "works of literature" and Christian "good works." Good works, of course, are individual, at least in principle. No one else can perform them for you and they only count if they are done voluntarily. The influence exercised through patronage, by contrast, is both borrowed ("It is him alone . . . that you have to thank for the little esteem that you possess") and coercive ("[he] encouraged his friends to speak favorably about your works").

Hélène Merlin has analyzed the political language of legitimacy and tyranny that underlies the quarrel.[17] In the *Lettre du Des-interessé*, it is the transfer of authority from the social sphere to the sphere of aesthetic judgment that raises the specter of illegitimacy. Aristocrats may deserve our deference in social, even political matters; they cannot, however, create aesthetic value *ex nihilo*. In the realm of literary glory, who you are (as an author) should be entirely independent of whom you know. The *Advertissement au Besançonnois Mairet* continues this line of attack, insinuating that Mairet's dramatic successes are the result of his cultivation of powerful patrons. To win applause, he cynically trades in occasional sonnets and compliments. "Your petty little dealings are well-known. You buy all of your applause with sonnets and compliments."[18] This attachment to patronage, the *Advertissement* suggests, is a legacy of Mairet's lack of creativity and financial penury.

Defending Mairet, the anonymous author of the *Apologie pour M. Mairet* responds that poverty is not inherently ignoble. Indeed Mairet, he claims, has spent more on clothing and licit pleasures (*honnestes desbauches*) than Corneille paid for his magnificent office. Acknowledging the fruits that Mairet has reaped from patronage, he argues that these favors are not substitutes for merit, but rather a sign of it. "You must acknowledge that this success in managing without either an inheritance or mischief is proof of his merit, just as your petty fortune is proof of your good luck and the obscure stinginess of your parents, who would have left you in difficulty if they had been inclined, by desire or by birth, to live nobly like the father of my friend."[19] Merit is not a matter of laboriously accumulating wealth but rather of living generously—without concern for the cost of maintaining a dignified lifestyle. It is thus more proper to accept the benevolence of patrons (such as Montmorency and Belin) than to amass a fortune through avarice or to buy a public office. The conflict between Corneille and Mairet, in sum, revolves around two contrasting notions of merit. Whereas the former places the emphasis on independent achievement, the latter stresses aristocratic taste and aloofness.

The stakes of this debate were not purely discursive. At least twice during the quarrel, the influence of prominent patrons was invoked to intimidate Corneille and his allies. In his *Lettre apologitique*, Corneille alludes to letters from Scudéry that accuse him of having offended "a person of condition." Henri Chardon, in his study of Rotrou, has identified this individual as the comte de Belin, Mairet's patron and the protector of the Théâtre du Marais (see below).[20] Chardon attributes Belin's hostility to Corneille to the latter's decision to publish *Le Cid* almost immediately after its first run, depriving the Marais company of its customary monopoly by making the text available to other companies. Assuming that Chardon's hypothesis is correct, the claims of the *Excuse* must have added insult to injury. In particular, the assertion of the primacy of text over performance could easily be seen as a justification of Corneille's violation of his tacit contract with the actors. The playwright, however, prudently refused to play this game, responding that he had no intention of offending the person in question. "Although I apparently lack judgment, if you are to be believed, I am not so foolish as to offend a person of such high condition."[21]

A similar accusation was published by Mairet in his *Épître familière*, where he insinuated that the anonymous *Lettre pour monsieur de Corneille contre les mots de la lettre sous le nom d'Ariste* had targeted a person of quality from Corneille's province, assumed to be the author of another letter in the quarrel. The rank of this person, according to Mairet, was so elevated that Corneille was obliged to seek his pardon so as to avoid disgrace. A later, rather scurrilous piece alludes to Corneille narrowly escaping a beating (*bastonnade*) from a "person of condition" as a result of this episode.[22] The person of condition is referred to as "Faucon," identified by Chardon as Jean-Louis Faucon de Ris, seigneur de Charleval.[23] Regardless of whether the episode in question is historical or apocryphal, it suggests the social forces that were mobilized in the quarrel. In their attacks, Mairet and his allies sought to move the debate into an arena where Corneille would be forced to respond to his social superiors. As we have seen, Corneille resisted this strategic maneuver, as least until the intervention of Richelieu and his French Academy (see chapter 6).

The differences between Corneille and Mairet should not be exaggerated, however. Corneille, by either election or necessity, would soon take a softer line toward patronage, famously dedicating *Horace* to Richelieu and *Cinna* to the financier Montauron, and taking a room at the Hôtel de Guise toward the end of his career.[24] Mairet, for his part, was perfectly capable of satirizing patronage while reaping its benefits.[25] In the end, the opposing discourses of Corneille and Mairet in the quarrel are largely attributable to their economic and social positions at the time. Corneille was a royal officer (an *avocat du roi*), which meant that his material welfare was well established. In 1637, moreover, his father was granted a title of nobility, enhancing the son's social standing by giving him an additional *quartier de noblesse*. Although he could still benefit from the protection of powerful aristocrats, Corneille was thus in a relatively autonomous financial and social position, which goes a long way toward explaining his relatively independent authorial stance. Mairet's situation, by contrast, was much more precarious. Lacking a remunerative profession, his welfare was closely dependent on patrons whose protection and beneficence he managed to win, most notably the duc de Montmorency and comte de Belin. He thus provides an exemplary case study of the effects of patronage on dramatic practice.

Between the Hôtel de Montmorency and the Hôtel de Bourgogne: Jean Mairet and His Patrons

Mairet's early theater is strongly marked by the influence of Montmorency. Although *Chryséide et Arimand* bears no dedication, critics have commented on the influence of the duke and his entourage at Chantilly on the play's liberal ideas, particularly its assertive individualism and flirtation with religious freethinking.[26] The political subtext becomes more explicit in Mairet's second play, *La Sylvie*. By affirming the individual's right to marry for love rather than for dynastic reason, this *pièce à clé* takes the side of Montmorency's ally Gaston d'Orléans against Richelieu and Louis XIII in the political battle over Gaston's proposed marriage to Marie de Montpensier.[27] The dedication to Montmorency, moreover, extends the general spirit of aristocratic liberalism to the protection of writers. "Where will we find a lord other than you who, in the corruption of our times, is still so enamored of good letters that he establishes pensions for them on the most reliable part of his income [*le plus clair de son revenue*]? All France saw what you did for one of the finest minds [of our century], who was only able to prove his innocence thanks to your protection."[28] The duke is presented as the antithesis of the tyrannical king of the play. He is a liberal-minded lover of good letters, willing to expend both material and social capital on behalf of authors in need. The unnamed author is of course Théophile de Viau, who had been Mairet's mentor and predecessor as Montmorency's household poet. It can hardly be coincidental that the title of the play echoes the title of Théophile's famous hymn to the Montmorencys' generosity (see chapter 4 on *La Maison de Silvie*).

La Silvanire is probably the most intriguing example of the intersection of patronage and stagecraft in Mairet's work. The genesis of the play, the first in the seventeenth century to put the dramatic unities and proprieties (*bienséances*) into practice, is explained in a preface addressed to the comte de Cramail (Montmorency's lieutenant, an enemy of Richelieu, and a former disciple and protector of the executed libertine Vanini). "Perhaps two years ago, you and Cardinal La Valette persuaded me to compose a pastoral with all of the rigor that the Italians customarily bring to this pleasant genre."[29] The case of *La Silvanire* illustrates the extent to which aristocratic tastes influenced the direction of seventeenth-century drama. The decisive impetus behind the unities came not only from literary critics, but also from a desire to emulate the refinement of Italian manners and culture, as reflected in the Italian pastoral. Giovanni Dotoli has convincingly demonstrated the Italianophile connections of the main players in this story. Cardinal La Valette was one of the central figures of Madame de Rambouillet's salon, where Italian influences were strong—owing, in part, to the hostess's Italian origins. The court at Chantilly had a strong Italian flavor, as well. In particular, Maria Felicia Orsini, Montmorency's wife (and the Silvie of Théophile's *Maison de Silvie*), was herself of Italian birth. As Dotoli has pointed out, her Italian relations had protected both Torquato Tasso and Giovanni Battista Guarini, the author of the *Pastor fido*, a regular Italian pastoral that influenced Mairet and other French authors.[30]

The example of *La Silvanire* illustrates the dynamic role played by patronage in introducing literary innovation. Contrary to a common misconception, the dramatic unities did not come into French theater through a conspiracy between royal power (in the hands of Richelieu) and academic pedants, but rather, as Henry Carrington Lancaster and Antoine Adam pointed out long ago, through the intervention of Richelieu's aristocratic enemies.[31] Erudite debates around the dramatic rules between the likes of Jean Chapelain and François Ogier could only go so far; if dramatic practice was to change, social energies would have to be mobilized that would overcome the inertia of acting companies and theatrical audiences.

Commenting on the length of *La Silvanire* in his preface to the play, Mairet wrote that "as for its length, it is true that it is a little longer than average, and since I composed it for the Hôtel de Montmorency rather than for the Hôtel de Bourgogne, I did not worry too much about how long it was."[32] The comparison between the two *hôtels* has an ironic edge. By the early seventeenth century, the term *hôtel* was by and large reserved for aristocratic or princely residences (such as the Hôtel de Montmorency); its presence in the name of a public playhouse (the Hôtel de Bourgogne) conforms to an earlier, broader usage. In other words, whereas the Hôtel de Bourgogne is a *hôtel* in name only, the Hôtel de Montmorency is an aristocrat's townhouse and thus a legitimate source of social value. As described by Mairet, *La Silvanire* is a new, more demanding kind of play, written, in part at least, for a different kind of audience—the discerning, elite members of Montmorency's circle. According to this logic, which sheds light on Mairet's position in the quarrel, writing for an enlightened patron offers the writer a paradoxical margin of freedom, liberating him from the necessity of catering to the short attention span of popular audiences. Although it runs counter to our modern tendency of equating patronage with limitations on artistic freedom, there is no reason why we should not take Mairet's claim seriously. Artistic freedom is a slippery and relative concept. After all, as many a contemporary writer can attest, the public can be an unforgiving and intransigent master.

The dynamic link between patronage and poetic creation is echoed in the dedication of *La Silvanire* to Maria Felicia Orsini (the duchesse de Montmorency). "I have always considered my Silvanire as a beauty whom I raised in order to appear one day before the eyes of one of the most virtuous and perfect ladies in the world. Considering this, I was not so overly concerned with making her beautiful that I forgot that she should be virtuous, so that she could be worthy of appearing before you."[33] Following a common convention of dedications, Mairet equates the protagonist of his play (the character Silvanire) with the play itself (*La Silvanire*). Just as La Valette and Cramail provide Mairet with an aesthetic model to which he could aspire, the duchess serves as his model of physical and moral perfection. It is the thought of her judgment that guides him as he crafts his play, much as a father might raise a daughter to appear before a court lady. Even when the play is described as being successful with the "people," the protection of the patron is invoked. "She [*La Silvanire*] has learned from the mouths of the people [*la voix du peuple*] the fortunate and warm reception her elder sister, the shepherdess Sylvie, had enjoyed under Milord's protection. She expects nothing less from yours."[34] Although the causal logic of the sentence is ambiguous, the positive reception of *La Sylvie* is as much a token of the people's good will toward Montmorency as toward Mairet and his work.

In contrast to spectators and critics, guided by opinion (*doxa*) rather than sound principles, a single enlightened individual provides the poet with a clear sense of artistic direction. "I swear to you, Madame (and I say it without flattery), that the sole esteem that you accord to my work will determine the good or bad opinion that I have of it . . . It has repeatedly been observed that your mind, which is not weighed down by any kind of matter, possesses a remarkable sense of judgment that is superior to the judgment invoked by the 'experts' of our time who evaluate things according to their own opinions."[35] Here, Mairet puts his own spin on two related trends in the seventeenth century: the Cartesian appeal to individual reason and the increased emphasis placed on the literary tastes of aristocrats and *honnêtes gens*.³⁶

Like the theoretical preface to *La Silvanire*, finally, the dedication ties the value of the play to a private, residential space. This time, however, it is not the Hôtel de Montmorency that is evoked, but rather the duke's château at Chantilly. "To conclude, Madame, here is that MORTE VIVE [living dead, literally] who must now pass from the shady park of your magnificent house at Chantilly to the bright stage of the court [*la clarté de la cour*], where it is important, as you know, to make a graceful entrance."³⁷ Together with the preface addressed to Cramail, the dedication suggests an imaginary topography of concentric circles. At the center is the personal relationship between writer and patron/protector, in which the latter provides the model from which the literary work is generated. The next level is the immediate social *milieu* of the patron, and by extension, the writer. Taken together, Chantilly (the rural château) and the Hôtel de Montmorency (the urban mansion) provide a protective, aristocratic backdrop for the initial performances of the play before the duke's entourage. From there, the play moves to the more public arena of the court, where it is performed before Montmorency's peers. Literary authority radiates out from the person of the patron. Only at the end, almost as an afterthought, does the play reach the general public of the playhouse.

After Montmorency's execution in 1632 for plotting against the crown, Mairet sought out the protection of other influential patrons of the theater, including François II d'Averton, comte de Belin, whom we have already encountered in conjunction with the *querelle du Cid*. Belin was not a grandee of the stature of Montmorency, and he did not provide the playwright with a long-term position within his household or a regular pension.³⁸ Mairet referred to him as a "friend" and such is generally the role that Belin played with respect to both playwrights and actors (such as Montdory).³⁹ According to Guérin de La Pinelière, Belin welcomed Mairet and other men of letters into his home. "In his household, he has two of the most beautiful and most eloquent muses who appear upon the stage [Mairet and Rotrou]. Instead of hosting a group of braggarts, hooligans, and brutes, as men of his condition typically do, he has attracted the finest minds and assembled a little court of poets."⁴⁰ Through his hospitality and connections to both political power and culturally influential salon circles (such as the Hôtel de Rambouillet), Belin helped create an intellectual and cultural climate that lent dignity to dramatic authors and actors.[41]

Mairet spent six years under Belin's protection, until the latter's death in 1638. During this period, the playwright, who could undoubtedly sense which way the wind was blowing, turned his sights on Montmorency's old nemesis, Richelieu. Using Chapelain and Conrart as intermediaries, he mended his relationship with Boisrobert, whom he had offended during his Montmorency days.[42] According to Tallemant, Boisrobert urged the cardinal to grant Mairet a pension on the grounds that he would win points with the ladies.[43] Richelieu obliged, giving him a pension of 200 *écus*. Mairet thus joined the company of Corneille and Rotrou, also protegés of the cardinal. With his journey from aristocratic resistance (Montmorency) to official conformity (Richelieu), Mairet exemplifies the broader trend toward the consolidation of state control of patronage during this period (see the end of this chapter).

The Private Life of the Theater

Mairet's career provides some suggestions as to how we might write a history of the private life of early seventeenth-century theater. As we have seen, Mairet attributed the length of his *Silvanire* to the fact that it was written for the Hôtel de Montmorency rather than the Hôtel de Bourgogne. His implication, we saw, was that aristocrats had more patience than popular audiences and could therefore handle more challenging material.[44] In fact, theatrical performances in private residences appear to have been quite common during this period. Numerous instances of the phenomenon have been documented: from a visit by the *comédiens du roi* to Montmorency's country palace at Chantilly in 1626; to performances of *Le Cid*, *L'Amour tyrannique*, and the work of the "Five Authors" at the private residence of Richelieu; to a production of Théophile's *Pyrame et Thisbé* for/by Mme de Rambouillet and her friends, to name but a few.[45] Lancaster, moreover, has compiled a list of the numerous references in Héroard's *Journal* to theatrical performances at court during the reign of Louis XIII. While not exactly private, performances at court were not entirely public, either. We must consider, finally, that plays were often read out loud in intimate settings, sometimes before they were publicly performed.[46]

As we observed in the case of *La Silvanire*, dedicatory epistles can similarly reorient the intelligibility of dramatic works. With the movement from stage to page, the meanings of "audience" and "performance" are inflected. Whereas the actors address themselves to their spectators, to the public space of the playhouse, the dedication to a printed work posits the patron as its privileged audience. This is not to say, of course, that the patron is the *only* audience. It would be more accurate to say that a dedication functions as the public display of a private relationship. The writer *performs* his relationship with one audience (the patron) in front of another (the broader reading public).

In a probing reading of Pierre Corneille's dedication to his tragedy *Horace*, Christian Jouhaud has demonstrated how this text constructs a complicity between the dramatist and the cardinal—an exchange between literature and power.[47] By evoking the scene of a private reading (*récit*) of *Horace* for Richelieu in his *cabinet*, Corneille strips the dramatic art down to the text and its effects, bypassing the mediation of a public performance and the appropriation of the play by actors and stage designers. Attuned to the seductive effects of the theater and to its political uses, Richelieu serves as the perfect audience:

> [L]isant sur son visage ce qui lui plaît et ce qui ne lui plaît pas, nous nous instruisons avec certitude de ce qui est bon et de ce qui est mauvais, et tirons des règles infaillibles de ce qu'il faut suivre et de ce qu'il faut éviter.[48]

> [By reading the signs of pleasure and displeasure in his countenance, we learn with certainty what is good and what is deficient, and from this we deduce infallible rules for what we should and should not do.]

The signs of pleasure on the cardinal's face are a testimony to the efficacy of Corneille's stagecraft, to his mastery of the secrets of dramatic art. The playwright does not, however, reveal what these secrets might be or offer any theory of theatrical representation. What is important, rather, is the *relationship* between writer and patron—a relationship that provides Corneille with recognition of his elevated status as dramatic author.

Jouhaud's argument depends on a rather tenuous lexical reading. When Corneille refers to the *récit de nos poèmes*, he takes this as meaning that the playwright read *Horace* to the cardinal in private. Such examples, as we have seen, were not unusual and constitute another chapter in the private life of the theater in seventeenth-century France.[49] Although this could be Corneille's meaning, the language of the passage is hardly clear and the *récit de nos poèmes* could simply refer to recitation by the actors on stage. For our purposes, however, it hardly matters whether Corneille is talking about a private reading or a public performance. What is significant is the importance attributed to the reaction of an individual audience member:

> Vous avez ennobli le but de l'art, puisqu'au lieu de celui de plaire au peuple que nous prescrivent nos maîtres . . . vous nous avez donné celui de vous plaire et vous divertir.[50]

> [You have ennobled the goal of art, for instead of having to please the people, as our masters instruct us . . . You have given us the higher calling of pleasing and entertaining you.]

As we have seen, this notion that the success of a play depends on a single audience member, or a small number of spectators, is a recurring *leitmotif* in seventeenth-century dramatic dedications, reflecting the aspiration of playwrights to elevate theater above its popular origins.[51]

Another factor is the evolution of staging practices. The growing popularity of Italian-style theaters (*la scène à l'italienne*), especially with the construction of the *salle de la comédie* of the Palais Cardinal in 1641, offers a model of patronage intelligibility within the larger context of public performance.[52] The *décor multiple,* in which different locations were represented simultaneously on the stage, had been equally intelligible to spectators occupying different positions in the playhouse. By contrast, the *trompe l'œil* illusion provided by the single-point perspective of the *scène à l'italienne* implied an ideal vantage point, a *place royale* to be occupied by the prince. In his 1638 treatise on stage design, Sabbattini describes this position as follows:

> It seems reasonable to me, after having described the stage setting, to discuss how and in what position should be located the seat of the prince or other dignitary who is to witness the performance. You will have to choose a location as near as possible to the point of distance, and elevated sufficiently from the floor of the hall so that when seated his eye will be as high as the vanishing point, for all the objects in the scene appear better from that position than from any other place. You then make a kind of palisade, fixed to the ground with strong beams and se-

cured with stout pegs and nailed, so that the crowd of people, who on these occasions show little discretion, cannot injure it.[53]

Above and apart from the crowd, the prince became not only the sole ideal spectator of a play, but also the very condition of its existence. Without the eye of the patron, who provides a stable ("fixed to the ground") and unique position, there would be no mathematically perfect illusion. Timothy Murray has described this mechanism at work during the performance of Desmarets de Saint-Sorlin's *Mirame* in Richelieu's *salle de la comédie*. "The cardinal's dais, located in the middle of the *salle* and centered by the proscenium arch, placed Richelieu in the only position of perfect perspective in the house. For the other spectators, the theatrical experience was directed away from the stage toward the one point in the playhouse from which the perspective achieved its greatest effect. They could enjoy the vanishing point only by imagining how it must look from Richelieu's place."[54] For Murray, Richelieu's unique position within the playhouse functions as a simulacrum of the prince's privileged epistemological position in the absolutist imaginations (all-seeing, all-knowing, and thus all-powerful). Although the *salle de la comédie* was not open to the public, it provided a model that other theater designers followed.[55]

Patronage Behind the Scenes: Du Ryer's *Les Vendanges de Suresnes*

In the following pages, I will explore this personal dimension of seventeenth-century theater in a theatrical plot—Pierre Du Ryer's pastoral comedy *Les Vendanges de Suresnes* (1636), dedicated to César de Vendôme.[56] Through a close reading of the play, I will examine the relationship between authorship and performance and its implications for a poetics of patronage. In particular, I will show how the play dramatizes the various ways in which dramatic texts communicate with different kinds of audiences—spectators, readers, and others. Du Ryer, I will argue, bases his authority as dramatic author not on his relationship with the theatrical audience, but rather on his personal bond with the "audience of one" represented by the patron.

In *Les Vendanges de Suresnes,* Du Ryer sets an essentially pastoral plot in a historical context: the place is Suresnes, famous in the seventeenth century for its vineyards and a favorite country retreat for bourgeois families from nearby Paris who owned property there. With the exception of Palmédor (a noble) and Guillaume and Lisette (who are villagers), the protagonists all ostensibly share a Parisian, middle-class background. This social framework is relatively superficial, however. On the one hand, the characters speak the fashionable gallant language of Parisian polite society; on the other, they conform more or less to the familiar pastoral typology of lovers. Polidor is the Céladon of the play, the perfect lover who admires his mistress, Dorimène, from afar. He has two rivals for her affection, the rich and cynical Tirsis and Palmédor (the aforementioned noble). On the female side, the inconstant Florice, Tirsis's former love-interest, is in love with Polidor. Dorimène's parents, finally, have their own agendas. Her mother, Doripe, is a sort of female M. Jourdain, eager to use her daughter's marriage to advance her social pretensions:

> On ne sçauroit trouver de plus grande richesse,
> Qu'en la possession de la seule noblesse.[57]
>
> [One cannot find any greater riches
> Than the possession of true nobility.]

The father, Crisère, is much more down to earth:

> Un homme est assez noble alors qu'il a de l'or. (Du Ryer, 49)
>
> [A man is noble enough if he has gold.]

Polidor, however, is neither rich (like Tirsis) nor of noble birth (like Palmédor) and thus his aspirations meet with the opposition of both parents. This indeterminate social status will prove important in our reading of the play.

The plot is structured around a series of courtships by proxy, in which one character delegates the advancement of his or her amorous interests to another. Tirsis sends Philémon to speak to Dorimène's father on his behalf; Florice's confidante Lisette invites Polidor to a social gathering on the false pretext that Dorimène will be there; and the timid Polidor asks his unbeknownst rival Tirsis to approach Dorimène and, as Polidor puts it:

>   Monstrer à Dorimene
>   Que ses yeux ont esté l'auteur de ma peine.
>
>   [Show Dorimène
>   That her eyes are the author of my torment.]

The last of these episodes illustrates the problematic nature of performance and spectatorship within the play. Pledging to help Polidor in act 1, scene 3, Tirsis invokes the authority of visual evidence:

> Amy, je te promets de t'ayder au besoin
> Et je veux que ton *œil* te serve de *tesmoin*. (Du Ryer, 11; emphasis added)
>
> [Friend, I promise to help you if you need me
> Let your eyes be your witnesses.]

Polidor is thus literally cast as an eyewitness (*témoin oculaire*): he will watch Tirsis court Dorimène on his behalf. Lest he doubt that Tirsis has his best interests at heart, he need only believe his eyes. When Dorimène arrives, Tirsis hides Polidor behind a rock, close enough to see Dorimène's reactions, but just out of earshot, provoking Polidor to complain:

>   Je n'entendray pas ma grace ou ma disgrace. (Du Ryer, 14)
>
>   [I will not hear my favor or disgrace.]

Tirsis again appeals to visual evidence:

>   Voy ce qu'elle fera, ses seules actions
>   Te pourront tesmoigner de ses intentions. (Du Ryer, 15)
>
>   [Watch what she does, her actions alone
>   Will reveal her intentions to you.]

Now that he has Polidor exactly where he wants him, Tirsis takes advantage of the occasion to court Dorimène for himself. With Polidor looking on, he engages her in a verbal sparring match, assuming the traditional role of the unrequited lover who implores his cruel mistress to abandon her rigors. Tirsis's pleading, however, has no effect on Dorimène (who is in fact in love with Polidor). Indeed, when he attempts to take her hand, she angrily withdraws and leaves the stage. Polidor, predictably, misinterprets the whole scene from his observation post, taking Dorimène's cool response as a rejection of *his* advances, a (mis)interpretation which Tirsis soon reinforces. Through a series of *double entendres,* the rest of the scene uses Polidor's misapprehension to comic effect. Tirsis assures Polidor:

> Sçache que j'ay parlé de mesme que pour moy
> [Be assured that I spoke as I would have for myself]

adding:

> Je m'offre à te servir comme j'ay desja fait. (Du Ryer, 20–21)
> [I offer to continue serving you as I have already done.]

Polidor responds:

> J'entreprendray pour toy ce que tu viens de faire
> [I will do for you what you have done for me]

provoking a hasty rejoinder from Tirsis:

> Je ne merite rien n'ayant rien fait pour toy. (Du Ryer, 21)
> [I don't deserve anything since I haven't done anything.]

The episode serves as a kind of cautionary tale about visual spectacle. Polidor is the victim of a theatrical illusion, a "play within the play" staged by Tirsis.[58] His vulnerability derives from his passivity—his willingness to assume the role of a spectator and to delegate his interests to other actors. This metatheatrical dimension of *Les Vendanges* is explicit elsewhere in the play, most notably in the next scene, when Tirsis comments to Philémon that his stratagem was

> Un trait assez plaisant pour une comedie (Du Ryer, 23)

> [A ploy worthy of a comedy]

Against other commentators, who have tended to interpret such allusions as poorly integrated nods to the audience, I would like to suggest that they are central to our understanding of how the play dramatizes its own intelligibility.[59] This point will become clearer as we examine a second key episode, which extends from the end of the second act through the entirety of the third act. Now that Polidor has discovered Tirsis's treachery and Dorimène's love, he is confronted with a new obstacle. After discovering an anonymous letter of denunciation penned by Florice, Dorimène's parents have forbidden her to see not only Polidor, but any member of his household. Polidor and Dorimène are thus denied the age-old solution of star-crossed lovers: the clandestine exchange of letters. Polidor, nevertheless, comes up with a novel solution:

Polidor
Mais je viens de trouver un moyen pour escrire
Sans que les plus subtils y trouvent rien à dire.
Dorimène
Comment donc?
Polidor
        Je feindray d'aimer auprès d'Autueil
Une jeune beauté qui me fait bon accueil,
Phillis sera son nom . . .
Dorimène
        Je ne vous puis comprendre.
Polidor
Quatre mots seulement me peuvent faire entendre,
Sous ce nom de Phillis, je traceray des vers
Que je sçauray donner en mille endroits divers,
Tant de monde en aura par tout dans le village
Que vous les pourrez voir sans donner de l'ombrage.
Là vous reconaistres que ma fidelité
Semblable à vos beautez n'a rien de limité. (Du Ryer, 57–58)

[**Polidor**
But I have just found a way of writing
That will escape the reproach of the nosiest persons.
Dorimène
How?
Polidor
        I will pretend to love a young beauty
From Auteuil who welcomes my advances.
Phillis will be her name . . .
Dorimène
        I don't get it.
Polidor
I can explain myself in a few words.
Under the name "Phillis," I will write verses
That I will distribute in a thousand different places.

So many people in the village will have them
That you will be able to see them without disgrace.
There you will discover that my fidelity,
Like your beauty, is unlimited.]

The lesson of Tirsis's treachery has not been lost on Polidor, who now deploys a strategy of dissimulation to his own ends, inventing the fiction of an Auteuil beauty as a cover for his courtship of Dorimène. The success of his stratagem depends on a kind of publication, evident in expressions such as *en mille endroits divers* (in a thousand different places) and *tant de monde* (so many people). This publication simultaneously enables and disguises private exchange. On the one hand, by widely disseminating his verses, he guarantees that they will reach Dorimène. On the other hand, the very public nature of their dissemination, coupled with the fiction of Phillis, serves to veil their true, private meaning.

Polidor's choice of diction is suggestive. He has found *un moyen pour escrire*, a mode of writing that depends on indirection—a kind of public mask, so to speak—for its efficacy. Between the first and third acts, Polidor's itinerary has thus taken him from the status of mere spectator to that of writer. Tirsis confirms this transformation in act 3, scene 2, when Polidor reads him his verses, joking that "Polidor est Poëte" (Du Ryer, 66). Polidor is careful, however, to distinguish himself from the greater mass of writers:

Polidor
                    Amour ma fait conaistre
Qu'un veritable Amant est tout ce qu'il veut estre;
Mais si je faits des vers, c'est pour me faire aimer,
Et non pas Philémon pour me faire estimer,
Le nombre est assez grand de ces melancoliques,
Qui cherchent par leurs vers des loüanges publiques. (Du Ryer, 66; emphasis added)

[**Polidor**
                    Love has taught me
That a true lover is whatever he wishes;
But if I write verse, it is to win love
And not, Philémon, esteem.
There are already enough melancholics
Who try to garner public praise with their poetry.]

The ensuing discussion between Polidor, Tirsis, and Philémon further develops the distinction between two kinds of audience:

Philémon.
À propos, l'autre jour je m'y trouvay surpris,
Et comme prisonnier entre *ces beaux esprits:*
La piece qu'on joüoit estoit incomparable,
Les plus judicieux la trouvoient admirable:
Toutesfois *ces rimeurs moins doctes qu'envieux*
N'y pouvoient rien trouver qui ne fust ennuyeux.
L'un faisoit de l'habile (& pour moy je m'en moque)
L'autre disoit tout haut cette rime me choque,
Ce mot n'est pas François, & m'estonne comment
On luy vient de donner tant d'applaudissement.
Ainsi parlent ces gens dont l'esprit populaire
Ne sçauroit rien souffrir comme il ne peut rien faire. (Du Ryer, 68–69; emphasis added)

[Philémon
By the way, the other day, I was trapped
Like a prisoner between two of these *so-called experts:*
The play being performed was without peer,
The most discerning found it admirable.
Nevertheless, *those ignorant but jealous rhymers*
Found things to criticize everywhere.
One of them tried to be subtle (but I'm not easily impressed),
Another said aloud "that rhyme shocks my sensibilities.
That word isn't even French. I'm surprised
That he is receiving so much applause."
See how *these people, with their vulgar tastes,*
Are as narrow–minded as they are untalented.]

This scene is a testimony to the dramatic increase in the popularity of theater in French society during the 1630s, particularly in aristocratic circles. Speaking through his characters, Du Ryer advances an elite conception of literature in which the judgment of the happy few (*les plus judicieux*) is more valued than public accolades or the approbation of semiprofessional critics and other writers. Although Du Ryer's voice is clearly audible here, it is important to remember that the conversation takes place against a narrative background that reinforces its message. Unbeknownst to Tirsis and Philémon, Polidor's stratagem similarly implies a distinction between two audiences, a privileged audience (Dorimène) who alone possesses the requisite knowledge to penetrate the real signification of his verses and an ignorant audience that takes them at face value (Philémon, Tirsis, Dorimène's parents, and all of the other inhabitants of Suresnes).

Eager to exploit an opportunity to sow discord between the two lovers, Tirsis grabs Polidor's verses and heads off to show them to Dorimène, which he does in act 3, scene 4. Since the verses are in fact intended for Dorimène, Polidor has effectively made Tirsis his unwitting messenger:

> Dieux! qui pourroit me nuire & me desobliger,
> Si mesme mon rival se rend mon messager! (Du Ryer, 70)

> [Heavens! who will be able to hurt and disoblige me,
> If even my rival becomes my messenger!]

Pursuing the metatheatrical analogy, Tirsis now becomes Polidor's actor, delivering the text to its audience. In fact, this is precisely how Polidor describes Tirsis in act 3, scene 5:

Guillaume
Il a monstré . . .
Polidor
   Des vers . . .
Guillaume
      dont il vous dit l'Auteur.
Polidor
J'ay composé la piece il n'en est que l'Acteur. (Du Ryer, 80)

[**Guillaume**
He showed [her] . . .
Polidor
   Some verses . . .
Guillaume
      He said you were the Author.
Polidor
I composed the play, he is but the Actor.]

Polidor has complely turned the tables on Tirsis, who is no longer in control of the spectacle in which he is an actor. Clearly, the authority for the intelligibility of dramatic practice is no longer vested in the actor, but rather in the dramatic author who constructs meaning behind the scenes. The privileged interpreter, similarly, is no longer the public (the village), but rather the informed reader who knows how to decipher and appreciate the equivocal authorial sign (Dorimène).

The rivalry between Polidor and Tirsis can be read as an allegory for the rivalries between acting companies and playwrights in the 1630s. At the beginning of the decade, playwrights were little more than *poètes à gages* (salaried poets) with little, if any, control over the performance and publication of their plays.[60] They were the indentured servants of the cultural sphere and the fruits of their labor belonged contractually to the acting companies who commissioned them. Actors, however, were highly reticent to allow authors to publish their works, as this would make them available to competing companies. Alexandre Hardy's contract with the *comédiens du roi* denied him virtually any control over the publication of his plays. In exchange for monetary compensation, he agreed not to let the texts pass into the hands of a third party.[61] And Jean Rotrou was only able to publish his plays in 1637 after an epic battle with Bellerose and the *comédiens du roi*.[62] By the middle of the 1630s, many authors began to publish their works. Judging by the delays between performance and publication, we can nonetheless infer that some kind of exclusive contract still existed in order to protect the interests of the actors.[63] And even when writers' works were published, they typically surrendered rights to booksellers in exchange for a lump-sum payment or a handful of copies. Corneille would try to change this situation by obtaining *privilèges* in his own name and attempting unsuccessfully to register letters patent that would control the performance of his plays.[64] However, for many practical purposes, authorship went virtually unremunerated.

Through a narrative in which Polidor reappropriates the act of publication, *Les Vendanges de Suresnes* reaffirms the prerogatives of authorship and writing over performance. If Polidor is a figure of dramatic authorship and Tirsis stands in for the actors who performed plays, Dorimène—the audience of one whom Polidor seeks above all to please—evokes the figure of the patron. Unlike the theatrical public, who is seduced by the visual spectacle of the theater, she—like Richelieu in the dedication to *Horace*—sees beyond the illusion and apprehends its rationale and purpose. By establishing a structural analogy between Dorimène and the figure of the patron, Du Ryer calls attention to the areas where gallantry and patronage overlap. Both are affectively charged and both affirm the value of service and loyalty.

Following Jouhaud, I would argue that patronage offered writers trying to construct an authorial position an alternative to dramatic spectacle (which was the territory of actors) and traditional publication (where publishers reigned supreme). First of all, patronage provided material advantages, relieving the perennial poverty of authors.[65] Of equal importance, I would suggest, was the elitist model of intelligibility and reception offered by patronage, which enhanced the author's social standing. In the dedication of the earlier *Clarigène* to the duc de Mercœur, Du Ryer writes, "There is undoubtedly much satisfaction in seeing one's work succeed. The greatest rapture, however, comes from giving pleasure to illustrious personages."[66]

Du Ryer advertises his relationship to his patron, the duc de Vendôme, on the frontispiece on the 1636 edition of *Les Vendanges:* "Les Vendanges de Suresnes, Comédie, par P. du Ryer, Secrétaire de Monseigneur le Duc de Vandosme." The dedication, for its part, picks up on a number of themes related to our analysis of the play. The genesis of the text, for instance, is presented as follows:

> Cet ouvrage est un divertissement que j'ay tasché de vous preparer durant ces fascheuses journées ou la fievre me rendait inutile au service de vostre grandeur.

> [This work is an entertainment that I attempted to put together during the unpleasant days when my fever rendered me useless to your greatness.]

The allusions to Du Ryer's illness and Vendôme's entertainment situate their relationship on a personal, almost familiar basis. The intelligibility of the aesthetic act derives not from the playhouse, but rather from the personal exchange between author and patron. Similarly, Du Ryer flatteringly suggests that Vendôme's protection of the *vendangeurs* (grape harvesters) will elevate their dignity and social status because "there is greater glory to serve a virtuous Prince than to command anywhere else" ("il y a plus de gloire à servir un Prince vertueux qu'à commander autre part").

Colette Schérer has labeled *Les Vendanges* a bourgeois play, and she is right—to a point.[67] The setting of the play within a middle class *milieu* and Polidor's victory over the noble Palmédor (who attempts to abduct Dorimène) certainly point in this direction. As Schérer acknowledges, however, Polidor is hardly a typical bourgeois. He practices no discernible profession other than *Poëte* and, like many Parisian youth of his generation, he has picked up sophisticated language and manners. He carries a sword and uses it twice during the play, once in a duel, and once to save Dorimène from Palmédor. He is thus very different from his miser uncle Phillargire, whose name literally means "lover of money." The nephew may find it useful when he inherits money at the end of the play, but he never pursues profit. Polidor, in sum, embodies the ideal of the gentleman (*honnête homme*) who combines physical prowess and refined manners.[68] As his name suggests (*poli*/polite + *d'or*/golden), he is representative of an upwardly mobile bourgeoisie with increasingly aristocratic values—the class that produced the majority of writers during this period.

Du Ryer's relationship with Vendôme lasted roughly from 1634 to 1640, during which time Du Ryer dedicated three plays to his patron, and one each to the latter's daughter and son.[69] Advertising a relationship with Vendôme was a risky strategy. He was one of the leaders of the aristocratic resistance to Richelieu and could easily have ended up in exile or in prison any number of times during the 1630s.[70] That the dedications to the children come chronologically after those to the father suggest that Du Ryer may have considered hedging his bets by wooing a new generation of Vendômes. After all, leveraging a current position for future advantage is one of the hallmarks of patronage culture. In 1640, Du Ryer dedicated his *Lucrèce* to the duchesse d'Aiguillon, Richelieu's niece. This may indicate a break with Vendôme; at the very least, it suggests that Du Ryer was seeking safer protectors with connections to the cardinal. Richelieu's well-earned reputation for protecting the theater must have been attractive, as well. While playing up Vendôme's protection may have made sense for a young poet who had to take risks to establish his reputation, it would be risky for a playwright trying to consolidate a reputation.[71] As it turns out, Du Ryer was prescient, as Vendôme was forced to flee France in disgrace in 1641.

After 1642, with the dedication to his tragedy *Saül*, Du Ryer seems to more or less break with the traditional forms of patronage:

> Je ne dedie cet ouvrage à personne, parce que je le dedie à tout le monde. Je le donne aux Grands & aux Petits, aux Profanes & aux Religieux, parce que les uns & les autres peuvent trouver dans son subjet une instruction sans aigreur, & un divertissement sans scandale. Si ces Illustres Personnes à qui nous avons accoustumé de presenter nos ou-

vrages, & de qui les noms venerables sont les premiers charmes, & bien souvent les seules beautez que l'on remarque dans nos Livres, sont en quelque façon obligées de nous donner leur protection, quand nous leur faisons des hommages, des productions de nostre esprit; Il semblera sans doute que je veuille interesser tout le monde en la deffense & la protection de Saül, puisque chacun peut dire que je luy en fais un present, & que c'est à luy que je le dedie.[72]

[I dedicate this work to no one, for I dedicate it to everyone. I give it to the great and the humble, to laymen and men of the cloth, because everyone can find in it instruction without sharp rebukes and entertainment without scandal. If those illustrious persons to whom we are accustomed to present our works, and whose venerable names are the primary charms and often the sole beauties that are found in our books, are obligated, so to speak, to give us their protection when we honor them by dedicating our works to them, it will seem that I am trying to recruit everyone in the defense and protection of *Saul,* for anyone can say that I am giving and dedicating it to him or her.]

Casting the widest net possible, Du Ryer includes every estate and every social rank, from commoner to grandee, in the dedication. This shift from patron to reading public can in part be explained by Du Ryer's position as established poet, and in part by the fact that *Saül* is a Christian play. What is most remarkable about this passage, however, is the way in which Du Ryer adapts the language of patronage to the reading public: the literary text is a gift bestowed on the latter to secure its "protection" and "defense." We have thus come around 180 degrees from *Les Vendanges de Suresnes.* Rather than being opposed to the patron, the public now *is* the patron.

In her *Public et littérature au XVIIe siècle,* Hélène Merlin has examined the ways in which the public was reimagined in the seventeenth century. She shows how the older, ontologicotheological conception of the public was gradually supplanted by the more familiar notion of a literary public as a fictional person, a virtual grouping (*ensemble virtuel*) of particulars who share a common aesthetic experience.[73] Having separated the patron from the undifferentiated mass of spectators in *Les Vendanges,* Du Ryer uses the pseudodedication to *Saül* to reconstruct a public of particulars out of his readers. The assimilation of reader to patron is possible because a reader has a relationship to the dramatic text that is simultaneously more critical and more particularistic than a typical theatrical audience, with its susceptibility to spectacle. The reading of a play takes place in private and silently, or with a relatively small group of friends. Free from the interference of actors, the reader has the leisure to examine the language and architecture of the play. With his notion of a public-patron, Du Ryer thus hints at a model of literary production in which literary works are purchased, judged, and protected by informed public opinion, rather than by the influence of an aristocratic patron.

RICHELIEU AND THE "FIVE AUTHORS"

Public opinion (or at least public sentiment) was of increasing interest to the state, as well. The last section of this chapter will examine the official dimension of seventeenth-century theatrical patronage, tracing how the tradition of princely patronage, in which a prince personally protected a writer or theatrical company, was gradually transformed into a mechanism by which the state could represent itself before its subjects.

As soon as two theater companies became permanently established in the capital (Bellerose's *comédiens du roi* at the Hôtel de Bourgogne in 1629 and Mondory's company at the Théâtre du Marais in 1634), the state became involved in their affairs. Both companies received funding from the crown, and both were expected to contribute to the recreations of the court. In Gougenot's *Comédie de comédiens* (1633), Bellerose's company is described as "a company of comedians for the service and private pleasures of the king [*le service et contentement particulier du roy*], with permission by the king to perform in public as well."[74] The emphasis, here, is primarily on the actors' service to the king, with public performance treated as secondary. On more than one occasion, moreover, the king decreed that actors be transferred from one company to the other. In the two most famous instances (1634 and 1642), the fashionable Marais theater was raided so as to revitalize the *comédiens du roi*.[75]

In supporting "his" company, the king was continuing a venerable tradition of the personal protection of acting companies by princes. Because their trade was considered disreputable, actors were vulnerable to persecution by civil and religious authorities. The protection of a prominent patron could protect a company from persecution by the civil authorities, banishment, or worse. Two of the most famous companies of the seventeenth century, Mondory's company at the Théâtre du Marais and Molière's Illustre théâtre, were initially protected by princes (the Prince of Orange and the duc d'Orléans, respectively). Being affiliated with an influential patron could play both ways, however. A company sponsored by the Prince of Condé was banished from Paris in 1615, possibly for political reasons (Condé was in conflict with the crown at the time).[76]

At the king's side, Richelieu contributed to the development of the French stage on multiple levels: by granting pensions to authors and companies; by encouraging an official dramatic doctrine (classicism); by building the most advanced theater of the time (the *salle de la comédie* of the Palais Cardinal); and by sponsoring, and participating in, specific theatrical projects.[77] One of the most famous episodes in the official history of the French theater during this period is the creation of the "Five Authors," which brought together Pierre Corneille, Jean Rotrou, Claude de L'Estoille, Guillaume Colletet, and François Le Métel de Boisrobert under the direction of the cardinal and Jean Chapelain.[78] This association produced three plays: *La Comédie des Tuileries, La Grande pastorale,* and *L'Aveugle de Smyrne.* Typically, it is assumed that general outlines for the plays were provided by Richelieu and Chapelain, with the "Five Authors" assigned to the job of putting these plot outlines into verse (one act to an author).[79]

One of the peculiarities of the two surviving plays to come out of this collaboration is the curious effacement of both the authors themselves and Richelieu. Jean Baudoin's dedications are addressed not to Richelieu himself, or even to prominent members of the court, but rather to foreigners. *La Comédie des Tuileries* is dedicated to the English Kenelm Digby and *L'Aveugle de Smyrne* to the marquis de Coualin, a colonel in the Swiss guards. As for the content of the dedications, it is more or less conventional, praising the dedicatees for their taste and virtue. They leave out, however, precisely what we would normally expect to find: an account of the power relationships at the origin of the play's composition and production.

To get a grasp on these relationships, we need to be attentive to the silences and lacunae in the texts. The "To the Reader" of *La Comédie de Tuileries* mentions the "Five Authors" but does not name them. Instead, it hints tantalizingly at their identities. "You should know, furthermore, that it was written by five different authors who, although they are not named, are nevertheless quite renowned, and whose other works are famous enough to force you to acknowledge the worth of this one."[80] Unnamed, the authors are nonetheless famous enough to lend credence to the preface's laudatory claims regarding the *La Comédie des Tuileries*. This raises a perplexing paradox. Either the reader is expected to take the "To the Reader" at its word regarding the prominence of the authors (on what grounds?), or he or she is presumed to already know who the "Five Authors" are, in which case the reason for their continued anonymity is puzzling. The silence is especially surprising given Paul Pellisson's claim, in his history of the *Académie,* that the "Five Authors," along with Chapelain, were mentioned in a lost prologue that was read during the original performance, and that they were given a place of honor in the theater.[81] Curiously, the names of the "Five Authors" were not printed until Pellisson's mention in 1653, suggesting a deliberate practice of official (if not actual) anonymity on the part of the various players (cardinal, authors, and publishers). The difficulties that literary historians have encountered in trying to identify the relative participation of the authors are thus not an accident, but the result of a policy that bears investigation.[82]

The title pages of both plays identify the authors as "*les* Cinq Auteurs" (*the* Five Authors). The definite article suggests that this association is not merely a temporary alliance of *any* five authors, but rather that it is a coherent entity, a corporation transcending particular members and possessing a kind of permanence. In a sense, then, the identity of the individual members, while not irrelevant, is not essential. Indeed in neither *La Comédie des Tuileries* nor *L'Aveugle de Smyrne* are these "authors" credited with the success of their plays. While *La Comédie des Tuileries* mentions the "beauty of the verse" and the "diversity of invention," it reserves its highest praise for what it calls the *scène:*

> If I am not mistaken, you will also confess that the refinements and ornaments of this poem derive from the *scène* which gives it all of its brilliance. It is a delicate place, charming beyond all other marvels, where the bright colors of spring can be seen even in the depths of winter, where everything the poets describe in their marvelous gardens can be found, and where the graces and deities converse innocently about love, to which they pay homage. This will not seem so strange when, in order to convince you, I tell you that this place is called THE TUILERIES.[83]

Scène could be translated as either "stage" or "setting" (the Tuileries gardens)—an ambiguity that is particularly productive when we consider that the play was performed at the Louvre, only a few steps away. The Tuileries, where the colors of spring can be seen in the depths of winter, embody the miraculous creative power to which the theater aspires: what are mere words to the poets become material reality in the royal gardens. For it is none other than the king himself who is the source of this restorative power and, by extension, the true author of all that is "charming," "brilliant," and "marvelous" in the play. (The play itself, a comedy of disguise and recognition, makes the most of the supposedly marvelous character of the gardens and, in particular, its famous "echo.")

The liminary texts that accompany *L'Aveugle de Smyrne* take a similar direction, but with a twist. Following a pattern that should be familiar by now, the "To the Reader" accords the "Authors" the limited role of elocution (here, versification). "You can judge the worth of this work either by the excellence of its matter, or by the form which was given to it by four famous minds."[84] This passage, needless to say, raises more questions than it answers. In addition to the curious reference to "four" authors, which we will examine below, the passage raises the issue of who exactly is responsible for invention, the "matter" of the text. The "To the Reader" acknowledges the significance of this question, noting that "invention is the soul of poetry." Rather than answering, however, it shifts the question to an allegorical register. "Although its title is L'AVEUGLE [*The Blind Man*], its lights are nonetheless so brilliant that they force our muses to confess that Apollo himself is behind them."[85] In a paradoxical maneuver, the text reveals a secret. Behind the "Four Authors" stands an unnamed, mysterious creative force without which there would be no dramatic material, and therefore no *Aveugle de Smyrne* and no "Four Authors." The latter, ultimately, are only authors in the second degree, dependent on a creative intent that gives their association its substance (just as the king's will, in the form of letters patent, gave substance to *ancien régime* corporations). With the allusions to Apollo and luminosity, the "To the Reader" resurrects the Renaissance myth of poetic inspiration, only to attribute it to a shadowy Author rather than to professional poets.

There is no real mystery, however. Even if a contemporary reader did not know the role assumed by Richelieu in the creation and direction of these projects, the cardinal, with his well-publicized interest in the theater, would be the obvious candidate. It has often been assumed that Richelieu intended to hide his identity behind Chapelain and the "Five Authors."[86] The evidence for this claim is an undated letter from Chapelain to Boisrobert, probably written in 1634 or 1635. There, alluding to Richelieu only as "the great man whose orders you communicated to me yesterday," Chapelain mentions his uneasiness at the cardinal's wish that he assume the public authorship of *La Comédie des Tuileries*. "If I am taken to be the author, people will think that I have been the recipient of a miracle, and that my weaknesses have been suddenly transformed into great strengths."[87] Another letter to Boisrobert (January 24, 1635), gives a quite different account of the matter, however. Chapelain describes himself as working on a court comedy (*une comédie d'apparat*) and assumes responsibility for "invention" and "disposition."[88] When he uses the expression "our work" (*nostre ouvrage*), it is not to include Richelieu, but rather Boisrobert as his collaborator.[89] The cardinal appears simply as the person who commissioned the work.

Christian Jouhaud has shown that Chapelain's correspondence cannot be treated as a homogenous corpus.[90] Certain letters were private, intended only for the eyes of his correspondent. In such instances, Chapelain develops a tone of intimacy and complicity with his interlocutors. Others, however, were destined for a wider distribution and were read aloud, recopied, and distributed in various other ways. The January 24 letter to Boisrobert, with its allusion to "our work," seems to fit into the first category. The case of the undated letter where Chapelain discusses Richelieu's refusal to accept the paternity for "his" play is less clear. The personal relationship between the two men of letters gives way to a hyperbolic celebration of the merits of the cardinal himself, possibly for the benefit of a broader audience. That Richelieu is not named might well be taken as a sign of his anonymity, if it were not for the fact that his identity would have been clear to anyone who saw the letter. Even if Boisrobert's relationship to the cardinal had not been well known, the fact that it was addressed to "M. de Boisrobert, à *Ruël* [that is, Rueil, Richelieu's estate]" would have made it clear that the *grand homme* and Richelieu were one and the same. In sum, Chapelain's letter to Boisrobert would seem to follow a similar strategy as the liminary prefaces and dedications, ostentatiously hiding (that is, revealing) the mystery of the cardinal's authorship.[91]

What about the mysterious reference to "*four* famous minds"? The last lines of *L'Aveugle de Smyrne*'s "To the Reader" hint at a possible explanation for this inconsistency. "This tragicomedy will earn the approval that it deserves, and that is owed to such plays, in judgments committed to paper rather than from the applause of an audience."[92] The notion that a play is better judged by a reader than by a theatrical spectator was an argument of Corneille's opponents in the *querelle du Cid* and, most notably, the *Sentiments* offered by Richelieu's Academy. This puts the elimination of one of the five authors in a sinister light. Did Corneille's independent stance during the *querelle*, one wonders, cause him to be excluded from the "Five Authors"? Unfortunately, we do not have enough documentation to answer this question. As we have seen, however, Corneille, went well beyond the traditionally limited authorial role by claiming *sole* authorship of *Le Cid*. It is thus tempting to see the mention of four authors in the "To the Reader" as an attempt to put Corneille back in his place by demonstrating the superfluity of any given member of the "Five Authors" (or of having any fixed number of members, for that matter).

To summarize, there are two kinds of anonymity operative in the texts surrounding the "Cinq Auteurs." The anonymity of the "Five Authors" and the hesitation regarding the number of authors serve to define the latter as a corporate entity, independent of the identity of any single person and thus ideally suited to serve the demands of royal propaganda. The ostentatious anonymity of the king and the cardinal, by contrast, serves to create a sense of mystery and to convey the message that neither is a "writer" in the pejorative, technical sense of the term; rather they are quasidivine Creators, omnipresent yet invisible. These plays, in other words, offer a kind of hypertrophied version of the *topos* of patron as author that we have been exploring throughout this essay.

Henri de Campion's famous description of Richelieu's attitude during the 1641 performance of *Mirame* (written by Desmarets de Saint-Sorlin, possibly on the basis of an outline provided by the cardinal) should probably be read in this light. "I found myself," he writes "sitting quite close to the cardinal, who was so transfixed by the plot of his comedy that he could do nothing save admire himself in his own work."[93] Campion's language ("*his* comedy," "he could do nothing save *admire himself* in *his own* work") would appear to suggest a degree of narcissism in Richelieu's self-contemplation. It would be difficult, indeed, to imagine a more personal conception of the theater, nor one that allows for less reciprocity and dynamism. Desmarets, the actors, and the stage settings of the brand-new *salle de la comédie* have all become mere reflections of the cardinal, who is both author and spectator, judge and judged.[94]

Toward Bureaucratic Patronage

For Richelieu's enemies, his patronage of the theater was a sign that he had turned away from France's real problems and was retreating into a fantasy world. The anonymous anti-Richelieu *Milliade* thus draws a sharp contrast between France's dire military and economic situation and the cardinal's frivolous comedic pursuits:

> Il descrit de fausses douleurs
> Quant l'Estat sent de vrays malheurs . . .
> Et consulte encor Bois-Robert
> Quand une province se pert.[95]
>
> [While the state is experiencing real misfortune.
> He describes fake suffering . . .
> And consults with Boisrobert
> While a province is being lost.]

Here, the language of theatricality and illusion expresses not the mystery of power, but rather the affinity between self-deception and political impotence.

Of course, there is another, more familiar way of understanding Richelieu's patronage of the stage, reflected in the 1641 royal decree on the theater. This famous text, undoubtedly sponsored by the cardinal himself, presents the rehabilitation of the theatrical profession within the context of public utility. "If actors amend their dramatic performances so as to completely avoid all filthiness, we desire that the exercise of their profession, which can distract our people from various harmful activities with innocent entertainment, not be held to be reprehensible or prejudicial to their public reputation."[96] The primary function of the theater, here, is not to distract the cardinal, or even a small group of enlightened patrons, but rather to present a salutary diversion for the people (presumably in times of war or economic crisis). This suggests another way of reading Campion's description of Richelieu's fascination with "his" play. Rather than take it at face value, as a symptom of narcissism, we might consider the possibility that what fascinates Richelieu is precisely the theater's power of fascination. His own enjoyment, according to this reading, would be double: that of the perfect (that is, entertained) spectator and that of the canny statesman who enjoys a private joke.

In his *Projet du rétablissement du théâtre français* (1657), Richelieu's ally, the abbé d'Aubignac, proposed a state theater, complete with its own director, professionally designed stage sets, and housing for actors. In this manner, he wrote, the people would not be jealous of the court, for they would have their own versions of the magnificent decorations that graced the Palais Cardinal and the Petit Bourbon, in the Louvre.[97] These comments reveal an anxiety about the dangers of an insular court culture, set apart from the general public. To avoid class envy, the remarkable technical developments of the French stage must be made available to the French people. D'Aubignac is not explicit regarding the source of funding for such an ambitious endeavor, specifying only that "a sufficient fund will be found without impinging upon the royal treasury." A few pages earlier, however, he gives a hint as to the sort of solution he would prefer. "Among the Ancients, the magistrates and other great lords who provided the theatrical entertainment for the people, either because this was part of their office or in order to win public goodwill, paid for all of the decorations out of their pockets."[98]

If d'Aubignac did indeed expect nobles and royal officers to contribute to his state theater, he anticipated a new *régime* of patronage, unlike anything seen before. His state theater immediately brings to mind the Comédie Française, whereas the contributions of the noble and/or wealthy recall the progressive taxes used by modern states to support their cultural politics. Gone, for better or worse, is the personal aspect of patronage, replaced by the logic of bureaucracy. We are not far from what Marc Fumaroli has derisively labeled the "culture state" (*l'état culturel*): government-sponsored culture/propaganda for everyone.[99] Richelieu's involvement in the theater, in sum, reflects a trend toward the officialization of theatrical patronage: the individual relationship between patron and author is occulted (though not eliminated), and the relationship between the state (in the persons of its sovereign and his minister) and its subjects is moved into the foreground. Henceforth, one of the functions of the theater will be to represent sovereign authority not just before the court, but also before the people.

This chapter began with a question, inspired by Maynard's refusal to write for the theater: how does our understanding of earlier seventeenth-century drama change if we foreground the personal relationship between playwright and patron, rather than the relationships between playwrights or actors and their various audiences? The legitimate limits of the relationship between author and patron, we discovered, was a subject of polemic in the *querelle du Cid*. Whereas Corneille claimed to dispense with actors and aristocratic supporters, Mairet repeatedly stressed the role of aristocrats as arbiters of taste. An examination of the latter's career revealed the extent to which not just his plays, but indeed seventeenth-century drama as a whole was shaped by the interventions of aristocratic patrons. The second half of the chapter examined two divergent ways that dramatic patronage could be leveraged. Du Ryer's *Les Vendanges de Suresnes* developed the idea that it could be a dynamic force in the creation of new forms of authorship, freeing the dramatic poet from his dependence on actors. Richelieu, finally, reconfigured and transformed the patronage relationship in another direction altogether. The entity known as the "Five Authors" served to paradoxically hide and reveal the authorship of the minister himself, signaling a new political role for theater in mediating the relationship between the royal state and its subjects and anticipating one of the themes of the next chapter: the progressive institutionalization of patronage.

6
Beyond Patronage

> On m'en escrit comme d'une Comete fatale qui nous menace; comme d'une chose terrible, & plus redoutable que la saincte Inquisition. On me mande que c'est une tyrannie qui se va establir sur les Esprits, & à laquelle il faut que nous autres Faiseurs de Livres, rendions une obeïssance aveugle. Si cela est, je suis Rebelle, je suis Heretique.
>
> [I am informed that it is a comet that bodes ill for us, a terrible thing, worse than the Holy Inquisition. I am told that it will establish a tyranny of thought, and that authors of books such as we will be required to show blind obedience. If this be the case, I am a rebel and a heretic.]
> —Guez de Balzac, on the Académie Française

> Il est vrai que les manières polies donnent cours au mérite, et le rendent agréable; et qu'il faut avoir de bien éminentes qualités pour se soutenir sans la politesse.
>
> [Politeness tends, undoubtedly, to advance merit and to render it agreeable; a man must have very eminent qualities to hold his own without being polite.]
> —La Bruyère, *Les Caractères*

THIS FINAL CHAPTER SEEKS TO PUT THE PRECEDING ANALYSES INTO A broader historical perspective. Two questions will predominate:

1) How did the patronage system develop and change over the course of the seventeenth century?
2) What role did a patronage rhetoric play outside the Republic of Letters, in the relationships among members of the social elite?

To provide some preliminary answers to these questions, I will examine academic sociability and conversation, two very different but extremely important practices of the period.¹ These practices reflect two significant and complementary trends with broad implications: the bureaucratization of literary patronage and the diffusion of particularistic rhetoric within polite society. As we explore these topics, and the general evolution of patronage culture in the seventeenth century, we will occasionally wander beyond the ostensible chronological scope of this study ("the age of Louis XIII").

I. THE FOUNDATION(S) OF THE ACADÉMIE FRANÇAISE (1635)

Most of the information we possess today regarding the origins of the Académie Française is derived from Paul Pellisson's lively *Histoire de l'Académie* (1653). In a narrative that has been faithfully repeated by generations of literary historians, Pellisson describes how a group of men of letters began to gather at the home of Valentin Conrart around 1629 to discuss "all sorts of matters, affairs, news, and fine letters."² This period, as he tells it, was the "Golden Age" of the French Academy. Since the participants were friends, they had little need for rules or elaborate ceremony. The relaxed and informal tone of the gatherings lent itself to a free exchange of ideas, with each member of the company voluntarily submitting his own works to the candid judgment of the group. This state of affairs, however, could only last as long as the meetings remained secret. The first to breach the pact of silence was Claude Malleville, who told Nicolas Faret about the gatherings. Faret, in turn, informed Boisrobert and Desmarets de Saint-Sorlin, both of whom were close to Richelieu. Apprised of the situation, the cardinal offered the company his personal protection and the official status conferred by royal letters patent.³

From one day to the next, Conrart's circle of friends thus found itself in negotiations with the most powerful minister in the kingdom. According to Pellisson, the company was almost universally displeased at this turn of events, which threatened to disrupt the informal spirit of the meetings (*la douceur & la familiarité de leurs conférences*).⁴ Jean Chapelain, however, persuaded them that there was no turning back and that they should make the best of a difficult situation. A refusal, he argued, would only serve to offend the cardinal, who could suppress any association that did not have the express authorization of the king. Boisrobert was thus delegated to inform Richelieu that they had accepted the offer and that the

"Conrart circle" would become the Académie Française. A private, democratic entity had been co-opted within a system of royal patronage.

Pellisson's account is appealing, largely because it conforms to the familiar stereotype of an autocratic Richelieu recruiting reluctant writers for his cynical propaganda campaigns. A number of recent commentators, however, have raised doubts about his version of the origins of the French Academy. They point out that Pellisson was seeking to be admitted to the Academy when he wrote his *Histoire* and thus had good reason to offer the academicians a flattering portrait of the institution's early years.[5] The unpopular Richelieu, on the other hand, had been dead for nearly a decade, so he was a safe target. (If the cardinal had still been alive, Pellisson would presumably have adopted a different tone.) Unfortunately, his account cannot be checked against documentary sources since the official *régistres,* which recorded the day-to-day activities of the Academy during the first two decades of its existence, disappeared after Pellisson's arrest in 1661 during the Fouquet affair. We are thus left with the extremely coherent, but somewhat suspect, *Histoire de l'Académie* on the one hand and the fragmentary evidence that can be gleaned from correspondences, memoirs, and dedications on the other. In the following pages, I will consider a number of recent reinterpretations of the French Academy with an end to understanding it as a patronage institution. Without taking Pellisson as an unimpeachable source, I will attempt to salvage some of the more important aspects of his account. The foundation of the Academy, I will argue, was a significant attempt to redirect the energies of patronage.

Reconfiguring Patronage: The 1635 Engraving

Hélène Merlin has recently advanced an alternative account of the genesis of the French Academy. Rather than seeking to unearth factual evidence that would contradict Pellisson's version of the events, Merlin uses a wide range of contemporary literary sources—from Théophile de Viau's poems to the polemic over Guez de Balzac's letters—to explore the possible historical significance of the Academy's limited mandate to deal with matters of language and style. The Academy, she argues, had contrasting meanings for different historical actors. Merlin's Richelieu is not so much an autocrat as a canny politician who recognized the exceptional—and thus precarious—nature of his power. Lacking the symbolic trappings of kingship and the customary privileges of high birth, he cultivated an institution (the Academy) that was as exceptional as he was. For the business of the Academy was precisely not the weighty business of state or religion, but rather matters of language and style. The result was a conception of culture that, because it dealt with words (*mots*) rather than things (*choses*), was diametrically opposed to both the Neoplatonizing and civic strands of Renaissance humanism. Henceforth, men of letters would devote themselves not to truth or politics, but rather to language as form.

Men of letters, Merlin argues, stood to gain as much as Richelieu from this novel institution, but for different reasons. Because literary culture was concerned with words rather than things, style rather than politics, it was accorded what Merlin characterizes as a kind of "immunity." "In other words, contrary to the usual interpretation of the creation of the Academy, it is because language is not an affair of state that it can . . . be detached from royal sovereignty."[6] By giving up his political and moral pretensions, the man of letters gained a margin of freedom. He could exercise a kind of free speech—free not because the voicing of political dissent was considered a democratic check on the state, but rather because the speech was explicitly apolitical. Merlin points out that language was considered a matter of usage, and usage was customarily determined not by the king, but rather by his subjects (or rather a subset thereof). The statutes of the Academy reflected this fundamental right of the French nation to its common linguistic property. For instance, the academicians might decide that the conjunction *car* (because) was not proper usage, but they could not ban its use by individuals. Seen in this light, the French Academy appears not as an instrument of power, but rather as a form of resistance to overreaching power, a zone of tolerance within the coercive structures of the absolutist state.[7] It is the paradoxical institutionalization of noninstitutional literary life.

Merlin's reading of the history of the Academy is at least partially inspired, as she herself acknowledges, by René Démoris's analysis of a 1635 engraving (figure 3) depicting Richelieu in three-quarter profile at the center of a sun motif, connected by rays to stars representing thirty-eight academicians (the full contingent of academicians had not been elected at the time). Directly above sits a crowned fleur-de-lis which, together with the sun motif, is enclosed within a crown of laurel. Merlin, following Démoris, attributes a pro-

Fig. 3. Richelieu surrounded by the members of the French Academy. Cabinet des Estampes QB[1] 1635. Bibliothèque Nationale de France.

found significance to the fact that the sun is off center with respect to the crown of laurel, suggesting the "eccentricity" (ex-centricity) of both Richelieu and the new literary institution he sponsored. The cardinal, Démoris argues, embodies a different kind of representational order than the king. Whereas the king is depicted using the conventional symbolic language of the fleur-de-lis and the crown, Richelieu enjoys an advantage. He is the only person in the engraving to be represented by a likeness that renders his body (or rather a simulacrum of his body) present. Despite the fact that he is spatially below the king, he appears as more real because he is represented in historical, embodied form. Démoris sees the desire to be written (or "inscribed," as he puts it) into history as one of the de-

Fig. 4. Richelieu surrounded by the members of the French Academy. From Jacques d'Auzoles (sieur de Lapeyre), *Esclaircissemens chronologiques et nécessaires pour les véritables positions des matières qui sont dans les poëtes et autres historiens fabuleux* (Paris: Alliot, 1635). Bibliothèque Nationale de France.

fining characteristics of modern consciousness. As religious certitudes became subject to doubt, individuals sought metaphorical immortality through books. This "desire for inscription" is shared by both Richelieu and the academicians and would be embraced in the latter half of the seventeenth century by Louis XIV, who appears in Le Brun's paintings as a historical person, rather than in the trappings of mythological iconography.[8]

Merlin picks up on this thread of Démoris's argument but, demonstrating a poststructuralist sensibility that runs throughout her essay, insists on the fundamental impossibility of using language to project a stable presence. The great secret that all academicians share is that their immortality (and that of their protectors, from Richelieu to Louis XIV and beyond) is built on language, that is, arbitrary convention. "Between us, you are only *presumed* to be be immortal," she imagines one academician saying to another.[9] For Merlin, the classical discourse of praise always operates within the ambiguous and unstable territory of the "as if": "I will praise you *as if* you were a hero/great writer." Beyond the surface of words (*verba*), the French Academy thus suffers from a thing (*res*) deficit. Merlin suggests that this emptiness, or "rottenness" (*pourriture*), as she calls it, is the flip side of the Academy's immunity. Built on words, it rises or falls depending on the efficacy attributed to words.

This insight that the French Academy is built on a fragile foundation of words is hardly new. From its inception, the institution was attacked as an empty form, without content or legitimacy. Reacting to the news of Chapelain's election to the Academy, for example, Guez de Balzac questioned the basis of the new institution's authority. "You tell me that you have been honored by being received into the Academy of great minds. But I would like to ask you who received the 'great minds' who received you?"[10] If the problem is put this way, only two answers are possible. Either the Academy's authority is the product of an empty vicious circle ("I will consecrate you if you consecrate me") or we have to look outside of the Republic of Letters to a political authority. It is not clear, however, how a political authority can authorize a literary institution. Language, as we have seen, belongs to the French people, not to the state.

Démoris's interpretation of the engraving and Merlin's extrapolation to the broader context of seventeenth-century culture and beyond are ingenious, but do they hold up to close scrutiny? In fact, both depend upon a flawed premise. Although it is hard to tell from the reproduction, the image analyzed by Démoris is not a creation of the seventeenth century at all, but rather an eighteenth-century collage in which the crown of laurel (taken from an ornament used by the Imprimerie royale) was combined with an engraving from Jacques d'Auzoles de Lapeyre's *Esclaircissemens chronologiques* (figure 4).[11] This latter image (with sun and crowned fleur-de-lis, but without the crown of laurel) is mentioned in a number of seventeenth-century texts. including Pellisson's *Histoire,* Tallemant des Réaux's *Historiettes,* and Balzac's *Lettres.*[12] In all three of these texts, moreover, the idea for the engraving is attributed to Auzoles, not to Richelieu or one of his propagandists.

The absence of the crown of laurel in this apparently well-known version of the engraving raises serious questions about the pertinence of the Démoris/Merlin interpretation. Rather than being decentered with respect to a graphical device, Auzoles's engraving is surrounded by text. The images of the sun and crowned fleur-de-lis are preceded by a formula of address—"A l'EMINENTE" (TO THE EMINENT)—and followed by a kind of signature: "IACQVES D'AVZOLES LAPEYRE." The engraving, in other words, appears as part of a dedication. If we take the page as a semantic whole, it becomes possible, and indeed productive, to read the surrounding text as part of the engraving and vice-versa. Assuming the engraving is part of the text and functions as a representation of the Academy, the dedication reads, "To the Eminent [Academy], Jacques d'Auzoles Lapeyre." In the subsequent pages, Auzoles explains that Richelieu is the only worthy dedicatee for his work, but he recognizes that the prerogative of praising the cardinal is henceforth reserved exclusively to members of the Academy. "To his EMINENCE, then, and to no other, are rightfully due these *Esclaircissemens chronologiques,* which we have been so presumptuous as to dedicate to him, as we did before with our *Job.* But realizing that Apelles alone is allowed to paint Alexander the Great, and that only the Eminent [Academy] is competent to give the GREAT ARMAND [Richelieu] the praise that is his due, I am humbly addressing myself to them and submitting myself to their examination and censure."[13] The use of the term "Eminent" for the French Academy suggests that the company participates in the cardinal's dignity (*Son Éminence Ducale*). This affinity makes it possible for the Academy to produce the cardinal's immortal praise. Praising the cardinal, however, is not the company's sole function. It also sits in judgment ("examination and censure") of works submitted to it by aspiring writers. The Academy has become a kind of intermediary between Richelieu and writers (such as Auzoles), taking the brute literary material provided by the latter and converting it into a form suitable to be presented to the cardinal.

If we attempt, inversely, to read Auzoles's name as part of the engraving, a complex hierarchy becomes apparent. At the top is the king, who is connected to the Richelieu-sun configuration by a flame that is longer than the others and attached to "M. le Garde des Sceaux" (that is, Pierre Séguier). It is significant that Séguier is named not by his family name, but rather by his function as keeper of the seals, the official charged with administering the machinery of royal justice on behalf of the king.[14] The Academy is thus subordinated to the king in much the same way as the chancellery, through the intermediary of the chancellor or, in the event that the chancellor is stripped of his duties, a keeper of the seals (*garde des sceaux*).[15] The analogy between the two institutions is suggestive. Both examine and censure works destined for publication, with the difference that the Academy's censure is stylistic and linguistic (and thus, as Merlin points out, non-binding) whereas the official censors of the chancellery are the guardians of orthodoxy and political conformity. The role of the Academy thus fits within the larger context of efforts by the royal state, during this period, to gain exclusive control over censorship (formerly shared with the university and the *parlements*).[16] It is worth recalling, in this context, that Séguier became the protector of the Academy after Richelieu's death in 1642.

A second, more prominent, intermediary is Richelieu, in whose person all of the connecting lines of the engraving converge. This topological centrality becomes more visible if we assume that the engraving has collapsed an essentially three-dimensional structure into a two–dimensional representation. It would clearly be difficult, if not impossible, to draw such a figure in perspective while keeping the names of the academicians legible; nevertheless, the possibility of such a reading is suggested by the three-dimensional royal crown, which introduces depth into the engraving. If we imagine the academicians as forming a disk traversed through its center by a perpendicular axis defined by Auzoles, Richelieu, and the fleur-de-lis (like a child's top), a number of contradictions in the engraving disappear. For one thing, it does not appear that Vaugelas is closer to the king than the cardinal. Moreover, all of the members of the company occupy the same level, as the supposedly democratic structure of the institution would seem to require.[17]

This solution is not entirely satisfactory, either, as it does not account for the two extended flames. In addition to the flame at the top, already mentioned, a second one extends from Abel Servien's name toward Auzoles, connecting the latter to Richelieu through the intermediary of the Academy. There is a tension between the relatively horizontal, democratic structure of the Academy itself, suggested by the figure of the circle and the orientation of the academician's names (it is necessary to turn the engraving to read them easily), and the hierarchical patronage system within which it is inscribed, suggested by the chain of being that extends from the top of the engraving (the crown) to the bottom (Auzoles).

Tallemant's later description of the engraving implies that he, at least, perceived a latent hierarchy within the representation of the Academy: "A nut of sorts, by the name of la Peyre, had the idea of prefacing a book with a big sun, with the cardinal in the middle, surrounded by forty rays extending out to the names of the forty academicians. The chancellor, as the most prominent [member of the company], had a direct ray. I think that M. Servien, a *secrétaire d'état* at the time, had the other, followed by Bautru, and the others, pro-rated according to their status."[18] Although the notion of a "direct ray" seems to make some sense in the case of Séguier, it is difficult to see how it could be applied to Servien. The ray attaching him to Richelieu is neither longer nor any more direct than those of his colleagues and the elongated flame, as we we have seen, connects him to Auzoles, not the cardinal. More likely, Servien's flame is an allusion to his weight, as *secrétaire d'état* for war, in dispensing pensions to writers. It is hard to see, moreover, how the distance of the academicians from the central axis would correlate with their prominence or the degree of favor they enjoyed. (Why should Bautru or Hay du Chastelet occupy a less prominent position than Vaugelas?) It nonetheless remains significant that the engraving could have been understood as the representation of a system of social relations and distinctions.

A passing comment made by Merlin suggests another possible dimension to the engraving's verticality. Following up on some remarks by Démoris, she observes a visual similarity between the cardinal's disk-shaped portrait at the center of the sun and a communion wafer inside a monstrance.[19] By analogy with the communion of the faithful, the French Academy becomes a social body (corporation) by communing around the physical body of Richelieu. This implicit analogy between Richelieu and Christ is worth pursuing. Most obviously, Richelieu's mediating position between the king and his subjects mirrors Christ's role as mediator between

God and man. This analogy is reinforced by Démoris's observation that Richelieu is represented by a recognizable portrait (that is, as a man) while the king is represented by an impersonal, abstract, fleur-de-lis. Within the representational scheme of the painting, he appears as the incarnation of royal power—royal power "made flesh" so to speak. The engraving would thus reproduce the dialectic between the king's two bodies that Ernst Kantorowicz and Louis Marin, among others, have analyzed.[20] Richelieu would correspond to the king's mortal, human body, while the crowned fleur-de-lis would be his immortal, sacred body.

By focusing on the vertical organization of the engraving and the *personal* character of Richelieu's role as mediator, I am suggesting that the engraving might fruitfully be read as an allegorized representation of a patronage dynamic—a hierarchical network of interpersonal relations. What makes this dynamic different from those we have analyzed in previous chapters is the specific role played by the French Academy as institution. Here, as in Auzoles's dedication, the Academy is both the beneficiary of patronage, radiating out from Richelieu, and a kind of institutional patron itself (Auzoles addresses his dedication to the institution, whose approval and protection he seeks).

It may seem like a stretch to extend the notion of patronage to an institution, especially since I have repeatedly sought to stress the personal nature of patronage. What makes this extension plausible, I would suggest, is the size of the Academy, which has remained constant from its foundation to the present. As is well known, the French Academy is made up of forty members. Although adding or subtracting ten members would hardly change matters much, I would suggest that the general order of magnitude is significant. If we were to attempt to reproduce Auzoles's engraving with a hundred or more names, it would become illegible at its current size (approximately 10 centimeters × 8 centimeters). This is not to suggest, of course, that the number of members of the Academy was chosen as a function of its suitability for graphic representation; rather, the question of graphic legibility raises the larger question of the intelligibility of the institution as a whole.

To put it in contemporary terms: A teacher can plausibly learn the names of forty students in a class (although it might take a few weeks) and attempt to conduct the class as a discussion. One hundred students, however, would be unmanageable and require teaching assistants and discussion groups. Forty is somewhere in the nebulous intermediary zone between "a few" and "many." It makes the Academy small enough to maintain the essentially personal bonds characteristic of patronage—it is conceivable that Richelieu would maintain some kind of personal relationship with forty individuals. However, it is also large enough to be a *corps* (corporation) and thus to serve as a plausible representation of the Republic of Letters as a whole, broadly defined to include aristocrats as well as professional or semiprofessional men of letters. My argument, in the pages that follow, will be that the French Academy reflects an initial, tentative stage in the progressive transformation of networks of literary patronage into a more stable and permanent institutional system. As we will see, the question of whose interests are best served by such a transformation will prove to be rather complicated.

Pellisson provides a useful starting point for examining the role of the French Academy as a patronage institution. While discussing the company's reaction to Richelieu's offer of protection, he specifically mentions the reticence of two of the members. "Some [members], and especially M. de Serizay and M. de Malleville, felt that they [the Academy] should decline the cardinal's offer as gracefully as they could. These two, in addition to the common reasons that they shared with the others, had a reason that especially concerned them. M. de Serizay was the intendant for the duc de La Rochefoucauld's household and M. de Malleville was Marshal Bassompierre's secretary. These two lords were considered enemies of the cardinal."[21] According to Pellisson, the creation of the new Academy did not merely affect the company as whole; the particular interests of individual members were implicated as well. To the extent that an individual might have already been entangled in other patronage networks, there was the possibility for conflicts of interest. Within the broader context of the narrative, the singling out of Serizay and Malleville is fraught with ironies. As we have already seen, it was Malleville who revealed the secret meetings of the "Conrart circle," leading to the cardinal's intervention. Serizay, for his part, would become the first director of the Academy, an unusual position for someone who was supposedly allied with one of the cardinal's enemies—unless, of course, Richelieu's intention in transforming the Conrart circle into an official Academy was to use his patronage to assert a more forceful control over the Republic of Letters. Although Pellisson's account should always be taken with a grain of salt, this idea seems perfectly plausible, and indeed has been mentioned by a number of commentators.[22] If we accept this premise, the fact that Serizay was promoted to the position of first among equals can be interpreted as either a favor from the new patron to gain his loyalty or an attempt on the part of the academicians to assert their independence.

The statutes of the Academy explicitly stated that no member could be elected without the protector's approval, thereby establishing a link between his patronage of individuals and his support of the institution. According to Pellisson, this rule was established after the election of Honorat de Porchères Laugier, who was allied with Richelieu's enemies. To smooth things over, Porchères Laugier reportedly gave a *discours de réception* on the subject of "praise of the Academy and its protector" and the cardinal was given his veto.[23] As the *Histoire* written by Pellisson and his successor d'Olivet shows, Richelieu and later protectors did not hesitate to use their power to influence elections. Indeed, the Academy occasionally became a battleground of competing patronages, as in the contested election of Antoine Furetière's successor in 1688.[24]

Civilizing Literature: Faret's *Projet de l'Académie*

Other than Pellisson's *Histoire* and the *lettres patentes,* perhaps the most valuable document that we possess regarding the foundation of the French Academy is Nicolas Faret's *Projet de l'Académie pour servir de préface à ses statuts,* a text that was printed and circulated among the academicians, but not published in its entirety until the twentieth century. It was intended, Pellisson tells us, for publication along with the statutes of the Academy, but withheld, he speculates, because it was considered stylistically and organizationally deficient.[25] Passages from the *Projet* appear in Pellisson's *Histoire* and, in substantially modified form, in the letters patent drafted by Conrart.

The *Projet* revolves around the *topos* of the rivalry between the Moderns (the French) and the Ancients (the Romans and Greeks), depicted as a struggle over memory and history. As Faret describes them, the ancient Gauls (the ancestors of the French nation) were fearsome warriors who often defeated their Greek and Roman enemies. The latter, however, found a means to avenge themselves for their inadequacies on the field of battle by characterizing the Gauls as "barbarians" in their written histories:

> If, in addition to their natural ardor for battle, these valiant men [the Gauls] had possessed the art of immortalizing their conquests in writing,

their glory would undoubtedly have come down to us much more brilliantly and beautifully than their enemies', despite the latter's attempts to use eloquence to arrogate to themselves the right to judge such matters. And certainly this is the only way they have found to avenge themselves for the defeats of their armies and the invasion of their lands. They have tried to erase the shame of defeat by obscuring the valor of the victors.[26]

Faret pits the strong Gauls (and, implicitly, the Germanic hordes who eventually overran the Roman empire) against the decadent, eloquent Greeks and Romans. In the hands of the weak, history functions as a kind of compensation for their lack of physical valor. The characterization of the Gauls as "barbarian" was thus part of an enormous historical fraud perpetuated by the Greeks and Romans to exact revenge on their enemies. Lacking valor, they resorted to the ruses ("artifices" and "disguises") of eloquence. The *Projet* thus puts an almost Nietzschian twist on the old *topos* of the rivalry of Arms and Letters.

The figure of the barbarian haunts the text as an object of both repulsion and identification. Ironically, Faret acknowledges a degree of truth to the Ancients' characterization of the Gauls as barbarians. If the version of history that has come down to us today reflects the biases of the Greeks and Romans, it is largely because the Gauls lacked the eloquence to write their own account. In a profound sense, therefore, they were the inarticulate barbarians that their enemies depicted them to be. This reputation of the French language as barbaric, Faret notes, continues to the present day. Despite the fact that France has prospered while Greece and Rome have fallen, the French language has not kept up. "[T]he king's language, which promulgates his ordinances and is charged with singing his glory, is still considered by some as barbaric" (Faret, 32). To compete with the great civilizations of antiquity, it is not enough to demonstrate military prowess or to have survived where they have perished; it is necessary to establish the cultural prestige of one's language so as to immortalize present deeds as future history.

Barbarity, in this context, is synonymous with amnesia, with the passage of time that threatens to wipe out civilizations and their memory. By an "extraordinary privilege," France has heretofore escaped the "almost inevitable revolutions" that destroy all things (Faret, 22). Cardinal Richelieu, however, has the foresight to look to the future. "He deems that it is principally by arms that kings make a name for themselves and make their authority feared; but without the assistance of the sciences and the arts, the luster of this reputation gradually fades away and ultimately disappears either through barbarity or with the passing of the centuries" (Faret, 26). Richelieu recognizes the priority of arms over letters in the here and now. A prince establishes his authority over his subjects and his enemies not by cultivating letters and surrounding himself with humanists, as Henry III had attempted to do, but through force. If letters are of little importance in the short run, however, they remain more durable over time. We take pleasure in the stories that poets tell, and thus we continue to tell them, passing them on to future generations. This capacity to survive by seducing new readers constitutes the political efficacy of literature for Faret.

Now that Richelieu and Louis XIII have reestablished political order within France and fortified its borders against enemies, it is time, therefore, to "resuscitate [*faire revivre*] the eloquence [of the Ancients]" (Faret, 22). By fixing language in a permanent form, men of letters can forge a weapon against the ravages of time (Faret, 54). The problem, however, is that letters in France continue to be characterized by a persistent and entrenched barbarity. "How powerful is this mad love that dazzles authors when they contemplate their own works? Even the most talented let themselves be blinded, and if they do not have good and faithful guides, they fall . . . dangerously" (Faret, 34). In the sixteenth and seventeenth centuries, language was often singled out as the human faculty that raised man above brute animals. As Faret himself puts it, "it is through the gift of language that God distinguished most clearly between the nature of men and that of beasts" (Faret, 52). Here, however, the Republic of Letters is presented as being in a primitive state of nature: men of letters are blinded by their passions, lacking clear direction and dependent on natural instinct. At the same time, there is a recognition that powerful passions are at work in the literary world. By according writers official protection, Richelieu seeks to *redirect* and harness these passions, to sublimate them into forms that are useful to the state. The most effective way to create a new eloquence that is both French and royal is to play off the ambitions of men of letters. "[I]t appears that great minds acquire or lose that vigor which permits them to rise to high and bold speculations to the extent that they receive or are denied the favors of Princes. Only their approval, which today takes the place formerly occupied by the applause of an entire people, can give men courage, which otherwise flags and becomes idle when the hope for reward is frustrated" (Faret, 26–28). It is favor that contemporary men of letters desire, and this desire can be turned to positive effect by keeping their energies directed toward honest labor such as praising the achievements of the king and his minister.[27] By offering writers a substitute for the patronage of feuding aristocrats, Richelieu has a provided a solid foundation for both the state and writers alike. The sublimation of barbaric passion has become the basis for civilization.[28]

The image of the Moderns pillaging the treasures of the Ancients eloquently captures Faret's dialectic of barbarity and civilization. "Who will prevent us," he asks "from pillaging both [the Romans and the Greeks] and using all of the treasures that are available to us in their writings?" (Faret, 42). Like the Germanic hordes that swarmed down onto the Roman peninsula, looting valuable treasures from that formerly great civilization, the new French eloquence takes booty freely from the riches of Roman and Greek literature, thereby getting its revenge on antiquity. Faret's *Projet*, like the engraving of Richelieu surrounded by the academicians, is an attempt to create an institutional framework that would channel the energies and desires generated by patronage (such as the desire for recognition and the desire for immortality) toward an explicitly royalist and nationalist project.

A Central Place for Literature

Ultimately, any balanced account of the French Academy needs to consider that it responds to a desire on the part of *both* Richelieu *and* the writers whom he patronized. Although the *coup de force* theory, according to which the new institution was merely imposed on writers by Richelieu, contains a grain of truth, it fails to take into full account the advantages that it offered men of letters.[29] If the Academy was an object of desire on the part of writers, as Faret suggests, it was undoubtedly because it reduced some of the ambiguities and uncertainties of patronage culture. An academician's interests were tied to the institution as a whole, which had a permanence that other patronage relationships often lacked. Pellisson devotes a good portion of his account to the laws and statutes governing the Academy. Although such rules could certainly be perceived as an unwelcome departure from the free and easy days of the Golden Age before Richelieu's intervention, they nevertheless introduced some predictability and stability into the lives of writers. Elections, although they were subject to the approval of the protector, were for life (except in exceptional cases), and the duties imposed on members were relatively light. Although membership in the Academy did not guarantee a pension, it provided a notoriety that an author could leverage to gain the favor of other patrons. Most important, perhaps, the Academy provided a support network for its members. As Nicolas Schapira has shown, the members of the "Conrart circle" exchanged information regarding everything from patrons to publishers.[30] Membership in the Academy similarly gave a man of letters access to patronage networks and potentially profitable connections. The Academy, finally, provided men of letters with a kind of official recognition *as men of letters*—a point that has been made forcefully by Alain Viala.[31] As we saw in earlier chapters, the roles of author, secretary, and ghost writer could easily become confused in patronage culture, leaving a writer's labor unrecognized. Whatever services he might be asked to perform, however, an academician could always point to his status as academician as evidence of his cultural capital. As such, the Academy contributed to what Viala has called the "autonomization" of the literary sphere—the recognition that literature was an independent field of human endeavor.

The French Academy has often been understood as the cultural manifestation of a propensity toward centralization that is attributed either to the French monarchy or to a deeply seated facet of the French character.[32] There is no particular reason, however, to assume that this centralization worked exclusively in the interests of the state.[33] If we focus on the geographical concentration of power in the capital, rather than the concentration of power in the hands of one person, we can understand how the Academy might have been effective not only as a relay between the state and men of letters, but also among men of letters themselves. It provided a common reference point, a central place where information could be exchanged and relationships developed. Schapira has speculated that the "Conrart circle" may have been little more than an informal gathering of secretaries and similar personnel who exchanged information in the context of their duties on behalf of their patrons.[34] If we accept this plausible theory, Richelieu's intervention appears in a very different light. He did not co-opt the autonomy of a nascent literary institution; rather, he transformed an informal networking session into a literary institution under his own patronage.

A central location, moreover, contributes to an institution's prestige. The history of the French Academy during the seventeenth century is, to a large extent, the history of the places it occupied. From its inception, it was a Parisian institution, rooted in the life of the city. Paris was the royal city, the site of the king's primary palace, his council, the *parlement de Paris* (the highest court in the realm), and the University of Paris (which possessed France's greatest faculty). In the beginning, however, the men of letters in Conrart's circle bad no place to gather, according to Pellisson. "Around the year 1629, several private persons who lived in various parts of Paris, finding nothing more frustrating than constantly missing each other in this vast city, resolved to start meeting once a week at one of their houses."[35] Initially, the group was itinerant, moving from private residence to private residence. Soon, however, Conrart's residence on the rue Saint-Martin was chosen because it was the most centrally located ("the most suitably lodged for receiving company, and in the middle of the city, more or less equidistant from the others").[36] The earliest headquarters of the proto-Academy thus seem to have been chosen with an eye to convenience, to facilitating exchange. In 1634, however, Conrart got married and the group was forced to move to the home of Desmarets de Saint-Sorlin. This was the same period during which the Academy was entertaining the cardinal's offer, a connection that Pellisson highlights in his narrative. "During this same period, M. Conrart, in whose home the company had met until this time, got married. All of these gentlemen, invited to the signing of his marriage contract in their capacity as personal friends, decided among themselves that his house would no longer be as suitable as before for their meetings. Thus they began to gather at the home of M. Desmarets and to think seriously, at the urging of the cardinal, about the establishment of the Academy."[37] The fact of being forced to move, in other words, seems to have been a decisive factor in the decision to reconsider Richelieu's suggestion and reflect on the future of the Academy. The disadvantage of a circle based purely on "personal" connections, Conrart's friends realized, was that it was vulnerable to the disruptions of private life.

No permanent meeting place seems to have been established, however, until after Richelieu's death in 1642 when Séguier, the company's new protector, offered his residence. This gives Pellisson the opportunity for a digression on the significance of place in the life of an institution:

> [W]hen I think of the different locations, from one end of the city to the other, occupied by this company during the ten years preceding the arrival of this new protector, it seems to me that I see the poets' Isle of Delos, which floated and wandered [the seas] until Apollo's birth. It is truly surprising that Cardinal Richelieu, who founded it, did not make more of an effort to find it a home. If it is true, as jurists say, that lawcourts, temples, public squares, theaters, stadia—all public places, in a word—are so many bonds of civil society that join us together and unite us intimately, surely a fixed location for the Academy would strengthen the ties of this pleasant society and contribute greatly to its longevity.[38]

The fable of Delos, the island that floated freely until after Apollo's birth when Zeus fixed it to the earth with four pillars, provides Pellisson with a myth that associates the notion of place and the desire for permanence. He thus resurrects the ancient principle according to which the dignity of eloquence is attached to a physical place, a notion we have already touched on in our discussion of Balzac's letters. In the ancient city, temples, public places, theaters, and stadia were all microcosms of the *polis*. By bringing men together in a single place, they strengthened the fundamental bonds of civil society. If the French Academy was to become an institution of eloquence that could compete with the *parlement de Paris*, it needed its own place too. The culmination of this process was reached in 1672 when the Academy gained the protection of Louis XIV and was granted space within the Louvre. The Academy had finally found a definitive, royal location and the ultimate protector—a monarch whose individual body might perish, but whose sacred person was immortal. The abbé d'Olivet, Pellisson's continuator, comments on the academicians' reaction to this favor. "They did not forget to include this event in their history, *as much for the glory of the king as for that of their company.*"[39] Harkening back to Pellisson's Delos myth, the medal commemorating this event depicts Apollo in front of the *colonnade du Louvre*, the latest and most ambitious royal project in the capital (figure 5). Of course, by this time, the Apollo myth had gained a new set of connotations by virtue of its association with Louis XIV and the emerging iconographic program at Versailles.

As we have seen, the *Histoire de l'Académie* should not necessarily be taken as the definitive source on the history of the French Academy. Even if we take the interpretations given by Pellisson and d'Olivet with a certain caution, however, the progressive centralization of the Academy remains an important historical fact. It is telling, for instance, that the one prerogative that was granted to the academi-

Fig. 5. Medal commemorating the installation of the Academy in the Louvre. From *Medailles sur les principaux evenements du regne de Louis le Grand* (Paris: Imprimerie Nationale, 1702), plate 119. Reproduced from the Collections of the Library of Congress.

cians in the original letters patent was the right of *committimus*—the right to have lawsuits decided before the royal council or the *parlement de Paris,* rather than in regional jurisdictions. The rationale for this privilege is explained in the letters patent:

> And whereas the work of the members will be of great public utility, and since it will be necessary for them to devote a great deal of their leisure to this undertaking, and being that our cousin has brought it to our attention that several of them would not be able to attend meetings of the Academy very often unless we exempted them from some of the onerous

responsibilities with which they may be burdened, like our other subjects, and unless we gave them the means to avoid having to plead in person lawsuits in provinces distant from our fine city of Paris, where such meetings are to take place, [therefore] at the request of our cousin, we have by the present letters henceforth exempted the members of the Académie Française, up to the number of forty persons, from all guardianship [*tutelle et curatelle*], and accorded to them the right of *committimus*.[40]

This passage demonstrates that the right of *committimus* was granted to the academicians precisely so that they would be able to remain in Paris and fulfill their academic responsibilities without having to return to the provinces to defend their material interests. It is easy to see how such an arrangement would work in the academicians' favor, as it gave them a strategic advantage over adversaries who were not familiar with, or present in, the capital. The letters patent, incidentally, explicitly mention that they shared this right with the domestic officers and table companions (*les officiers domestiques et commensaux*) of the king, who were similarly deemed to be so necessary to the crown as to deserve special consideration. This parallel between domestic service in the king's household and literary service in the Academy is an important clue to the latter's status.

Hélène Merlin's remarks regarding the French Academy's "eccentricity" thus need to be put in perspective. Whatever marginality the Academy might have had by virtue of its linguistic mandate, both the academicians and their protectors perceived that it was advantageous to give the Academy a central position in the capital. This centralization, however, was both gradual and relative. Since the king, as we have seen, did not become its protector until 1672, it is premature to talk about the early Academy as a manifestation of the concentration of power in the hands of the king. The realignment of patronage networks was a slow process, and that it progressed in the direction it did can undoubtedly be attributed to the fact that the increased institutionalization of the patronage system served writers and the crown alike.

Immunity Revisited

That leaves the question of "immunity." Merlin is certainly correct to stress the specifically linguistic role assigned to the French Academy (its trade in words rather than things) as well as its limited authority (its linguistic decrees were not binding). Her strict divide between the spheres of public and private, political power and literary exchange fails to account, however, for the extralegal nature of power in seventeenth-century France. She is thus hard pressed to explain the first major literary event in the history of the Academy—its intervention in the *querelle du Cid*. In 1637, the *Sentiments de l'Académie sur le Cid* were published at Richelieu's instigation. If the Academy was essentially a tolerant institution committed to the respect of linguistic (though perhaps not ideological) difference, its judgment of Corneille's play becomes a paradox. As Merlin concedes, "The first action of the Academy in the seventeenth century was to immediately betray its charter."[41] One of the most significant limitations on the power of the Academy, inserted into the letters patent by Richelieu's parliamentary adversaries, was the stipulation that authors consent that their works be submitted to its censure. Following the letter of the law, then, Corneille would have been within his rights to withhold his work from consideration. When he finally submitted to the Academy's authority, however, it was in terms that hardly suggest free consent. "[S]ince you have informed me that Milord wishes to see their [the Academy's] judgment and His Eminence will find this entertaining, I have nothing to say."[42] Later in his career, Corneille would go so far as to deny that he ever submitted to the Academy's authority. While it is true that he does not exactly give his consent in this passage, neither does he *explicitly* withhold his consent. Rather, his "I have nothing to say" points to the fundamental ambivalence inherent in the notion of consent. If consent can be coerced, or if silence can be interpreted as "tacit consent," what exactly does it mean to consent?

However immune the French Academy and its activities were from formal state power, they were obviously not exempt from the informal, but very real, personal power that Richelieu exerted on writers and their production. There is no question that the early seventeenth century, as Merlin suggests, witnessed a sharpening divide between the public and private. I have argued that patronage was becoming progressively institutional, rather than personal. These categories, however, were hardly stable or watertight. Richelieu's position as minister of state, for instance, could still be leveraged in coercive ways that would be unimaginable today. The fact that he had no legal authority over Corneille or the Academy did not prevent him from exerting substantial influence. If we understand the Academy as a patronage institution, not yet fully disengaged from the personal influence of its protector, the paradox disappears, because patronage by its very nature challenges the boundaries between the political and the personal, the public and the private.

In conclusion, the foundation of the French Academy is best seen neither as a *coup de force* nor as the creation of a space of literary immunity, but rather as the first, tentative step toward reorganizing and leveraging the existing patronage system. On the one hand, by bringing together authors in a single institution, the state was able to leverage its patronage to advance an aggressive propaganda campaign that would reach its peak under Louis XIV. In the latter years of the seventeenth century, this "official patronage" would be expanded with the creation of other academies, including the Académie des Inscriptions and the Académie des Sciences, and the system of royal pensions would be instituted by Colbert with the help of Chapelain between 1662 and 1664. On the other hand, the academicians could leverage the new authority accorded to them as a group to advance the cause of the Republic of Letters and the social status of the writer.

Conversation and the Diffusion of Rhetoric

Polite conversation, needless to say, operates differently from an academy. It does not have letters patent, a director, or a fixed membership, and it is difficult to determine where it begins or ends in either space or time. Roland Barthes has described conversation as an "objet vague, sorte de 'bruit' interlocutoire" (vague object, a sort of interlocutory "noise").[43] Just as patronage subverts traditional social and historical categories such as public and private, conversation forces the linguist to reexamine notions such as "grammar," "reference," and "competency." In particular, it resists the linguistic reductionism that would characterize language as an autonomous system of signs distinct from social and political considerations. In conversation, we are never merely dealing with signs, but rather with persons or bodies who are in some degree of physical contact. Such relationships are as much social as they are semiotic. To borrow a formula coined by Pierre Bourdieu, the codes that govern conversation are not merely systems of arbitrary signs (that is, a cipher) but also social codes that govern conduct.[44] However informal it may be, conversation always has its rules, which govern who has the right to speak, on what topics, in what manner, and for how long.

This connection between speech and social practice is embedded in the history of the term *conversation*. The most primitive meaning of the verb *converser* is to be *with* someone on a regular basis—*estre ordinairement avec quelqu'un*, to quote from the *Dictionnaire de l'Académie*. Until at least the latter half of the seventeenth century, therefore, conversation did not refer to a primarily linguistic activity; like the Latin *conversatio*, it was synonym of *fréquentation*.[45] The art of conversation that flourished in the seventeenth century was extremely broad in scope, and it would be a mistake to restrict it to the confines of salon culture. Beyond the narrow framework of linguistic prescriptions, it attempted to embrace as a totality the art of living together in society.

The seminal early modern text on conversation is Stefano Guazzo's *Civil Conversation* (translated into French, from the Italian, in 1580). The modifier "civil" in the title suggests the ambitious scope of the work. Going beyond polite discussion to deal more generally with civic life, Guazzo attempts to resurrect the cosmopolitan spirit of Greek and Roman antiquity. Following Cicero, he defends the active life against a more contemplative/philosophical conception of virtue. Virtue and wisdom are of little interest unless they are deployed in the arena of social life. "It is not enough for a man to be esteemed for some dignity or principal virtue if he does not also pursue the friendship and goodwill of others, which are the true bonds of conversation."[46] Based on the notion that the function of discourse is to create personal relationships and affective bonds between human beings, the history of conversation intersects with our study of patronage. Indeed, I will argue that the flourishing culture of conversation, like the Academy, illustrates the gradual dissolution and transformation of patronage culture in the seventeenth century.

An Art of the Particular

Setting aside the humanist fantasy of resurrecting the orators of antiquity who roused the citizens of Athens and Rome with their speeches, the seventeenth-century theorists of conversation sought to valorize the intimate linguistic encounters between individuals. Some theorists took great pains to insist that conversation was entirely unrelated to rhetoric. In his *Lycée* (1642), for example, Pierre Bardin distinguished between "Moral Science," the subject of his book, and the art of "remonstrances."[47] Similarly, Antoine Gombaud, chevalier de Méré (1607–84) dismissed traditional rhetoric as a superfluous art whose principles were either trivial or wrongheaded. "This art . . . is easily learned, and there is not much to it, at least as it is usually taught. Most of those who are well versed in it are no more capable for that, either because the precepts that have been drilled into them are not worthwhile, or because they have not been taught to apply them."[48] Seventeenth-century theorists were less inclined than their sixteenth-century humanist counterparts to treat rhetoric as a difficult, arcane science that required extensive training. As Latin culture went into a steady decline, the art of syllogisms and figures gave way to an art of pleasing (*art de plaire*) based on taste and commonsense reason. Taste might not be easy to acquire (if it could be acquired at all), but it was certainly not a technical capacity, and it could not be taught exclusively through books. At the end of the century (1698), Pierre d'Ortigue de Vaumorière excluded public discourse dealing with *les grandes Affaires* from the purview of conversation because the language of those who generally spoke in public—lawyers, university professors, and others—was characterized by obscurity, technical *arcana,* and demagoguery.[49] Public speakers had forgotten how to delight their audiences, a skill that the art of conversation attempted to revive.

Despite these efforts to repudiate the technical and stylistic aspects of traditional rhetoric, conversation theory, by placing the use of the word at the heart of the social bond, nevertheless constituted an attempt to reconnect with the great principles of eloquence.[50] Although Bardin, for instance, insisted that rhetoric was not part of his subject, he nonetheless expounded on the importance of the art of mastering good speech. "There is nothing that we should work at more diligently than acquiring a form of discourse that is pleasant to others."[51] Here, the traditional focus on persuasion is shifted toward gratification. Men do not come together in society to make their lives more orderly and rational, but rather because of the pleasure they can give one another. Bardin rewrites Cicero's myth of the origin of society in terms of courtesy. "If you were to ask me what [the role of courtesy] were, I would tell you that it is the heir to the charms of Orpheus and Amphion, who tamed savage beasts and moved the stones from which the walls of cities were built. It is the reason why men seek each other out and form societies. It is thus the basis of the most honorable pleasures of human existence."[52] Absent from this account is the word as the foundation of the order of law. In Cicero's *De inventione* (see the introduction), men "cried out" against the orator's attempts to educate them in the ways of society, resisting the novelty of the "useful and honorable" occupations he offered them. Rhetoric, in other words, was seen as a necessary civilizing tool for overcoming man's bestial nature. For Bardin, by contrast, society is not the product of the persuasive work of the orator, but rather of a natural social instinct that causes man to take pleasure in the company of other men.

Another defining aspect of the rhetoric of conversation, and one of its primary affinities with the rhetoric of patronage that we have been examining, is its attentiveness to particularity. If conversation cannot be codified in the same manner as traditional oratory, it is in part because of the multitude of persons and circumstances with which the conversationalist must deal. The public orator need only master a relatively limited set of circumstances that recur with predictable frequency according to the rhythms of public life. Conversation, by contrast, is an art of expression: the speaker must adapt his or her subject, demeanor, and linguistic register to his or her interlocutor(s). The technical questions of invention and disposition (the creation and ordering of arguments) assume a lesser importance in such interactions. Since a conversation requires at least two partners, and since it is necessary to respond to the contributions of others, it is impossible to know in advance in which direction the exchange will progress. A good conversationalist can do without a sonorous voice or an extensive technical knowledge of the types of arguments and figures of discourse. There is no such thing, however, as a conversationalist who is good in theory—in front of the mirror in his bedroom, for example—but not in practice.[53]

The rhetorical principle of *aptum* (that is, *bienséance* or appropriateness) thus assumes an importance in conversation that it does not possess in traditional oratory. The insistence that the speaker adjust his discourse to time, place, and circumstance is reiterated by nearly every author who writes on conversation during this period. For Bardin, such considerations are paramount. "Time, place, and the other circumstances give our actions the imprint of goodness or malevolence."[54] The perfect gentleman "must be the master of his character and know how to adjust it according to the humor of those with whom his condition requires him to live."[55] Nearly identical passages can be found in Eustache de Refuge, Nicolas Faret, Chalesme, Antoine de Courtin, and Vaumorière.[56] Although *aptum* was an important principle in classical rhetoric, the conversation theorists of the seventeenth century assign it a more central place in human interactions. Indeed, Vaumorière goes so far as to assert that it is more difficult to be engaging with a single person than in a large company. "Do you not find that the most important skill to have in the commerce of daily life is to be able to find something to say to others in private conversation that suits them personally? As for me, I have always thought that it is easier to manage in a large company than when one is conversing with a single person."[57] He thus effectively reverses the traditional hierarchy of rhetoric, which privileged public occasions before large audiences.

The Italian Baldesar Castiglione, in his highly influential *Book of the Courtier* (1528), concluded that the great variety of persons in the world made it impossible to lay down precepts for a systematic art of conversation. There are at least as many kinds of conversation, in other words, as there are individual characters. It is left to the speaker's judgment to attempt to identify the character (*ingenium* or *génie*) of his or her interlocutor and to adjust his or her discourse accordingly.[58] Closely following Castiglione, Nicolas Faret picks up this idea in his *L'Honnête homme* (1630). "Because of the infinite diversity of encounters in polite society, it is impossible to give fixed rules regarding the manner of one's speech . . . He who wants to adapt himself to the conversation of others must use his judgment as a guide, so that distinguishing between different types of character, he can constantly adjust his language and his principles accordingly."[59] A science of conversation would thus seem to be an oxymoron, as there can be no systematic science of the particular.[60]

The art of conversation thus reflected an increased sensitivity to what was unique in the individual (his or her individual genius/*ingenium*). Following the example of Guazzo, Eustache de Refuge (1616) attempted to establish a set of principles for distinguishing among circumstances and persons and adjusting one's speech accordingly.[61] This required more than simply recognizing the gender or age of one's interlocutor, however. Every aspect of the situation had to be analyzed. If the conversationalist wanted to create a certain *mouvement* (passion) in someone to whom he was speaking, he had to consider the general causes that could produce passions, the causal relationships between them, and the susceptibility of the person to whom he was speaking. When considering the person, he further had to consider the listener's humor (melancholic, sanguine, choleric or phlegmatic), his or her prejudices, and the state of his or her affairs—not to mention the fine gradations between social ranks. The result was a kind of "generative grammar" of conversation in which a potentially infinite variety of situations could be reduced to a number of basic principles.[62]

The chevalier de Méré, by contrast, viewed the skill of adjusting one's discourse to the character of another as an *art*, analogous to portraiture. "Since eloquence is often compared to painting, it seems to me that most conversations in polite society are nothing other than tiny portraits, which do not require spectacular views [*grandes vuës*]."[63] Indeed, the status of conversation in the history of rhetoric recalls art historian John Pope-Hennessy's account of the emergence of the Renaissance portrait.[64] Pope-Hennessy shows how an increased interest in likenesses in history and religious painting gradually gave birth to portraiture, which was an art of the particular. We can speak, similarly, of a kind of miniaturization of rhetoric, linked to an increased awareness of the individual or, rather, with the subject as a site of strategic intervention. This miniaturization reaches its culmination in the science of miniscule detail that we find in midcentury treatises on conversation and manners. Méré speaks of the "almost imperceptible things" (*choses presque imperceptibles*)[65] that make all the difference in conversation, echoing Vincent Voiture's famous formula:

> Les véritables grâces, et qui touchent le plus, consistent principalement en de petites choses.[66]

> [True grace, the kind that is most touching, consists principally in little things.]

In contrast to Refuge, Voiture and Méré do not attempt to systematize circumstances, insisting instead on the role of *intuition*. Using Pascal's famous distinction, *l'esprit de géométrie* may be sufficient for traditional rhetoric; in conversation, only *l'esprit de finesse* will do. Like "high" patronage rhetoric (as opposed to conventional flattery), conversation combines the mystique of good taste with a heightened sensitivity to particularity and circumstance.

THE STAKES OF CONVERSATION

If men have assembled together for reasons of pleasure, it follows that the worth of the individual is measured by his ability to please others through conversation. Seventeenth-century treatises on manners are virtually unanimous in treating verbal conversation skills as essential to social success. What constitutes success, however, differs dramatically from author to author. The patronage model, in which success is a matter of winning the support of social superiors, continues to find spokesmen throughout the century. It has increasing competition, however, from an anticourtly strand of aristocratic egalitarianism in which pleasure is put ahead of profit.

For some authors, conversation is simply a means for climbing the social ladder. Guazzo already anticipated this idea in the sixteenth century by remarking that "it is in companies that we acquire the goodwill and favor of others."[67] Nicolas Pasquier, whose treatise *Le Gentilhomme* (1614) seeks to build a model of aristocratic conduct on the example of Montaigne's essays, similarly insists that candor of speech and action are not sufficient to earn a reputation. "It is true that he [the gentleman] should not content himself with good deeds and good speech; he should try to please others with his good deeds and good speech. For reputation is not acquired by the candor of our speech and actions alone, but by gentility."[68] The idea that a gentleman must heed the opinion of his peers and betters, and that conversation can win over opinion, is a recurrent theme in the texts of this period.[69] Nicolas Faret, whose *L'Honnête homme* is tinged with bourgeois moralism, nonetheless acknowledges that reputation has little to do with virtue or inherent worth. "Our renown depends upon conventional opinion, which is so powerful that reason can do nothing to change it."[70] Faret's treatise is written for nonnobles seeking social advancement at the court. Success thus depends on supplementing virtue with carefully calculated strategies of self-presentation. It is not enough to have merit; you must know how to put it in a favorable light (*il le faut sçavoir debiter et le faire valoir*).[71] The *honnête homme* is thus a master of what Erving Goffman has called "impression management."[72] He must present a "front" that is compatible with the station that he claims to occupy in society. This requires, in particular, that he become an expert in fashion, as nothing shocks opinion so much as a disregard for current tastes in language, manners, clothes, and other trends. This pandering is permissible, Faret explains, for the simple reason that such matters are by their very nature superficial and "indifferent" and do not hamper the exercise of virtue. To gain the affection of others, it is necessary to understand and even embrace their prejudices. Nearly all of Faret's successors in the area of *honnêteté* reiterate this imperative of heeding the dictates of fashion.[73]

In the second half of the century, Chalesme (1671) has an even more pragmatic orientation. For him, eloquence is simply a way to "get ahead" and obtain prestigious appointments. "It is quite necessary for a man of quality to devote himself as much as he can to perfecting his speech and his writing. If he does not successfully acquire this advantage, he runs the risk of not being very pleasant and not having any chance of winning prestigious appointments."[74] In particular, it is important to be pleasing to your protector, as the latter puts your services in a favorable light, enhancing your reputation. "We must choose a protector for ourselves. Indeed, given the distance between us and the person of the sovereign, a patron is a sort of middleman [*milieu*] who creates a kind of communication between these two extremes—that is to say, he brings the rumors of our services to the ear of the Prince and passes down from the prince to us the benefits that we have earned . . . It is thus necessary to please this protector."[75] Society, for Chalesme, consists of a chain of interlocking relationships. It is through conversations that reputations are made and broken, not only because one's own conversation wins over protectors, but also because one's reputation circulates through the conversations of others, eventually reaching the ear of the prince—the locus of legitimacy, power, and favor. Chalesme thus illustrates a point that should be obvious by now: "patronage rhetoric" had broad applications outside the Republic of Letters. In a society where refinement and grace were gradually replacing military valor as aristocratic values, men of letters had something to offer elite society as a whole. Integrated into the art of conversation, rhetoric ceased to be an arcane, erudite discipline and became a concrete social skill.[76]

This was especially true at court. Following Castiglione in his *Courtier,* a number of seventeenth-century authors take it for granted that the courtier's ultimate aspiration is to become counselor to the ruler. Such is especially the case in the first half of the seventeenth century, when Castiglione's influence was particularly strong in France. Thus Louis Guyon writes that the "the goal of the courtier should be to educate the prince," a sentiment echoed by early seventeenth-century theorists such as Pasquier, Refuge, and Faret, among others.[77] Conversation with the prince, however, requires no less finesse and judgment than conversation in polite society. The prince, like any other interlocutor, has a particular character that must be taken into account.[78] If he is inclined toward mischief, the counselor must act carefully so as not to lose his confidence. "If he is prone to doing unbecoming things, [the courtier] should contradict him gracefully in order to divert him from this harmful path and put him gradually onto the path of virtue by showing him how much honor and profit is showered upon him, as well as his subjects, when he is just, liberal, and magnanimous."[79] Such passages recall Balzac's portrait of Maecenas, the minister-patron who won over Augustus to the side of virtue (see chapter 1), as well as Budé's man of letters/counselor. More generally, they reflect the persistence of a humanist model in which rhetoric shapes the exercise of power by the ruler.

Pasquier, Refuge, Faret, Chalesme and, to some extent, Bardin represent one strand of the seventeenth-century literature on manners. For them, conversation is a practical skill—a means for realizing one's social ambitions. Another strand, increasingly prevalent later in the century, is represented by authors such as the chevalier de Méré, Madeleine de Scudéry, and Jean Baptiste Morvan de Bellegarde, who take great pains to remove conversation from the sordid world of competition for favors. For Bellegarde (1698), conversation is not a means to an end (favor, appointments). It is the very essence of aristocratic life. "Most persons of quality, who are usually quite idle and have few occupations, pass the time by making and receiving visits. It is very important for them to learn everything they need to know to sustain their character. The worth of a man is judged according to his ability to carry off a conversation."[80] Here, the aristocracy is neither a military nor even a political class. Its business, rather, is leisure: visits, conversations, and other social interactions. The worth of an individual is a function of the grace and finesse that he or she brings to the art of doing nothing.

For Méré, similarly, the function of conversation is not to provide a path up the social ladder toward the king, but rather to build horizontal affective bonds between kindred souls. It is the best way, he writes, to win friends (*le plus seur moyen de se faire aimer*).[81] To do this, each individual must efface his or her own particularity and attempt to adapt himself or herself to the character of others. "The best way to win over people whom we like," he writes "is to share all of their pleasures [*entrer dans tous leurs plaisirs*]."[82] Like Faret's courtier, Méré's *honnête homme* is an actor who crafts a performance to please his audience.[83] It may even be necessary, sometimes, to sacrifice either moral propriety or stylistic perfection to cater to the tastes of others. It would be a mistake, however, to assume that his performance is cynical. As his language ("winning friends") suggests, Méré is less interested in credit and influence than affection. What he is proposing is a kind of polite charity in which each person sacrifices himself or herself to provide pleasure to others. Nor is his acting hypocritical. Since the most convincing performances are those that are truest to life, the actor must internalize his role. "Nothing contributes so much [to winning friends] as appearing like a gentleman in every situation, and to appear like a gentleman, you must actually be one."[84] Méré rejects the metaphysical stance that forces us to divide the world into the categories of the real and the apparent, the ethical and the aesthetic. "Our actions are only pleasant to the extent that they are virtuous, unless you want to turn it around: they are only virtuous to the extent that they are pleasant, which seems more accurate to me."[85] Virtue pleases and pleasing is virtuous. Because of this interchangeability of ethical and aesthetic criteria, the *honnête homme*'s performance transforms him, making him better.

Daniel Gordon has noted a similar ethical orientation in Madeleine de Scudéry, who pushes an apolitical model of conversation to its logical limits.[86] All serious subjects, including politics and religion, are banned for fear of the boredom that would ensue. Devoid of political content, the group is nonetheless egalitarian in its functioning. "Everyone in the company has the same right to change it [the subject of conversation] as he/she sees fit."[87] For Scudéry, ultimately, content matters less than the dynamic of give and take. To quote Elizabeth Goldsmith, "What is important in conversation is that all participants allow the form and flow of talk to continue without paying too much attention to what is being said or weighing too carefully the value of each contribution."[88]

In Bellegarde, Méré, and Scudéry, conversation remains the measure of a man (or woman), but the opinion it seeks to seduce no longer carries the vaguely pejorative connotations present in Faret or Pasquier. It is simply the consensus of the group of one's peers. This consensus, in sharp contrast to the dogmas of politics and religion, is flexible and tolerant, the product of negotiation and compromise. Conversation thus provides a refuge for aristocrats fleeing the court. Egalitarianism and reciprocity within the conversational group are only possible, however, because of the group's exclusivity. As Goldsmith has written, "Exclusive groups counterbalance their collective sense of superiority with the conviction that they themselves are a community of equals." Democratic within, the group is elitist with respect to the outside world.[89]

Many scholars who have written on conversation have identified

Bellegarde, Méré, and Scudéry as the most compelling theorists of conversation, dismissing Pasquier, Refuge, Faret, Bardin, Chalesme, and Vaumorière as belonging to a distinct court literature. They side, in other words, with those theorists who seek to idealize conversation, rather than those who treat it as a practical social skill. For them, conversation is by its very nature egalitarian, disinterested, unserious, and only loosely organized.[90] Such scholars have undoubtedly fallen under the sway of the idealizing tendency because it appeals simultaneously to their desire to find formal coherence in conversational practice and because it seems to fit into a neat historical narrative—either harkening back to a gentler time or anticipating the Enlightenment. Nostalgic for the tolerant spirit of the Renaissance, Marc Fumaroli has called conversation a "counter-institution," a kind of apolitical resistance to the official culture of absolutism.[91] From a different perspective, Daniel Gordon has used these texts to refute Norbert Elias's influential thesis in the *Court Society*. For Elias, the mechanisms of obedience that underlie the modern state were first developed in the princely courts, where aristocrats learned self-control and violent competition was sublimated into the cult of etiquette.[92] For Gordon, by contrast, the literature of sociability has little to do with the court; rather, it is a reaction against the expansion of the state and the decline of corporate structures. Whereas theorists of absolutism embraced an Augustinian view of man's corrupt nature (thus justifying the absolute authority of monarchy as a "check on the passions"), the theorists of polite sociability explored the notion that "some meaningful activities are self-instituting, that in some situations human beings can band together of their own accord; that humans, in short, are sociable creatures."[93] Abandoning politics to the state and rejecting the hegemony of the court, salon culture developed the values of communication and reciprocity that would become the hallmark of the French Enlightenment. Gordon thus puts a new spin on Habermas's famous description of the "public sphere in apolitical form." Before the public was a political player, it was a space of conversation.

My purpose here is not to contest the conclusions of either Fumaroli or Gordon. I merely wish to question the validity of their construction of conversation as a historical object. Using an author such as Scudéry as a model for understanding the role of conversation in seventeenth-century culture can be misleading. As a woman, Scudéry could exert substantial cultural influence, but she could not aspire to an appointment at the court. Her vision of an exclusive circle of friends unconcerned with politics and public life can be at least partly explained in terms of the limitations placed on women in seventeenth-century society. None of her male counterparts, however, provide a model that is nearly so idealized. Not even Méré is immune to the attraction of the court and the possibility of influencing the prince. In his *Conversations,* he has his spokesman, the Chevalier, express precisely this aspiration. "My sentiment, the Chevalier continued, is that those who are intelligent and courteous be not only well-received by the Prince, but that an effort be made to seek them out and attract them [to court]."[94] The more general idea that the partners in conversation are on an unequal social footing is a recurrent theme of one of the most important late seventeenth-century treatises on the subject: Pierre d'Ortigue de Vaumorière's *L'Art de plaire dans la conversation* (1698). "To give [our conversation partners] the deference that is their due, it is enough that we know their rank."[95] Vaumorière testifies to the persistence of a practical orientation toward conversation. In a social climate where birth and military valor were on the decline as markers of status, the aristocrat or bourgeois who wanted to succeed at court could not afford to neglect the social graces.

Commentators such as Peter Burke and Christoph Strosetzki who have adopted a descriptive approach to seventeenth-century conversation offer a broader picture that takes courtly texts such as Vaumorière's into account. To quote Burke, "A reading of these texts that provides a truly general theory of conversation should discuss the tension and the balance between the competitive and cooperative principles, between equality and hierarchy, between inclusion and exclusion, and between spontaneity and study, rather than placing all the weight on the first item in each of these pairs."[96] A broad perspective such as Burke's is compatible, moreover, with the premise on which I have been operating in these pages, that is, that the culture of conversation was closely related to the culture of patronage I described in the first five chapters of this study. As writers were admitted to aristocratic salons and as aristocrats became more polite and artful, their interests converged. To some extent, we can say that rhetorical culture overflowed the literary milieu in which it was first articulated and became integrated into a wide range of social practices. The precepts of "personalized" rhetoric thus became principles of elite social comportment applicable in a variety of contexts. One such context, obviously, was the court, where winning over protectors and presenting a compelling image of the self were essential to social success. Indeed, many of the examples cited above come from treatises on how to succeed at court. These principles of courtesy would later become the basis for good manners in increasingly broad segments of society.[97]

If we limit our focus to the idealizing texts on conversation and sociability, another process comes to the fore. Once the group is substituted for the protector, once the speaker is solely concerned with pleasing his or her peers, we are no longer dealing with something recognizable as classic patronage. The vertical dynamic disappears and, as Gordon would put it, a new "self-instituting" social order emerges. By positing the principle that "who you are is a function of whom you know," patronage culture arguably helped create the conditions for this new conception of the social. The necessary leap was the assumption that certain *external* factors outside the scope of the group could be excluded from consideration and that all that mattered were the relationships that members of the group constructed with each other.[98] In reality, of course, access to salons such as those of Mme de Rambouillet and her successors was a matter of having the right connections and obtaining the support of an influential sponsor. It is hardly plausible that the participants in such groups ever entirely forgot the social standing of their peers; more likely, the egalitarian conversation was an "ideal type" that never really existed. The elaboration of an ostensibly autonomous and egalitarian salon culture, in other words, was predicated on a kind of ideological blindness. Like any political order, it forgot the injustices at its origin.

The particularistic, hierarchical culture of patronage described in these pages corresponds to a transitional moment in French history that coincided with the acceleration during the early seventeenth century of the long process that transformed France from a feudal kingdom into a modern state. Literary patronage, of course, did not die after 1661, or even at the end of the seventeenth century. Patronage, however, changed in significant ways over the course of the seventeenth and eighteenth centuries. As we have seen, the diffuse culture of patronage resolved in two different directions as its personal and the hierarchical aspects were increasingly decoupled from each other. On the one hand, as the example of the French Academy suggests, official (that is, bureaucratic and impersonal) patronage assumed an increasingly important role, serving both the professional interests of writers and the political interests of the state. On the other hand, the culture of literary patronage gradually merged into practices of polite sociability and conversation. The rhetorical art of negotiating personal relationships gradually lost its literary character and became the foundation of polite society, whether at the court or in salons. The new theorists of egalitarian sociability, meanwhile, increasingly downplayed the hierarchical nature of such contacts. These trends become more pronounced in the latter half of the seventeenth century. By the end of the eighteenth century, they help create the conditions of the French Revolution, most notably a high degree of centralization of political power and the emergence of a "public sphere."

Conclusion

> [P]our déployer tous les efforts dont on est capable, ce n'est pas à un petit cercle d'amis ou de complaisans adulateurs qu'il faut se borner lorsqu'on écrit: il faut . . . se produire au grand jour.
>
> [If you want to demonstrate your abilities, you should not limit yourself to writing for a small circle of friends or accommodating admirers; instead, you should . . . expose your work to the light of public opinion.]
>
> —Jean le Rond d'Alembert

THE MID-SEVENTEENTH CENTURY REPRESENTS A MOMENT OF TRANSITION poised between a highly personalized culture of patronage and newer, more familiar cultural forms such as commercial publishing and state patronage. Writers still had a strong sense of being embedded in networks of interpersonal relations, and indeed much of my argument has been devoted to studying how this sense of personal "connectedness" shaped seventeenth-century literary discourse. Boisrobert's *Épîtres*, Balzac's *Lettres*, Théophile's *Maison de Silvie*, Mairet's *La Silvanire*, and Du Ryer's *Les Vendanges de Suresnes*, to take the most striking examples, all illustrate that the bonds of patronage could engender resentment, but they could also be a rich source of inspiration.

At the same time, I have tried to emphasize the relative looseness and adaptability of patronage relationships in the first half of the seventeenth century, as well as the liminality of patronage—the way that it sits on the threshold between public and private, self and other. During this period when authors and the state alike were experimenting with new models of culture, the patronage "system" (for lack of a better word) served as a kind of "primordial soup" out of which new configurations of culture and power emerged: authors such as Du Ryer and Sorel pushed the limits of patronage as they imagined new models of authorship; the state began to build an official, national culture that reached an apogee at Versailles under

Louis XIV; and disaffected aristocrats developed networks of egalitarian sociability. None of these developments would have been possible without the existing framework of patronage, and yet each anticipates its declining relevance.

Antoine Furetière's *Roman bourgeois* (1666) illustrates the extent to which the delicate equilibrium between idealism and self-interest that had characterized patronage before 1650 became increasingly untenable in the second half of the century. The novel ends with a *Somme dédicatoire*, a satirical treatise on dedicatory epistles that lays down rules for the relationships between writers and the patrons to whom they dedicate their books. Is a writer in the household service of a patron required to dedicate his works exclusively to him or her, Furetière wonders? If he does not receive a *gratification*, can he withdraw his dedication? What if a patron falls out of favor? The absurdity reaches its culmination with a table of prices for different kinds of dedications, according to genre (for example, 3 *livres* for a sonnet or 2,000 *livres* for an epic poem).[1] With its specific prices and rules and its spirit of calculation, the *Somme* undermines the informal character of patronage, rooted in an aristocratic culture of magnanimity and personal honor.

This trend becomes even more pronounced in the eighteenth century. Jean le Rond d'Alembert's *Essai sur la société des gens de lettres et des grands, sur la réputation, sur les mécènes, et sur les récompenses littéraires* (1753) presents a cynical portrait of the personal relationship between men of letters and aristocrats. He mercilessly dissects the self-interested bond between artistic creator and elite audience that underlies the aesthetics of patronage. While aristocrats seek out men of letters because of the *chic* associated with the new philosophical spirit, the latter seek out the former not only to gain material advantages, but also because they provide an ideal audience to satisfy their vanity. Literature, d'Alembert observes, is a rather subjective discipline: unlike the hard sciences, it has no right or wrong answer, and thus no objective standard by which to measure individual achievement and aesthetic value. This creates a space of ambiguity where men of letters can fabricate literary reputations with the help of protectors. The alliance between aristocrats and men of letters is thus revealed to be a ploy of vanity on both sides. The true value of aesthetic works, according to d'Alembert, is assigned by the market of public opinion. "A man who feels that his talents and genius should earn him fame need only let public opinion do its work."[2]

For Voltaire, writing on the subject of "men of letters" for the *Encyclopédie* (1753), the only worthwhile patronage is the bureaucratic *régime* introduced by Louis XIV. "Men of letters . . . are ordinarily more independent-minded than other men, and those who are born without a fortune to their name can easily use the foundations created by Louis XIV to strengthen this independence; we no longer see, as we once did, dedicatory epistles offered up to vanity by self-interest and servility."[3] Although he is coming from a very different perspective than d'Alembert, Voltaire similarly takes aim at the personal aspect of patronage. Because it is rational and impersonal, royal patronage offers writers a margin of independence that the informal networks of nobiliary patronage could not provide. It frees men of letters from the need to ingratiate themselves with individual patrons and bestows on them the *imprimatur* of the French crown. A monarchist at heart, Voltaire has nothing to say about the sacrifices to official ideology and style that men of letters must make to earn their pensions. He assumes that monarchs will be of the enlightened variety and that they will view good letters and philosophical reason as the basis for solid statecraft. Just as Louis XIV established peace within his kingdom, his academies and royal pensions bring order to the Republic of Letters.

Patronage did not disappear in the eighteenth century: we need only think of Voltaire at the courts of Stanislas and Frederick the Great or Malesherbes's protection of the *Encyclopédie*.[4] Indeed, as recent research on modernism has shown, patronage never really disappeared in either its official or personal variations.[5] The specifically local, informal, particularistic, and hierarchical patronage characteristic of the early seventeenth-century, however, became progressively less visible and central to the self-image of writers and patrons.[6] Increasingly, both justified their existence by appealing to universal, rational principles (the example of the *Encyclopédie* is particularly telling), and the public (in the Habermasian sense of public opinion, but also in the economic sense of a buying public) became a growing preoccupation of both writers and the state. Eventually, with the advent of Romanticism, the solitary genius would become the central figure of the literary imagination (if not of the sociological reality). Nostalgic for a slower, gentler time, Marc Fumaroli has devoted much of his work to attempts to rehabilitate the personal culture of patronage characteristic of the period studied in this book.[7] I suspect that it is neither possible nor desirable to turn back the clock. Nevertheless, in an age when the author has supposedly died, public reason has come under attack, and writers and readers are increasingly seeking more personal ways of relating to each other (through direct marketing, the internet, book clubs, and other avenues), it is instructive to remember how writers and readers related to texts in another time.[8]

Notes

Introduction

1. Margaret Jane Wyszomirski, "From Accord to Discord: Arts Policy During and After the Culture Wars," in *America's Commitment to Culture, Government, and the Arts*, ed. Kevin V. Mulcahy and Margaret Jane Wyszomirski (Boulder, CO: Westview Press, 1995), 23–24.

2. Jürgen Habermas, *The Structural Transformation of the Public Sphere: An Inquiry into a Category of Bourgeois Society*, trans. Thomas Burger, Studies in Contemporary German Social Thought (Cambridge, MA: MIT Press, 1989), 7. See also Orest A. Ranum, *Artisans of Glory: Writers and Historical Thought in Seventeenth-Century France* (Chapel Hill: University of North Carolina Press, 1980), 31; Roger Chartier, *On the Edge of the Cliff: History, Language, and Practices*, trans. Lydia G. Cochrane (Baltimore: Johns Hopkins University Press, 1997), 86–87.

3. Hélène Merlin, *Public et littérature en France au XVIIe siècle* (Paris: Les Belles Lettres, 1994), 25–29.

4. Ranum, *Artisans of Glory*, 31.

5. Alain Viala and Christian Jouhaud, eds., *De la publication: entre Renaissance et Lumières* (Paris: Fayard, 2002).

6. Stephen Greenblatt, "Toward a Poetics of Culture," in *Learning to Curse* (New York: Routledge, 1990), 158.

7. S. N. Eisenstadt and Louis Roniger, "Patron-Client Relations as a Model of Structuring Social Exchange," *Comparative Studies in Society and History* 22, no. 1 (1980): 47–48.

8. Ibid., 47.

9. Sharon Kettering, *Patrons, Brokers, and Clients in Seventeenth-Century France* (New York: Oxford University Press, 1986). See also Katia Béguin, *Les Princes de Condé: rebelles, courtisans et mécènes dans la France du grand siècle* (Seyssel: Champ Vallon, 1999).

10. Ronald Weissman, "Taking Patronage Seriously: Mediterranean Values and Renaissance Society," in *Patronage, Art, and Society in Renaissance Italy*, ed. F. W. Kent, Patricia Simons, and J. C. Eade (New York: Oxford University Press, 1987), 44. See also Priscilla Parkhurst Ferguson, *Literary France: The Making of a Culture* (Berkeley and Los Angeles: University of California Press, 1987), 39.

11. For examples of a similar approach, see Arthur F. Marotti, *John Donne, Coterie Poet* (Madison: University of Wisconsin Press, 1986); Lauro Martines, *Strong Words: Writing and Social Strain in the Italian Renaissance* (Baltimore: Johns Hopkins University Press, 2001).

12. Ernst Hartwig Kantorowicz, *The King's Two Bodies: A Study in Mediaeval Political Theology* (Princeton, NJ: Princeton University Press, 1957); Jean-Marie Apostol-

idès, *Le Roi-machine: spectacle et politique au temps de Louis XIV* (Paris: Minuit, 1981); Louis Marin, *Le Portrait du roi* (Paris: Minuit, 1981); Peter Burke, *The Fabrication of Louis XIV* (New Haven, CT: Yale University Press, 1992); Abby E. Zanger, *Scenes from the Marriage of Louis XIV: Nuptial Fictions and the Making of Absolutist Power* (Stanford, CA: Stanford University Press, 1997).

13. Marc Fumaroli, *L'Âge de l'éloquence: rhétorique et "res literaria", de la Renaissance au seuil de l'époque classique* (Geneva: Droz, 1980), x.

14. Marcus Tullius Cicero, *De inventione*, trans. H. M. Hubbell (Cambridge, MA: Harvard University Press, 1949), 5–7.

15. Daniel de Priézac, *Discours politiques* (Paris: Foucault, 1666), 2.

16. See Ranum, *Artisans of Glory*, 48; Donald R. Kelley, *Foundations of Modern Historical Scholarship: Language, Law, and History in the French Renaissance* (New York: Columbia University Press, 1970), 53–85.

17. Guillaume Budé, *De l'institution du prince* (Paris: Maistre Nicole Paris, 1547), 16.

18. Ibid., 67.

19. Ibid., 54–55.

20. Roger Chartier, *Forms and Meanings: Texts, Performances, and Audiences from Codex to Computer* (Philadelphia: University of Pennsylvania Press, 1995), 29.

21. Examples of this intimate gesture of presenting a patron with a unique, specially bound copy, often in manuscript form, can be documented through the seventeenth century. See Alain Viala, *Naissance de l'écrivain: sociologie de la littérature à l'âge classique*, Le Sens Commun (Paris: Minuit, 1985), 167.

22. Fumaroli, *Âge de l'éloquence*, 101–6.

23. Michel de Montaigne, *Complete Essays*, trans. Donald M. Frame (Stanford, CA: Stanford University Press, 1958), 2.

24. Baldesar Castiglione, *Book of the Courtier*, trans. Charles S. Singleton (Garden City, NJ: Anchor, 1959), 109.

25. Reinhart Koselleck, *Critique and Crisis: Enlightenment and the Pathogenesis of Modern Society*, Studies in Contemporary German Social Thought (Cambridge, MA: MIT Press, 1988), 20; Merlin, *Public et littérature*, 19.

26. Robert C. Evans, "Poetry and Power: Ben Jonson and the Poetics of Patronage" (PhD diss., Princeton University, 1984), 567.

CHAPTER 1. THEORIZING PATRONAGE

1. Roland Mousnier, *The Institutions of France under the Absolute Monarchy, 1598–1789* (Chicago: University of Chicago Press, 1979), 1:99. See also Thierry Rentet, "Fidélités et clientèles en France de 1500 à 1660," *L'Information historique*, no. 57 (1995): 89–99.

2. Mousnier, *Institutions*, 1:6.

3. Ibid., 1:99.

4. Ibid., 1:100 (emphasis added).

5. Ibid., 1:105.

6. Ibid., 1:107.

7. Marc Fumaroli, "Introduction," in *L'Âge d'or du mécénat (1598–1661): actes du*

colloque international CNRS (mars 1983), ed. Roland Mousnier and Jean Mesnard (Paris: CNRS, 1985), 1–11.

8. William Beik, *Absolutism and Society in Seventeenth-Century France: State Power and Provincial Aristocracy in Languedoc*, Cambridge Studies in Early Modern History (Cambridge: Cambridge University Press, 1985); Sharon Kettering, *Patrons, Brokers, and Clients in Seventeenth-Century France* (New York: Oxford University Press, 1986); David Parker, "Class, Clientage and Personal Rule in Absolutist France," *Seventeenth-Century French Studies*, no. 9 (1987). For an approach that attempts to dispense with patronage entirely, see Kristen Brooke Neuschel, *Word of Honor: Interpreting Noble Culture in Sixteenth-Century France* (Ithaca, NY: Cornell University Press, 1989).

9. Kettering, *Patrons, Brokers, and Clients*, 9.

10. Ronald Weissman, "Taking Patronage Seriously: Mediterranean Values and Renaissance Society," in *Patronage, Art, and Society in Renaissance Italy*, ed. F. W. Kent, Patricia Simons, and J. C. Eade (New York: Oxford University Press, 1987), 36–37.

11. Orest A. Ranum, *Artisans of Glory: Writers and Historical Thought in Seventeenth-Century France* (Chapel Hill: University of North Carolina Press, 1980), 149.

12. Antoine Adam, *Théophile de Viau et la libre pensée française en 1620* (Geneva: Droz, 1935; reprint, Geneva: Slatkine Reprints, 1966), 430.

13. Henri-Jean Martin, *Livres, pouvoirs et société à Paris au XVIIe siècle (1598–1701)* (Geneva: Droz, 1969), 430.

14. Georges Mongrédien, *La Vie de société aux XVIIe et XVIIIe siècles* (Paris: Hachette, 1950), 13; C. A. J. Armstrong, "The Golden Age of Burgundy," in *The Courts of Europe: Politics, Patronage and Royalty, 1400–1800,* ed. A. G. Dickens (London: Thames & Hudson, 1977), 55–75; A. G. Dickens, "Monarchy and Cultural Revival: Courts in the Middle Ages," in *The Courts of Europe: Politics, Patronage and Royalty, 1400–1800,* ed. A. G. Dickens (London: Thames & Hudson, 1977), 8–30; R. J. Knecht, *Renaissance Warrior and Patron: The Reign of Francis I* (Cambridge: Cambridge University Press, 1994); Johan Huizinga, *The Autumn of the Middle Ages,* trans. Rodney J. Payton (Chicago: University of Chicago Press, 1996); Emmanuel Bourassin, *François Ier: le roi et le mécène* (Paris: Tallandier, 1997). For an influential interpretation of the transformation in patronage relations brought on by print culture during the late Middle Ages, see Cynthia J. Brown, *Poets, Patrons, and Printers* (Ithaca, NY: Cornell University Press, 1995).

15. John Lough, *Writer and Public in France: from the Middle Ages to the Present Day* (Oxford: Clarendon Press, 1978), 99.

16. Maurice Magendie, *La Politesse mondaine et les théories de l'honnêteté en France au XVIIe siècle, de 1600 à 1660* (Paris: Presses Universitaires de France, 1925; reprint, Geneva: Slatkine Reprints, 1970), 4. See, for instance, François Maynard, *Poésies,* ed. Ferdinand Gohin (Paris: Garnier, 1927), 80.

17. Gédéon Tallemant des Réaux, *Historiettes* (Paris: Gallimard, 1961), 1:344.

18. Mongrédien, *La Vie de société aux XVIIe et XVIIIe siècles*, 14.

19. Claude Kurt Abraham, *Gaston d'Orléans et sa cour: étude litteraire* (Chapel Hill: University of North Carolina Press, 1963).

20. On the pensions see P. Desmolets, *Mémoires de littérature et d'histoire*, vol. 2 (Paris: Nyon fils, 1749), 21–56, 318–63; Jean Chapelain, *Lettres de Jean Chapelain de l'Académie française,* ed. Philippe Tamizey de Larroque (Paris: Imprimerie Nationale, 1880–1883; reprint, Paris: Bibliothèque Nationale, 1968.), 2:273–77; Lough, *Writer and Public,* 107; Ranum, *Artisans of Glory,* 162–63. The project had its origins in 1655, when Colbert asked Pierre Costar to draw up a list of worthy writers.

21. Philip Tomlinson, *Jean Mairet et ses protecteurs: une œuvre dans son milieu*, Biblio 17 (Paris: Papers on French Seventeenth Century Literature, 1983).
22. Tallemant des Réaux, *Historiettes*, 1:362–63.
23. Nicolas Schapira, *Un Professionnel des lettres au XVIIe siècle: Valentin Conrart, une histoire sociale*, Époques (Seyssel: Champ Vallon, 2003), 51.
24. André Tuilier, ed., *Richelieu et le monde de l'esprit* (Paris: Imprimerie nationale, 1985); Roland Mousnier, ed., *Richelieu et la culture: actes du colloque international en Sorbonne* (Paris: CNRS, 1987); Hilliard Todd Goldfarb, ed., *Richelieu: l'art et le pouvoir* (Montreal: Musée des Beaux-Arts de Montréal, 2002); Hugh Gaston Hall, *Richelieu's Desmarets* (Oxford: Clarendon Press, 1990).
25. Mark Bannister, "The Crisis of Literary Patronage in France, 1643–1655," *French Studies* 39, no. 1 (1985): 18–30. Some writers who sought and/or received Mazarin's protection include Jean-Louis Guez de Balzac, Pierre Corneille, Jean Chapelain, François Maynard, Guillaume Colletet, and Marin Le Roy de Gomberville. On the writers' involvement in the Fronde, see Christian Jouhaud, *Mazarinades: la Fronde des mots* (Paris: Aubier, 1985), 37.
26. Paul Scarron, *Poésies diverses*, ed. Maurice Cauchie (Paris: Marcel Didier, 1947), 2:57.
27. Ibid., 2:59.
28. François Le Métel de Boisrobert, *Épistres en vers* (Paris: Hachette, 1921), 2:29.
29. Tallemant des Réaux, *Historiettes*, 1:614.
30. Schapira, *Un Professionnel des lettres*, 98–151.
31. René Kerviler, *Le Chancelier Séguier, second protecteur de l'Académie française* (Paris: Marcel Didier, 1874); Urbain Chatelain, *Le Surintendant Foucquet, protecteur des lettres, des arts et des sciences* (Paris: Perrin, 1905); Wolfgang Leiner, "Nicolas Fouquet au jeu des miroirs," in *Études sur la littérature française du XVIIe siècle*, ed. Volker Schröder and Rainer Zaiser, Biblio 17 (Paris: Papers on French Seventeenth Century Literature, 1996), 251–73; Marc Fumaroli, *Le Poète et le roi: Jean de La Fontaine en son siècle* (Paris: Éditions de Fallois, 1997); Madeleine de Seudéry, *Clélie, histoire romaine*, vol. 6, bk. 2 (Paris: Augustin Courbé, 1660), 860–64.
32. Tallemant des Réaux, *Historiettes*, 2:537–41; Georges Mongrédien, "Le Mécène de Corneille: M. de Montauron," *Revue de France*, 15 novembre 1928.
33. See Roger Chartier, *The Order of Books: Readers, Authors, and Libraries in Europe between the Fourteenth and Eighteenth Centuries*, trans. Lydia G. Cochrane (Stanford, CA: Stanford University Press, 1994), 47. As Chartier has pointed out, publishers often paid writers by giving them copies of their books that they could give as gifts to friends and protectors.
34. Lough, *Writer and Public*, 99.
35. Ranum, *Artisans of Glory*, 149.
36. Alain Viala, *Naissance de l'écrivain: sociologie de la littérature à l'âge classique*, Le Sens Commun (Paris: Minuit, 1985), 58. See also Mathurin Régnier, *Œuvres complètes*, ed. Gabriel Raibaud (Paris: Marcel Didier, 1958), 15. Régnier satirizes this practice in his second *Satire*.
37. Émile Magne, *Le Plaisant abbé de Boisrobert* (Paris: Mercure de France, 1909); Lough, *Writer and Public*, 97.
38. Viala, *Naissance de l'écrivain*, 58.
39. Tallemant des Réaux, *Historiettes*, 1:326.
40. Lough, *Writer and Public*, 116. Mme de La Sablière, similarly, housed Jean de La Fontaine.

41. Marc Antoine Girard de Saint-Amant, *Œuvres*, ed. Jacques Bailbé and Jean Lagny (Paris: Marcel Didier, 1967), 60. See also Antoine Furetière, *Le Roman bourgeois*, Folio (Paris: Gallimard, 1981), 227. Furetière imagines an "Almanach de disners," a sort of guidebook for writers to the best tables in Paris.

42. Tallemant des Réaux, *Historiettes*, 2:326.

43. Viala, *Naissance de l'écrivain*, 147–50; Priscilla Parkhurst Ferguson, *Literary France: The Making of a Culture* (Berkeley and Los Angeles: University of California Press, 1987), 45–48.

44. Viala, *Naissance de l'écrivain*, 54. On the aristocratic household as social unit, see Mousnier, *Institutions*, 91–95.

45. If the distinction between *mécénat* and *clientélisme* proves so tenuous, it is perhaps because the notion of "pure gift" invites suspicion. See chapter 2.

46. Norbert Elias, *The Court Society* (New York: Pantheon Books, 1983); Domna C. Stanton, *The Aristocrat as Art: A Study of the Honnête Homme and the Dandy in Seventeenth- and Nineteenth-Century French Literature* (New York: Columbia University Press, 1980).

47. Louis Althusser, *Lenin and Philosophy and Other Essays*, trans. Ben Brewster (London: New Left Books, 1971), 153.

48. Viala, *Naissance de l'écrivain*, 62 (emphasis added).

49. Ibid., 316.

50. D. V. Kent, *Cosimo de' Medici and the Florentine Renaissance: The Patron's Œuvre* (New Haven, CT: Yale University Press, 2000), 8 (emphasis added). See also Christian Jouhaud and Hélène Merlin, "Mécènes, patrons et clients: les médiations textuelles comme pratiques clientélaires au XVIIe siècle," *Terrain*, no. 21 (1993): 48.

51. Pierre Richelet, *Dictionnaire françois contenant les mots et les choses* (Geneva: Widerhold, 1680; reprint, Geneva: Slatkine Reprints, 1970), s.v. "Patron."

52. Antoine Furetière, *Le Dictionnaire universel d'Antoine Furetière* (Rotterdam: Arnout et Reinier Leers, 1690; reprint, Paris: S.N.L.-Le Robert, 1978), s.v. "Patron."

53. Académie française, *Le Dictionnaire de l'Académie françoise* (Paris: J. B. Coignard, 1694), s.v. "Patron."

54. Antoine Furetière, *Le Dictionnaire universel*, 2nd ed. (The Hague: Pierre Husson et al., 1927; reprint, Hildesheim: G. Olms Verlag, 1972), s.v. "Patron."

55. Robert Muchembled, *Popular Culture and Elite Culture in France* (Baton Rouge: Louisiana State University Press, 1985).

56. Jonathan Dewald, *Aristocratic Experience and the Origins of Modern Culture: France, 1570–1715* (Berkeley and Los Angeles: University of California Press, 1993), 86–94.

57. Antoine de Courtin, *Nouveau traité de la civilité qui se pratique en France parmi les honnestes gens*, ed. Marie-Claire Grassi (Saint-Étienne: Publications de l'Université de Saint-Étienne, 1998), 61. See also Nicolas Pasquier, *Le Gentilhomme* (Paris: Champion, 2003), 171.

58. Richelet, *Dictionnaire françois*, s.v. "Mécenas."

59. Furetière, *Le Dictionnaire universel d'Antoine Furetière*, s.v. "Mecenas."

60. Furetière, *Le Dictionnaire universel*, s.v. "Mecenas."

61. Nicolas Boileau-Despréaux, *Œuvres* (Paris: Garnier-Flammarion, 1969), 1:51.

62. Wolfgang Leiner, *Der Widmungsbrief in der französischen Literatur (1580–1715)* (Heidelberg: Winter, 1965), 19–20.

63. Jean-Louis Guez de Balzac, *Œuvres diverses (1644)*, ed. Roger Zuber (Paris: Champion, 1995), 137. Further citations to this work are given in the text.

64. Elias, *The Court Society*. On this ethic of prosperity and tranquillity, which was prevalent among the equestrian order to which Maecenas belonged, see Jean-Marie André, *Mécène, essai de biographie spirituelle* (Paris: Les Belles Lettres, 1967), 68.

65. For the tradition of comparison between Agrippa and Maecenas, which dates back to Tacitus, see Bernard Beugnot, "La Figure du Mécénas," in *L'Âge d'or du mécénat (1598–1661): actes du colloque international CNRS (mars 1983)*, ed. Roland Mousnier and Jean Mesnard (Paris: CNRS, 1985), 286. See also Nicolas Coëffeteau, *Histoire romaine* (Paris: Antoine Maurry, 1680), 1:433.

66. Viala, *Naissance de l'écrivain*, 69.

67. On Maecenas's Epicurean leanings, see André, *Mécène*, 75.

68. Beugnot, "La Figure du Mécénas," 260.

69. In this respect, he is faithful to the the historical Maecenas. See André, *Mécène*, 75.

70. Hélène Merlin, *Public et littérature en France au XVIIe siècle* (Paris: Les Belles Lettres, 1994), 140.

71. See François de La Motte le Vayer, *Considérations sur l'éloquence françoise de ce temps* (Paris: S. Cramoisy, 1638), 85. These critiques are picked up La Mothe le Vayer, who criticizes Maecenas for his "harmonie trop affectée." La Mothe le Vayer and other regulars of the *cabinet* Dupuy aligned themselves against Balzac in the quarrels following the publication of his letters (see chapter 2).

72. Balzac, *Œuvres diverses*, 142.

73. For Balzac's bitter feelings toward Richelieu, see Jean-Louis Guez de Balzac, *Lettres de Jean-Louis Guez de Balzac publiées par Philippe Tamizey de Larroque*, Mélanges historiques (Paris: Imprimerie Nationale, 1873), 462.

74. Jean-Louis Guez de Balzac, *Les Entretiens (1657)*, ed. Bernard Beugnot (Paris: Marcel Didier, 1972), 319.

75. Ibid., 320.

76. Tallemant des Réaux, *Historiettes*, 1:272.

77. Balzac, *Œuvres diverses*, 74.

78. Émile Magne, *Voiture et les origines de l'hôtel de Rambouillet: portrait et documents inédits* (Paris: Mercure de France, 1911); Émile Magne, *Voiture et les années de gloire à l'hôtel de Rambouillet: portrait et documents inédits* (Paris: Mercure de France, 1912).

79. Henry Carrington Lancaster, *A History of French Dramatic Literature in the Seventeenth Century* (Baltimore: Johns Hopkins University Press, 1929–1942; reprint, New York: Gordian Press, 1966), 1:526.

80. Boisrobert, *Épistres*, 1:46. Further citations to this work are given in the text.

81. On Boisrobert's role at Richelieu's side, see Chapelain, *Lettres de Jean Chapelain*, 1:678, 1:129–30, 1:208–9; Jean-Louis Guez de Balzac, *Œuvres de Monsieur de Balzac divisées en deux tomes* (Paris: T. Jolly, 1665), 1:246–47, 1:716–17.

82. Patronage was as important in getting pensions paid as it was in obtaining pensions in the first place.

83. Christian Jouhaud, *Les Pouvoirs de la littérature: histoire d'un paradoxe* (Paris: Gallimard, 2000), 108–9.

84. Larry F. Norman, *The Public Mirror: Molière and the Social Commerce of Depiction* (Chicago: University of Chicago Press, 1999).

85. Viala, *Naissance de l'écrivain*, 176.

86. Jouhaud, *Pouvoirs*, 19.

87. Mario Biagioli, *Galileo, Courtier: The Practice of Science in the Culture of Absolut-*

ism, Science and its Conceptual Foundations (Chicago: University of Chicago Press, 1993), 90.

88. Ferguson, *Literary France*, 37.

Chapter 2. Reinventing Eloquence

1. Charles-Augustin Sainte-Beuve, *Port-Royal* (Paris: Hachette, 1860), 2:80.
2. Ibid., 2:77–78.
3. Ibid., 2:46.
4. Gaston Guillaumie, *J. L. Guez de Balzac et la prose française* (Paris: Picard, 1927), 55–58.
5. Ibid., 58. See also F. E. Sutcliffe, *Guez de Balzac: littérature et politique* (Paris: Nizet, 1959); Jean Jéhasse, *Guez de Balzac et le génie romain* (Saint-Étienne: Publications de l'Université de Saint-Étienne, 1977); Marc Fumaroli, *L'Âge de l'éloquence: rhétorique et "res literaria", de la Renaissance au seuil de l'époque classique* (Geneva: Droz, 1980); Christian Jouhaud, *Les Pouvoirs de la littérature: histoire d'un paradoxe* (Paris: Gallimard, 2000); Hélène Merlin-Kajman, *L'Excentricité académique: littérature, institution, société* (Paris: Les Belles Lettres, 2001).
6. For detailed biographical information, see Sutcliffe, *Guez de Balzac*; Zobeidah Youssef, *Polémique et littérature chez Guez de Balzac* (Paris: Nizet, 1972); Jéhasse, *Guez de Balzac*.
7. Jean-Louis Guez de Balzac, *Les Premières lettres de Guez de Balzac*, ed. H. Bibas and K. T. Butler, Société des Textes Français Modernes (Paris: Droz, 1933), 1:237. Further citations to this work are given in the text.
8. Jouhaud, *Pouvoirs*, 62.
9. Benedict R. Anderson, *Imagined Communities: Reflections on the Origin and Spread of Nationalism* (London: Verso, 1991).
10. Fumaroli, *Âge de l'éloquence*, 419.
11. Hélène Tierchant, *Le Duc d'Épernon: le favori de Henri III* (Paris: Pygmalion, 2002).
12. Jean Jéhasse, "Jean-Louis Balzac et l'esthétique de la pastorale," in *Le Genre pastoral en Europe du XVe au XVIIe siècle*, ed. Claude Longeon (Saint-Étienne: Publications de l'Université de Saint-Étienne, 1980), 245.
13. Honoré d' Urfé, *L'Astrée*, ed. Louis Mercier (Lyon: Pierre Masson, 1925), 1:9. On the pastoral, see Marc Fumaroli, *Le Poète et le roi: Jean de La Fontaine en son siècle* (Paris: Éditions de Fallois, 1997), 113; Jean-Pierre van Elslande, *L'Imaginaire pastoral du XVIIe siècle: 1600–1650* (Paris: Presses Universitaires de France, 1999). On the *locus amoenus*, see Ernst Robert Curtius, *European Literature and the Latin Middle Ages* (Princeton, NJ: Princeton University Press, 1973), 183–202.
14. See Frances Amelia Yates, *Astraea: The Imperial Theme in the Sixteenth Century* (London: Routledge, 1975).
15. Fumaroli, *Âge de l'éloquence*, 427–29.
16. Christian Jouhaud, "Power and Literature: The Terms of the Exchange 1624–42," in *The Administration of Aesthetics: Censorship, Political Criticism, and the Public Sphere*, ed. Richard Burt (Minneapolis: University of Minnesota Press, 1994), 47.
17. Bernard Beugnot, "L'Écriture du paysage de Balzac: imaginaire et genèse," *XVIIe siècle* 42, no. 3 (1990): 359–69.

18. Youssef, *Polémique et littérature*.

19. Natalie Zemon Davis, *The Gift in Sixteenth-Century France* (New York: Oxford University Press, 2000), 42; Marcel Mauss, *The Gift: Forms and Functions of Exchange in Archaic Societies* (Glencoe, IL: Free Press, 1954), 44–45.

20. Pierre Bourdieu, *Outline of a Theory of Practice* (Cambridge: Cambridge University Press, 1977), 197.

21. Georges Bataille, *La Part maudite* (Paris: Minuit, 1967), 138.

22. Pierre Bourdieu, *Les Règles de l'art: genèse et structure du champ littéraire* (Paris: Seuil, 1992).

23. See Jean-Pierre Camus, *Conférence académique sur le différent des belles-lettres de Narcisse et de Phyllarque par le sieur de Musac* (Paris: J. Cottereau, 1630); Youssef, *Polémique et littérature*; Jéhasse, *Guez de Balzac*; Jouhaud, *Pouvoirs*.

24. François Garasse, *Response du sieur Hydaspe au sieur de Balzac sous le nom de Sacrator, touchant l'anti-Théophile et ses écrits* (N.p.: 1624); André de Saint-Denis, *Conformité de l'eloquence de Mr de Balzac avec celle des plus grand personnages du temps present et passé* (N.p.: 1627); Charles Sorel, *Histoire comique de Francion*, ed. Fausta Garavini (Paris: Gallimard, 1996). See also Youssef, *Polémique et littérature*.

25. See Camus, *Conférence académique*, 46.

26. François Ogier, *Apologie pour Monsieur de Balzac* (Saint-Étienne: Publications de l'Université de Saint-Étienne, 1977), 296.

27. Ibid., 289.

28. Ibid., 297.

29. Pierre Zoberman, *Cérémonies de la parole: l'éloquence d'apparat en France dans le dernier quart du XVIIe siècle* (Paris: Champion, 1999).

30. Le Père Jean Goulu, *Lettres de Phyllarque à Ariste, où il est traité de l'éloquence française* (Paris: N. Buon, 1627–1628), 2:17.

31. Ibid., 2:369.

32. Ibid., 1:33.

33. Ibid., 2:352.

34. Ibid., 1:145 (emphasis added). See also Camus, *Conférence académique*, 125–28, 298.

35. Cornelius Tacitus, *The Complete Works of Tacitus*, trans. Alfred John Church, William Jackson Brodribb, and Moses Hadas (New York: Modern Library, 1942), 764.

36. Ibid., 767.

37. Ibid., 768.

38. Garasse, *Response*, 24.

39. Christian Jouhaud, *La Main de Richelieu, ou le pouvoir cardinal* (Paris: Gallimard, 1991), 81; Hélène Merlin, *L'Absolutisme dans les lettres et la théorie des deux corps: passions et politique* (Paris: Champion, 2000), 258.

40. Goulu, *Lettres de Phyllarque à Ariste*, 1:164–65.

41. On friendship and patronage, see Ullrich Langer, *Perfect Friendship: Studies in Literature and Moral Philosophy from Boccaccio to Corneille* (Geneva: Droz, 1994); Alan Bray, "Homosexuality and the Signs of Male Friendship in Elizabethan England," in *Queering the Renaissance*, ed. Jonathan Goldberg (Durham, NC: Duke University Press, 1994), 40–61; Frédéric Charbonneau and Normand Doiron, eds., "L'Amitié," special issue, *XVIIe siècle* 3, no. 3 (1999).

42. Goulu, *Lettres de Phyllarque à Ariste*, 1:86–87.

43. Ibid., 1:369.

44. Guillaumie, *J. L. Guez de Balzac*, 394–410; Youssef, *Polémique et littérature*, 61–62, 66, 80; Jéhasse, *Guez de Balzac*, 191–92; Bernard Bray, "La Louange, exigence de civilité et pratique épistolaire," *XVIIe siècle* 42, no. 2 (1990): 148–50; Jean Lafond, "Guez de Balzac et Descartes," *XVIIe siècle* 42, no. 3 (1990): 307, 310; Roger Zuber, "Singularité du Barbon: le comique et la critique," *XVIIe siècle* 42, no. 3 (1990): 321; Gilles Declercq, "Bouhours lecteur de Balzac, ou du naturel," *Littératures classiques*, no. 33 (1998): 93–113; Jouhaud, *Pouvoirs*, 349.

45. Camus, *Conférence académique*, 111; Maurice Magendie, *La Politesse mondaine et les théories de l'honnêteté en France au XVIIe siècle, de 1600 à 1660* (Paris: Presses Universitaires de France, 1925; reprint, Geneva: Slatkine Reprints, 1970), 451.

46. Quintilian, *The Institutio oratoria of Quintilian*, trans. H. E. Butler (Cambridge, MA: Harvard University Press, 1921–1936), 3:339.

47. Ibid., 3:343.

48. Ibid., 3:345.

49. Jean Rousset, *La Littérature de l'âge baroque en France: Circé et le paon* (Paris: José Corti, 1953). See also Gérard Genette, "Hyperboles," in *Figures I* (Paris: Seuil, 1966), 252.

50. Patrick Dandrey, *L'Éloge paradoxal: de Gorgias à Molière* (Paris: Presses Universitaires de France, 1997).

51. Goulu, *Lettres de Phyllarque à Ariste*, 1:56–59.

52. Goulu would seem to contradict himself later, when (following Quintilian) he allows for hyperbole in extraordinary circumstances. Ibid., 1:299.

53. Ogier, *Apologie pour Monsieur de Balzac*, 90.

54. Ibid., 80–81.

55. Ibid., 87.

56. Ibid., 71–72.

57. Ibid., 69.

58. Jéhasse, *Guez de Balzac*, 191.

59. Ogier, *Apologie pour Monsieur de Balzac*, 81.

60. Ibid., 92.

61. Goulu, *Lettres de Phyllarque à Ariste*, 1:302.

62. Ibid., 1:300–301.

63. Camus, *Conférence académique*, 112.

64. Bernard de Javersac, *Discours d'Aristarque à Nicandre* (Rouen: 1628), 33.

65. Sorel, *Francion*, 542–46. See also L. Du Peschier, *La Comédie des comédies*, in *Le Théâtre français au XVIe et au XVIIe siècle*, ed. Edouard Fournier (Paris: Garnier, 1874), 237–56.

66. Camus, *Conférence académique*, 122.

67. Ogier, *Apologie pour Monsieur de Balzac*, 94.

68. Ibid., 92–93.

69. Ibid., 104.

70. Quintilian, *Institutio oratoria*, 3:401.

71. Ogier, *Apologie pour Monsieur de Balzac*, 85.

72. Ibid., 86.

73. Ibid., 168–204.

74. Ibid., 177.

75. Goulu, *Lettres de Phyllarque à Ariste*, 1:231.

76. Ogier, *Apologie pour Monsieur de Balzac,* 164.
77. Alain Viala, *Naissance de l'écrivain: sociologie de la littérature à l'âge classique,* Le Sens Commun (Paris: Minuit, 1985), 60.
78. Lafond, "Guez de Balzac et Descartes," 307.
79. Jouhaud, "Power and Literature," 332–52; P. Watter, "Jean-Louis Guez de Balzac's *Prince,* a Revaluation," *Journal of the Wartburg and Courtault Institutes* 20 (1957): 215–47; Jéhasse, *Guez de Balzac,* 221–344; Hélène Merlin, *Public et littérature en France au XVIIe siècle* (Paris: Les Belles Lettres, 1994), 141–50; Philippe J. Salazar, "Balzac lecteur de Pline le Jeune: la fiction du Prince," *XVIIe siècle* 42, no. 3 (1990): 293–302.
80. Jouhaud, *La Main de Richelieu,* 81.
81. Balzac, *Le Prince* (Paris: Toussainct du Bray, Pierre Roccolet et Claude Sonnius, 1631), 200.
82. Gédéon Tallemant des Réaux, *Historiettes* (Paris: Gallimard, 1961), 1:43.
83. Bernard Beugnot, "Trois lettres de Jean-Louis Guez de Balzac," *Revue d'histoire littéraire de la France,* no. 69 (1969): 110–11.
84. Jean-Louis Guez de Balzac, *Œuvres de Monsieur de Balzac divisées en deux tomes* (Paris: T. Jolly, 1665), 1:520.
85. Ibid.
86. Ibid., 1:351.

Chapter 3. His Master's Voice

1. Paul Sonnino, "The Dating and Authorship of Louis XIV's Mémoires," *French Historical Studies* 3, no. 3 (1964): 303–37.
2. On art patronage see Francis Haskell, *Patrons and Painters: A Study in the Relations Between Italian Art and Society in the Age of the Baroque* (New Haven, CT: Yale University Press, 1980); Peter Burke, *The Italian Renaissance: Culture and Society in Italy* (Princeton, NJ: Princeton University Press, 1987), 88–123; D. V. Kent, *Cosimo de' Medici and the Florentine Renaissance: The Patron's Œuvre* (New Haven, CT: Yale University Press, 2000).
3. Jacques Thuillier, *Rubens, la Galerie Médicis au Palais du Luxembourg* (Paris: Robert Laffont, 1969), 98.
4. Ibid.
5. Ronald Forsyth Millen and Robert Erich Wolf, *Heroic Deeds and Mystic Figures: A New Reading of Rubens's Life of Maria de' Medici* (Princeton, NJ: Princeton University Press, 1989), 8.
6. Ibid., 184.
7. Ibid., 187.
8. Guillaume Girard, *Histoire de la vie du duc d'Épernon* (Paris: Montalant, 1730), 3:113.
9. Ibid., 3:106. For a discussion of the hand as an emblematic representation of the secretary, see Salvatore S. Nigro, "The Secretary," in *Baroque Personae,* ed. Rosario Villari (Chicago: University of Chicago Press, 1995), 82–99.
10. Jean-Louis Guez de Balzac, *Les Premières lettres de Guez de Balzac,* ed. H. Bibas and K. T. Butler, Société des Textes Français Modernes (Paris: Droz, 1933), 1:87–88.
11. Ibid., 1:81.

12. Arlette Jouhanna, *Le Devoir de révolte: la noblesse française et la gestation de l'état* (Paris: Fayard, 1989).

13. Christian Jouhaud, *Les Pouvoirs de la littérature: histoire d'un paradoxe* (Paris: Gallimard, 2000), 235.

14. Le Père Jean Goulu, *Lettres de Phyllarque à Ariste, où il est traité de l'éloquence française* (Paris: N. Buon, 1627–1628), 1:166.

15. Jouhaud, *Pouvoirs*, 234.

16. Christian Jouhaud, "Power and Literature: The Terms of the Exchange 1624–42," in *The Administration of Aesthetics: Censorship, Political Criticism, and the Public Sphere*, ed. Richard Burt (Minneapolis: University of Minnesota Press, 1994), 239–40.

17. See Hélène Merlin-Kajman, *L'Excentricité académique: littérature, institution, société* (Paris: Les Belles Lettres, 2001), 107–14. In an intriguing but slightly strained reading, Hélène Merlin has interpreted Balzac's republication of his letters for Épernon as a critical moment in the history of the subject: disconnected from its historical referent, the pronoun "je" acquires its own, sovereign authority.

18. Jouhaud, *Pouvoirs*, 241.

19. Gédéon Tallemant des Réaux, *Historiettes* (Paris: Gallimard, 1961), 1:169.

20. Nigro, "The Secretary," 86. See also Georges Couton, *Richelieu et le théâtre* (Lyon: Presses Universitaires de Lyon, 1986), 22.

21. For a discussion of the privileges of the secretary's position, see Louis Marin's prefatory essay to Gabriel Naudé, *Considérations politiques sur les coups d'Etat, précédé de Pour une théorie baroque de l'action politique, par Louis Marin* (Paris: Éditions de Paris, 1989).

22. Jean Chapelain, *La Pucelle ou la France delivrée*, 3rd ed. (Paris: Augustin Courbé, 1657), Avj4v. See also Roger Chartier, *Forms and Meanings: Texts, Performances, and Audiences from Codex to Computer* (Philadelphia: University of Pennsylvania Press, 1995), 47. Chartier describes dedication as "a figure by means of which the prince seems himself praised as the primordial inspiration and the first author of the book that is being presented to him, as if the writer or the scholar were offering him a work that was in fact his own. In this extreme figure of sovereignty, the king becomes a poet or a scholar."

23. Maurice Magendie, *La Politesse mondaine et les théories de l'honnêteté en France au XVIIe siècle, de 1600 à 1660* (Paris: Presses Universitaires de France, 1925; reprint, Geneva: Slatkine Reprints, 1970), 55. For a parody of this practice, see Jean Desmarets de Saint-Sorlin, *Les Visionnaires*, ed. H. Gaston Hall (Paris: Marcel Didier, 1963), 71–83.

24. Margaret McGowan, *L'Art du ballet de cour en France* (Paris: CNRS, 1963).

25. Paul Lacroix, *Ballets et mascarades de cour de Henri III à Louis XIV* (Turin: J. Gay et Fils, 1870), 2:99.

26. Ibid.

27. Antoine Adam, *Théophile de Viau et la libre pensée française en 1620* (Geneva: Droz, 1935; reprint, Geneva: Slatkine Reprints, 1966), 281.

28. Marie-Claude Canova-Green, "Créatures et créateurs: les écrivains patronnés et le ballet de cour sous Louis XIII," *Papers on French Seventeenth Century Literature* 15, no. 28 (1988): 101–13.

29. Lacroix, *Ballets et mascarades*, 2:52.

30. Michel Foucault, "What Is an Author?," in *The Foucault Reader*, ed. Paul Rabinow (London: Penguin, 1984), 107.

31. For a sympathetic critique of some of the details of Foucault's argument, see "Figures of the Author" in Roger Chartier, *The Order of Books: Readers, Authors, and Libraries in Europe between the Fourteenth and Eighteenth Centuries*, trans. Lydia G. Cochrane (Stanford, CA: Stanford University Press, 1994), 25–59.

32. Foucault, "What Is an Author?," 108.

33. Chartier, *Order of Books*, 43.

34. René Pintard, *Le Libertinage érudit dans la première moitié du XVIIe siècle* (Paris: Boivin, 1943), 34. On Vanini's problems with patrons, see John Stephenson Spink, *French Free-Thought from Gassendi to Voltaire* (London: Athlone Press, 1960), 28.

35. Jacques Prévot, ed., *Libertins du XVIIe siècle* (Paris: Gallimard, 1998), 131.

36. Théophile de Viau, *Œuvres complètes*, ed. Guido Saba (Paris: Nizet, 1978), 4:212. See also the "Apologie de Théophile" in Prévot, ed., *Libertins du XVIIe siècle*, 63.

37. Viau, *Œuvres complètes*, 4:81.

38. Ibid., 4:11–12, 4:42–43.

39. Marc Antoine Girard de Saint-Amant, *Œuvres*, ed. Jacques Bailbé and Jean Lagny (Paris: Marcel Didier, 1967), 2:46.

40. Here Saint-Amant appears to be speaking through the *poète crotté*. In other passages, the poet appears as the *object* of satire. It is generally believed that the *poète crotté* is Marc de Maillet, a court poet and client of Marguerite de Valois.

41. Académie française, *Le Dictionnaire de l'Académie françoise* (Paris: J. B. Coignard, 1694), s.v. "Happelourde."

42. For a sixteenth-century forerunner, see Joachim Du Bellay, "Le Poete courtisan," in *La Monomachie de David et de Goliath, ensemble plusieurs autres œuvres poétiques*, ed. E. Caldarini (Geneva: Droz, 1981), 152–56.

43. Mathurin Régnier, *Œuvres complètes*, ed. Gabriel Raibaud (Paris: Marcel Didier, 1958), 24–25.

44. See Frédéric Lachèvre, *Bibliographie des recueils collectifs de poésies publiés de 1597 à 1700* (Paris: H. Leclerc, 1901–1905).

45. Adam, *Théophile de Viau*, 429.

46. See the excellent treatment of Renaissance occasional poetry in O. B. Hardison, *The Enduring Monument: A Study of the Idea of Praise in Renaissance Literary Theory and Practice* (Chapel Hill: University of North Carolina Press, 1962), 107–21.

47. Predrag Matvejevitch, *La Poésie de circonstance* (Paris: Nizet, 1971), 148–52.

48. Georg Wilhelm Friedrich Hegel, *Aesthetics: Lectures on Fine Art*, trans. T. M. Knox (Oxford: Clarendon Press, 1975), 996. Brackets in original.

49. Pierre Bourdieu, *Les Règles de l'art: genèse et structure du champ littéraire* (Paris: Seuil, 1992).

50. Matvejevitch, *La Poésie de circonstance*, 47.

51. Pierre Zoberman, *Les Panégyriques du roi prononcés dans l'Académie française* (Paris: Presses de l'Université Paris-Sorbonne, 1991).

52. Harold Bloom, *The Anxiety of Influence: A Theory of Poetry* (New York: Oxford University Press, 1973).

53. A number of recent studies have attempted to reappraise the role of the occasion in modernist verse. See for example Marian Zwerling Sugano, *The Poetics of the Occasion: Mallarmé and the Poetry of Circumstance* (Stanford, CA: Stanford University Press, 1992).

54. Francis Ponge, *Œuvres complètes*, ed. Bernard Beugnot (Paris: Gallimard, 1999), 2:38.

55. Ibid., 2:35.
56. See Ibid., 2:176.
57. Ibid., 1:98.
58. René Fromilhague, *La Vie de Malherbe: apprentissage et luttes (1555–1610)* (Paris: Armand Colin, 1954), 225–46.
59. Ponge, *Œuvres complètes*, 132.
60. For biographical information on Sigogne see Charles Timoléon de Beauxoncles seigneur de Sigogne, *Œuvres satyriques du Sieur de Sigogne*, ed. Fernard Fleuret and Louis Perceau (Paris: Bibliothèque de Curieux, 1920).
61. Ibid., xxi.
62. Joseph-François Michaud and Jean-Joseph-François Poujoulat, eds., *Nouvelle collection des mémoires pour servir à l'histoire de France: première série*, vol. 11 (Paris: Éditeur du commentaire analytique du code civil, 1838), 596.
63. René Girard, *Deceit, Desire, and the Novel: Self and Other in Literary Structure* (Baltimore: Johns Hopkins University Press, 1965).
64. Sigogne, *Œuvres satyriques du Sieur de Sigogne*, xxvii.
65. Ponge, *Œuvres complètes*, 157.
66. François de Malherbe, *Œuvres*, Bibliothèque de la Pléiade (Paris: Gallimard, 1971), 73–78.
67. Ponge, *Œuvres complètes*, 2:204.

Chapter 4. The Anxiety of Influence

1. These pieces were first published in *La Revue littéraire* in 1833–34.
2. Jean Rousset, *La Littérature de l'âge baroque en France: Circé et le paon* (Paris: José Corti, 1953); Jean Serroy, *Poètes français de l'âge baroque: anthologie (1571–1677)* (Paris: Imprimerie nationale, 1999).
3. Théophile Gautier, *Les Grotesques* (Paris: Michel Lévy frères, 1853), vi.
4. Ibid., 339.
5. For the kinds of misreading engendered by this pervasive account, see Edwin M. Duval, *Poesis and Poetic Tradition in the Early Works of Saint-Amant* (York, SC: French Literature Publications Company, 1981), 3–16.
6. Joan E. DeJean, *Libertine Strategies: Freedom and the Novel in Seventeenth-Century France* (Columbus: Ohio State University Press, 1981), 8. See also Maurice Laugaa, *La Pensée du pseudonyme* (Paris: Presses Universitaires de France, 1986).
7. DeJean, *Libertine Strategies*, 184.
8. Ibid., 190.
9. Ibid., 185.
10. See also Joan E. DeJean, *The Reinvention of Obscenity: Sex, Lies, and Tabloids in Early Modern France* (Chicago: University of Chicago Press, 2002); Mitchell Greenberg, *Detours of Desire: Readings in the French Baroque* (Columbus: Ohio State University Press, 1984).
11. Marc Antoine Girard de Saint-Amant, *Œuvres*, ed. Jacques Bailbé and Jean Lagny (Paris: Marcel Didier, 1967), 1:154. Further citations to this work are given in the text.
12. John D. Lyons, *The Listening Voice: An Essay on the Rhetoric of Saint-Amant* (Lexington, KY: French Forum, 1982), 12. See also Nathalie Negroni, "Poésie et altérité

dans l'œuvre de Saint-Amant," in *L'Autre au XVIIe siècle,* ed. Ralph Heyndels and Barbara R. Woshinsky (Tübingen: Gunter Narr, 1999), 403–23.

13. For Tristan's biography, see Amédée Carriat, *Tristan, ou l'éloge d'un poète* (Limoges: Rougerie, 1955); Claude Kurt Abraham, *Tristan L'Hermite* (Boston: Twayne, 1980). Overviews of Tristan's panegyric poetry can be found in Jean-Pierre Chauveau, "Tristan L'Hermite et la célébration des héros," *Baroque* 3 (1969): 117–26; Claude Kurt Abraham, "Tristan et la geste de Gaston," in *Diversité, c'est ma devise,* ed. Jürgen Grimm, et al., Biblio 17 (Paris: Papers on French Seventeenth Century Literature, 1994), 9–15.

14. François Tristan L'Hermite, *Les Vers héroïques* (Paris: Jean Baptiste Loyson & Nicolas Portier, 1648), 60. Further citations to this work are given in the text.

15. Abraham, "Tristan et la geste de Gaston," 13.

16. Alain Viala and Christian Jouhaud, eds., *De la publication: entre Renaissance et Lumières* (Paris: Fayard, 2002).

17. For Théophile's career, see Antoine Adam, *Théophile de Viau et la libre pensée française en 1620* (Geneva: Droz, 1935; reprint, Geneva: Slatkine Reprints, 1966); Christian Jouhaud, *Les Pouvoirs de la littérature: histoire d'un paradoxe* (Paris: Gallimard, 2000), 44–49.

18. Théophile de Viau, *Œuvres complètes,* ed. Guido Saba (Paris: Nizet, 1978), 1: 280. Théophile's editor, Guido Saba, agrees with Antoine Adam that Théophile's "Cloris, ma franchise est perdue" is one such poem, written for Candale who was in love with Marguerite de Béthune. See also Théophile's Latin letter to Candale in Viau, *Œuvres complètes,* 4:283. Further citations to this work are given in the text.

19. James S. Baumlin and Tita French Baumlin, *Ethos: New Essays in Rhetorical and Critical Theory* (Dallas, TX: Southern Methodist University Press, 1994); Hélène Merlin-Kajman, *L'Excentricité académique: littérature, institution, société* (Paris: Les Belles Lettres, 2001), 75, 81.

20. Jacqueline Lichtenstein, *The Eloquence of Color: Rhetoric and Painting in the French Classical Age* (Berkeley and Los Angeles: University of California Press, 1993), 3–6.

21. Adam, *Théophile de Viau,* 151.

22. See Geoffrey Turnovsky, "The Enlightenment Literary Market: Rousseau, Authorship, and the Book Trade," *Eighteenth-Century Studies* 36, no. 3 (2003): 294–95. In some respects, Théophile anticipates Rousseau.

23. Jean Tortel, "Quelques constantes du lyrisme préclassique," in *Le Préclassicisme français,* ed. Jean Tortel (Paris: Cahiers du Sud, 1952), 153; Jean-Pierre Chauveau, "Vie et mort d'un genre sous les règnes de Louis XIII et de Louis XIV: la poésie encomiastique," *Papers on French Seventeenth Century Literature* 5, no. 9 (1978): 77.

24. Natalie Zemon Davis, *The Gift in Sixteenth-Century France* (New York: Oxford University Press, 2000), 11. For the classical tradition see "De beneficiis" in Lucius Anneaeus Seneca, *Moral Essays,* trans. John Basore, vol. 3 (Cambridge, MA: Harvard University Press, 1935), 7.

25. He picks up this idea elsewhere in his poetry, such as in "Au Roy, Estreine," where a discussion of New Year's gifts (*étrennes*) becomes a pretext for the discussion of nature's gifts, which are compared to the king's generosity and the poet's own offer of a (poetic) gift to the monarch (Théophile, 1:181).

26. See, for example, "Quand la Divinité, qui formoit ton essence" (Théophile, 1:347–366).

27. Henri Lafay, *La Poésie française du premier XVIIe siècle (1598–1630): esquisse pour un tableau* (Paris: Nizet, 1975), 158.

28. Jacques Morel, "La Structure poétique de la *Maison de Silvie* de Théophile de Viau," in *Mélanges d'histoire littéraire (XVIe–XVIIe siècle), offerts à Raymond Lebègue* (Paris: Nizet, 1969), 149.

29. For Théophile's trial see Frédéric Lachèvre, *Le Libertinage devant le parlement de Paris: le procès du poète Théophile de Viau* (Paris: Champion, 1909); DeJean, *The Reinvention of Obscenity;* Stéphane Van Damme, "Libertinage de mœurs/libertinage érudit," *Libertinage et philosophie au XVIIe siècle*, no. 8 (2004): 161–80.

30. François Garasse, *La Doctrine curieuse des beaux esprits de ce temps, ou prétendus tels* (Paris: S. Chappelet: 1623), 55.

31. Chauveau, "Vie et mort," 78; Guido Saba, *Théophile de Viau: un poète rebelle* (Paris: Presses Universitaires de France, 1999), 98; Guido Saba, "La Poésie de Théophile de Viau," *Papers on French Seventeenth Century Literature* 9, no. 17 (1982): 532; Marie-Odile Sweetser, "Mirrors of Affectivity and Aesthetics: Gardens, Parks, and Landscapes as Seen by Théophile de Viau and La Fontaine," in *Gardens and the Passion for the Infinite*, ed. Anna-Teresa Tymieniecka (Dordecht: Kluwer, 2003), 14.

32. David Michael Roberts, "Théophile's Cygnus and the Vulnerable *locus amoenus*," in *Actes de Las Vegas*, ed. Marie-France Hilgar (Paris: Papers on French Seventeenth Century Literature, 1991), 123.

33. Sweetser, "Gardens and the Passion for the Infinite," 13.

34. Jean Serroy, *Roman et réalité: les histoires comiques au XVIIe siècle* (Paris: Minard, 1981); Wolfgang Leiner and Volker Schröder, eds., *Charles Sorel: Histoire comique de Francion* (Paris: Klincksieck, 2000).

35. Charles Sorel, *Histoire comique de Francion,* ed. Fausta Garavini (Paris: Gallimard, 1996), 238. Further citations to this work (the 1633 edition of *Francion*) are given in the text.

36. Charles Sorel, *The Comical History of Francion* (London: Francis Leach, 1655), 5:10. Further citations to this translation are given in the text.

37. Charles Sorel, *Histoire comique de Francion,* ed. Yves Giraud (Paris: Garnier-Flammarion, 1979), 367. Translations from this dedication are my own.

38. Ibid., 369. On Sorel's attitude toward dedications, see Charles Sorel, *De la connoissance des bons livres*, ed. Lucia Moretti Cenerini (Rome: Bulzoni Editore, 1974), 35. On dedications in general, see Wolfgang Leiner, *Der Widmungsbrief in der französischen Literatur (1580–1715)* (Heidelberg: Winter, 1965).

39. Adam, *Théophile de Viau.*

40. Jean Tardieu, "Étienne Durand, poète supplicié," in *Le Préclassicisme français*, ed. Jean Tortel (Paris: Cahiers du Sud, 1952), 189–95.

41. Clérante is often assumed to be the duc de Montmorency, Théophile de Viau's protector.

42. Gédéon Tallemant des Réaux, *Historiettes* (Paris: Gallimard, 1961), 1:362–63.

43. On the evolution of aristocratic manners in France during this period, see Maurice Magendie, *La Politesse mondaine et les théories de l'honnêteté en France au XVIIe siècle, de 1600 à 1660* (Paris: Presses Universitaires de France, 1925; reprint, Geneva: Slatkine Reprints, 1970); Norbert Elias, *The Civilizing Process* (Oxford: Blackwell, 1994); Domna C. Stanton, *The Aristocrat as Art: A Study of the Honnête Homme and the Dandy in Seventeenth- and Nineteenth-Century French Literature* (New York: Columbia University Press, 1980).

44. See Walter Ong, *Interfaces of the Word* (Ithaca, NY: Cornell University Press, 1977). Ong argues that speech, by contrast, was necessarily embodied, at least prior to modern recording and data transmission technologies.

45. Roger Chartier, *The Order of Books: Readers, Authors, and Libraries in Europe between the Fourteenth and Eighteenth Centuries*, trans. Lydia G. Cochrane (Stanford, CA: Stanford University Press, 1994), 36.

46. Daniel Roche, *Les Républicains des lettres: gens de culture et lumières au XVIIIe siècle* (Paris: Fayard, 1988); Alain Viala, *Naissance de l'écrivain: sociologie de la littérature à l'âge classique*, Le Sens Commun (Paris: Minuit, 1985); Jouhaud, *Pouvoirs;* Pierre Bourdieu, *Les Règles de l'art: genèse et structure du champ littéraire* (Paris: Seuil, 1992).

47. Sorel, *De la connoissance des bons livres*, 40–41.

48. Ibid., 41.

49. Martine Debaisieux, *Le Procès du roman: écriture et contrefaçon chez Charles Sorel*, Stanford French and Italian Studies (Saratoga, CA: Anma Libri, 1989), 136.

50. Alain Viala and Denis Saint-Jacques, "A Propos du champ littéraire," *Annales: économies, sociétés, civilisations* 49, no. 2 (1994): 400.

Chapter 5. Public and Private Lives

1. Jean Desmarets de Saint-Sorlin, *Europa*, ed. Anna Lia Franchetti (Florence: Alinea, 2002); Hugh Gaston Hall, *Richelieu's Desmarets* (Oxford: Clarendon Press, 1990).

2. Ralph E. Giesey, *The Royal Funeral Ceremony in Renaissance France*, Travaux d'Humanisme et Renaissance 37 (Geneva: Droz, 1960); Sarah Hanley, *The Lit de Justice of the Kings of France: Constitutional Ideology in Legend, Ritual, and Discourse* (Princeton, NJ: Princeton University Press, 1983); Richard A. Jackson, *Vive le Roi!: A History of the French Coronation from Charles V to Charles X* (Chapel Hill: University of North Carolina Press, 1984).

3. See Georges Couton, *Richelieu et le théâtre* (Lyon: Presses Universitaires de Lyon, 1986), 24–27; Frances Amelia Yates, *The Art of Memory* (Chicago: University of Chicago Press, 1966).

4. Jean-Pierre Camus, *Conférence académique sur le différent des belles-lettres de Narcisse et de Phyllarque par le sieur de Musac* (Paris: J. Cottereau, 1630), 307.

5. François Maynard, *Œuvres* (Paris: Augustin Courbé, 1646).

6. Ibid., 63.

7. Ibid., 194.

8. Armand Gasté, *La Querelle du Cid: pièces et pamphlets publiés d'après les originaux* (Paris: H. Walter, 1898; reprint, Geneva: Slatkine Reprints, 1970), 64.

9. Alain Viala, "Corneille et les institutions littéraires de son temps," in *Pierre Corneille: Actes du colloque tenu à Rouen (2–6 octobre 1984)*, ed. Alain Niderst (Paris: Presses Universitaires de France, 1985), 200–202.

10. Académie française, *Le Dictionnaire de l'Académie françoise* (Paris: J. B. Coignard, 1694), s.v. "Appui."

11. On the all-important alliance between *cour* and *ville* see Erich Auerbach, "La Cour et la ville," in *Scenes from the Drama of European Literature* (Minneapolis: University of Minnesota Press, 1984), 179.

12. Antoine Furetière, *Le Dictionnaire universel d'Antoine Furetière* (Rotterdam: Ar-

nout et Reinier Leers, 1690; reprint, Paris: S.N.L.-Le Robert, 1978), s.v. "Réduit." The *ruelle* is the space between a lady's bed and the wall.

13. Gasté, *Querelle*, 63–64.
14. Ibid., 72.
15. Ibid., 288–89.
16. Ibid., 317.
17. Hélène Merlin, *Public et littérature en France au XVIIe siècle* (Paris: Les Belles Lettres, 1994). See also Dalia Judovitz, "La Querelle du Cid: Redefining Poetic Authority," *Papers on French Seventeenth Century Literature* 16, no. 31 (1989): 491–504; Milorad R. Margitic, "Sociological Aspects of 'La Querelle du Cid'," in *Homage to Paul Benichou* (Birmingham, AL: Summa, 1994), 59–74.
18. Gasté, *Querelle*, 324.
19. Ibid., 332.
20. Ibid., 147; Henri Chardon, *La Vie de Rotrou, mieux connue* (Paris: Picard, 1884; reprint, Geneva: Slatkine Reprints, 1970), 108.
21. Gasté, *Querelle*, 147.
22. Ibid., 344.
23. Chardon, *Vie de Rotrou*, 239–40.
24. Viala, "Corneille et les institutions littéraires de son temps," 198.
25. See, for example, his "Épître" to Antoine Brun in Jacques Schérer, ed., *Théâtre du XVIIe siècle*, vol. 1, Bibliothèque de la Pléiade (Paris: Gallimard, 1975), 597.
26. Philip Tomlinson, *Jean Mairet et ses protecteurs: une œuvre dans son milieu*, Biblio 17 (Paris: Papers on French Seventeenth Century Literature, 1983), 118.
27. Claude Kurt Abraham, *Gaston d'Orléans et sa cour: étude littéraire* (Chapel Hill: University of North Carolina Press, 1963), 12; Antoine Adam, *Théophile de Viau et la libre pensée française en 1620* (Geneva: Droz, 1935; reprint, Geneva: Slatkine Reprints, 1966), 279–84, 410–14; Giovanni Dotoli, "L'Idéologie baroque et libertine des pastorales de Jean Mairet," in *Le Genre pastoral en Europe du XVe au XVIIe siècle* (Saint-Étienne: Publications de l'Université de Saint-Étienne, 1980), 301; Philip Tomlinson, "Jean Mairet et Gaston d'Orléans," *XVIIe siècle* 33, no. 130 (1981): 25–35.
28. Schérer, ed., *Théâtre*, 393. For concrete details regarding the financial terms of Mairet's relationship with Montmorency, see Philip Tomlinson, "Jean Mairet and Henri II de Montmorency, or What's a Poet Worth? Some New Evidence," *Papers on French Seventeenth Century Literature* 28, no. 54 (2001): 31–44.
29. Schérer, ed., *Théâtre*, 497.
30. Giovanni Dotoli, "Jean Mairet et/ou la naissance d'une dramaturgie: éléments historiques et esthétiques," in *Critique et création littéraire en France au XVIIe siècle*, ed. Marc Fumaroli (Paris: CNRS, 1977), 155–68.
31. Henry Carrington Lancaster, *A History of French Dramatic Literature in the Seventeenth Century* (Baltimore: Johns Hopkins University Press, 1929–1942; reprint, New York: Gordian Press, 1966), 1:374; Antoine Adam, *Histoire de la littérature française au XVIIe siècle* (Paris: Del Duca, 1962), 1:436–37.
32. Schérer, ed., *Théâtre*, 488.
33. Ibid., 475.
34. Ibid.
35. Ibid., 477.
36. Alain Viala, *Naissance de l'écrivain: sociologie de la littérature à l'âge classique*, Le Sens Commun (Paris: Minuit, 1985), 169–70.

37. Schérer, ed., *Théâtre*, 475.
38. Tomlinson, *Jean Mairet et ses protecteurs*, 217. See also Chardon, *Vie de Rotrou*.
39. Schérer, ed., *Théâtre*, 597. On Belin's relationship with Montdory, see Jean Chapelain, *Lettres de Jean Chapelain de l'Académie française*, ed. Philippe Tamizey de Larroque (Paris: Imprimerie Nationale, 1880–1883; reprint, Paris: Bibliothèque Nationale, 1968), 1:131.
40. Pierre Guérin de La Pinelière, *Le Parnasse ou le critique des poètes: suitte des visions de Quevedo* (Paris: T. Quinet, 1635; reprint, Geneva: Slatkine, 1973), 62–63. See also the dedication to Jean Mairet, *Le Roland furieux* (Paris: Augustin Courbé, 1640).
41. Gédéon Tallemant des Réaux, *Historiettes* (Paris: Gallimard, 1961), 1:89.
42. Chapelain, *Lettres de Jean Chapelain*, 1:131, 1:80, 1:328.
43. Tallemant des Réaux, *Historiettes*, 1:397.
44. See Maurice Descotes, *Le Public de théâtre et son histoire* (Paris: Presses Universitaires de France, 1964), 72.
45. Lancaster, *History of French Dramatic Literature*, 1:68–69, 1:169, 1:233, 2:8–9. See also Gasté, *Querelle*, 148, 90, 94; Katia Béguin, *Les Princes de Condé: rebelles, courtisans et mécènes dans la France du grand siècle* (Seyssel: Champ Vallon, 1999), 346–49; Vincent J. Pitts, *La Grande Mademoiselle at the Court of France: 1627–1693* (Baltimore: Johns Hopkins University Press, 2000), 106; Benedetta Craveri, *The Age of Conversation*, trans. Teresa Waugh (New York: New York Review Books, 2005), 146–47.
46. Lancaster, *History of French Dramatic Literature*, 68–69; Georges Forestier, "Du spectacle au texte: les pratiques d'impression du texte du théâtre au XVIIe siècle," in *Du spectateur du lecteur: imprimer la scène aux XVIIe et XVIIIe siècles*, ed. Larry Norman and Philippe Desan (Paris: Presses de l'Université de Paris-Sorbonne, 2002), 95.
47. Christian Jouhaud, *Les Pouvoirs de la littérature: histoire d'un paradoxe* (Paris: Gallimard, 2000), 292–304. See also Timothy Murray, *Theatrical Legitimation: Allegories of Genius in Seventeenth-Century England and France* (New York: Oxford University Press, 1987), 125; Wolfgang Leiner, *Der Widmungsbrief in der französischen Literatur (1580–1715)* (Heidelberg: Winter, 1965), 243–50.
48. Pierre Corneille, *Œuvres complètes*, ed. Georges Couton (Paris: Gallimard, 1980), 248.
49. See, for instance, the dedications to Pierre Du Ryer's *Alcionée* and Jean Mairet's *Solyman*.
50. Corneille, *Œuvres*, 248.
51. For one example among many, see the dedication to Mairet's *Sidonie*.
52. M. A. Lawrenson, *The French Stage in the XVIIth Century: A Study in the Advent of the Italian Order* (Manchester: Manchester University Press, 1957).
53. Nicola Sabbattini, "Manual for Constructing Theatrical Scenes and Machines," in *The Renaissance Stage*, ed. Barnard Hewitt (Coral Gables, FL: University of Miami Press, 1958), 87–88.
54. Murray, *Theatrical Legitimation*, 120.
55. See Jean Duvignaud, *Les Ombres collectives* (Paris: Presses Universitaires de France, 1973), 289; Jean Duvignaud, *Lieux et non-lieux* (Paris: Galilée, 1977), 70–85; François Hédelin abbé d'Aubignac, *La Pratique du théâtre* (Alger: J. Carbonel, 1927), 379.
56. First performance in 1633.

57. Pierre Du Ryer, *Les Vendanges de Suresnes* (Paris: Antoine de Sommaville, 1636), 48. Further citations to this work are given in the text.

58. Georges Forestier, *Le Théâtre dans le théâtre: sur la scène française du XVIIe siècle* (Geneva: Droz, 1981).

59. Veronica Sternberg, "Les Vendanges de Suresnes et la modernité comique," *Littératures classiques*, no. 42 (2001): 150.

60. John Lough, *Seventeenth-Century French Drama: The Background* (Oxford: Clarendon Press, 1979), 33; Alain Viala, ed., *Le Théâtre en France: des origines jusqu'à nos jours* (Paris: Presses Universitaires de France, 1997), 169; Jacqueline de Jomaron, *Le Théâtre en France* (Paris: Armand Colin, 1988–1989), 1:201.

61. Forestier, "Du spectacle au texte," 85.

62. Jean-Claude Vuillemin, *Baroquisme et théâtralité: le théâtre de Jean Rotrou* (Paris: Papers on French Seventeenth Century Literature, 1994), 111–19.

63. Forestier, "Du spectacle au texte," 91–93. Publication delays disappear around the middle of the century, suggesting that this practice had ended.

64. Viala, ed., *Théâtre en France*, 169–70; Henri-Jean Martin, *Livres, pouvoirs et société à Paris au XVIIe siècle (1598–1701)* (Geneva: Droz, 1969), 424–29; Viala, "Corneille et les institutions littéraires de son temps," 199. On *privilèges* generally, see Bernard Barbiche, "Le Régime de l'édition," in *Histoire de l'édition française*, ed. Henri Jean Martin and Roger Chartier (Paris: Promodis, 1983), 1:457–71.

65. Viala, ed., *Théâtre en France*, 170. See also Jomaron, *Le Théâtre en France*, 206–7.

66. Pierre Du Ryer, *Clarigène* (Paris: Antoine de Sommaville, 1639).

67. Colette Schérer, *Comédie et société sous Louis XIII: Corneille, Rotrou et les autres* (Paris: Nizet, 1983).

68. Nicolas Faret, *L'Honnête homme, ou l'art de plaire à la cour*, ed. Maurice Magendie (Paris: Presses Universitaires de France, 1925; reprint, Geneva: Slatkine Reprints, 1970).

69. James F. Gaines, *Pierre Du Ryer and His Tragedies* (Geneva: Droz, 1987), 19–22; Henry Carrington Lancaster, *Pierre Du Ryer, Dramatist* (Washington, DC: Carnegie Institution of Washington, 1912).

70. Philippe Bousquet, "Pierre du Ryer: une stratégie de l'oubli," *Littératures classiques*, no. 42 (2001): 42; Gaines, *Pierre Du Ryer and His Tragedies*, 19.

71. Bousquet, "Pierre du Ryer: une stratégie de l'oubli," 43.

72. Pierre Du Ryer, *Saül* (Paris: Antoine de Sommaville & Augustin Courbé, 1642), *aiiir*.

73. Merlin, *Public et littérature*, 385.

74. L. Du Peschier, "La Comédie des comédies," in *Le Théâtre français au XVIe et au XVIIe siècle*, ed. Edouard Fournier (Paris: Garnier, 1874), 292.

75. For this, and other details on Paris's professional companies, see Alan Howe and Madeleine Jurgens, *Le Théâtre professionnel à Paris, 1600–1649* (Paris: Centre historique des Archives Nationales, 2000). See also Viala, ed., *Théâtre en France*; S. Wilma Deierkauf-Holsboer, *Le Théâtre de l'Hôtel de Bourgogne* (Paris: Nizet, 1968); S. Wilma Deierkauf-Holsboer, *Le Théâtre du Marais* (Paris: Nizet, 1954); Jomaron, *Le Théâtre en France*; Lancaster, *History of French Dramatic Literature*; Lough, *Seventeenth-Century French Drama*.

76. Howe and Jurgens, *Le Théâtre professionnel*, 66–68.

77. Léopold Lacour, *Richelieu dramaturge et ses collaborateurs* (Paris: Librairie Ol-

lendorff, 1925); Couton, *Richelieu et le théâtre;* Robert Garapon, "Mécènes et auteurs dramatiques," in *L'Âge d'or du mécénat (1598–1661): actes du colloque international CNRS (mars 1983),* ed. Roland Mousnier and Jean Mesnard (Paris: CNRS, 1985), 315–18.

78. See Lacour, *Richelieu dramaturge;* Couton, *Richelieu et le théâtre.*
79. Paul Pellisson and Pierre-Joseph Thoulier d'Olivet, *Histoire de l'Académie françoise* (Paris: Coignard, 1743), 105–6. *La Grande pastorale* was not published and has not survived.
80. Cinq Auteurs, *Comédie des Tuilleries* (Paris: Augustin Courbé, 1638).
81. Pellisson and Olivet, *Histoire de l'Académie françoise,* 109–10.
82. Lacour, *Richelieu dramaturge.*
83. Cinq Auteurs, *Comédie des Tuilleries.*
84. Cinq Auteurs, *L'Aveugle de Smyrne* (Paris: Augustin Courbé, 1638).
85. Ibid.
86. Couton, *Richelieu et le théâtre,* 27.
87. Chapelain, *Lettres de Jean Chapelain,* 1:84.
88. Ibid., 1:89.
89. Ibid., 1:90.
90. Christian Jouhaud, "Sur le statut d'homme de lettres au XVIIe siècle: la correspondance de Jean Chapelain (1595–1674)," *Annales: histoire, sciences sociales* 49, no. 2 (1994): 311–47.
91. Christian Jouhaud, *La Main de Richelieu, ou le pouvoir cardinal* (Paris: Gallimard, 1991).
92. Cinq Auteurs, *L'Aveugle de Smyrne.*
93. Henri de Campion, *Mémoires de Henri de Campion, suivies d'un choix des lettres d'Alexandre de Campion* (Paris: Plon, 1857), 354.
94. Murray, *Theatrical Legitimation,* 124.
95. Edouard Fournier, ed., *Variétés historiques et littéraires,* vol. 9 (Paris: Pagnerre, 1859), 16–17.
96. François-André Isambert, ed., *Recueil général des anciennes lois françaises,* vol. 16 (Paris: Leprieur, 1829), 537.
97. Aubignac, *La Pratique du théâtre,* 397.
98. Ibid., 393.
99. Marc Fumaroli, *L'État culturel: une religion moderne* (Paris: Éditions de Fallois, 1991).

Chapter 6. Beyond Patronage

1. Marc Fumaroli, *Trois institutions littéraires* (Paris: Gallimard, 1994).
2. Paul Pellisson and Pierre-Joseph Thoulier d'Olivet, *Histoire de l'Académie françoise* (Paris: Coignard, 1743), 1:12.
3. François-André Isambert, ed., *Recueil général des anciennes lois françaises,* vol. 16 (Paris: Leprieur, 1829), 418–20.
4. Pellisson and Olivet, *Histoire de l'Académie françoise,* 1:16.
5. Nicolas Schapira, *Un Professionnel des lettres au XVIIe siècle: Valentin Conrart, une histoire sociale,* Époques (Seyssel: Champ Vallon, 2003), 74; Hélène Merlin-Kajman,

L'Excentricité académique: littérature, institution, société (Paris: Les Belles Lettres, 2001), 28.

6. Merlin-Kajman, *Excentricité*, 35.

7. See Marc Fumaroli, "La Coupole," in *Realms of Memory*, ed. Pierre Nora and Lawrence D. Kritzman (New York: Columbia University Press, 1997), 249–306. Although she is coming from a very different ideological and theoretical perspective, Merlin picks up numerous aspects of Fumaroli's defense of the Academy. Like Merlin, Fumaroli stresses the values of tolerance and moderation incarnated by the new institution, its relatively heterogeneous and "impure" character, and the emphasis on "words" rather than "things." By contrast, his nostalgic yearning for a sense of belonging on the part of writers, imperiled by the corrosive individualistic and bureaucratic tendencies of modern society, reveals a fundamentally conservative perspective that Merlin does not seem to share. Unlike Fumaroli, Merlin is aware of the Academy's will to tyranny and exclusion, exemplified by its refusal to admit women until the late twentieth century.

8. René Démoris, "Le Portrait du roi par Félibien," *Revue des sciences humaines* 44, no. 172 (1978): 9–30.

9. Merlin-Kajman, *Excentricité*, 199.

10. Jean-Louis Guez de Balzac, *Œuvres de Monsieur de Balzac divisées en deux tomes* (Paris: T. Jolly, 1665), 1:727.

11. Jacques d'Auzoles (sieur de Lapeyre), *Esclaircissemens chronologiques et nécessaires pour les véritables positions des matières qui sont dans les poëtes et autres historiens fabuleux* (Paris: Alliot, 1635). Maxime Préaud, of the Bibliothèque Nationale de France helped settle the question of the two "versions."

12. Balzac, *Œuvres de Monsieur de Balzac*, 1:982–83; Gédéon Tallemant des Réaux, *Historiettes* (Paris: Gallimard, 1961), 1:272; Pellisson and Olivet, *Histoire de l'Académie françoise*, 1:177.

13. Auzoles, *Esclaircissemens chronologiques*.

14. Démoris, "Le Portrait du roi," 11.

15. On the chancellery in general, see Roland Mousnier, *The Institutions of France under the Absolute Monarchy, 1598–1789* (Chicago: University of Chicago Press, 1979).

16. Schapira, *Un Professionnel des lettres*, 110–12.

17. See, for instance, Pellisson and Olivet, *Histoire de l'Académie françoise*, 1:201.

18. Tallemant des Réaux, *Historiettes*, 1:272.

19. Merlin-Kajman, *Excentricité*, 39.

20. Ernst Hartwig Kantorowicz, *The King's Two Bodies: A Study in Mediaeval Political Theology* (Princeton, NJ: Princeton University Press, 1957); Louis Marin, *Le Portrait du roi* (Paris: Minuit, 1981).

21. Pellisson and Olivet, *Histoire de l'Académie françoise*, 1:16–17.

22. Christian Jouhaud, *Les Pouvoirs de la littérature: histoire d'un paradoxe* (Paris: Gallimard, 2000), 16; Claudette Delhez-Sarlet, "L'Académie française au temps de Cardinal de Richelieu," *Marche romane* 29, no. 2 (1979): 41–60.

23. Pellisson and Olivet, *Histoire de l'Académie françoise*, 1:200.

24. On this election, and the academic praise of patrons in general, see Pierre Zoberman, *Cérémonies de la parole: l'éloquence d'apparat en France dans le dernier quart du XVIIe siècle* (Paris: Champion, 1999), 149–64.

25. Pellisson and Olivet, *Histoire de l'Académie françoise*, 1:34.

26. Nicolas Faret, *Projet de l'Académie pour servir de préface à ses statuts,* ed. Jean Rousselet (Saint-Étienne: Publications de l'Université de Saint-Étienne, 1983), 18–22. Further citations to this work are given in the text.

27. Orest A. Ranum, *Artisans of Glory: Writers and Historical Thought in Seventeenth-Century France* (Chapel Hill: University of North Carolina Press, 1980), 153.

28. The idea that the Academy could be an object of desire for writers resurfaces in one of the contemporary satires of the Academy, Saint-Évremond's *Comédie des Académiens.* In his ironical dedication "To the Authors of the Academy," Saint-Évremond describes the academicians as blinded by passion (*prévenus de passion*), self-interested (*intéressés*), and "engaged" (*engagés*). See Charles de Marguetel de Saint-Denis seigneur de Saint-Évremond, *Œuvres en prose,* ed. René Ternois (Paris: Marcel Didier, 1962), 1:10–11.

29. For an example of this type of interpretation, see Delhez-Sarlet, "L'Académie française."

30. Jouhaud, *Pouvoirs,* 18; Schapira, *Un Professionnel des lettres,* 78.

31. Alain Viala, *Naissance de l'écrivain: sociologie de la littérature à l'âge classique,* Le Sens Commun (Paris: Minuit, 1985), 50.

32. Robert Muchembled, *La Société policée: politique et politesse en France du XVIe au XXe siècle,* Univers historique (Paris: Seuil, 1998), 74–97.

33. Delhez-Sarlet, "L'Académie française," 58.

34. Schapira, *Un Professionnel des lettres,* 78.

35. Pellisson and Olivet, *Histoire de l'Académie françoise,* 1:11–12.

36. Ibid., 1:12.

37. Ibid., 1:19.

38. Ibid., 1:12.

39. Ibid., 2:24 (emphasis added).

40. Isambert, ed., *Recueil général des anciennes lois françaises,* 420.

41. Merlin-Kajman, *Excentricité,* 173.

42. Pierre Corneille, *Œuvres complètes,* ed. Georges Couton (Paris: Gallimard, 1980), 850.

43. Roland Barthes and Frédéric Berthet, "Présentation," *Communications,* no. 30 (1979): 3.

44. Pierre Bourdieu, *Language and Symbolic Power,* trans. John B. Thompson (Cambridge, MA: Harvard University Press, 1991), 45.

45. Alain Montandon, "Conversation," in *Dictionnaire raisonné de la politesse et du savoir-vivre: du moyen âge à nos jours,* ed. Alain Montandon (Paris: Seuil, 1995), 125; Christoph Strosetzki, *Rhétorique de la conversation: sa dimension littéraire et linguistique dans la société française du XVIIe siècle* (Paris: Papers on French Seventeenth Century Literature, 1984), 22; Maurice Magendie, *La Politesse mondaine et les théories de l'honnêteté en France au XVIIe siècle, de 1600 à 1660* (Paris: Presses Universitaires de France, 1925; reprint, Geneva: Slatkine Reprints, 1970), 250.

46. Stefano Guazzo, *La Civile conversation* (Lyon: Jean Beraud, 1580), 175; Marcus Tullius Cicero, *De officiis,* trans. Walter Miller (Cambridge, MA: Harvard University Press, 1913), 156.

47. Pierre Bardin, *Le Lycée du sieur Bardin* (Paris: Camusat, 1632), 2:918.

48. Antoine Gombaud de Méré, *Œuvres complètes,* ed. Charles Henri Boudhors (Paris: F. Roches, 1930), 1:46.

49. Pierre d'Ortigue de Vaumorière, *L'Art de plaire dans la conversation* (Paris: Chez Jean and Michel Guignard, 1701), 5.

50. Domna C. Stanton, *The Aristocrat as Art: A Study of the Honnête Homme and the Dandy in Seventeenth- and Nineteenth-Century French Literature* (New York: Columbia University Press, 1980), 16; Marc Fumaroli, *La Diplomatie de l'esprit: de Montaigne à La Fontaine* (Paris: Hermann, 1994), 289; Strosetzki, *Rhétorique de la conversation*, 89, 91; Emmanuel Bury, "Langage," in *Dictionnaire raisonné de la politesse et du savoir-vivre: du Moyen Âge à nos jours*, ed. Alain Montandon (Paris: Seuil, 1995), 531–42.

51. Bardin, *Lycée*, 2:978.

52. Ibid., 2:970.

53. Dominique Bertrand, "Circonstances," in *Dictionnaire raisonné de la politesse et du savoir-vivre: du Moyen Âge à nos jours*, ed. Alain Montandon (Paris: Seuil, 1995), 73–89.

54. Bardin, *Lycée*, 1:65–66.

55. Ibid., 1:438.

56. Strosetzki, *Rhétorique de la conversation*, 37; Chalesme, *L'Homme de qualité ou les moyens de vivre en homme de bien, & en homme du monde* (Paris: André Parlard, 1671); Eustache de Refuge, *Traicté de la cour* (N.p.: 1617), 9; Nicolas Faret, *L'Honnête homme, ou l'art de plaire à la cour*, ed. Maurice Magendie (Paris: Presses Universitaires de France, 1925; reprint, Geneva: Slatkine Reprints, 1970), 86; Antoine de Courtin, *Nouveau traité de la civilité qui se pratique en France parmi les honnestes gens*, ed. Marie-Claire Grassi (Saint-Étienne: Publications de l'Université de Saint-Étienne, 1998), 51; Vaumorière, *Art de plaire*, 16, 171, 270.

57. Vaumorière, *Art de plaire*, 385.

58. Baldesar Castiglione, *Book of the Courtier*, trans. Charles S. Singleton (Garden City, NJ: Anchor, 1959), 109.

59. Faret, *Honnête homme*, 47–48.

60. Bertrand, "Circonstances," 78.

61. Guazzo, *La Civile conversation*, 188–89.

62. Refuge, *Traicté de la cour*, 16–17.

63. Méré, *Œuvres complètes*, 3:107.

64. John Wyndham Pope-Hennessy, *The Portrait in the Renaissance* (London: Phaidon, 1966).

65. Méré, *Œuvres complètes*, 2:14.

66. Magendie, *Politesse mondaine*, 465.

67. Guazzo, *La Civile conversation*, 134.

68. Nicolas Pasquier, *Le Gentilhomme* (Paris: Champion, 2003), 189.

69. Bardin, *Lycée*, 1:204–5.

70. Faret, *Honnête homme*, 62.

71. Ibid., 59.

72. Erwin Goffman, *The Presentation of Self in Everyday Life* (Garden City, NJ: Anchor, 1959).

73. Faret, *Honnête homme*, 92; Vaumorière, *Art de plaire*, 27; Bardin, *Lycée*, 2:955; Courtin, *Nouveau traité*, 106.

74. Chalesme, *L'Homme de qualité*, 147.

75. Ibid., 156–57. See also Refuge, *Traicté de la cour*, 100; Faret, *Honnête homme*, 59.

76. Strosetzki, *Rhétorique de la conversation*, 154, 210–13.

77. Louis Guyon, *Les Diverses leçons* (Lyon: Claude Morillon, 1610), 200; Pasquier, *Le Gentilhomme*, 187; Refuge, *Traicté de la cour*, 79; Chalesme, *L'Homme de qualité*, 161.

78. Faret, *Honnête homme*, 50.
79. Pasquier, *Le Gentilhomme*, 276–77. See also Refuge, *Traicté de la cour*, 118; Chalesme, *L'Homme de qualité*, 165; Faret, *Honnête homme*, 50.
80. Jean Baptiste Morvan de Bellegarde, *Modeles de conversations pour les personnes polies*, 2nd ed. (Paris: Guignard, 1698).
81. Méré, *Œuvres complètes*, 1:151.
82. Ibid., 3:79.
83. Ibid., 3:157–58.
84. Ibid., 3:141.
85. Ibid., 3:94.
86. Daniel Gordon, *Citizens without Sovereignty: Equality and Sociability in French Thought, 1670–1789* (Princeton, NJ: Princeton University Press, 1994), 122.
87. Madeleine de Scudéry, *Conversations sur divers sujets*, vol. 1 (Paris: Barbin, 1680), 34. See Montandon, "Conversation," 143.
88. Elizabeth C. Goldsmith, *Exclusive Conversations: The Art of Interaction in Seventeenth-Century France* (Philadelphia: University of Pennsylvania Press, 1988), 12.
89. Ibid., 10. See also Montandon, "Conversation," 149; Stanton, *The Aristocrat as Art*, 83.
90. Montandon, "Conversation," 129–30; Gordon, *Citizens without Sovereignty*, 243; Stanton, *The Aristocrat as Art*, 52; Elena Russo, *La Cour et la ville de la littérature classique aux lumières: l'invention de soi*, Écriture (Paris: Presses Universitaires de France, 2002), 5–22.
91. Fumaroli, *Diplomatie de l'esprit*, 283–320.
92. Roger Chartier, *Cultural History: Between Practices and Representations*, trans. Lydia G. Cochrane (Ithaca, NY: Cornell University Press, 1989), 85.
93. Gordon, *Citizens without Sovereignty*, 5.
94. Méré, *Œuvres complètes*, 1:44.
95. Vaumorière, *Art de plaire*, 172. See Strosetzki, *Rhétorique de la conversation*, 71.
96. Peter Burke, *The Art of Conversation* (Ithaca, NY: Cornell University Press, 1993), 92.
97. Roger Chartier, "Distinction et divulgation: la civilité et ses livres," in *Lectures et lecteurs dans la France d'Ancien Régime* (Paris: Seuil, 1987), 45–86.
98. Gordon calls this the "rule of irrelevance."

Conclusion

1. Antoine Furetière, *Le Roman bourgeois*, Folio (Paris: Gallimard, 1981), 234–45.
2. Jean le Rond d'Alembert, *Œuvres*, vol. 4 (Paris: A. Belin, 1822), 347.
3. Voltaire, "Gens de lettres," in *Encyclopédie: dictionnaire raisonné des sciences, des arts et des métiers*, ed. Jean le Rond d'Alembert and Denis Diderot (Paris: Briasson, 1751–1772; reprint, Parma: F. M. Ricci, 1970), 9:599.
4. Robert Darnton, *L'Aventure de l'Encyclopédie, 1775–1800: un best-seller au siècle des Lumières*, trans. Marie-Alyx Revellat (Paris: Perrin, 1982), 28, 30. On patronage in the Enlightenment, see Robert Darnton, *The Literary Underground of the Old Régime* (Cambridge, MA: Harvard University Press, 1982), 6–7, 13–14.
5. Frances Stonor Saunders, *Who Paid the Piper?: The CIA and the Cultural Cold*

War (London: Granta Books, 1999); Paul Delany, "Who Paid for Modernism?," in *The New Economic Criticism: Studies at the Intersection of Literature and Economics,* ed. Martha Woodmansee and Mark Osteen (London: Routledge, 1999), 335–51.

6. Geoffrey Turnovsky, "The Enlightenment Literary Market: Rousseau, Authorship, and the Book Trade," *Eighteenth-Century Studies* 36, no. 3 (2003): 387–410.

7. Marc Fumaroli, "Introduction," in *L'Âge d'or du mécénat (1598–1661): actes du colloque international CNRS (mars 1983),* ed. Roland Mousnier and Jean Mesnard (Paris: CNRS, 1985), 1–11; Marc Fumaroli, *L'État culturel: une religion moderne* (Paris: Éditions de Fallois, 1991); Marc Fumaroli, *Le Poète et le roi: Jean de La Fontaine en son siècle* (Paris: Éditions de Fallois, 1997).

8. It is worth pondering, moreover, whether the old debate over patronage and the market will be rendered moot by new technologies. The emergence of interactive information networks raises the possibility of new, more "personal" forms of cultural exchange. Today, a book or essay can be distributed on the internet to a relatively small audience/market with highly particular tastes. The public sphere, moreover, is becoming increasing fragmented, as news and opinion outlets proliferate and common reference points disappear. It is too early to guess what such technologies might eventually bring us, but it is not out of the question that we may see the emergence of less commodified forms of cultural production and consumption.

Bibliography

ANCIENT AND EARLY MODERN PRIMARY SOURCES

Académie française. *Le Dictionnaire de l'Académie françoise.* 2 vols. Paris: J. B. Coignard, 1694.

Alembert, Jean le Rond d'. *Œuvres.* Vol. 4. Paris: A. Belin, 1822.

Amyot, Jacques. *Projet d'éloquence royale.* Edited by Philippe-Joseph Salazar. Paris: Les Belles Lettres, 1992.

Aristotle. *Rhetoric.* Translated by W. Rhys Roberts and Ingram Bywater. New York: Modern Library, 1984.

Aubignac, François Hédelin, abbé d'. *La Pratique du théâtre.* Alger: J. Carbonel, 1927.

Auzoles (sieur de Lapeyre), Jacques d'. *Esclaircissemens chronologiques et nécessaires pour les véritables positions des matières qui sont dans les poëtes et autres historiens fabuleux.* Paris: Alliot, 1635.

Balzac, Jean-Louis Guez de. *Les Entretiens (1657).* Edited by Bernard Beugnot. 2 vols. Paris: Marcel Didier, 1972.

———. *Lettres de Jean-Louis Guez de Balzac publiées par Philippe Tamizey de Larroque.* Mélanges historiques. Paris: Imprimerie Nationale, 1873.

———. *Œuvres de Monsieur de Balzac divisées en deux tomes.* 2 vols. Paris: T. Jolly, 1665.

———. *Œuvres diverses (1644).* Edited by Roger Zuber. Paris: Champion, 1995.

———. *Les Premières lettres de Guez de Balzac.* Edited by H. Bibas and K. T. Butler. 2 vols. Société des Textes Français Modernes. Paris: Droz, 1933.

———. *Le Prince.* Paris: Toussainct du Bray, Pierre Roccolet et Claude Sonnius, 1631.

Bardin, Pierre. *Le Lycée du sieur Bardin.* Paris: Camusat, 1632.

Bary, René. *L'Esprit de cour ou les conversations galantes.* Paris: C. de Sercy, 1662.

Bellegarde, Jean Baptiste Morvan de. *Modeles de conversations pour les personnes polies.* 2nd ed. Paris: Guignard, 1698.

Boileau-Despréaux, Nicolas. *Œuvres.* 2 vols. Paris: Garnier-Flammarion, 1969.

Boisrobert, François Le Métel de. *Épistres en vers.* 2 vols. Paris: Hachette, 1921.

———, ed. *Le Parnasse royal ou les immortelles actions du tres-chrestien et tres-victorieux monarque Louis XIII.* Paris: S. Cramoisy, 1635.

———, ed. *Le Sacrifice des muses au grand cardinal de Richelieu.* Paris: S. Cramoisy, 1635.

Budé, Guillaume. *De l'institution du prince.* Paris: Maistre Nicole Paris, 1547.

Castiglione, Baldesar. *Book of the Courtier.* Translated by Charles S. Singleton. Garden City, NJ: Anchor, 1959.

Campion, Henri de. *Mémoires de Henri de Campion, suivies d'un choix des lettres d'Alexandre de Campion.* Paris: Plon, 1857.

Camus, Jean-Pierre. *Conférence académique sur le différent des belles-lettres de Narcisse et de Phyllarque par le sieur de Musac.* Paris: J. Cottereau, 1630.

Chalesme. *L'Homme de qualité ou les moyens de vivre en homme de bien, & en homme du monde.* Paris: André Pralard, 1671.

Chapelain, Jean. *Lettres de Jean Chapelain de l'Académie française.* Edited by Philippe Tamizey de Larroque. 2 vols. Paris: Imprimerie Nationale, 1880–1883. Reprint, Paris: Bibliothèque Nationale, 1968.

———. *La Pucelle ou la France delivrée.* 3rd ed. Paris: Augustin Courbé, 1657.

Chappuzeau, Samuel. *Le Théâtre françois.* Edited by Georges Monval. Paris: Jules Bonnaissies, 1876.

Chetardye, Joachim Trotti de la. *Instructions pour un jeune seigneur ou l'idée d'un galant homme.* Paris: Théodore Girard, 1686.

Cicero, Marcus Tullius. *Cicero on Oratory and Orators.* Translated by J. S. Watson. Landmarks in Rhetoric and Public Address. Carbondale: Southern Illinois University Press, 1970.

———. *De inventione.* Translated by H. M. Hubbell. Cambridge, MA: Harvard University Press, 1949.

———. *De officiis.* Translated by Walter Miller. Cambridge, MA: Harvard University Press, 1913.

Cinq Auteurs. *L'Aveugle de Smyrne.* Paris: Augustin Courbé, 1638.

———. *Comédie des Tuilleries.* Paris: Augustin Courbé, 1638.

Coëffeteau, Nicolas. *Histoire romaine.* Paris: Antoine Maurry, 1680.

Corneille, Pierre. *Œuvres complètes.* Edited by Georges Couton. Paris: Gallimard, 1980.

Courtin, Antoine de. *Nouveau traité de la civilité qui se pratique en France parmi les honnestes gens.* Edited by Marie-Claire Grassi. Saint-Étienne: Publications de l'Université de Saint-Étienne, 1998.

Della Casa, Giovanni. *Galateo.* Translated by Konrad Eisenbichler and Kenneth R. Bartlett. Toronto: Center for Reformation and Renaissance Studies, 1986.

Desmarets de Saint-Sorlin, Jean. *Europa.* Edited by Anna Lia Franchetti. Florence: Alinea, 2002.

———. *Les Visionnaires.* Edited by H. Gaston Hall. Paris: Marcel Didier, 1963.

Desmolets, P. *Mémoires de littérature et d'histoire.* Vol. 2. Paris: Nyon fils, 1749.

Dinet, François. *Le Théâtre françois des seigneurs et dames illustres.* Paris: Nicolas & Jean de la Coste, 1642.

Du Bellay, Joachim. "Le Poete courtisan." In *La Monomachie de David et de Goliath, ensemble plusieurs autres œuvres poétiques,* edited by E. Caldarini, 152–56. Geneva: Droz, 1981.

Du Peschier, L. *La Comédie des comédies.* In *Le Théâtre français au XVIe et au XVIIe siècle,* edited by Edouard Fournier, 237–56. Paris: Garnier, 1874.

Du Pré de la Porte, J. *Le Pourtrait de l'éloquence françoise avec X actions oratoires.* Paris: Jean L'Évesque, 1621.

Du Ryer, Pierre. *Clarigène*. Paris: Antoine de Sommaville, 1639.

———. *Saül*. Paris: Antoine de Sommaville & Augustin Courbé, 1642.

———. *Les Vendanges de Suresnes*. Paris: Antoine de Sommaville, 1636.

Du Vair, Guillaume. *Les Œuvres de Messire Guillaume du Vair*. Paris: Sébastien Cramoisy, 1641.

Faret, Nicolas. *L'Honnête homme, ou l'art de plaire à la cour*. Edited by Maurice Magendie. Paris: Presses Universitaires de France, 1925. Reprint, Geneva: Slatkine Reprints, 1970.

———. *Projet de l'Académie pour servir de préface à ses statuts*. Edited by Jean Rousselet. Saint-Étienne: Publications de l'Université de Saint-Étienne, 1983.

Fournier, Edouard, ed. *Variétés historiques et littéraires*. Vol. 9. Paris: Pagnerre, 1859.

Furetière, Antoine. *Le Dictionnaire universel*. 2nd ed. 4 vols. The Hague: Pierre Husson et al., 1927. Reprint, Hildesheim: G. Olms Verlag, 1972.

———. *Le Dictionnaire universel d'Antoine Furetière*. 3 vols. Rotterdam: Arnout et Reinier Leers, 1690. Reprint, Paris: S.N.L.-Le Robert, 1978.

———. *Le Roman bourgeois*. Folio. Paris: Gallimard, 1981.

Garasse, François. *La Doctrine curieuse des beaux esprits de ce temps, ou prétendus tels*. Paris: S. Chappelet, 1623.

———. *Response du sieur Hydaspe au sieur de Balzac sous le nom de Sacrator, touchant l'anti-Théophile et ses écrits*. N.p., 1624.

Gasté, Armand. *La Querelle du Cid: pièces et pamphlets publiés d'après les originaux*. Paris: H. Walter, 1898. Reprint, Geneva: Slatkine Reprints, 1970.

Girard, Guillaume. *Histoire de la vie du duc d'Épernon*. 4 vols. Paris: Montalant, 1730.

Goulu, Le Père Jean. *Lettres de Phyllarque à Ariste, où il est traité de l'éloquence française*. 2 vols. Paris: N. Buon, 1627–28.

Guazzo, Stefano. *La Civile conversation*. Lyon: Jean Beraud, 1580.

Guéret, Gabriel. *La Carte de la cour*. Paris: Jean-Baptiste Lyson, 1663.

———. *La Guerre des auteurs anciens et modernes*. Paris: Théodore Girard, 1671.

———. *Le Parnasse réformé*. Paris: Thomas Jolly, 1671.

———. *La Promenade de Saint-Cloud*. Edited by Georges Monval. Paris: Librarie des Bibliophiles, 1888. Reprint, Geneva: Slatkine Reprints, 1968.

Guérin de La Pinelière, Pierre. *Le Parnasse ou le critique des poètes: suitte des visions de Quevedo*. Paris: T. Quinet, 1635. Reprint, Geneva: Slatkine, 1973.

Guyon, Louis. *Les Diverses leçons*. Lyon: Claude Morillon, 1610.

Idao-Justiniani, J. E. *L'Esprit classique et la préciosité au XVIIe siècle, avec le Discours contre l'amour & le Dialogue sur la gloire de Chapelain*. Paris: Picard, 1914.

Isambert, François-André, ed. *Recueil général des anciennes lois françaises*. Vol. 16. Paris: Leprieur, 1829.

Javersac, Bernard de. *Discours d'Aristarque à Nicandre*. Rouen, 1628.

———. *Recueil curieux touchant l'éloquence françoise*. Paris, 1628.

La Bruyère, Jean de. *Les Caractères, ou, les mœurs de ce siècle*. Paris: Garnier-Flammarion, 1965.

———. *Characters*. Translated by Henri van Laun. New York: Howard Fertig, 1992.

La Fontaine, Jean de. *Œuvres complètes*. Paris: Seuil, 1965.

La Motte le Vayer, François de. *Considérations sur l'éloquence françoise de ce temps*. Paris: S. Cramoisy, 1638.

La Serre, Jean Puget de. *Le Secrétaire à la mode*. Brussels: I. Mommart, 1650.

Lacroix, Paul. *Ballets et mascarades de cour de Henri III à Louis XIV*. 6 vols. Turin: J. Gay et Fils, 1870.

Lamy, Bernard. *De l'art de parler*. Paris: André Pralard, 1672.

Le Faucheur, Michel, and Valentin Conrart. *Traitté de l'action de l'orateur ou de la prononciation et du geste*. Paris: Augustin Courbé, 1657.

Mairet, Jean. *Le Roland furieux*. Paris: Augustin Courbé, 1640.

Malherbe, François de. *Œuvres*. Bibliothèque de la Pléïade. Paris: Gallimard, 1971.

Maynard, François. *Œuvres*. Paris: Augustin Courbé, 1646.

———. *Poésies*. Edited by Ferdinand Gohin. Paris: Garnier, 1927.

Ménage, Gilles. *Menagiana*. Paris: Florentin et Pierre Delaulne, 1693.

Méré, Antoine Gombaud de. *Œuvres complètes*. Edited by Charles Henri Boudhors. 3 vols. Paris: F. Roches, 1930.

Michaud, Joseph-François, and Jean-Joseph-François Poujoulat, eds. *Nouvelle collection des mémoires pour servir à l'histoire de France: première série*. Vol. 11. Paris: Éditeur du commentaire analytique du code civil, 1838.

Montaigne, Michel de. *Complete Essays*. Translated by Donald M. Frame. Stanford, CA: Stanford University Press, 1958.

———. *Essais*. Edited by Alexandre Micha. 3 vols. Paris: Garnier-Flammarion, 1969.

Naudé, Gabriel. *Considérations politiques sur les coups d'Etat, précédé de Pour une théorie baroque de l'action politique, par Louis Marin*. Paris: Éditions de Paris, 1989.

Ogier, François. *Apologie pour Monsieur de Balzac*. Saint-Étienne: Publications de l'Université de Saint-Étienne, 1977.

Pasquier, Nicolas. *Le Gentilhomme*. Paris: Champion, 2003.

Pellisson, Paul. "Projet de l'histoire de Louis XIV." In *Œuvres diverses*, Vol. 2, 323–28. Paris: Didot, 1735.

Pellisson, Paul, and Pierre-Joseph Thoulier d'Olivet. *Histoire de l'Académie françoise*. 2 vols. Paris: Coignard, 1743.

Plato. *Collected Dialogues*. Edited by Edith Hamilton. Princeton: Princeton University Press, 1961.

Priézac, Daniel de. *Discours politiques*. Paris: Foucault, 1666.

Quintilianus, Marcus Fabius. *The Institutio oratoria of Quintilian*. Translated by H. E. Butler. Cambridge, MA: Harvard University Press, 1921–36.

Prévot, Jacques, ed. *Libertins du XVIIe siècle*. Paris: Gallimard, 1998.

Refuge, Eustache de. *Traicté de la cour*. N.p., 1617.

Régnier, Mathurin. *Œuvres complètes*. Edited by Gabriel Raibaud. Paris: Marcel Didier, 1958.

Richelet, Pierre. *Dictionnaire françois contenant les mots et les choses*. Geneva: Widerhold, 1680. Reprint, Geneva: Slatkine Reprints, 1970.

Sabbattini, Nicola. "Manual for Constructing Theatrical Scenes and Machines." In *The Renaissance Stage*, edited by Barnard Hewitt, 37–177. Coral Gables, FL: University of Miami Press, 1958.

Saint-Amant, Marc Antoine Girard de. *Œuvres.* Edited by Jacques Bailbé and Jean Lagny. Paris: Marcel Didier, 1967.

Saint-Denis, André de. *Conformité de l'eloquence de Mr de Balzac avec celle des plus grand personnages du temps present et passé.* N.p., 1627.

Saint-Évremond, Charles de Marguetel de Saint-Denis, seigneur de. *Œuvres en prose.* Edited by René Ternois. 3 vols. Paris: Marcel Didier, 1962.

Scarron, Paul. *Poésies diverses.* Edited by Maurice Cauchie. 2 vols. Paris: Marcel Didier, 1947.

Schérer, Jacques, ed. *Théâtre du XVIIe siècle.* Vol. 1. Bibliothèque de la Pléïade. Paris: Gallimard, 1975.

Scudéry, Madeleine de. *Clélie, histoire romaine.* Vol. 6, bk. 2. Paris: Augustin Courbé, 1660.

———. *Conversations sur divers sujets.* Vol. 1. Paris: Barbin, 1680.

Seneca, Lucius Anneaeus. *Moral Essays.* Translated by John Basore. Vol. 3. Cambridge, MA: Harvard University Press, 1935.

Serroy, Jean. *Poètes français de l'âge baroque: anthologie (1571–1677).* Paris: Imprimerie nationale, 1999.

Sigogne, Charles Timoléon de Beauxoncles, seigneur de. *Œuvres satyriques du Sieur de Sigogne.* Edited by Fernard Fleuret and Louis Perceau. Paris: Bibliothèque de Curieux, 1920.

Sorel, Charles. *La Bibliothèque françoise.* 2nd ed. Paris: Compagnie des Librairies du Palais, 1667. Reprint, Geneva: Slatkine Reprints, 1970.

———. *The Comical History of Francion.* London: Francis Leach, 1655.

———. *De la connoissance des bons livres.* Edited by Lucia Moretti Cenerini. Rome: Bulzoni Editore, 1974.

———. *Histoire comique de Francion.* Edited by Yves Giraud. Paris: Garnier-Flammarion, 1979.

———. *Histoire comique de Francion.* Edited by Fausta Garavini. Paris: Gallimard, 1996.

Tacitus, Cornelius. *The Complete Works of Tacitus.* Translated by Alfred John Church, William Jackson Brodribb, and Moses Hadas. New York: Modern Library, 1942.

Tallemant des Réaux, Gédéon. *Historiettes.* 2 vols. Paris: Gallimard, 1961.

Tristan L'Hermite, François. *Les Vers héroïques.* Paris: Jean Baptiste Loyson & Nicolas Portier, 1648.

Urfé, Honoré d'. *L'Astrée.* Edited by Louis Mercier. 5 vols. Lyon: Pierre Masson, 1925.

Valdor, Jean. *Triomphes de Louis le Juste.* Paris: A. Estienne, 1649.

Vaumorière, Pierre d'Ortigue, sieur de. *L'Art de plaire dans la conversation.* Paris: Chez Jean and Michel Guignard, 1701.

Viau, Théophile de. *Œuvres complètes.* Edited by Guido Saba. 4 vols. Paris: Nizet, 1978.

Voltaire. "Gens de lettres." In *Encyclopédie: dictionnaire raisonné des sciences, des arts et des métiers,* Vol. 7, edited by Jean le Rond d'Alembert and Denis Diderot, 599. Paris: Briasson, 1751–1772. Reprint, Parma: F. M. Ricci, 1970.

SECONDARY SOURCES

Abraham, Claude Kurt. *Gaston d'Orléans et sa cour: étude litteraire.* Chapel Hill: University of North Carolina Press, 1963.

———. "Tristan et la geste de Gaston." In *Diversité, c'est ma devise,* edited by Jürgen Grimm, Frank-Rutger Hausmann, Christoph Miething and Margarete Zimmermann, 9–15. Paris: Papers on French Seventeenth Century Literature, 1994.

———. *Tristan L'Hermite.* Boston: Twayne, 1980.

Adam, Antoine. *Histoire de la littérature française au XVIIe siécle.* Paris: Del Duca, 1962.

———. *Les Libertins au XVIIe siècle.* Paris: Buchet Chastel, 1964.

———. *Théophile de Viau et la libre pensée française en 1620.* Geneva: Droz, 1935. Reprint, Geneva: Slatkine Reprints, 1966.

Althusser, Louis. *Lenin and Philosophy and Other Essays.* Translated by Ben Brewster. London: New Left Books, 1971.

Altman, Janet Gurkin. *Epistolarity, Approaches to a Form.* Columbus: Ohio State University Press, 1982.

———. "The Letter Book as a Literary Institution, 1539–1789: Toward a Cultural History of Published Correspondances in France." *Yale French Studies,* no. 71 (1986): 17–62.

Anderson, Benedict R. *Imagined Communities: Reflections on the Origin and Spread of Nationalism.* London: Verso, 1991.

André, Jean-Marie. *Mécène, essai de biographie spirituelle.* Paris: Les Belles Lettres, 1967.

———. *L'Otium dans la vie morale et intellectuelle romaine, des origines à l'époque augustéenne.* Paris: Presses Universitaires de France, 1966.

Apostolidès, Jean-Marie. *Le Prince sacrifié: théâtre et politique au temps de Louis XIV.* Paris: Minuit, 1985.

———. *Le Roi-machine: spectacle et politique au temps de Louis XIV.* Paris: Minuit, 1981.

Armstrong, C. A. J. "The Golden Age of Burgundy." In *The Courts of Europe: Politics, Patronage and Royalty, 1400–1800,* edited by A. G. Dickens, 55–75. London: Thames & Hudson, 1977.

Asse, Eugène. *L'Académie française.* Paris: F. Didot, 1890.

Auerbach, Erich. "La Cour et la ville." In *Scenes from the Drama of European Literature.* Minneapolis: University of Minnesota Press, 1984.

Austin, J. L. *How to Do Things with Words.* Oxford: Clarendon Press, 1962.

Bannister, Mark. "The Crisis of Literary Patronage in France, 1643–1655." *French Studies* 39, no. 1 (1985): 18–30.

———. *Privileged Mortals: The French Heroic Novel, 1630–1660.* Oxford Modern Languages and Literature Monographs. New York: Oxford University Press, 1983.

Barbiche, Bernard. "Le Régime de l'édition." In *Histoire de l'édition française,* Vol. 1, edited by Henri Jean Martin and Roger Chartier, 457–71. Paris: Promodis, 1983.

Barthes, Roland. "La Bruyère." In *Essais critiques,* 221–37. Paris: Seuil, 1964.

Barthes, Roland, and Frédéric Berthet. "Présentation." *Communications,* no. 30 (1979): 3–5.

Bataille, Georges. *La Part maudite.* Paris: Minuit, 1967.

Bates, Catherine. "Poetry, Patronage, and the Court." In *The Cambridge Companion to English Literature, 1500–1600,* edited by Arthur F. Kinney, 90–103. Cambridge: Cambridge University Press, 2000.

Baumlin, James S., and Tita French Baumlin. *Ethos: New Essays in Rhetorical and Critical Theory.* Dallas, TX: Southern Methodist University Press, 1994.

Béguin, Katia. *Les Princes de Condé: rebelles, courtisans et mécènes dans la France du grand siècle.* Seyssel: Champ Vallon, 1999.

Beik, William. *Absolutism and Society in Seventeenth-Century France: State Power and Provincial Aristocracy in Languedoc.* Cambridge Studies in Early Modern History. Cambridge: Cambridge University Press, 1985.

Bellenger, Yvonne, ed. *Le Mécénat et l'influence des Guises: actes du colloque organisé sur la littérature de la Renaissance de l'Université de Reims et tenu à Joinville du 31 mai au 4 juin 1994.* Paris: Champion, 1997.

Bénichou, Paul. *Morales du grand siècle.* Paris: Gallimard, 1948.

Berger, Harry. *The Absence of Grace: Sprezzatura and Suspicion in Two Renaissance Courtesy Books.* Stanford, CA: Stanford University Press, 2000.

Berger, Robert W. *A Royal Passion: Louis XIV as Patron of Architecture.* Cambridge: Cambridge University Press, 1994.

Bergin, Joseph. *Cardinal Richelieu: Power and the Pursuit of Wealth.* New Haven, CT: Yale University Press, 1985.

Berrendonner, Alain. *Éléments de pragmatique linguistique.* Propositions. Paris: Minuit, 1981.

Bertrand, Dominique. "Circonstances." In *Dictionnaire raisonné de la politesse et du savoir-vivre: du Moyen Âge à nos jours,* edited by Alain Montandon, 73–89. Paris: Seuil, 1995.

Beugnot, Bernard. "Avant-propos, Balzacius recidivus." *XVIIe siècle* 42, no. 3 (1990): 287–92.

———. *Le Discours de la retraite au XVIIe siècle.* Paris: Presses Universitaires de France, 1996.

———. "L'Écriture du paysage de Balzac: imaginaire et genèse." *XVIIe siècle* 42, no. 3 (1990): 359–69.

———. "Les Études sur J. L. Guez de Balzac: renouveau présent et perspectives de recherches." *Société archéologique et historique de la Charente, Mémoires pour l'année 1970* (1971): 1–11.

———. "La Figure du Mécénas." In *L'Âge d'or du mécénat (1598–1661): actes du colloque international CNRS (mars 1983),* edited by Roland Mousnier and Jean Mesnard, 285–93. Paris: CNRS, 1985.

———. *Guez de Balzac.* Rome: Memini, 2001.

———. *Jean-Louis Guez de Balzac: bibliographie générale.* Montreal: Presses de l'Université de Montréal, 1967.

———. *Jean-Louis Guez de Balzac: bibliographie générale; supplément.* Montreal: Presses de l'Université de Montréal, 1969.

———. "La Leçon de Balzac." *Littératures classiques,* no. 33 (1998): 265–77.

———. "Style ou styles épistolaires." *Revue d'histoire littéraire de la France* 78, no. 6 (1978): 939–57.

———. "Trois lettres de Jean-Louis Guez de Balzac." *Revue d'histoire littéraire de la France*, no. 69 (1969): 101–11.

Biagioli, Mario. *Galileo, Courtier: The Practice of Science in the Culture of Absolutism.* Science and its Conceptual Foundations. Chicago: University of Chicago Press, 1993.

Blocker, Deborah, and Dinah Ribard. "Du Ryer ou l'écriture indirecte." *Littératures classiques*, no. 42 (2001): 29–58.

Bloom, Harold. *The Anxiety of Influence: A Theory of Poetry.* New York: Oxford University Press, 1973.

Boissevain, Jeremy. *Friends of Friends: Networks, Manipulators and Coalitions.* New York: St. Martin's Press, 1974.

Boissier, Gaston, and Edmond Courbaud. *L'Académie française sous l'ancien régime.* Paris: Hachette, 1909.

Bourassin, Emmanuel. *François Ier: le roi et le mécène.* Paris: Tallandier, 1997.

Bourdieu, Pierre. *Language and Symbolic Power.* Translated by John B. Thompson. Cambridge, MA: Harvard University Press, 1991.

———. "Marginalia: Some Additional Notes on the Gift." In *The Logic of the Gift*, edited by Alan D. Schrift, 231–41. London: Routledge, 1997.

———. *Outline of a Theory of Practice.* Cambridge: Cambridge University Press, 1977.

———. *Les Règles de l'art: genèse et structure du champ littéraire.* Paris: Seuil, 1992.

Bousquet, Philippe. "Pierre du Ryer: une stratégie de l'oubli." *Littératures classiques*, no. 42 (2001): 29–58.

Boutang, Pierre. *La Fontaine politique.* Paris: Albin Michel, 1981.

Bouyer, Christian. *Gaston d'Orléans (1608–1660): séducteur, frondeur et mécène.* Paris: Albin Michel, 1999.

Bowditch, Phebe Lowell. *Horace and the Gift Economy of Patronage.* The Joan Palevsky Imprint in Classical Literature. Berkeley and Los Angeles: University of California Press, 2001.

Bray, Alan. "Homosexuality and the Signs of Male Friendship in Elizabethan England." In *Queering the Renaissance,* edited by Jonathan Goldberg, 40–61. Durham, NC: Duke University Press, 1994.

Bray, Bernard. "L'Épistolier et son public en France au XVIIe siècle." *Travaux de linguistique et de littérature* 11, no. 2 (1973): 8–17.

———. "La Louange, exigence de civilité et pratique épistolaire." *XVIIe siècle* 42, no. 2 (1990): 135–53.

Bray, Bernard, and Christoph Strosetzki, eds. *Art de la lettre, art de la conversation, à l'époque classique en France: actes du colloque de Wolfenbüttel, octobre 1991.* Paris: Klincksieck, 1995.

Brown, Cynthia J. *Poets, Patrons, and Printers.* Ithaca, NY: Cornell University Press, 1995.

Burke, Peter. *The Art of Conversation.* Ithaca, NY: Cornell University Press, 1993.

———. *The Fabrication of Louis XIV.* New Haven, CT: Yale University Press, 1992.

———. *The Fortunes of the Courtier: The European Reception of Castiglione's Cortegiano.* University Park: Pennsylvania State University Press, 1996.

———. *The Italian Renaissance: Culture and Society in Italy.* Princeton, NJ: Princeton University Press, 1987.

Bury, Emmanuel. "Langage." In *Dictionnaire raisonné de la politesse et du savoir-vivre: du Moyen Âge à nos jours,* edited by Alain Montandon, 531–42. Paris: Seuil, 1995.

———. *Littérature et politesse: l'invention de l'honnête homme (1580–1750).* Perspectives littéraires. Paris: Presses Universitaires de France, 1996.

Caldicott, C. E. J. *La Carrière de Molière: entre protecteurs et éditeurs.* Amsterdam: Rodopi, 1998.

Canova-Green, Marie-Claude. "Créatures et créateurs: les écrivains patronnés et le ballet de cour sous Louis XIII." *Papers on French Seventeenth Century Literature* 15, no. 28 (1988): 101–13.

Caput, Jean Pol. *L'Académie française.* Paris: Presses Universitaires de France, 1986.

Carriat, Amédée. *Tristan, ou l'éloge d'un poète.* Limoges: Rougerie, 1955.

Charbonneau, Frédéric, and Normand Doiron, eds. "L'Amitié." Special issue, *XVIIe siècle* 51, no. 3 (1999).

Chardon, Henri. *La Vie de Rotrou, mieux connue.* Paris: Picard, 1884. Reprint, Geneva: Slatkine Reprints, 1970.

Chartier, Roger. *Cultural History: Between Practices and Representations.* Translated by Lydia G. Cochrane. Ithaca, NY: Cornell University Press, 1988.

———. "Distinction et divulgation: la civilité et ses livres." In *Lectures et lecteurs dans la France d'Ancien Régime,* 45–86. Paris: Seuil, 1987.

———. *Forms and Meanings: Texts, Performances, and Audiences from Codex to Computer.* Philadelphia: University of Pennsylvania Press, 1995.

———. "The Oldest Hath Borne Most." *French Politics, Culture and Society* 20, no. 1 (2002): 95–99.

———. *On the Edge of the Cliff: History, Language, and Practices.* Translated by Lydia G. Cochrane. Baltimore: Johns Hopkins University Press, 1997.

———. *The Order of Books: Readers, Authors, and Libraries in Europe between the Fourteenth and Eighteenth Centuries.* Translated by Lydia G. Cochrane. Stanford, CA: Stanford University Press, 1994.

———. *Publishing Drama in Early Modern Europe.* The Panizzi Lectures. London: British Library, 1999.

Chartier, Roger, and Alain Boureau, eds. *La Correspondance: les usages de la lettre au XIXe siècle.* Nouvelles études historiques. Paris: Fayard, 1991.

Chartier, Roger, and Christian Jouhaud. "Pratiques historiennes des textes." In *Interpretation des textes,* edited by Claude Reichler, 53–79. Paris: Minuit, 1989.

Chatelain, Urbain. *Le Surintendant Foucquet, protecteur des lettres, des arts et des sciences.* Paris: Perrin, 1905.

Chauveau, Jean-Pierre. "Tristan L'Hermite et la célébration des héros." *Baroque* 3 (1969): 117–26.

———. "Vie et mort d'un genre sous les règnes de Louis XIII et de Louis XIV: la poésie encomiastique." *Papers on French Seventeenth Century Literature* 5, no. 9 (1978): 67–82.

Chomarat, Jacques. *Grammaire et rhétorique chez Érasme.* Paris: Les Belles Lettres, 1981.

Christout, Marie Françoise. *Le Ballet de cour en France, 1581–1671.* Aix-en-Provence: Pavillon de Vendôme, 1971.

Church, William Farr. *Richelieu and Reason of State.* Princeton, NJ: Princeton University Press, 1973.

Clarke, David. "Pierre Corneille's Occasional and Circumstantial Writings Relating to Cardinal Richelieu." *Seventeenth-Century French Studies* 41, no. 1 (1987): 20–36.

Conesa, Gabriel. "Comique et enjouement dans *Les Vendanges de Suresnes.*" *Littératures classiques,* no. 42 (2001): 137–44.

Conley, Thomas M. *Rhetoric in the European Tradition.* Chicago: University of Chicago Press, 1994.

Cornette, Joël. *Les Années cardinales.* Paris: Armand Colin, 2000.

Couton, Georges. *Corneille.* Paris: Hatier, 1969.

———. *Corneille et la Fronde: théâtre et politique il y a trois siècles.* Clermont-Ferrand: G. de Bussac, 1951.

———. *Richelieu et le théâtre.* Lyon: Presses Universitaires de Lyon, 1986.

Craveri, Benedetta. *The Age of Conversation.* Translated by Teresa Waugh. New York: New York Review Books, 2005.

Cruickshank, John, ed. *French Literature and its Background.* 6 vols. London: Oxford University Press, 1968.

Curtius, Ernst Robert. *European Literature and the Latin Middle Ages.* Princeton, NJ: Princeton University Press, 1973.

Dandrey, Patrick. *L'Éloge paradoxal: de Gorgias à Molière.* Paris: Presses Universitaires de France, 1997.

Darmon, Jean-Charles. *Philosophie épicurienne et littérature au XVIIe siècle en France: études sur Gassendi, Cyrano de Bergerac, La Fontaine, Saint-Évremond.* Perspectives littéraires. Paris: Presses Universitaires de France, 1998.

Darnton, Robert. *L'Aventure de l'Encyclopédie, 1775–1800: un best-seller au siècle des Lumières.* Translated by Marie-Alyx Revellat. Paris: Perrin, 1982.

———. *The Literary Underground of the Old Régime.* Cambridge, MA: Harvard University Press, 1982.

Davidson, Hugh McCullough. *Audience, Words, and Art: Studies in Seventeenth-Century French Rhetoric.* Columbus: Ohio State University Press, 1965.

Davies, Joan. "History, Biography, Propaganda, and Patronage in Early Seventeenth-Century France." *Seventeenth-Century French Studies,* no. 13 (1991): 5–17.

Davis, Natalie Zemon. *The Gift in Sixteenth-Century France.* New York: Oxford University Press, 2000.

Debaisieux, Martine. *Le Procès du roman: écriture et contrefaçon chez Charles Sorel.* Stanford French and Italian Studies. Saratoga, CA: Anma Libri, 1989.

Declercq, Gilles. "Bouhours lecteur de Balzac, ou du naturel." *Littératures classiques,* no. 33 (1998): 93–113.

Deierkauf-Holsboer, S. Wilma. *L'Histoire de la mise en scène dans le théâtre français à Paris de 1600 à 1673.* Paris: Nizet, 1968.

———. *Le Théâtre de l'Hôtel de Bourgogne*. 2 vols. Paris: Nizet, 1968.

———. *Le Théâtre du Marais*. 2 vols. Paris: Nizet, 1954.

DeJean, Joan E. *Libertine Strategies: Freedom and the Novel in Seventeenth-Century France*. Columbus: Ohio State University Press, 1981.

———. *The Reinvention of Obscenity: Sex, Lies, and Tabloids in Early Modern France*. Chicago: University of Chicago Press, 2002.

Delany, Paul. "Who Paid for Modernism?" In *The New Economic Criticism: Studies at the Intersection of Literature and Economics*, edited by Martha Woodmansee and Mark Osteen, 335–51. London: Routledge, 1999.

Delhez-Sarlet, Claudette. "L'Académie française au temps de Cardinal de Richelieu." *Marche romane* 29, no. 2 (1979): 41–60.

Démoris, René. "Le Portrait du roi par Félibien." *Revue des sciences humaines* 44, no. 172 (1978): 9–30.

Derrida, Jacques. *La Dissémination*. Paris: Seuil, 1972.

———. *Donner le temps*. Paris: Galilée, 1991.

Descotes, Maurice. *Le Public de théâtre et son histoire*. Paris: Presses Universitaires de France, 1964.

Dessert, Daniel. *Argent, pouvoir et société au Grand Siècle*. Paris: Fayard, 1984.

Dewald, Jonathan. *Aristocratic Experience and the Origins of Modern Culture: France, 1570–1715*. Berkeley and Los Angeles: University of California Press, 1993.

Dickens, A. G. "Monarchy and Cultural Revival: Courts in the Middle Ages." In *The Courts of Europe: Politics, Patronage and Royalty, 1400–1800*, edited by A. G. Dickens, 8–30. London: Thames & Hudson, 1977.

Dolan, John. *Poetic Occasion from Milton to Wordsworth*. Early Modern Literature in History. New York: Palgrave, 2000.

Dort, Bernard. *Pierre Corneille, dramaturge*. Paris: L'Arche, 1957.

Dotoli, Giovanni. "L'Idéologie baroque et libertine des pastorales de Jean Mairet." In *Le Genre pastoral en Europe du XVe au XVIIe siècle*, 299–310. Saint-Étienne: Publications de l'Université de Saint-Étienne, 1980.

———. "Jean Mairet et/ou la naissance d'une dramaturgie: éléments historiques et esthétiques." In *Critique et création littéraire en France au XVIIe siècle*, edited by Marc Fumaroli, 155–68. Paris: CNRS, 1977.

Duchêne, Roger. "Lettre et portrait au 17e siècle." In *Le Portrait littéraire*, edited by K. Kupisz, G.-A. Pérouse, and J. Y. Debreuille, 121–30. Lyon: Presses Universitaires de Lyon, 1988.

Dufournet, Jean, Adelin Fiorato, and Augustin Redondo, eds. *Le Pouvoir monarchique et ses supports idéologiques aux XIVe–XVIIe siècles*. Paris: Publications de la Sorbonne Nouvelle, 1990.

Dumont, Louis. *Homo hierarchicus: essai sur le système des castes*. Bibliothèque des sciences humaines. Paris: Gallimard, 1967.

Dunn, Kevin. *Pretexts of Authority: The Rhetoric of Authorship in the Renaissance Preface*. Stanford, CA: Stanford University Press, 1994.

Duval, Edwin M. *Poesis and Poetic Tradition in the Early Works of Saint-Amant*. York, SC: French Literature Publications Company, 1981.

Duvignaud, Jean. *Lieux et non-lieux*. Paris: Galilée, 1977.

———. *Les Ombres collectives*. Paris: Presses Universitaires de France, 1973.

Eisenstadt, S. N., and Louis Roniger. "Patron-Client Relations as a Model of Structuring Social Exchange." *Comparative Studies in Society and History* 22, no. 1 (1980): 42–77.

———. *Patrons, Clients, and Friends: Interpersonal Relations and the Structure of Trust in Society*. Cambridge: Cambridge University Press, 1984.

Elias, Norbert. *The Civilizing Process*. Oxford: Blackwell, 1994.

———. *The Court Society*. New York: Pantheon Books, 1983.

Elslande, Jean-Pierre van. *L'Imaginaire pastoral du XVIIe siècle: 1600–1650*. Paris: Presses Universitaires de France, 1999.

Evans, Robert C. *Ben Jonson and the Poetics of Patronage*. Lewisburg, PA: Bucknell University Press, 1989.

———. "Poetry and Power: Ben Jonson and the Poetics of Patronage." PhD diss., Princeton University, 1984.

Ferguson, Priscilla Parkhurst. *Literary France: The Making of a Culture*. Berkeley and Los Angeles: University of California Press, 1987.

Ferrier-Caverivière, Nicole. *L'Image de Louis XIV dans la litterature française de 1660 à 1715*. Paris: Presses Universitaires de France, 1981.

Fish, Stanley. "Authors-Readers: Jonson's Community of the Same." In *Representing the English Renaissance*, edited by Stephen Greenblatt, 231–63. Berkeley and Los Angeles: University of California Press, 1988.

Forestier, Georges. "Du spectacle au texte: les pratiques d'impression du texte du théâtre au XVIIe siècle." In *Du spectateur du lecteur: imprimer la scène aux XVIIe et XVIIIe siècles*, edited by Larry Norman and Philippe Desan, 85–110. Paris: Presses de l'Université de Paris-Sorbonne, 2002.

———. *Le Théâtre dans le théâtre: sur la scène française du XVIIe siècle*. Geneva: Droz, 1981.

Foucault, Michel. "What Is an Author?" In *The Foucault Reader*, edited by Paul Rabinow, 101–20. London: Penguin, 1984.

Fourcade, Pierrette. "Guez de Balzac et les plaisirs de la vie retirée. Mode ou art de vivre?" *Marseille* 109, no. 2 (1977): 123–28.

France, Peter. *Rhetoric and Truth in France: Descartes to Diderot*. Oxford: Clarendon Press, 1972.

Fromilhague, René. *La Vie de Malherbe: apprentissage et luttes (1555–1610)*. Paris: Armand Colin, 1954.

Fumaroli, Marc. *L'Âge de l'éloquence: rhétorique et "res literaria", de la Renaissance au seuil de l'époque classique*. Geneva: Droz, 1980.

———. "La Coupole." In *Realms of Memory*, Vol. 2, edited by Pierre Nora and Lawrence D. Kritzman, 249–306. New York: Columbia University Press, 1997.

———. *La Diplomatie de l'esprit: de Montaigne à La Fontaine*. Paris: Hermann, 1994.

———. *L'État culturel: une religion moderne*. Paris: Éditions de Fallois, 1991.

———. "Genèse de l'épistolographie classique: rhétorique humaniste de la lettre, de Pétrarque à Juste Lipse." *Revue d'histoire littéraire de la France* 78, no. 6 (1978): 886–905.

———. *Héros et orateurs: rhétorique et dramaturgie cornéliennes*. Geneva: Droz, 1990.

———. "Introduction." In *L'Âge d'or du mécénat (1598–1661): actes du colloque international CNRS (mars 1983)*, edited by Roland Mousnier and Jean Mesnard, 1–11. Paris: CNRS, 1985.

———. *Le Poète et le roi: Jean de La Fontaine en son siècle*. Paris: Éditions de Fallois, 1997.

———. *Trois institutions littéraires*. Paris: Gallimard, 1994.

Gaines, James F. *Pierre Du Ryer and His Tragedies*. Geneva: Droz, 1987.

Garapon, Robert. *La Fantaisie verbale et le comique dans le théatre français du moyen âge à la fin du XVIIe siècle*. Paris: Armand Colin, 1957.

———. "Mécènes et auteurs dramatiques." In *L'Âge d'or du mécénat (1598–1661): actes du colloque international CNRS (mars 1983)*, edited by Roland Mousnier and Jean Mesnard, 315–18. Paris: CNRS, 1985.

Gautier, Théophile. *Les Grotesques*. Paris: Michel Lévy frères, 1853.

Gaxotte, Pierre. *L'Académie française*. Paris: Hachette, 1965.

Génétiot, Alain. *Poétique du loisir mondain, de Voiture à La Fontaine*. Paris: Champion, 1997.

———. "Les Romains de Balzac." *Littératures classiques*, no. 33 (1998): 45–66.

Genette, Gérard. "Complexe de Narcisse." In *Figures I*, 21–28. Paris: Seuil, 1966.

———. "Hyperboles." In *Figures I*, 245–52. Paris: Seuil, 1966.

———. *Seuils*. Paris: Seuil, 1987.

Giesey, Ralph E. *The Royal Funeral Ceremony in Renaissance France*. Travaux d'Humanisme et Renaissance 37. Geneva: Droz, 1960.

Girard, René. *Deceit, Desire, and the Novel: Self and Other in Literary Structure*. Baltimore: Johns Hopkins University Press, 1965.

Goffman, Erwin. *The Presentation of Self in Everyday Life*. Garden City, NJ: Anchor, 1959.

Goldberg, Jonathan. *James I and the Politics of Literature*. Baltimore: Johns Hopkins University Press, 1983.

Goldfarb, Hilliard Todd, ed. *Richelieu: l'art et le pouvoir*. Montreal: Musée des Beaux-Arts de Montréal, 2002.

Goldsmith, Elizabeth C. *Exclusive Conversations: The Art of Interaction in Seventeenth-Century France*. Philadelphia: University of Pennsylvania Press, 1988.

Gordon, Alex L. *Ronsard et la rhétorique*. Travaux d'Humanisme et Renaissance. Geneva: Droz, 1970.

Gordon, Daniel. *Citizens without Sovereignty: Equality and Sociability in French Thought, 1670–1789*. Princeton, NJ: Princeton University Press, 1994.

Gossman, J. Lionel. "Molière's *Misanthrope*: Melancholy and Society in the Age of the Counterreformation." *Theatre Journal* 34, no. 3 (1982): 323–43.

Greenberg, Mitchell. *Detours of Desire: Readings in the French Baroque*. Columbus: Ohio State University Press, 1984.

Greenblatt, Stephen. "Culture." In *Critical Terms for Literary Study*, edited by Frank Lentricchia and Thomas McLaughlin, 225–34. Chicago: University of Chicago Press, 1990.

———. "Invisible Bullets: Renaissance Authority and its Subversion, Henry IV and

Henry V." In *Political Shakespeare: New Essays in Cultural Materialism*, edited by Jonathan Dollimore and Alan Sinfield, 18–47. Ithaca, NY: Cornell University Press, 1985.

———. *Renaissance Self-Fashioning: From More to Shakespeare*. Chicago: University of Chicago Press, 1980.

———. "Toward a Poetics of Culture." In *Learning to Curse*, 146–60. New York: Routledge, 1990.

Guerre, Pierre. "Pouvoir et poésie." In *Le Préclassicisme français*, edited by Jean Tortel, 79–88. Paris: Cahiers du Sud, 1952.

Guichemerre, Roger. *Quatre poètes du XVIIe siècle*. Paris: SEDES, 1991.

Guillaumie, Gaston. *J. L. Guez de Balzac et la prose française*. Paris: Picard, 1927.

———. "Quelques variantes du 'Prince' de Guez de Balzac." In *Mélanges de littérature, d'histoire et de philologie offerts à Paul Laumonier*, 377–86. Paris: Droz, 1935. Reprint, Geneva: Slatkine Reprints, 1972.

Habermas, Jürgen. *The Structural Transformation of the Public Sphere: An Inquiry into a Category of Bourgeois Society*. Translated by Thomas Burger. Studies in Contemporary German Social Thought. Cambridge, MA: MIT Press, 1989.

Hall, Hugh Gaston. *Richelieu's Desmarets*. Oxford: Clarendon Press, 1990.

Hanley, Sarah. *The Lit de Justice of the Kings of France: Constitutional Ideology in Legend, Ritual, and Discourse*. Princeton, NJ: Princeton University Press, 1983.

Hardison, O. B. *The Enduring Monument: A Study of the Idea of Praise in Renaissance Literary Theory and Practice*. Chapel Hill: University of North Carolina Press, 1962.

Harth, Erica. *Ideology and Culture in Seventeenth-Century France*. Ithaca, NY: Cornell University Press, 1983.

Haskell, Francis. *Patrons and Painters: A Study in the Relations Between Italian Art and Society in the Age of the Baroque*. New Haven, CT: Yale University Press, 1980.

Hegel, Georg Wilhelm Friedrich. *Aesthetics: Lectures on Fine Art*. Translated by T. M. Knox. Oxford: Clarendon Press, 1975.

Howe, Alan, and Madeleine Jurgens. *Le Théâtre professionnel à Paris, 1600–1649*. Paris: Centre historique des Archives Nationales, 2000.

Huizinga, Johan. *The Autumn of the Middle Ages*. Translated by Rodney J. Payton. Chicago: University of Chicago Press, 1996.

Huppert, George. *Les Bourgeois Gentilshommes: An Essay on the Definition of Elites in Renaissance France*. Chicago: University of Chicago Press, 1977.

Iser, Wolfgang. *The Implied Reader: Patterns of Communication in Prose Fiction from Bunyan to Beckett*. Baltimore: Johns Hopkins University Press, 1974.

Jackson, Richard A. *Vive le Roi!: A History of the French Coronation from Charles V to Charles X*. Chapel Hill: University of North Carolina Press, 1984.

Jaeger, C. Stephen. *The Origins of Courtliness: Civilizing Trends and the Formation of Courtly Ideals, 939–1210*. The Middle Ages. Philadelphia: University of Pennsylvania Press, 1985.

Jaouën, Françoise. *De l'art de plaire en petits morceaux: Pascal, La Rochefoucauld, La Bruyère*. Essais et savoirs. Saint-Denis: Presses Universitaires de Vincennes, 1996.

Jardine, M. D. "New Historicism for Old: New Conservatism for Old?: The Politics of Patronage in the Renaissance." *Yearbook of English Studies*, no. 21 (1991): 286–304.

Jéhasse, Jean. *Guez de Balzac et le génie romain*. Saint-Étienne: Publications de l'Université de Saint-Étienne, 1977.

———. "Guez de Balzac, poète chrétien." *XVIIe siècle* 42, no. 3 (1990): 371–79.

———. "Jean-Louis Balzac et l'esthétique de la pastorale." In *Le Genre pastoral en Europe du XVe au XVIIe siècle*, edited by Claude Longeon, 241–55. Saint-Étienne: Publications de l'Université de Saint-Étienne, 1980.

Jomaron, Jacqueline de. *Le Théâtre en France*. 2 vols. Paris: Armand Colin, 1988–1989.

Jouhanna, Arlette. *Le Devoir de révolte: la noblesse française et la gestation de l'état*. Paris: Fayard, 1989.

Jouhaud, Christian. "L'Écrivain et le ministre: Corneille et Richelieu." *XVIIe siècle* 46, no. 1 (1994): 135–42.

———. "Histoire et histoire littéraire: naissance de l'écrivain." *Annales: économies, sociétés, civilisations* 43, no. 4 (1988): 849–66.

———. *La Main de Richelieu, ou le pouvoir cardinal*. Paris: Gallimard, 1991.

———. *Mazarinades: la Fronde des mots*. Paris: Aubier, 1985.

———. *Les Pouvoirs de la littérature: histoire d'un paradoxe*. Paris: Gallimard, 2000.

———. "Power and Literature: The Terms of the Exchange 1624–42." In *The Administration of Aesthetics: Censorship, Political Criticism, and the Public Sphere*, edited by Richard Burt, 34–82. Minneapolis: University of Minnesota Press, 1994.

———. "Sur le statut d'homme de lettres au XVIIe siècle: la correspondance de Jean Chapelain (1595–1674)." *Annales: histoire, sciences sociales* 49, no. 2 (1994): 311–47.

Jouhaud, Christian, and Hélène Merlin. "'Aristippe' ou les équivoques de la publication." In *Ordre et contestation au temps des classiques*, Vol. 2, edited by Roger Duchêne, 155–65. Tübingen: Papers on French Seventeenth Century Literature, 1992.

———. "Mécènes, patrons et clients: les médiations textuelles comme pratiques clientélaires au XVIIe siècle." *Terrain*, no. 21 (1993): 47–62.

Judovitz, Dalia. "La Querelle du Cid: Redefining Poetic Authority." *Papers on French Seventeenth Century Literature* 16, no. 31 (1989): 491–504.

Kantorowicz, Ernst Hartwig. *The King's Two Bodies: A Study in Mediaeval Political Theology*. Princeton, NJ: Princeton University Press, 1957.

Kavanaugh, James H. "Ideology." In *Critical Terms for Literary Study*, edited by Frank Lentricchia and Thomas McLaughlin, 306–20. Chicago: University of Chicago Press, 1990.

Kelley, Donald R. *Foundations of Modern Historical Scholarship: Language, Law, and History in the French Renaissance*. New York: Columbia University Press, 1970.

Kent, D. V. *Cosimo de' Medici and the Florentine Renaissance: The Patron's Œuvre*. New Haven, CT: Yale University Press, 2000.

Keohane, Nannerl. *Philosophy and State in France*. Princeton, NJ: Princeton University Press, 1980.

Kerviler, René. *Le Chancelier Séguier, second protecteur de l'Académie française.* Paris: Marcel Didier, 1874.

Kettering, Sharon. *French Society.* London: Longman, 2001.

———. "Patronage in Early Modern France." *French Historical Studies* 17, no. 4 (1992): 839–62.

———. *Patrons, Brokers, and Clients in Seventeenth-Century France.* New York: Oxford University Press, 1986.

Kibédi-Varga, Aron. *Rhétorique et littérature: études de structures classiques.* Paris: Marcel Didier, 1970.

Knecht, R. J. *Renaissance Warrior and Patron: The Reign of Francis I.* Cambridge: Cambridge University Press, 1994.

Koselleck, Reinhart. *Critique and Crisis: Enlightenment and the Pathogenesis of Modern Society.* Studies in Contemporary German Social Thought. Cambridge, MA: MIT Press, 1988.

Lachèvre, Frédéric. *Bibliographie des recueils collectifs de poésies publiés de 1597 à 1700.* 4 vols. Paris: H. Leclerc, 1901–1905.

———. *Disciples et successeurs de Théophile de Viau.* 5 vols. Paris: Champion, 1911–1924.

———. *Le Libertinage devant le parlement de Paris: le procès du poète Théophile de Viau.* 2 vols. Paris: Champion, 1909.

Lacour, Léopold. *Richelieu dramaturge et ses collaborateurs.* Paris: Librairie Ollendorff, 1925.

Lafay, Henri. *La Poésie française du premier XVIIe siècle (1598–1630): esquisse pour un tableau.* Paris: Nizet, 1975.

Lafond, Jean. "Guez de Balzac et Descartes." *XVIIe siècle* 42, no. 3 (1990): 302–15.

———. *L'Homme et son image.* Paris: Champion, 1996.

Lagarde, François. *La Persuasion et ses effets: essai sur la réception en France au dix-septième siècle.* Biblio 17. Paris: Papers on French Seventeenth Century Literature, 1995.

Lagny, Jean. *Le Poète Saint-Amant, 1594–1661: essai sur sa vie et ses œuvres.* Paris: Nizet, 1964.

Lancaster, Henry Carrington. *A History of French Dramatic Literature in the Seventeenth Century.* 9 vols. Baltimore: Johns Hopkins University Press, 1929–1942. Reprint, New York: Gordian Press, 1966.

———. *Pierre Du Ryer, Dramatist.* Washington, DC: Carnegie Institution of Washington, 1912.

Langer, Ullrich. *Perfect Friendship: Studies in Literature and Moral Philosophy from Boccaccio to Corneille.* Geneva: Droz, 1994.

Laugaa, Maurice. *La Pensée du pseudonyme.* Paris: Presses Universitaires de France, 1986.

Lawrenson, M. A. *The French Stage in the XVIIth Century: A Study in the Advent of the Italian Order.* Manchester: Manchester University Press, 1957.

Le Gall, André. *Pierre Corneille en son temps et en son œuvre: enquête sur un poète de théâtre au XVIIe siècle.* Paris: Flammarion, 1997.

Leiner, Wolfgang. *Der Widmungsbrief in der französischen Literatur (1580–1715)*. Heidelberg: Winter, 1965.

———. *Études sur la littérature française du XVIIe siècle*. Biblio 17. Paris: Papers on French Seventeenth Century Literature, 1996.

———. "Nicolas Fouquet au jeu des miroirs." In *Études sur la littérature française du XVIIe siècle*, edited by Volker Schröder and Rainer Zaiser, 251–73. Paris: Papers on French Seventeenth Century Literature, 1996.

Leiner, Wolfgang, and Volker Schröder, eds. *Charles Sorel: Histoire comique de Francion*. Paris: Klincksieck, 2000.

Lentricchia, Frank, and Thomas McLaughlin, eds. *Critical Terms for Literary Study*. Chicago: University of Chicago Press, 1990.

Levi, Anthony. *Cardinal Richelieu and the Making of France*. New York: Carroll and Graf, 2000.

Lichtenstein, Jacqueline. *The Eloquence of Color: Rhetoric and Painting in the French Classical Age*. Berkeley and Los Angeles: University of California Press, 1993.

———. "Socrate à la cour de Louis XIV." *XVIIe siècle* 38, no. 1 (1986): 3–18.

Lopez, Denis. "Effets de l'atticisme chez Guez de Balzac." *XVIIe siècle* 42, no. 3 (1990): 329–43.

Lough, John. *An Introduction to Seventeenth Century France*. New York: David McKay, 1966.

———. *Seventeenth-Century French Drama: The Background*. Oxford: Clarendon Press, 1979.

———. *Writer and Public in France: From the Middle Ages to the Present Day*. Oxford: Clarendon Press, 1978.

Lux, David Stephan. *Patronage and Royal Science in Seventeenth-Century France: The Académie de physique in Caen*. Ithaca, NY: Cornell University Press, 1989.

Lyons, John D. *The Listening Voice: An Essay on the Rhetoric of Saint-Amant*. Lexington, KY: French Forum, 1982.

Lytle, Guy Fitch, and Stephen Orgel. *Patronage in the Renaissance*. Folger Institute Essays. Princeton, NJ: Princeton University Press, 1981.

Magendie, Maurice. *La Politesse mondaine et les théories de l'honnêteté en France au XVIIe siècle de 1600 à 1660*. Paris: Presses Universitaires de France, 1925. Reprint, Geneva: Slatkine Reprints, 1970.

Magne, Émile. *Le Plaisant abbé de Boisrobert*. Paris: Mercure de France, 1909.

———. *La Vie quotidienne au temps de Louis XIII*. Paris: Hachette, 1942.

———. *Voiture et les années de gloire à l'hôtel de Rambouillet: portrait et documents inédits*. Paris: Mercure de France, 1912.

———. *Voiture et les origines de l'hôtel de Rambouillet: portrait et documents inédits*. Paris: Mercure de France, 1911.

Maingueneau, Dominique. *Pragmatique pour le discours littéraire*. Paris: Bordas, 1990.

Margitic, Milorad R. "Sociological Aspects of 'La Querelle du Cid'." In *Homage to Paul Benichou*, 59–74. Birmingham, AL: Summa, 1994.

Marin, Louis. *Le Portrait du roi*. Paris: Minuit, 1981.

———. *Utopiques: jeux d'espaces*. Paris: Minuit, 1973.

Marotti, Arthur F. *John Donne, Coterie Poet.* Madison: University of Wisconsin Press, 1986.

———. "Patronage, Poetry, and Print." *The Yearbook of English Studies* 21 (1991): 1–26.

Martin, Henri-Jean. *Livres, pouvoirs et société à Paris au XVIIe siècle (1598–1701).* 2 vols. Geneva: Droz, 1969.

Martines, Lauro. *Strong Words: Writing and Social Strain in the Italian Renaissance.* Baltimore: Johns Hopkins University Press, 2001.

Maskell, David. *The Historical Epic in France, 1500–1700.* London: Oxford University Press, 1973.

Masseau, Didier. *L'Invention de l'intellectuel dans l'Europe du XVIIIe siècle.* Perspectives littéraires. Paris: Presses Universitaires de France, 1994.

Mathieu-Castellani, Gisèle. *Mythes de l'Éros baroque.* Paris: Presses Universitaires de France, 1981.

———. *Les Thèmes amoureux dans la poésie française: 1570–1600.* Paris: Klincksieck, 1975.

Matvejevitch, Predrag. *La Poésie de circonstance.* Paris: Nizet, 1971.

Mauss, Marcel. *The Gift: Forms and Functions of Exchange in Archaic Societies.* Glencoe, IL: Free Press, 1954.

McGowan, Margaret. *L'Art du ballet de cour en France.* Paris: CNRS, 1963.

McLuskie, Kathleen E. "Commerce and Patronage in Early Modern Drama." *Yearbook of English Studies* 21 (1991): 53–62.

Merlin, Hélène. *L'Absolutisme dans les lettres et la théorie des deux corps: passions et politique.* Paris: Champion, 2000.

———. "L'Auteur et la figure absolutiste." *Revue des sciences humaines* 238 (1995): 85–96.

———. "Horace, l'équivoque et la dédicace." *XVIIe siècle* 46, no. 1 (1994): 121–34.

———. "Langue et souveraineté en France au XVIIe siècle: la production autonome d'un corps de langage." *Annales: histoire, sciences sociales* 49, no. 2 (1994): 369–94.

———. *Public et littérature en France au XVIIe siècle.* Paris: Les Belles Lettres, 1994.

———. "La Publication du particulier dans les *Lettres* de Guez de Balzac." In *Libertinage et philosophie au XVIIe siècle,* Saint-Étienne: Publications de l'Université de Saint-Étienne, 1999.

Merlin-Kajman, Hélène. *L'Excentricité académique: littérature, institution, société.* Paris: Les Belles Lettres, 2001.

Mesnard, Jean. *La Culture au XVIIe siècle.* Paris: Presses Universitaires de France, 1992.

Michalowsky, Ulrike. "La Vanité de Guez de Balzac: fiction critique ou réalité littéraire." *XVIIe siècle* 42, no. 3 (1990): 345–57.

Millen, Ronald Forsyth, and Robert Erich Wolf. *Heroic Deeds and Mystic Figures: A New Reading of Rubens's Life of Maria de' Medici.* Princeton, NJ: Princeton University Press, 1989.

Miller, Peter N. *Peiresc's Europe: Learning and Virtue in the Seventeenth Century.* New Haven, CT: Yale University Press, 2000.

Miller, Stephen. *Conversation: A History of a Declining Art.* New Haven, CT: Yale University Press, 2006.

Moncond'huy, Dominique. "Présentation: Pierre du Ryer." *Littératures classiques,* no. 42 (2001): 5–9.

Mongrédien, Georges. "Le Mécène de Corneille: M. de Montauron." *Revue de France,* 15 novembre 1928, 329–50.

———. *La Vie de société aux XVIIe et XVIIIe siècles.* Paris: Hachette, 1950.

Monod, Paul Kléber. *The Power of Kings: Monarchy and Religion in Europe, 1589–1715.* New Haven, CT: Yale University Press, 1999.

Montandon, Alain. "Conversation." In *Dictionnaire raisonné de la politesse et du savoir-vivre: du moyen âge à nos jours,* edited by Alain Montandon, 125–54. Paris: Seuil, 1995.

Montrose, Louis. "Of Gentlemen and Shepherds: The Politics of Elizabethan Pastoral Form." *English Literary History* 50, no. 3 (1983): 415–60.

Morel, Jacques. "La Structure poétique de la *Maison de Silvie* de Théophile de Viau." In *Mélanges d'histoire littéraire (XVIe–XVIIe siècle), offerts à Raymond Lebègue,* 147–53. Paris: Nizet, 1969.

Mousnier, Roland. *L'Homme rouge, ou la vie du cardinal de Richelieu.* Paris: R. Laffont, 1992. Chicago: University of Chicago Press, 1979.

———. *The Institutions of France under the Absolute Monarchy, 1598–1789.* 2 vols.

———. *Paris, capitale au temps de Richelieu et de Mazarin.* Paris: A. Pedone, 1978.

———, ed. *Richelieu et la culture: actes du colloque international en Sorbonne.* Paris: CNRS, 1987.

Mousnier, Roland, and Yves Durand, eds. *Hommage à Roland Mousnier: clientèles et fidélités en Europe à l'époque moderne.* Paris: Presses Universitaires de France, 1981.

Mousnier, Roland, and Jean Mesnard, eds. *L'Âge d'or du mécénat (1598–1661): actes du colloque international CNRS (mars 1983).* Paris: CNRS, 1985.

Muchembled, Robert. *Popular Culture and Elite Culture in France.* Baton Rouge, LA: Louisiana State University Press, 1985.

———. *La Société policée: politique et politesse en France du XVIe au XXe siècle.* Univers historique. Paris: Seuil, 1998.

Murray, Timothy. *Theatrical Legitimation: Allegories of Genius in Seventeenth-Century England and France.* New York: Oxford University Press, 1987.

Negroni, Nathalie. "Poésie et altérité dans l'œuvre de Saint-Amant." In *L'Autre au XVIIe siècle,* edited by Ralph Heyndels and Barbara R. Woshinsky, 403–23. Tübingen: Gunter Narr, 1999.

Neuschel, Kristen Brooke. *Word of Honor: Interpreting Noble Culture in Sixteenth-Century France.* Ithaca, NY: Cornell University Press, 1989.

Nigro, Salvatore S. "The Secretary." In *Baroque Personae,* edited by Rosario Villari, 82–99. Chicago: University of Chicago Press, 1995.

Norman, Larry F. *The Public Mirror: Molière and the Social Commerce of Depiction.* Chicago: University of Chicago Press, 1999.

O'Leary, Harriet Louise. "A Survey of Literary Patronage in France." PhD. diss., University of Cincinnati, 1966.

Ong, Walter. *Interfaces of the Word.* Ithaca, NY: Cornell University Press, 1977.

Osteen, Mark. *The Question of the Gift.* New York: Routledge, 2002.

Oster, Daniel. *Histoire de l'Académie française.* Paris: Vialetay, 1970.

Parker, David. "Class, Clientage and Personal Rule in Absolutist France." *Seventeenth-Century French Studies,* no. 9 (1987): 192–213.

Pintard, René. *Le Libertinage érudit dans la première moitié du XVIIe siècle.* Paris: Boivin, 1943.

Pitts, Vincent J. *La Grande Mademoiselle at the Court of France: 1627–1693.* Baltimore: Johns Hopkins University Press, 2000.

Ponge, Francis. *Œuvres complètes.* Edited by Bernard Beugnot. 2 vols. Paris: Gallimard, 1999.

Pope-Hennessy, John Wyndham. *The Portrait in the Renaissance.* London: Phaidon, 1966.

Prendergast, Christopher. "Circulating Representations: New Historicism and the Poetics of Culture." *SubStance* 28, no. 1 (1999): 90–104.

Ranum, Orest A. *Artisans of Glory: Writers and Historical Thought in Seventeenth-Century France.* Chapel Hill: University of North Carolina Press, 1980.

———. "Courtesy, Absolutism and the Rise of the French State, 1630–1660." *Journal of Modern History* 52 (1980): 426–41.

———. *The Fronde: A French Revolution, 1648–1652.* New York: Norton, 1993.

———. *Paris in the Age of Absolutism: An Essay.* Revised and expanded ed. University Park: Pennsylvania State University Press, 2002.

Rentet, Thierry. "Fidélités et clientèles en France de 1500 à 1660." *L'Information historique,* no. 57 (1995): 89–99.

Richmond, Hugh. "Personal Identity and Literary Personae: A Study in Historical Psychology." *PMLA* 90, no. 2 (1975): 209–21.

Rigolot, François. "Prolégomènes à une étude du statut de l'appareil liminaire des textes littéraires." *L'Esprit Créateur* 27, no. 3 (1987): 7–18.

Roberts, David Michael. "Théophile's Cygnus and the Vulnerable locus amoenus." In *Actes de Las Vegas,* edited by Marie-France Hilgar, 123–27. Paris: Papers on French Seventeenth Century Literature, 1991.

Roche, Daniel. *Les Républicains des lettres: gens de culture et lumières au XVIIIe siècle.* Paris: Fayard, 1988.

Rousset, Jean. *La Littérature de l'âge baroque en France: Circé et le paon.* Paris: José Corti, 1953.

Rubin, David Lee. *The Knot of Artifice.* Columbus: Ohio State University Press, 1981.

———, ed. *La Poésie française du premier 17e siècle: textes et contextes.* Tübingen: Gunter Narr Verlag, 1986.

Russo, Elena. *La Cour et la ville de la littérature classique aux lumières: l'invention de soi.* Écriture. Paris: Presses Universitaires de France, 2002.

Saba, Guido. *Fortunes et infortunes de Théophile de Viau: histoire de la critique, suivie d'une bibliographie.* Paris: Klincksieck, 1997.

———. "La Poésie de Théophile de Viau." *Papers on French Seventeenth Century Literature* 9, no. 17 (1982): 511–35.

———. "La Poétique de Théophile de Viau." *French Literature Series,* no. 18 (1991): 13–25.

———. *Théophile de Viau: un poète rebelle.* Paris: Presses Universitaires de France, 1999.

Sainte-Beuve, Charles-Augustin. *Port-Royal.* 5 vols. Paris: Hachette, 1860.

Salazar, Philippe J. "Balzac lecteur de Pline le Jeune: la fiction du Prince." *XVIIe siècle* 42, no. 3 (1990): 293–302.

———. *Le Culte de la voix au XVIIe siècle: formes esthétiques de la parole à l'âge de l'imprimé.* Lumière classique. Paris: Champion, 1995.

———. "L'Éclat et la catastrophe." *Seventeenth-Century French Studies,* no. 20 (1998): 1–16.

Saunders, Frances Stonor. *Who Paid the Piper?: The CIA and the Cultural Cold War.* London: Granta Books, 1999.

Schalk, Ellery. *From Valor to Pedigree: Ideas of Nobility in France in the Sixteenth and Seventeenth Centuries.* Princeton, NJ: Princeton University Press, 1986.

Schapira, Nicolas. *Un Professionnel des lettres au XVIIe siècle: Valentin Conrart, une histoire sociale.* Époques. Seyssel: Champ Vallon, 2003.

Schérer, Colette. *Comédie et société sous Louis XIII: Corneille, Rotrou et les autres.* Paris: Nizet, 1983.

Scott, James C. *Domination and the Arts of Resistance: Hidden Transcripts.* New Haven, CT: Yale University Press, 1990.

Serroy, Jean. *Roman et réalité: les histoires comiques au XVIIe siècle.* Paris: Minard, 1981.

Shoemaker, Peter William. "Guez de Balzac and the Eloquence of Patronage." PhD diss., Princeton University, 1997.

Sonnino, Paul. "The Dating and Authorship of Louis XIV's Mémoires." *French Historical Studies* 3, no. 3 (1964): 303–37.

Spink, John Stephenson. *French Free-Thought from Gassendi to Voltaire.* London: Athlone Press, 1960.

Stanton, Domna C. *The Aristocrat as Art: A Study of the Honnête Homme and the Dandy in Seventeenth- and Nineteenth-Century French Literature.* New York: Columbia University Press, 1980.

Sternberg, Veronica. "Les Vendanges de Suresnes et la modernité comique." *Littératures classiques,* no. 42 (2001): 145–63.

Strauss, Leo. *Persecution and the Art of Writing.* Glencoe, IL: Free Press, 1952.

Strosetzki, Christoph. *Rhétorique de la conversation: sa dimension littéraire et linguistique dans la société française du XVIIe siècle.* Paris: Papers on French Seventeenth Century Literature, 1984.

Stroup, Alice. *A Company of Scientists: Botany, Patronage, and Community at the Seventeenth-Century Parisian Royal Academy of Sciences.* Berkeley and Los Angeles: University of California Press, 1990.

Sugano, Marian Zwerling. *The Poetics of the Occasion: Mallarmé and the Poetry of Circumstance.* Stanford, CA: Stanford University Press, 1992.

Suozzo, Andrew G. *The Comic Novels of Charles Sorel.* Lexington, KY: French Forum, 1982.

Sutcliffe, F. E. *Guez de Balzac: littérature et politique.* Paris: Nizet, 1959.

———. *Politique et culture 1560–1660.* Paris: Marcel Didier, 1973.

Sweetser, Marie-Odile. "Mirrors of Affectivity and Aesthetics: Gardens, Parks, and Landscapes as Seen by Théophile de Viau and La Fontaine." In *Gardens and the Passion for the Infinite*, edited by Anna-Teresa Tymieniecka, 7–24. Dordecht: Kluwer, 2003.

Tansey, Joel, and Kiki Gounaridou. "The Fouquet Affair: The Politics of Patronage in Theatre and Painting under Louis XIV." *Seventeenth-Century News* 57, no. 1 (1999): 1–9.

Taormina, Michael. "Poetry and Power: Théophile's 'Franchise' and the Limits of Clientage, 1621–1623." *Romanic Review* 93, no. 4 (2002): 387–413.

Tapié, Victor. *France in the Age of Louis XIII and Richelieu*. Translated by D. Lockie. Cambridge: Cambridge University Press, 1984.

Tardieu, Jean. "Étienne Durand, poète supplicié." In *Le Préclassicisme français*, edited by Jean Tortel, 189–95. Paris: Cahiers du Sud, 1952.

Thuillier, Jacques. *Rubens, la Galerie Médicis au Palais du Luxembourg*. Paris: Robert Laffont, 1969.

Tierchant, Hélène. *Le Duc d'Épernon: le favori de Henri III*. Paris: Pygmalion, 2002.

Tomlinson, Philip. "Jean Mairet and Henri II de Montmorency, or What's a Poet Worth? Some New Evidence." *Papers on French Seventeenth Century Literature* 28, no. 54 (2001): 31–44.

———. "Jean Mairet et Gaston d'Orléans." *XVIIe siècle* 33, no. 130 (1981): 25–35.

———. *Jean Mairet et ses protecteurs: une œuvre dans son milieu*. Biblio 17. Paris: Papers on French Seventeenth Century Literature, 1983.

Tortel, Jean. "Quelques constantes du lyrisme préclassique." In *Le Préclassicisme français*, edited by Jean Tortel, 123–61. Paris: Cahiers du Sud, 1952.

Tuilier, André, ed. *Richelieu et le monde de l'esprit*. Paris: Imprimerie nationale, 1985.

Turnovsky, Geoffrey. "The Enlightenment Literary Market: Rousseau, Authorship, and the Book Trade." *Eighteenth-Century Studies* 36, no. 3 (2003): 387–410.

Van Damme, Stéphane. "Libertinage de moeurs/libertinage érudit." *Libertinage et philosophie au XVIIe siècle*, no. 8 (2004): 161–80.

Verdier, Gabrielle. *Charles Sorel*. Boston: Twayne, 1984.

Viala, Alain. "Corneille et les institutions littéraires de son temps." In *Pierre Corneille: actes du colloque tenu à Rouen (2–6 octobre 1984)*, edited by Alain Niderst, 197–204. Paris: Presses Universitaires de France, 1985.

———. "La Genèse des formes épistolaires en français (XVIe–XVIIIe siècles)." *Revue de littérature comparée* 55, no. 2 (1981): 168–83.

———. "Le Monarque obligé: figures du monarque et de l'écrivain dans l'encomiastique du XVIIe siècle français." In *Le Pouvoir monarchique et ses supports idéologiques aux XIVe–XVIIe siècles*, edited by Jean Dufournet, Adelin Fiorato, and Augustin Redondo, 245–56. Paris: Presses de la Sorbonne Nouvelle, 1990.

———. *Naissance de l'écrivain: sociologie de la littérature à l'âge classique*. Le Sens Commun. Paris: Minuit, 1985.

———. *Racine: la stratégie du caméléon*. Paris: Seghers, 1990.

———, ed. *Le Théâtre en France: des origines jusqu'à nos jours*. Paris: Presses Universitaires de France, 1997.

Viala, Alain, and Christian Jouhaud, eds. *De la publication: entre Renaissance et Lumières*. Paris: Fayard, 2002.

Viala, Alain, and Denis Saint-Jacques. "A Propos du champ littéraire." *Annales: économies, sociétés, civilisations* 49, no. 2 (1994): 395–406.

Vuillemin, Jean-Claude. *Baroquisme et théâtralité: le théâtre de Jean Rotrou*. Paris: Papers on French Seventeenth Century Literature, 1994.

Watter, P. "Jean-Louis Guez de Balzac's *Prince*, a Revaluation." *Journal of the Wartburg and Courtault Institutes* 20 (1957): 215–47.

Weissman, Ronald. "Taking Patronage Seriously: Mediterranean Values and Renaissance Society." In *Patronage, Art, and Society in Renaissance Italy*, edited by F. W. Kent, Patricia Simons, and J. C. Eade, 25–45. New York: Oxford University Press, 1987.

Woodmansee, Martha, and Peter Jaszi, eds. *The Construction of Authorship: Textual Appropriation in Law and Literature*. Post-Contemporary Interventions. Durham, NC: Duke University Press, 1994.

Wyszomirski, Margaret Jane. "From Accord to Discord: Arts Policy During and After the Culture Wars." In *America's Commitment to Culture, Government, and the Arts*, edited by Kevin V. Mulcahy and Margaret Jane Wyszomirski, 1–46. Boulder, CO: Westview Press, 1995.

Yates, Frances Amelia. *The Art of Memory*. Chicago: University of Chicago Press, 1966.

———. *Astraea: The Imperial Theme in the Sixteenth Century*. London: Routledge, 1975.

Youssef, Zobeidah. *Polémique et littérature chez Guez de Balzac*. Paris: Nizet, 1972.

Zanger, Abby E. *Scenes from the Marriage of Louis XIV: Nuptial Fictions and the Making of Absolutist Power*. Stanford, CA: Stanford University Press, 1997.

———. "The Spectacular Gift: Rewriting the Royal Scenario in Molière's *Les Amants Magnifiques*." *Romanic Review* 81, no. 2 (1990): 173–88.

Zoberman, Pierre. *Cérémonies de la parole: l'éloquence d'apparat en France dans le dernier quart du XVIIe siècle*. Paris: Champion, 1999.

———. *Les Panégyriques du roi prononcés dans l'Académie française*. Paris: Presses de l'Université Paris-Sorbonne, 1991.

Zuber, Roger. "Atticisme et classicisme." In *Critique et création littéraires en France au XVIIe siècle*, Paris: CNRS, 1977.

———. "Balzac poète? Balzac savant?" In *Mélanges offerts à Georges Couton*, edited by Jean Jéhasse, Claude Martin, Pierre Rétat, and Bernard Yon, 147–59. Lyon: Presses Universitaires de Lyon, 1981.

———. *Les "Belles infidèles" et la formation du goût classique*. Paris: Armand Colin, 1968.

———. "Littérature et urbanité." In *Les Émerveillements de la raison*. Paris: Klincksieck, 1997.

———. "La Notion d'ouvrier de classicisme: le cas de Guez de Balzac." In *Un Classicisme ou des classicismes?* Pau: Presses Universitaires de Pau, 1996.

———. "Singularité du Barbon: le comique et la critique." *XVIIe siècle* 42, no. 3 (1990): 317–28.

Index

absolutism, 17–18, 45, 171, 224
Académie des Inscriptions, 214
Académie des Sciences, 214
academies, 25, 30, 54, 79, 214
Academy, French, 25, 33, 162, 187–88, 192; advantages for men of letters, 207–12; central location, 208–12; *Dictionnaire*, 38, 40, 106, 215; eccentricity, 195, 199, 212; foundation, 32, 49, 54–55, 109, 193–94; immunity, 195–98, 212–14; intermediary, 199–201; letters patent, 204, 211–13; mandate restricted to language, 194–95, 212–13; patronage institution, 193–214, 226–27; and *querelle du Cid*, 213–14; statutes, 204, 207–8; and women, 252n7
Actaeon, 139–40
actio. See action
action, 154
actors. *See under* dramatic authors
Adam, Antoine, 30, 131, 165
adieu à la cour, 108
Agrippa, Marcus Vipsanius, 42, 45
Aiguillon, duchesse d' (Marie Madeleine de Vignerot du Pont de Courlay), 181
Alembert, Jean le Rond d', 228–29
Alexander the Great, 199
alienation, 106, 110, 119, 129, 142
Althusser, Louis, 37
Amphion, 216
Ancients and Moderns. *See* Quarrel of the Ancients and Moderns
André, Frère. *See* Saint-Denis, André de
Angoulême, 59, 68, 96–98
Anne of Austria (queen), 102–3
anonymity, 144, 184–88
anxiety of influence, 110, 117–51

Apelles, 199
Apollo, 139, 186, 210
appropriateness. See *aptum; bienséance*
appropriation, 99–100, 242n17; of literary labor, 107–8, 137, 179; penal, 104–5. *See also* intellectual property
appui, 38, 126, 158
aptum, 217–18
architecture: commissions today, 15–16; ephemeral, 68
aristocratic vs. bourgeois values, 180–81
Art pour l'art, L', 109
artistic freedom, 16, 122, 165, 195, 230
Assoucy, Charles d', 118
Astrea, 69
Aubignac, abbé d' (François Hédelin), 189–90
audience of one, 22, 23, 66, 171, 179
Auerbach, Erich, 247n11
Augustinianism, 224
Augustus, 36, 39, 40–48, 222
author function, 103–5
authorship, 94–151, 153, 191, 228; and autonomy, 54–56; collective, 96, 100–3, 105–8, 183–88; and friendship, 129; as literary labor, 150–51; and style, 148, 151. *See also* author function; dramatic authors
autonomy. *See* literary field
Auzoles de Lapeyre, Jacques d', 199–203

Bailleul, Nicolas, 50
ballet, court, 24, 30, 102–3, 105–6, 143, 153
Balzac, Jean-Louis Guez de, 31, 49, 56–93, 107–8, 155; ambivalent attitude toward rhetorical efficacy, 77, 90–91; on antiquity, 47–48; *De la conversation des Romains,* 47; education and early

INDEX

career, 59; failure, 93; and French Academy, 192, 194, 198; imprudence, 82–83; later career, 91–93; *Lettres,* 24, 46, 59–93, 98–100, 199, 210, 228, 242n17; and Mazarin, 235n25; *Mécénas,* 40–48, 222; *Œuvres,* 62, 78; patriotism, 66; political ideas, 41–44, 60, 64, 91–92; position within Republic of Letters, 70; *Le Prince,* 37, 91–93; *querelle des Premières Lettres,* 24, 45–46, 59, 77–93; reformer of French prose, 57, 89; reorientation of rhetoric, 57–65, 69–70, 77, 80, 91, 93; "Response à trois questions," 46; and Richelieu, 46–47, 60, 62–63, 70, 82–83, 91–92; 237n73; style, 64–67, 76, 83–91; superficiality, 57–58, 93
Bardin, Pierre, 215–17, 222, 224
baroque, 84, 117
Barthes, Roland, 214
Bassompierre, François, 203
Baudoin, Jean, 184
Bautru, Guillaume, 51, 201
Beaumarchais, Pierre Augustin Caron de, 150
Beckett, Samuel, 94
Beik, William, 28
Belin, comte de (François II d'Averton), 31, 152, 161–63; friend of the theater, 167–68
belle matineuse, 132
Bellegarde, Jean-Baptiste Morvan de, 222–24
Bellerose (Pierre Le Messier) 154–55, 179, 183
Bellona, 96
Benserade, Isaac de, 35
Bergerac, Cyrano Hercule Savien de, 117
Bertaut, Jean, 35, 114
Béthune, Hippolyte de, 127
Biagioli, Mario, 55–56
bible, 87
bienséance, 161. *See also* dramatic unities and *bienséances; aptum*
Big Bang, 133
birds: figure for poet, 138. *See also* nightingale

Blois, 98–100
Blot, baron de (Claude de Chouvigny), 30
Boileau-Despréaux, Nicolas, 117
Boisrobert, François Le Métel de, 30, 34, 35, 40, 56, 186–87, 189; career, 48–50; *Les Épîtres,* 33, 48–54, 228; and Five Authors, 184; and French Academy, 49, 52, 193; and Mazarin, 50–53; *Le Parnasse royal,* 49; and Richelieu, 32, 49–51; *Le Sacrifice des muses,* 49
Bordier, René, 102
Bouillon, duc de (Henri de La Tour d'Auvergne), 113
Bourdieu, Pierre, 74, 77, 150, 214
bourgeoisie, 179–80
Bouthillier, Claude, 96
Brown, Cynthia, 234n14
Brunetière, Ferdinand, 29
Bruno, Giordano, 133
Brye, Monsieur de, 93
Buckingham, Marquis and Duke of (George Villiers), 132–34
Budé, Guillaume, 20–21, 222
Burke, Peter, 225
burlesque, 88

cabinet, 58, 80, 169
caduceus, 96
Caesar, Julius, 21, 61–62
Camillus, Marcus Furius, 48
Campion, Henri de, 188
Camus, Jean-Pierre, 88, 154
Candale, comte de (Henri de Nogaret de La Valette, also duc de Candale), 127
Canova-Green, Marie-Claude, 103
capitalism. *See* market economy
capitan, 88
Cartesianism, 166–67
Castiglione, Baldesar, 22, 218, 221
Catelet fortress, 135
Cato, Marcus Porcius, 48
censorship, 33, 91, 103–5, 139, 144, 200
Cérisy, abbé de. *See* Habert de Cérisy, Germain
Chalesme (author of *L'Homme de qualité*), 217, 221–22
chancellery, 33, 200

Chantilly, 135–42, 164, 167, 168
Chapelain, Jean, 41–42, 49, 101, 165, 168, 235n25; and Five Authors, 184, 185, 186–87; and French Academy, 193, 198; and royal pensions, 31, 214
Chardon, Henri, 162–63
Charleval, Jean-Louis Faucon de Ris de, 162
Charlotte de Montmorency. *See* Montmorency, Charlotte de
Chartier, Roger, 21, 149, 242n22
Christ, Jesus, 201–2
Cicero, Marcus Tullius, 21, 59, 61–62, 81; ideal of eloquence, 20, 215–17; style, 57, 67
Cinq Auteurs. *See* Five Authors
circumstantial poetry. *See* occasional poetry
citation, 118–19
classicism, 117, 184
cliché, 131–32
clientélisme. *See under* patronage system
Colbert, Jean-Baptiste, 31, 214, 234n20
Colletet, Guillaume, 49, 102, 135, 184, 235n25
Comédie Française, 190
comédiens du roi, 155, 168, 179
committimus, 211–12
concordia discors, 96–97
Condé, prince de (Henry II de Bourbon), 112, 184
Condé, prince de (Louis II de Bourbon), 50–51
Conrart, Valentin, 49, 168; and French Academy, 193–94, 203–4, 208–9
consent, 213
content. *See* form
Conti, prince de (Armand de Bourbon), 51, 53
conversation, 23, 25, 192; among ancient Romans, 43–45; art of the particular, 22, 217–19; and circumstance, 217, 219, 224; egalitarian, 220, 222–26, 227, 229; informality, 217, 223; letter as, 61; and patronage, 214–27; and rhetoric, 215–19; and social advancement, 220–21, 225; stakes, 219–26; style, 64, 82

Corcoran Gallery, 16
Corneille, Pierre, 25, 31, 33, 34, 35, 168, 179, 187–88, 213, 235n25; *Cinna*, 163; comedies, 54; *Excuse à Ariste*, 156–60, 162; and Five Authors, 184, 187–88; *Horace*, 163, 169–70, 179; *Le Cid*, 160–61, 162, 168, 188; nobility, 163; political drama, 65, 100; primacy of text over performance, 153, 157–64, 169. See also *querelle du Cid*
Costar, Pierre, 234n20
Coualin, marquis de, 184
council, royal, 62, 211
counsel, political, 20, 44–45, 97, 221
Counter-Reformation, 135
court ballet. *See* ballet, court
Courtin, Antoine de, 39, 217
court society, 17, 37, 71, 111, 114–15, 190, 227, 247n11; aesthetic values, 52–54, 89; patronage in, 38–39; resistance against, 220; and rhetoric, 20, 79–80; Roman principate as, 41–43; satire of, 53; and science, 55; and sociability, 223–26; and spectacle, 68, 153, 183; writers' role in, 30, 103, 105–6, 114–15, 143. *See also* ballet, court
Cramail, comte de (Adrien de Monluc), 164–67
créateur vs. *créature*, 103
creativity, 104
créature, 38
Culture Wars, American, 16
Cycnus, 139

Davis, Natalie, 73–74, 133
Debaisieux, Martine, 151
decontextualization, 100
décor multiple, 170
dedications, 104, 199, 230, 242n22; dramatic, 166–67, 169–71, 180, 184–86; satire of, 144, 229
DeJean, Joan, 118–19
delivery. *See* action
Delos, Isle of, 210
Démoris, René, 195–99, 201–2
Des Barreaux, Jacques Vallée, 104, 139
Desmarets de Saint-Sorlin, Jean, 49, 102, 136; and French Academy, 193, 210;

Mirame, 171, 188; and Richelieu, 32, 101
Desportes, Philippe, 114
Diana, 139
Digby, Kenelm, 184
displacement, 97–98
dispositio. *See* disposition
disposition, 101, 102, 153, 187, 217
dissonance, 126–27, 151
Dotoli, Giovanni, 165
dramatic authors: and actors, 153, 156, 158, 171–80
dramatic literature. *See* theater
dramatic unities and *bienséances*, 164–65
dreams, 139
drinking songs, 122
Dubosc-Montandré, Claude, 37
duels, 61
Dunois, Jean de, 31, 101
duplicity, 90
Dupuy *cabinet*, 237n71
Du Perron, Jacques Davy, 48
Durand, Étienne, 102, 145
Du Ryer, Pierre, 31, 34, 100; aristocratic vs. bourgeois values, 180–81; break with patronage, 181–82; *Clarigène*, 180; *Saül*, 181–82; *Les Vendanges de Suresnes*, 25, 153, 171–83, 191, 228
Du Vair, Guillaume, 58

Eisenstadt, S. N., 17
Elias, Norbert, 41, 224
elitist aesthetic, 16–17, 19, 62, 77, 160–61, 164–68, 177
elocutio. *See* elocution
elocution, 101, 149, 153, 186
éloges paradoxaux, 85
eloquence. *See* rhetoric
Encyclopédie, L', 230
Enghien, duc d'. *See* Condé, prince de (Louis II de Bourbon)
enjambment, 123
Enlightenment, 27, 151, 224
Entragues, Henriette d', 113–14
Épernon, duc d' (Jean Louis de Nogaret de La Valette), 31, 59, 60, 62, 71, 77, 82–84, 90–91; campaign in Béarn, 66; conflict with Louis XIII, 66, 98–100; hero, 65–68, 100

Epicureanism, 43, 76, 84, 91
epideictic rhetoric. *See* panegyric
epistolary rhetoric, 60–65, 79–80, 93
Erasmus, Desiderius, 22, 59
eroticism and inspiration, 119–20
esprit de géométrie and *esprit de finesse*, 219
Esprit, Jacques, 33
Estates General, 60
ethos, 130
etiquette, 224
être and *paraître*, 106
eucharist, 201–2
Evans, Robert, 23
exaggeration. *See* hyperbole
excess. *See* hyperbole

Faret, Nicolas, 25, 193; *L'Honnête homme*, 217–18, 220–22, 224; *Projet de l'Académie*, 204–7
fashion, 220
Ferguson, Priscilla Parkhurst, 56
feudalism, 18, 27, 29, 226
Feydeau, Georges, 150
fiction, 85, 114–15
fidelity, 26–29, 65–66, 83, 179
figurative language. *See individual figures*
figures vs. tropes, 89
Five Authors, 168, 183–88, 191; *L'Aveugle de Smyrne*, 184, 186–87; *Comédie des Tuileries*, 184–87. *See also* Boisrobert, François Le Métel de; Colletet, Guillaume; Corneille, Pierre; L'Estoille, Claude de; Rotrou, Jean de
food as sign, 76
form and content, 73–74
fortune, 50, 134
Foucault, Michel, 103–5
Fouquet, Nicolas, 32, 33–34, 194
Francis I, 20–21
Frederick the Great, 230
freedom, artistic. *See* artistic freedom
French Academy. *See* Academy, French
French language: considered barbaric, 205; reform of, 32, 55, 57, 89, 206
French Revolution, 227
friendship, 167, 215; and conversation, 222–23; with patron, 128–29, 147–48; vs. patronage, 18, 27, 82, 239n41
Fronde, 31, 32, 35, 42, 124

Fumaroli, Marc, 19, 28, 190, 224, 230, 252n7
Furetière, Antoine, 204, 236n41; *Dictionnaire*, 38–40; *Roman bourgeois*, 229

Galilei, Galileo, 55–56
gallantry, 148, 172, 179
Garasse, François: and Balzac, 78, 82, 84; and Théophile, 104, 135
Gassendi, Pierre, 46
Gauls, 204–7
Gautier, Théophile, 117–18, 132
Genesis, 133
Genette, Gérard, 84
génie, 218
genius, solitary, 230
gesture, 154
ghostwriting, 119, 127, 208
gift economy, 36, 62, 65, 72–77, 132–35, 236n45; and art, 74; vs. market economy, 73–75; and nature, 133–34, 142, 245n25
Girard, Guillaume, 98
Godeau, Antoine, 35, 111
Goffman, Erving, 220
Golden Age, 69, 81
Gombauld, Jean Ogier de, 30, 49, 52
Gomberville, Marin Le Roy de, 235n25
Gondi, Henri de. *See* Retz, duc de
Gondi, Jean-François Paul de. *See* Retz, Cardinal de
Gordon, Daniel, 223–26
Gougenot, Nicolas, 183
Goulart, Claude, 113
Goulu, Jean, 46, 78, 79–83, 86–88, 90, 99, 240n52
grace, 53, 72–73, 76
Gravelines, siege of, 122–24
Greenblatt, Stephen, 17
Guarini, Giovanni Battista, 165
Guazzo, Stefano, 215, 218, 220
Guérin de La Pinelière, Pierre, 15, 167
Guez, Guillaume, 59, 70
Guillaumie, Gaston, 58–59
Guyon, Louis, 221

Habermas, Jürgen, 17, 224, 230
Habert de Cérisy, Germain, 33
hand, symbolism, 100, 241n9

happelourde, 106
happy few, 177
Hardy, Alexandre, 179
harmony, 124–26
Hay de Chastelet, Paul, 201
Hegel, Georg Wilhelm Friedrich, 109
Henrietta-Maria (queen consort of England), 48–49
Henry III, 206
Henry IV, 24, 30, 96, 111–16, 123, 135, 136–37
Hercule gaulois, 20
Héroard, Jean, 168
heroicomical. *See* mock heroic
heroism, 65–68, 71, 86–88, 91, 100
history: and literature, 100; and national identity, 204
Holland, 59–60
Hollywood, 156
honeybee: figure of poetic variety, 141
honnêteté, 42, 145, 147, 167, 181, 220, 222–23
Horace (Quintus Horatius Flaccus), 86, 108, 141
hôtel, 165
Hôtel de Bourgogne. *See comédiens du roi*
Hugo, Victor, 110
humanism. *See under* Renaissance
humors, theory of, 218
hyperbole, 66, 76, 78, 83–93

identity, 119
ideology, 37
Illustre Théâtre, 183
imagined community, 63
imitation, 79; poetic, 124, 125
immunity. *See under* Academy, French
impression management, 220
Indians, American, 69
individuality, 134. *See also* poet: individuality
ingenium, 218
inscription, desire for, 195–98, 253n28
inspiration and eroticism, 119–20
intellectual property, 17, 25, 30, 129, 179; and collective authorship, 102, 104; and style, 149, 151

intelligibility, private. *See* theater: private vs. public dimension
internet, 231, 256n8
intuition, 219
inventio. See invention
invention, 101, 102, 149, 153, 186–87, 217
irony, 88, 89, 93. See also *raillerie*
irréguliers, 24, 110, 117–19
irrelevance, rule of, 255n98
Isocrates, 81

Jansenism, 58
Javersac, Bernard de, 88
Jesuits, 59, 65, 84, 135
Joan of Arc, 101
Johnson, Ben, 23
Jouhaud, Christian: on Balzac, 70, 92, 99–100; on Corneille, 169–70; on *Fronde*, 235n25; on literary field, 52, 54–56, 150, 180, 187
journée des dupes, 92

Kant, Immanuel, 109
Kantorowicz, Ernst, 202
Kent, Dale, 38
Kettering, Sharon, 18, 28–29, 36
king's two bodies, 19, 201–2

La Bruyère, Jean de, 15, 192
La Croix du Maine, François, 104
Lafay, Henri, 134
La Fontaine, Jean de, 33, 136, 235n40
La Mothe Le Vayer, François de, 237n71
La Motte-Aigron, Jacques de, 60, 68, 77
Lancaster, Henry Carrington, 165, 168
landscape, 68–72, 115–16
language: defined by common usage, 195; and feeling, 130; and identity, 106, 118; inadequacy, 84, 198; Malherbian cult, 111, 115–16; pleasures, 76; raises man above animals, 206. *See also* rhetoric; French language: reform
Lanson, Gustave, 29
La Rivière, abbé de (Louis Barbier), 124–27
La Rochefoucauld, Cardinal (François): 96–97

La Rochefoucauld, duc de (François V), 203
La Roche-Guyon, duc de. *See* Liancourt, duc de (Roger du Plessis)
La Sablière, Marguerite de, 235n40
La Valette, Cardinal (Louis de Nogaret), 60, 62, 72–76, 77, 82, 84, 91, 164–66
La Varenne, Guillaume Fouquet de, 113
League, Catholic, 42
Le Brun, Charles, 34, 68, 94, 198
legitimacy and tyranny, 161
leisure, culture of, 41–44, 48, 237n64
Le Nôtre, André, 34
Lescot, Jacques, 101
L'Estoille, Claude de, 47, 184
Leszczyski, Stanislas, 230
letters. *See* epistolary rhetoric
Le Vau, Louis, 34
Leyden, University of, 59
L'Hôpital, Michel de, 32
Liancourt, duc de (Roger du Plessis, also duc de La Roche-Guyon), 104, 127
libertines, 24, 59, 78, 117–19, 135
liberty, political, 41–44
light, 120
Lionne, Hugues de, 50
Lipsius, Justus, 59
literary field, 54–56, 77, 150–51, 208
locus amoenus, 69
Longueville, duc de (Henri II d'Orléans), 31, 101
Lorraine, Marguerite de, 34
Louis XIII, 42, 49, 71, 91, 164, 168; as author, 102, 185–86; conflict with Épernon, 66; conflict with Marie de' Medici, 96–99; and Luynes, 127, 145; and French Academy, 206; as patron, 30
Louis XIV, 27 198, 214, 230; and Fouquet, 33; memoirs, 94; and Versailles, 48, 68, 210, 229
Louvre, 111, 185–86, 190, 210
lover vs. poet, 120–21
loyalty. *See* fidelity
Lully, Jean-Baptiste, 48
Luxembourg Palace, 94

Luynes, duc de (Charles d'Albert), 127, 145
Lyons, John D., 120
lyre, 111

Maecenas, Gaius, 22, 36, 39, 40–49, 237nn.64 and 69; and Augustus, 40–48; contrasted with contemporary patrons, 47; easy manner with poets, 47; eloquence, 44–45; figure of mediation, 44–46; Golden Age, 40, 46, 48; and Horace, 108
Maillet, Marc de, 30, 243n40
Mairet, Jean, 25, 31, 49, 100, 153, 160–68, 190; *Chyrséide et Arimand*, 164; *Épître familière*, 160–62; reliance on patronage, 163–71; *La Silvanire*, 164–69; *La Sylvie*, 164
Malesherbes, Guillaume-Chrétien de Lamoignon de, 230
Malherbe, François, 30, 34, 49, 57, 89, 108; "Alcandre cycle," 24, 110–16, 137, 139; political beliefs, 110
Malleville, Claude de, 193, 203
manners. *See honnêteté*
Mapplethorpe, Robert, 16
Marais, Théâtre du. *See* Théâtre du Marais
Mareschal, André, 30, 34
Marin, Louis, 202
Marino, Giambattista, 101
market economy, 15–16, 18, 27, 29, 256n8; vs. gift economy, 73–75
Martin, Henri-Jean, 30
masters and servants, 66, 99, 107, 125, 128, 147, 150
Matvejevitch, Predrag, 109
Mauss, Marcel, 74
Maynard, François, 30, 31, 153, 190, 235n25; rejection of theater, 154–56
Mazarin, Cardinal (Jules), 50–52; as patron, 32–33, 235n25
mazarinades, 235n25
mécénat. See patronage system: *clientélisme* and *mécénat*
mécène, 39–40
Medici, Marie de', 48, 59–60, 68, 71; conflict with Richeleu, 91–92; as patron, 30; and Rubens, 94–98

memoria. See memory
memory, 154, 206
Ménage, Gilles, 35
Mercury, 96–97
Méré, Antoine Gombaud de, 22, 25, 215–16, 219, 222–25
merit, 73, 162
Merlin, Hélène, 17, 161, 182, 194–203, 212–14, 242n17, 252n7
metatheatricality, 174–78
Middle Ages, 30, 234n14
mignon, 159
Millen, Ronald, 96–97
Milliade, La, 189
mimetic desire, 113
mirror, princely, 91
mock heroic, 122–23
mockery. See *raillerie*
modernism and patronage, 230
modernization theory, 18
Molé, Mathieu, 105
Molière (Jean-Baptiste Poquelin), 33, 53, 183
Mondory (Guillaume des Gilberts), 155–56, 167, 183
Montaigne, Michel de, 22, 69, 129, 142, 220
Montauron, Pierre Puget de, 34, 163
Montmorency, Charlotte de, 24, 112–14, 136–37
Montmorency, duc de (Henri II), 102–3, 118, 127, 135–42, 152, 161–68; literary court, 31; model for Sorel's Clérante, 146, 246n41; protection of Théophile de Viau, 105, 135, 164–66
Montpensier, Mademoiselle de (Marie de Bourbon), 164
Morgues, Matthieu de, 91
Mousnier, Roland, 26–29, 36
Murray, Timothy, 171
music. *See* harmony

Nantes, Edict of, 22, 58
nationalism, 207, 228
nature, 136–42; controlled, 139–40; diversity, 134; and gift economy: 133–34
Naudé, Gabriel, 37

NEA (National Endowment of the Arts), 16
neo-Aristotelian thought, 133
Neoplatonism, 195
Neufgermain, Louis de, 30, 154–55
New Science, 55
New World, 69
Nietzsche, Friedrich, 205
nightingale, 139–41
Nigro, Salvatore, 101
nobility: and art, 37, 75; evolution in seventeenth century, 146, 221; as performative, 77; prejudice against letters, 146

occasional poetry, 14, 48, 107–51
œuvres, 161
Ogier, François, 165; *Apologie pour Monsieur de Balzac*, 78–79, 81–82, 86–90
Olivares, Count-Duke of (Gaspar de Guzmán y Pimentel), 47
Olivet, abbé d' (Pierre-Joseph Thoulier), 210
Ong, Walter, 247n44
opinion, 220, 223. *See also* public: opinion
Orange, Prince of, 184
orator, 44–45, 61, 86–87, 93, 217; vs. actor, 87; in antiquity, 80–81; disappearing breed, 64; distinguished by delivery, 154; ideal of, 20–21; vs. writer, 80
orders, society of. *See under* patronage system
originality, 101
Orléans, Gaston d', 30, 118, 122–27, 164
Orléans, Philippe d', 184
Orpheus, 20, 216
Orsini, Maria Felicia, 135–42, 165
Ovid (Publius Ovidius Naso), 69, 101

painting: and patronage, 94–98, 100; and rhetoric, 68. *See also* portraiture
Palais Cardinal, 170–71, 184, 188, 189
panegyric, 36, 60, 61, 65–66, 109, 124, 136; academic, 79, 198–99; and hyperbole, 90–91; humorous, 123
Paris, 138, 209–12
Paris, University of, 209

Parker, David, 28
parlement de Paris, 55, 135, 140, 209–11
parlements, 54–55, 65, 69
Parnasse satyrique, Le, 135
Parnassus, Mount, 155–56, 159, 161
parti espagnol, 59
Pascal, Blaise, 58, 219
Pasquier, Nicolas, 220–24
passions, 218, 224
pastoral, 68–72, 164–65, 171–72
pathetic fallacy, 116
patriarchy, 39, 118
patron, 38–40
patronage system, 26–56, 256n8; *bénéfices*, 34–35, 49–51; bureaucratization, 25, 153, 168, 183, 193, 203–14, 226–28, 230; characteristics, 17–19; *charges*, 34–35; *clientélisme* and *mécénat*, 36–40, 77, 236n45; and conversation, 214–27; crisis after Richelieu, 32; declining relevance, 229; dynamism and flexibility, 29, 55–56, 77, 142, 164–66, 228; extension of familial relationships, 39; fringe benefits, 35; *gratifications*, 34, 36, 153, 229; institutionalization under Louis XIV, 25, 31, 214, 228–29, 230; and painting, 94–97; patriarchal character, 39; pensions, 30, 31, 33, 34, 50–51, 153, 214, 230, 237n82; persistence today, 16, 230; personal character, 28, 38, 50, 152, 161, 190, 202–3, 228, 230; problematic notion, 28, 30, 56; rewards, 34–36; and rhetoric, 23, 59, 62; satire of, 229; and self-interest, 28, 72, 74, 229–30; social mobility within, 52; and society of orders, 26–29; terminology, 38
patrons: aristocratic, 31; as authors, 101–2, 188–91; ministers and royal officers, 32–34; royal family, 30; types, 30–34
Pax Romana, 42, 81
Pellisson, Paul, 25, 33; *Histoire de l'Académie*, 152, 185, 193–94, 199, 203–4, 207, 209–12
pensions. *See under* patronage system
Petit Bourbon, 189

Petrarchism, 120
Phateon, 139
Philip IV (king of Spain), 47
Philomela, 140
Pintard, René, 104
Plato, 78, 130
pleasure, 75–76, 91; literary and sexual, 148–50. *See also* Epicureanism
Pliny the Younger, 78
poet: affinity with nature, 140; familiarity with patron, 139; as gatherer, 141; individuality, 117–18, 122, 125, 131, 132, 135; vs. lover, 120–21; manipulator of signs, 121; as rhymer, 138; role at court, 105–6, 114, 127, 139
poète à gages, 179, 250n63
poète crotté, 105, 243n40
poetic voice, 109–10, 115, 122–24, 151; and the Other, 24, 106, 118–19, 122, 125, 127, 131–32, 135, 141–42
poetry: epic, 122; vs. rhetoric, 86; therapeutic role, 140
politeness. See *honnêteté*
political function of art, 16, 30, 36
polyvocality, 124. *See also* poetic voice
Pompey (Gnaeus Pompeius Magnus), 88
Ponge, Francis, 110–16
Pont Neuf, 123
Pope-Hennessy, John, 219
Porchères Laugier, Honorat de, 204
portraiture and conversation, 219
Port-Royal, 58
poststructuralism, 118–19, 198
poulets, 106, 114, 148
power: delegation of, 97–98; local, 98; personal, 18; and representation, 17, 27
praise. *See* panegyric
Préaud, Maxime, 252n11
Priézac, Daniel de, 20, 33
print culture, 234n14
private sphere. *See* public and private spheres
privilèges, 33, 179
property intellectual. *See* intellectual property
propriety, poetic, 138–39

protecteur, 38
public: buying, 230; opinion, 31, 158, 228–30; as patron, 182–83; and private spheres, 17, 44–45, 61, 63, 65, 77, 80, 82, 93, 176, 182, 213–14, 224, 227, 256n8; theatrical, 153, 156, 157, 165, 167–69, 171, 178–79, 182, 187
publication, 68, 108, 120, 127, 151, 176, 179, 242n17
publicity, 17, 30, 31, 32, 37, 55, 66, 82, 121, 152, 158
publishers, 153

Quarrel of the Ancients and Moderns, 78, 204
querelle des Anciens et des Modernes. See Quarrel of the Ancients and Moderns
querelle des Premières Lettres. See *under* Balzac, Jean-Louis Guez de
querelle du Cid, 70, 160–63, 167, 190, 213–14; *Advertissement au Besançonnois Mairet*, 161–62; *Apologie pour M. Mairet*, 162; *Lettre apologitique*, 162; *Lettre du Des-interessé*, 161; *Lettre pour monsieur de Corneille contre les mots de la lettre sous le nom d'Ariste*, 162; *Les Sentiments de l'Académie Française sur la tragédie du Cid*, 160, 187–88
Quinault, Philippe, 33
Quintilian (Marcus Fabius Quintilianus), 84, 86, 89

Racan, Honorat de Bueil de, 49
Racine, Jean, 48
raillerie, 46, 88–90
Rambouillet, marquise de (Catherine Vivonne), 40, 92, 168; *chambre bleue*, 35, 165, 167, 226
Ranum, Orest, 29
Ravaillac, François, 135
reason of state, 92
reciprocity, 63, 72, 74, 76, 223–24
recueils collectifs, 108
réduit, 159
Refuge, Eustache de, 25, 217–19, 221–22, 224
Régnier, Mathurin, 26, 106–7, 109,
Renaissance, 224; humanism, 195, 216, 222; myth of poetic inspiration, 186;

notion of harmony, 124. *See also* rhetoric: in Renaissance
representation and power, 17, 27
Republic of Letters, 158, 192, 198, 203, 214, 221, 230; barbarity, 206
res vs. *verba*, 98
Retz, Cardinal (Jean-François Paul de Gondi), 35
Retz, duc de (Henri de Gondi), 31, 119
Revolution. *See* French Revolution, 227
rewriting, 101
rhetoric: affect vs. argumentation, 87; Asiatic vs. Attic, 97; civic, 58–59, 64; as coercion, 64; and conversation, 215–19; decline of, 79–80; diffusion within aristocratic society, 221, 225, 227; foundation of social order, 20, 216–17; and patronage, 23, 59, 62, 101; personal, 21–23, 61, 193, 217–19, 225; and place, 62, 70, 80, 210; vs. poetry, 86; reduced scope in monarchical culture, 58, 63, 79, 81–82; in Renaissance, 58–59, 216; under Roman Empire, 79
Rhetorica ad Herennium, 22
rhyme, 123–24
Richelet, Pierre: *Dictionnaire*, 38–39
Richelieu, Cardinal (Armand Jean du Plessis), 23, 42, 162, 179, 181; as author, 101; and Balzac, 46–47, 60, 62, 63, 70, 82–83, 91–92, 237n73; and Boisrobert, 32, 49–51; and French Academy, 187–89, 193–207, 210–11, 213; as patron, 30–33, 118; in Rubens's "Treaty of Angoulême," 96–97; and theater, 25, 152–53, 164, 168, 169–71, 181, 183–91
Roche, Daniel, 150
rodomontade, 87–88
Romanticism, 108–9, 111, 151, 230
Rome: passage from republic to principate, 40–44, 80–81
Roniger, Louis, 17
Rotrou, Jean de, 31, 100, 162, 167–68, 179, 184
Rousset, Jean, 84
royal entries, 68
Rubens, Peter Paul, 30; Medici cycle, 68, 94–98; "Treaty of Angoulême," 96–98
Rucellai, Luigi, 98, 117
Rueil, 187
ruelle, 159, 248n12

Sabbattini, Nicola, 170
Saint-Aignan, duc de (François de Beauvilliers), 125
Saint-Amant, Marc-Antoine Girard de, 31, 108–10, 117, 119, 125–26, 136, 151; biography vs. poetry, 120; "Le Contemplateur," 35; "L'Élégie à Damon," 119–22; "L'ÉpîtreHeroïcomique À Monseigneur le Duc d'Orléans," 122–24; "Les Nobles triolets," 124; "Le Poëte crotté," 105–6, 119, 129
Saint-Denis, André de, 78
Sainte-Beuve, Charles-Augustin: on Balzac, 57–58
Saint-Évremond, Charles de Marguetel de Saint-Denis de, 38, 253n28
salle de la comédie. *See* Palais Cardinal
salon culture, 23, 30, 35–36; and conversation, 215, 224–27; and theater, 158–59, 165, 167
satire, 53, 143–44; 145–46, 229
savants, erudite, 78
Scaliger, Joseph Justus, 59
Scarron, Paul, 32–33, 117
scène à l'italienne, 25, 170–71
Schapira, Nicolas, 208
Schérer, Colette, 180–81
Schiller, Johann Christoph Friedrich, 109
Schomberg, Henri de, 62, 63, 125–26
Scudéry, Georges de, 31, 49, 159, 162; *L'Amour tyrannique*, 168
Scudéry, Madeleine de, 33, 222–25
secrecy, 22, 101
secretaries, 24, 31, 34, 65, 80, 208; and collective authorship, 98–101; used by Roman emperors, 79
Séguier, Pierre, 32, 33, 51, 53; and French Academy 200, 209–10
self-fashioning, 17, 19, 56, 62, 70–71
self-interest. *See under* patronage system

290   INDEX

Seneca, Lucius Anneaeus, 45–46, 59, 101
senses, 120–21
Serizay, Jacques de, 203–4
servants and masters. *See* masters and servants
Servien, Abel, 20, 201
sexual licence, 138–40
sign, transparency of, 70
Sigogne, Charles Timoléon de Beauxoncles de, 113–15
Silvie. *See* Orsini, Maria Felicia
Soissons, comte de (Louis de Bourbon), 31
solitary genius, 230
Sorbonne, 91
Sorel, Charles, 37–38, 110, 117, 119, 151, 228; attitude toward patronage, 145; and Balzac, 78, 88; *De la connoissance des bons livres*, 150; *Histoire comique de Francion*, 24, 142–51; satire of literary culture, 143–44
spectacle, 153, 155, 157–58, 173–74, 182
speech and writing, 40, 148, 247n44
stage design. See *scène à l'italienne*
Stanton, Domna, 37
Stoicism, 43
Strosetzki, Christoph, 225
style: vs. thought, 89; *See also* Balzac, Jean-Louis Guez de: style; authorship: style
subjectivity, 104, 109–11, 125, 242n17; and language, 118; poetic, 24
sublimation of social desire, 206–7
sublime, 86–87
Sully, duc de (Maximilien de Béthune), 113
sun *motif*, 195–204
superfluity, 75–77
Suresnes, 171–72
surrealism, 84
symbolism, 109
sympathy, 125

Tacitus, Cornelius, 46, 80–81
Taine, Hippolyte, 29
Tallemant des Réaux, Gédéon, 30, 31, 33, 35, 92 101, 168, 199
Tasso, Torquato, 165

taste, 19, 31, 55, 77, 91, 146, 161, 216, 219
theater, 25, 31, 32, 100, 152–91; as mass entertainment, 155; morality of, 189; performances at court, 168; popularity in 1630s, 177; princely patronage, 183–84; private vs. public dimension, 25, 152–53, 159, 168–71, 174; public utility, 152, 189–91; state patronage, 183–91. *See also* dramatic authors; metatheatricality
Théâtre du Marais, 162, 183
Théophile. *See* Viau, Théophile de
Thirty Years War, 32
thought vs. style, 89
Thuillier, Jacques, 96
Trajan, 78
transgression, 139
transparency, 91
triangular lyric, 120
Tristan L'Hermite, François, 24, 30, 34, 108, 117, 119, 136, 142; "À M. l'Ab[b]é de la Rivière," 124, 126–27; "À Monsieur l'Ab[b]é de la Rivière, Stances," 126; "À Monseigneur le Mareschal de Schomberg," 125–26; "À Monsieur de Patris, Luy faisant voir l'ode que j'ay composée à la gloire de Monsieur l'Ab[b]é de la Rivière," 126; poetics of resonance, 126, 151; *Vers héroïques*, 124–27
tropes vs. figures, 89
Tuileries, 185–86
tyranny and legitimacy, 161

urbanity, 42
Urfé, Honoré d', 68–69
utility of art, 109

Valois kings, 30
Valois, Charles de, 113
Valois, Marguerite de, 30, 243n40
value: artistic, 75; cultural, 16; literary 19, 73, 77, 229
Vanini, Giulio Cesare, 104
Vaugelas, Claude Favre de, 30, 201
Vaumorière, Pierre d'Ortigue de, 25, 216, 217–18, 224–25
Vendôme, duc de (César), 31, 34, 171, 180–81

ventriloquism, 122–24
verba vs. *res*, 98
Versailles, 48, 68, 94, 210, 228
Viala, Alain, 36–40, 54–56, 90, 150, 208
Viau, Théophile de, 24, 102–3, 108, 110, 127–44, 151, 164, 194, 245n25; "À M. le marquis de Boquingant," 132–34, 136, 142; "À Monsieur de Fargis," 117, 119, 130; and Balzac, 59, 78; cannot write for others, 130; claim to individuality, 131; court poet and libertine, 127; deism and materialism, 133–34; "Desja trop longuement la paresse me flatte," 128–29; fusion with patron, 128–29; *La Maison de Silvie*, 134–42, 164–65, 228; "Première journée," 129–30; *Pyrame et Thisbé*, 168; trial and imprisonment, 31, 104–5, 135

Virgil (Publius Virgilius Maro), 101
vita activa, 20
voice, 94, 124, 154. *See also* poetic voice
Voisin, Father, 104
Voiture, Vincent, 30, 34, 219
Voltaire (François Marie Arouet), 230

Wars of Religion, 22, 42, 69
Weber, Max, 18
Weissman, Ronald, 18
Wolf, Robert, 96–97
women: role in seventeenth-century society, 224–25
writer vs. orator, 80
writing and speech, 40, 148, 247n44

Zeus, 210
Zuber, Roger, 46
Zuniga, Balthazar de, 113